A REPORT

OF THE

RECORD COMMISSIONERS

CONTAINING

CHARLESTOWN LAND RECORDS, 1638–1802.

SECOND EDITION.

BOSTON:

ROCKWELL AND CHURCHILL, CITY PRINTERS,

No. 39 ARCH STREET.

1883.

BOSTON:
Rockwell & Churchill
City Printers, No. 39 Arch Street.
1883

A Facsimile Reprint
Published 1999 by

HERITAGE BOOKS, INC.
1540E Pointer Ridge Place
Bowie, Maryland 20716
1-800-398-7709
http://www.heritagebooks.com

ISBN: 0-7884-1204-3

CITY OF BOSTON.

THIRD REPORT

OF THE

RECORD COMMISSIONERS.

IN BOARD OF ALDERMEN, Dec. 3, 1877.

Ordered, That the Record Commissioners be authorized to have transcribed the Charlestown Book of Possessions, and to have the same printed, bound, and distributed in the same manner as their first and second reports, at an expense not exceeding one thousand dollars; to be charged to the appropriation for Printing.

Sent down for concurrence.

Dec. 13, came up concurred.

Approved by the Mayor, Dec. 14, 1877.

A true copy.

Attest:

S. F. McCLEARY,
City Clerk.

To His Honor the Mayor and the City Council of Boston: —

In pursuance of the above vote, the Record Commissioners herewith submit a volume containing the early land grants and records of the town of Charlestown, being the documents comprised in one bound volume of the town and city archives as now arranged. In regard to this book the following statement has been made by Mr. Henry H. Edes, the gentleman who was selected by the City Government of Charlestown, prior to annexation, to arrange the records: —

" The volume which you have caused to be printed, and which is lettered ' Charlestown Archives 34 | Book of Possessions | 1638–1802,' comprises, besides the record of 1638, and the transfers made during the succeeding twenty years, all records relating to the laying out and conveyance of land and the survey of streets and highways, originally dispersed in several volumes of our public archives, which properly could be separated from the other matter contained in the volumes in which I found them in 1869. This breaking up of old volumes and creating of new ones has been done by authority and in pursuance of joint orders of tne City Council of Charlestown, passed in June, 1869, and April, 1870, directing a classification, arrangement, and binding of all the archives of the old town from 1629 to 1847, when it was incorporated a city. The result of these orders will be such a consolidation and chronological arrangement of our records under a few heads, such as (1) Town Records, (2) Treasury Records, (3) Vital Statistics, (4) Fire Department, (5) Poor Department, (6) Schools, (7) Voters, (8) Jurors, etc., etc., that, when my labors are completed, the future inquirer for information contained in our archives will readily find within a small compass the greater part at least of all that is extant concerning the department in which he shall be making special inquiry.

" Referring to the editorial note on page 186 of your report, permit me to say that it is perfectly accurate so far as the surveys of 1767 and 1802 are concerned; but, unfortunately, the original reports of the committees which made the surveys of 1670 and 1714 are not now extant among our archives.

" The first entry in the town records respecting the compilation of the 'Book of Possessions' occurs in volume ii. (generally referred to as ' Greene's Transcript'), folio 35 (old pagination), and is in these words : —

" ' 1638. The first month, The 26 : day | Abra: Palmer, chosen by the Towne for keepeing the Towne Booke, as also to Record all pprieties of Houses, Lands, Meadow or Pasture, as any Inhabitants of ye Towne are, or shall bee possest of accord^g : to an ord^r of Court provided in y^t. behalfe.'

" It is reasonable to presume that Mr. Palmer began his labors without unnecessary delay, and that the following entry was made on the completion of his work of engrossing the schedules handed in to him by the major portion of the inhabitants, since the mere clerical labor involved in executing this important commission was by no means inconsiderable.

" ' 1638.

" ' On the 28th day of the X month was taken A True Record of all such houses & Lands as are Possessed by the Inhabita^{nts} of Charlstown, wheth^r by purchase, by gift from the Towne, or by allottments as they were devided amongst them by A Joynt Consent aft^r the Gen^{ll} Court had setled theire Bounds, by granting eight miles from the old Meeting house into the Contry Northwest Northrly, &c. the bounds of the s^d Towne Lying or being bettwixt Cambridge *alias* New Towne, on the West South west, & Boston Land on the East as it app^{rs} upon Record by the sever^{ll} grants of Gen^{ll} Courts to all the affores^d Bounds.'

"Mr. Palmer recorded a large proportion of the ' Possessions' with his own hand; but there are many pages in the peculiar handwriting of Elder Nowell. Those persons who are familiar with the chirography of those gentlemen need no further confirmation of this fact than a glance at the record itself; but, as if to insure to posterity the fullest possible account of the preparation of this book, the town clerk of that period makes this entry : —

" ' 28 (11) 1638.

" ' Abra: Palmer was allowed £3 for wrighting this yeare past: & Mr. Nowell 20s. for helping in Acco : '

"Here we have a complete record of the authority under which the volume was prepared, and of the hands to which its compilation and engrossment were confided.

" An order, imposing a fine upon delinquents, is here transcribed : —

" ' 27 (11) 1639.

" ' It was ordrd the first of 8ber last, y^t any that have not dd in A note of theire Lands to Mr Abra: Palmer to have entered in ye booke shall pay to the Towns use 2s. A month aft^r notice given from the s^d first of the 8 month.'

"In this connection it should be remembered that Charlestown originally embraced within its limits the territory now contained in Woburn, Burlington, Stoneham, Malden, Somerville, and parts also of Reading, Medford, Cambridge, and West Cambridge.

" Nor was the importance of *maintaining* the completeness of the record lost sight of, for in 1643 we find the following entry : —

" ' 1643. The 23^d of the IV. month | .

" ' It is ordrd y^t all purchases & alienations of houses or Lands shall be Recorded in the Towne booke, & whosever shall neglect to Record any such purchase or Alienation for above A month shall forfeit five shillings.'

"This was followed by a more stringent order passed (probably in March) : —

" ' 1644.

" ' ' Whereas it was form^{rly} ordrd at A meeting an: *1643*, in the 4th mo: That all purchases, & Alienaçons of houses or Lands should bee Recorded in A Towne Booke upon a certaine penalty therein expresst, wch notwithstand^g hath beene neglected: It is now farther ordrd y^t all Purchases, & Alienations y^t have not beene form^{rly} Recorded, or shall hereafter bee made for time to come, shall within A month after the publication of this ord^r bee brought in to the Secretary for the Towne affaires, upon the forfeiture of sixe shillings eight pence for every deffect, to bee levied by A Towne officer, & for every such Record the Secretary to have foure Pence.'

" Much to be regretted is the loss of the folio — apparently the only one that is missing in the whole volume — on which, as we learn from the ancient index, were recorded the possessions of the Rev. John Harvard, the founder of the College. It seems, indeed, as though a strange fatality attended everything pertaining to Harvard's private life, his lineage and his possessions; and so few are the known facts concerning him that I have copied, verbatim, from our records the following entries certifying his admission as an Inhabitant and the esteem in which he was held by his contemporaries : —

" ' 1637. The 1st day of the vi. month. |
" ' ' Mr. John Harvard is admitted A Townsman with pmise of such accomodations as wee best Can.' "
" ' 1638. The 26 of the ii. month. |
" ' ' Mr. Increase Nowell, Mr. Zach^r Sims, Mr. Jno Greene, Mr. Jno Harvard, Lieft Ralph Sprague & Wm Learned were desired to consid^r of some things tending towards A body of Lawes, &c.'

" Since you have suggested that a full list of Town Clerks, or Recorders as they sometimes were termed, would give additional value to your report, I have prepared the following schedule, regretting that I have not at present at my command the time necessary to a scrutiny of the third and fourth volumes of our Town Records for the purpose of ascertaining if, buried in their obscure hieroglyphics which are intelligible only to a practised eye, the precise date is preserved of the appointment of Edward Burtt. Such an examination as I have been able to make of these volumes fails to afford more than the approximate date appended to his name.

"TOWN CLERKS OF CHARLESTOWN. 1629–1847.

" INCREASE NOWELL. — There is no record of his first appointment, but our earliest, extant, *original* records, dating from 1634, are in his handwriting. On the 22 (11) 1635–6, it was *Ordered*, 'That Mr. Increase Nowell have 40s. for writeing the ordinary Transactions of the Town Last yeare '

"ABRAHAM PALMER was chosen 26 (1) 1638.

"JOHN GREENE. — Mr. Palmer was one of the Selectmen, as well as Town Clerk as late as Jan. 12, 1643–4. At the succeeding election, 2 (11) 1645–6, Elder Greene was elected in his stead, and appears to have entered upon the office of Recorder at the same time, although the records are silent as regards his formal appointment to that service *at that time.*

"In fact the original record of the meeting held 2 (11) 1645–6 is in Greene's handwriting, and is the first record of municipal proceedings preserved *in the original,* which occurs after a hiatus of eleven years, and follows Elder Nowell's record of a meeting in January, 1635–6. It is, therefore, safe to conclude that Elder Greene's service as Recorder began 2 (11) 1645–6.

"SAMUEL ADAMS appears to have acted as Town Clerk at intervals between 1653 and 1661, and was honored with an election by the Inhabitants 3 (11) 1658–9, Elder Greene having died April 22, 1658, at the age of 65.

"EDWARD BURTT acted as Recorder in 1658, although I fail to find the precise date of his appointment. He served till about the year 1662.[1]

"JAMES CARY was chosen Nov. 3, 1662.

"LAURENCE HAMMOND was chosen Jan. 27, 1672–3.

"JAMES RUSSELL was chosen Jan. 14, 1677–8.

"JOHN NEWELL was chosen March 11, 1678–9.

"SAMUEL PHIPPS, *the Schoolmaster,* was chosen June 4, 1688 and Served till June 17, 1689.

"JOHN NEWELL recorded the proceedings, not as Recorder but as one of the Selectmen, from June 19, 1689, till Sept. 9, 1689, when he was chosen Recorder by his associates. He was reëlected till March 2, 1695–6.

"NATHANIEL DOWS [DOWSE] was chosen March 2, 1695–6.

"BENJAMIN DOWS, JR., [DOWSE] was chosen Sept. 4, 1719.

"THOMAS JENNER was chosen Sept. 12, 1720.

"SAMUEL PHIPPS was chosen March 7, 1725–6. He was a nephew of the *Schoolmaster.*

"JOSEPH PHILLIPS was chosen March 4, 1727–8.

"SETH SWEETSER was chosen Jan. 20, 1755.

"WALTER RUSSELL was chosen March 2, 1778, but had

---

[1] "It has been stated in print that Nicholas Shapley served as Town Clerk for a few months in 1662 — during the interval which elapsed between the retirement of Burtt and the election of Cary; but I doubt the accuracy of the statement, and am of opinion that Mr. Shapley served only as Clerk of the Writs, to which office he was chosen July 27, 1662." H. H. E.

acted as town clerk for several weeks previous to that time. Mr. Sweetser's last entry in the records bears date Jan. 13, 1778. He died Jan. 15, 1778.

" SAMUEL SWAN was chosen March 1, 1779.

" TIMOTHY TRUMBALL was chosen March 6, 1780.

" SAMUEL SWAN was chosen October 23, 1782.

" SAMUEL HOLBROOK was chosen March 3, 1783.

" SAMUEL PAYSON was chosen March 5, 1787.

" PHILLIPS PAYSON was chosen August 3, 1801.

" JOHN KETTELL was chosen March 3, 1806.

" SAMUEL DEVENS was chosen March 2, 1812.

" JOHN KETTELL was chosen March 1, 1813.

" DAVID DODGE was chosen March 7, 1814.

" JOHN KETTELL was chosen March 2, 1818.

" CHARLES DEVENS was chosen September 30, 1822.

" DAVID DODGE was chosen March 7, 1825.

" Mr. Dodge continued in office till the incorporation of the town as a city, and reluctantly consented to an election as first city clerk. The infirmities of age were upon him, and he retired from office before the close of the year for which he was elected, after more than twenty-six years of faithful service. To him we are deeply indebted for the excellent records of the period of his own term of service, and for the preservation and transmission of much valuable matter that would have been irretrievably lost but for his zeal and watchful care and untiring industry.

" I believe that the foregoing list includes the name of every person who held the office of Town Clerk or Recorder of the Town of Charlestown. It is possible, however, though not probable, that, for the reasons above stated, the name of some person who acted in that capacity for a few weeks or months by appointment of the Selectmen, may have been overlooked; but such an omission, if there be any, is of slight importance."[1]

---

[1] " Since I have had occasion to mention the Charlestown records, covering the period from 1658 to 1695, and the great difficulty in consulting them experienced even by those persons who are most familiar with the exceedingly bad chirography in which they are written, I beg leave, respectfully, to call the attention of the Record Commissioners to these volumes. They have been carefully repaired and bound during the past decade, but even now are in a frail and perishing condition.

" A single additional report, equal in size to the one you are about to issue, would suffice to present in type all the records now known to be extant of the municipal proceedings of the Town of Charlestown, from its settlement down to about the year 1695. These records treat largely of the grants made by the town to its early inhabitants, of boundaries, and the laying out of highways and commons; in fine, of matters which would greatly aid conveyancers and our City Engineers and Surveyors in the prosecution of their labors at the present time, could they but have the material in print. The Charlestown Records are unusually full as regards land matters; and when the extent of territory originally covered by the town, and the condition of the records themselves, are taken into consideration, the importance of printing them appears in the strongest possible light." H. H. E.

The Commissioners would add that, as in the previous volumes, they have not felt at liberty to insert any annotations. The liberality of the city is sufficiently taxed in placing the text of these records before the public in an accurate transcript. The only notes are such as relate to the text itself. It may also be added, that the index is not to be considered a part of the volume, not having been prepared at the cost of the city. It is hoped, however, that it is both accurate and comprehensive, and that it will be found of service.

It also seems proper to annex a statement of the cost of the volumes already issued : —

First report, pp. 183, estimated cost . . $900 00
Cost of 1,500 copies, 500 being bound in
    cloth 824 08

Second Report, pp. 299, estimated cost . $1,000 00
Cost of same number of copies . . . 736 87

Third Report, estimated cost . . . $1,000 00

The Commissioners may perhaps anticipate that other portions of the city, as Roxbury and Dorchester, may call for a similar publication of their records of early grants and possessions of land.

There has also been a feeling manifested in favor of printing the first volume of deeds for Suffolk County, inasmuch as the expense would be but little greater than that of a manuscript copy. Certainly the old town of Boston requires a second volume of extracts from its records, to complete the grants of lots and the laying out of streets.

Whilst the Commissioners will cheerfully discharge any duties of the above-named nature which may be assigned to them, they beg leave to repeat their previous notice that their main duty is still unfulfilled. The transcripts of the Church records, to supplement and complete the records preserved by the City Registrar, are still to be made. They hope, therefore, to receive instructions during the next year to make a beginning upon their most necessary and long-delayed work.

The preparation of the following volume has devolved solely upon the undersigned.

For the Record Commissioners,

WILLIAM H. WHITMORE.

BOSTON, December, 1878.

NOTE TO THE SECOND EDITION.

The first edition of the volume having been distributed, the City Council has directed the Record Commissioners to reprint and stereotype the same, in order to continue to supply copies to those interested. The opportunity has been availed of to make such slight corrections of errors in the text as have been noticed by Mr. Edes, but these have not caused any difference in the pagination.

WILLIAM H. WHITMORE,
WILLIAM S. APPLETON,
Record Commissioners.

BOSTON, July, 1883.

PREFATORY NOTE.

The pagination in brackets is that of the volume as now bound up and interleaved. The numbers are on the page facing the old leaves; but the original was numbered by folios only.

Page 1 of the bound volume is a new printed title-page. Page 2 (*i.e.* folio 1 of the original) contains the following random entry, evidently misplaced, as it is also found in the first volume of Town Records : —

"It is agreed that Thomas Beecher, William Jennings and Raphe Sprage are apoynted to bee at the meetings, and to bee of them to p'sent the towne at the generall court next In September."

Page 3 (reverse of folio 1) contains an old Index of the List of Possessions following; and, although folio 2 (pp. 4 and 5) is missing, we learn by this Index that on it were recorded the possessions of John Harvard and the Rev. Zechariah Symmes. The old Index also refers, without naming page, to the possessions of Major William Phillips. Probably they, too, were recorded on the missing folio, as he is elsewhere referred to as an abutter on the estates of other inhabitants. — W.H.W.

INDEX TO THE POSSESSIONS.

CHARLESTOWN LAND RECORDS.

[6.] *The possession of Rob[t] Long within the limits of Charltowne.*[1]

1. One Roode and a haulfe of grounde by estimation, more or lesse, scituate on the south of the mill hill, butting south east and north east upon the markett place, bounded on the north by the meeting house lane and on the south west by the high streete, with a dwelling house upon it and other aptinances.

2. One acre of meaddow by estimation, more or lesse, scituate in the south meade, butting north east upon Rob[t] Hayle as also on the south west and north weast, bounded on the south east by Samuell Carter.

3. Two acres of meaddow by estimation, more of lesse, scituate in the south meade, butting eastward upon the broad cove, bounded on the southwest by Sarah Ewer and on the northwest by Rob. Hayle.

4. Comones for eight milch Cowes.

5. Eight acres of earable land by estimation, more or lesse, scituate in the line feilde, butting northeast upon mistick River, south west upon the bridg way, bounded on the north west by a high way and on the south east by Rob[t] Rand, M[r] Simmes and Edw Convers.

6. ffoure acres of land, more or lesse, bought of Will Powell, butting northeast upon mistick river, southwest upon the Bridge-

---

[1] The record from this place to the bottom of our page 68 are in the handwriting of Abraham Palmer unless otherwise noted. — ED.

way, bounded on the northwest by Steeven fforsdick and on the southeast by Will. Batchellor.

7. ffoure acres of earable land, more or lesse, scituate in the line feilde bought of Isaac Cole, butting northeast upon mistick river, south west upon the bridg-way, bounded on the northwest by James Pemberton and on the south east by Ed. Carrington.

8. Tenn acres of meaddow by estimation, more or lesse, scituate in mistick marshes, butting eastward upon the south river, west upon Capt. Rob. Sedgwick, bounded upon the south by whitehands iland and on the north by Ed. Carington and the river.

9. One acre of meaddow by estimation, more or lesse, lying at the same place next beyond Ed. Carington bought of Rob. Haukines.

10. Eight acres of meaddow by estimation, more or lesse, scituate in mistick marshes, butting southeast upon the south river, north west upon the highway, bounded on the south west by Mr Nowell and on the northeast by

11. fflve acres of wood land, more or lesse, scituate in mistick feilde, butting south upon the high way betwixt that and the meaddow, north west upon an other high way [and] on the northeast by and on the southwest by

12. Thirtie acres of woodland, more or lesse, scituate in mistick feilde, butting southwest upon Mª Kathorin Coytemore and John Sibley, to the northeast upon Will. Ler[ned] and Sam Richardson, bounded on the northwest by Rob. Cutler and on the southeast by ffrancis Norton.

13. Seaventie and three acres of land by estimation, more or lesse, situated in waterfeilde, bounded on the southeast by George bunker and George Knowker, on southwest by ffrancis Norton, on the northeast by Rob. Cutler, and on the northwest by the comõon.

.[**7.**] *The possession of Captaine Rob. Sedgwick in Charltown limites.*

1. One roode of grounde by estimation, more or lesse, scituate in the middle row, butting northwest upon the markett place, southeast upon the marsh towards the harbour, bounded on the north east by Josseph Hiles, and on the southwest by Ed. Convers, with a dwelling-house, Brew house and other aptinances.

2. Two acres of earable land by estimation, more or lesse, scituate in the litle south feilde, butting southwest upon Charles river, northeast upon the Cove, bounded on the northwest by Abr Pratt, and on the southeast by Sarah Nash, Nicolas Stowers and Thõ. Lynde.

3. ffoure acres of earable land by estimation, more or lesse, scituate in the east feilde, butting north upon mistick river, south upon the comõon swamp, bounded on the east by Mr Nowell, and on the west by Ralph Sprague.

4. ffoure acres of earable land by estimation, more or lesse, scituate in the east feilde, bought of Mrs Ann Higginson, butting southwest upon Mr Simmes, bounded on the northeast by

5. Two acres of meaddow by estimation, more or lesse, scituate in the high feilde mead

6. Milch cow commones, eleven and a haulf ; ffoure of which he bought and 7 and ½ were his pportion in the divident of the comon. [One of these cows comons maior sedgwick sould to Susan Hewins. — *Greene*.[1]]

7. ffive acres of wood land, more or lesse, scituate in mistick feilde, butting south upon the high way towards the meaddow, north upon the land way, bounded on the on side by M[r]. Simmes.[2] [This is sould to Thomas Brigden. — *Greene*.]

8. Tenn acres of meaddow by estimation, more or lesse, scituate in mistick marshes, butting

9. Eight score acres of land by estimation, more or lesse, scituate at the northeast point of the towne bounds, bounded on the east by Boston line, and on the north by Lynne villiage.

[8.] *The possession of* [1638] *Ezechell Richardson in Charltowne.*

1. Ezechell Richardson hath in the high ffeilde one homesteede, containing three Acres by esteemation, more or lesse, butting to the south upon the high-way, and to the north upon the marsh to misticke river, Bounded on the west by Thomas Squire, and on the east by Thomas Richardson.

2. One Acre of meaddow by esteemation, more or lesse, lying at the North end of the aforesayd three Acres ; Bounded on the west by George Bunker ; and on the east by Ralph Moussell and butting to the north upon A Cove in Misticke river.

3. One half Acre of meaddow by esteemation, lying in the high feilde on the north side of Thomas Squire his homesteede Bounded by the comon fence upon the east, and by Edward Mellowes on the west, and butting to the north upon misticke river.

4. One Acre of meaddow by estimation, more or lesse, upon the northeast side of Gibbines feilde, butting to the west upon Samuell Richardson and bounded on the south by Prudence Wilknson and on the north by   and butting to the east upon Robt. Long his meaddow. this he bought of william nash to whom at first it fell by Lott.

5. One Acre of eareable Land lying in the East feilde, butting to the north upon misticke river, and to the south upon widdoe nash, bounded on the west by Edward mellowes, and on the east by Abr. Pratt.

6. Two Acres of meaddow by estimation, more or lesse, butting to the south upon Cambridge feilde, and to the north upon Gibbines river bounded on the west by Robt. Hayle, and on the est by Thomas Brigden. [This is sould to Thomas Brigden. — *Greene*.]

7. Sixe Acres of meaddow by estimation, more or lesse, lying in misticke feilde, butting to the east upon the south river ; bounded by Thomas Brigden on the southeast, and by Edward Joanes on the norwest, and soe along by the upland.

8. ffive Acres of woodland lying in Misticke feilde, N[o]. 11 butting south east upon the high way against Abr. Pratt his mead-

---

[1] Various interlineations were made on the original by Elder John Greene, who was the Town Clerk from 1645 to 1658. These will be placed in brackets in the text and marked *Greene*. — ED.

[2] Mr. Simmes's name is erased with a pen — evidently the Recorder's. — ED.

dow, and to the nor-west upon the comon 80 Pole in length and tenn pole in bredth, bounded by John fairefeilde on the east and by Micheall Bastow upon the west.

9. Thirtie five Acres of woodland lying in the litle hundreths in mistick feilde no. 31, bounded by Robt. Rande on the west and by John Hodges on the east, butting upon Thomas Peirce and Rich. Palgrave northeast   and south est upon Thomas Carter Thō wickes and Rob Blotte.   100 Pole in Length and 28 pole in bredth marked.

10. Three Acres of meaddow by esteemation, more or lesse, lying to the northward of mount prospect, bounded at the eastend with the great rocks and on the west with the fresh riverett, Edward conves his meaddow lying upon the North and George Bunker on the south.

11. Ninetie Acres of land lying in waterfeilde Nọ 31 butting to the southeast upon Edward Convers, and to the northwest upon the high rockes Thō Goble bounded by Robt. Rand upon the southwest, and by John Hodges on the noreast 100 pole in length and   pole in breadth marked.

12. Sixe milch cow comon and $\frac{1}{2}$, of which 4 and $\frac{3}{4}$ were given him in the devision of the sayde comon ; one and a qʳr he bought of william nash, and halfe a one he bought of George whitehand.

13. ffoure Acres of earable land lying in the line feilde, butting to the southwest upon Cambridge line ; and to the northeast upon the milch cow comon, bounded on the norwest by Samuell Richardson and on the south east by Thō Carter.

[9.] *The possession of Mr. Josseph Hills within Charlton limites.*
One Roode of grounde by estimation, more or lesse, scituate and being in the midle row, butting northwest upon the markett place, southeast upon the marsh towards the harbour, bounded on the southwest by Rob. Sedgwick, and on the northeast by Will Brakenbury, with A Dwelling house and other aptinances.

2. One roode of grounde by estimation, more or lesse, scituate on the southwest of the mill hill, butting south upon croocked lane, east upon the high streete, bounded on the west by Ed. Johnson and John Lewis.

3. One acre of meaddow by estimation, more or lesse, lying in the south meade.

4. Comones for three milch cowes.

5. Seaven acres of earable land by estimation, more or lesse, scituate in the line feilde, butting north upon mistick river, southwest upon the bridgeway, bounded on the southeast by a high way and on the northwest by John Goulde.

6. Six acres of meaddow by estimation, more or lesse, scituate in the meaddowes at wilsons point, butting east upon the north river.

7. Tenn acres of woodland by estimation, more or lesse, scituate in mistick feilde, butting west upon the drift way towards the north river to the east upon the land way bounded on the south by Ed Convers and George Hutchinson, and on the north by Ric. Palgrave and James Heyden.

8. ffoure acres of meaddow by estimation, more or lesse, scituate in mistick marshes, butting north upon the north river, east upon the woodland ; bounded on the south by Will. Nash and on the north by Will Brakenbury.

9. Two acres of meaddow by estimation, more or lesse, scituate in mistick feilde in long meaddow, bounded on the north and south by the lottes of upland ther lying, on the east by   , and on the west by

10 Twentie and ffive acres of woodland, more or lesse, scituate in mistick feilde, butting south upon long meaddow, north upon the comon ; bounded on the west by Thō Coytemore and on the east by Thō. Ruck.

11. Thirtie and ffive acres of woodland, scituate and being in mistick feilde, bought of Capt Sedgwick, butting southward upon Mr Nowell, northward upon the com̄, bounded on the east by Thō Higginson and on the west by ffaint Wines.

12. ffiftie acres of land by estimation, more or lesse, scituate and lying in

---

[**10.**] 1638. *The possession of Samuell Richardson in Charlstowne.*

1. 1638. Samuell Richardson hath in the east feilde one homesteed, by estimation two Acres, butting to the southwest upon the streete way, and to the northeast upon George Bunker, bounded on the southeast by Will. Bates and on the north west by Seth Sweetzer ; with A dwelling house and other out houses upon it.

2. Two Acres of eareable land lying in the east feilde, butting to the north upon misticke river, and to the south upon James Bemberton, bounded on the east by Will Bates and on the west by ffrancis willebey.

3. One Acre of meaddow by esteemation, more or lesse, lying at the east end of Gibbines feilde. butting towarde the east upon Ezecheall Richardson and toward the west upon Edward Sturges and John Hodges ; bounded on the north by John Moussell, and on the south by the com̄on and Gibbines river

4. Two milch cowes com̄on.

5. ffoure Acres of earablein the Line feilde, butting west south west upon Cambridg Line and eastward upon the com̄on bounded to the southward by Ezechell Richardson and to the northward by Thomas Richardson.

6. ffive Acres of woodland in misticke feilde Nº 10, butting to the south upon the highway toward Cap. Robert Sedgwicke his meaddow ; and to the north upon the misticke feilde, bounded on the west by the high way and upo the East by Micheall Bastow, 80 pole in length and tenn pole in bredth.

7. Two Acres of meaddow by esteemation, more or lesse, lying in misticke feild butting upon the upland to the west. and upon Edward Joanes to the east bounded on the south by the upland, and upon the north by widdow wilkin.

8. One acre of meaddow by estimation, more or lesse, lying in misticke feilde bounded on the north by Salem high way and on

the west by Thom Peirce and on the south by the fresh reverett which runes into the north river.

9.   ffifteene Acres of woodland lying in misticke feilde N° 96. 100 pole in length and   in breadth; buting southwest upon Rob. Long and Rob. Cutler, northeast upon the coṁon, bounded on the norwest by Will Lerned and on the southeast by Micheall Bastow and Boston line.

10.   ffortie Acres of land more or lesse situate   in Rock feilde N° 96 and butting to the river (westward) bounded on the south by Will Lernet on the north by Micheall Bastow and on the east by the coṁon.

———

[**11.**]   *The possession of Edward Converse within Charltowne Limites.*

One roode of grownde by estimation, more or lesse, scituate in the midle row, butting north west and southwest upon the markett place, south east upon the marsh towards the harbour, bounded on the north east by Capt. Sedgwick, with a dwelling house, store house, and other aptinances.

2.   ffive acres of earable land by estimation, more or lesse, scituate in the east feilde butting south west upon the long way; northeast upon Will Bates, bounded on the northwest by George Bunker, and on the southeast by Mr. Simmes, Capt. Sedgwick, and Rice Cole.

3.   One acre and haulfe of earable land by estimation, more or lesse, scituate in the east feilde. butting south west upon the back streete, northeast upon Will Johnson, bounded on the southeast by Will dade, and on the northwest by Saṁ. Carter.

4.   Three acres of meaddow by estimation, more or lesse, scituate in the south meaddowes butting northwest towards the streete way southeast upon a creeke bounded on the southwest by Mr. Simmes, and on the northeast by Rā. Sprague.

5.   One acre of meaddow by estimation, more or lesse, scituate in the south meade.

6.   Coṁons for milch cowes ffive and a quarter.

7.   Two acres of meaddow by estimation, more or lesse. scituate and being in the line feilde, with a p'cell of upland adioining on the west side of it, bounded on the west by the high way; on the east by winotamies river, on the south by Mr. Simmes, and on the north by George Bunker.

8.   Eight acres of earable land by estimation, more or lesse, scituate in the line feilde, butting east upon the high way; west upon Rob Long, bounded on the south by Mr. Simmes, and on the northe by Daniell Shepheardson and Will Brakenbury.

9.   Three acres of meaddow by estimation, more or lesse, lying on the north of mount p'spect, bounded on the west by the river, on the east by the coṁon, on the south by Ezecheall Richardson, and on the north by Thō. Lynde.

10.   ffive acres of woodland, more or lesse, scituate in mistick feilde, butting west and south upon the drift way east upon the landway, bounded on the north by George Hutchinson.

11.   Thirtie and ffive acres of woodland, more or lesse, scituate

in mistick feilde, butting southwest upon the reserved land, northeast upon Will Brakenbury, James Pemberton, and Peter Garland, bounded on the north west by Thō. Moulton, and on the southeast by John Martin.

12. Eightie acres of land by estimation, more or lesse, scituate in waterfeilde, bounded on the east by the river, on the northwest by Eze. Richardson, Rob. Rand, Thō Moulton, and John Crow ; on the northwest by Thō. Moulton, John Martin, and Mr. Simmes.

13. ffiv acres of woodland, more or lesse, scituate in mistick feilde, butting south west upon George Bunker, north east upon Ed. Mellowes, bounded on the north west by George Whitehand, and on the southwest by John Tedd.

[**12.**] 1638. *The Possession of Thomas Richardson in Charltown.*

1. Thomas Richardson hath, in the high feilde, one homesteede containing one Acre of ground by esteemation, butting to the south upon the high way ; to the north upon Ralph Mossell, his meaddow toward Mistike River, bounded on the east by Nicolas Davis, and on the west by Ezecheall Richardson.

2. One milch Cow comon.

3. One Acre of meaddow grounde lying in the high feilde marsh, butting to the norwest upon mistike river, and to the southeast upon   , bounded on the southwest by Thomas Carter, and on the northeast by Cap. Robt. Sedgwicke.

4. ffoure Acres in the line feilde butting to the southwest upon Cambridge line, to the northeast upon the comon, bounded on the southeast by Samuell Richardson, and on the northwest by John Brinsemeade.

5. ffive acres of woodland in mistike feilde, No. 25, butting to the   upon   and to the   upon   bounded on the   by   and on the

6. Seaventeene Acres of land, more or lesse, scituate in waterfeilde, butting to the norwest upon George Bunker, southeast upon James Browne, bounded on the southwest by Edward Burton, and on the northeast by John Moussall.

7. Haulfe an Acre of meaddow by esteemation, more or lesse, lying in misticke feilde, bounded on the   by George Bunker, and on the   by Thomas Carter, butting to the north towards Salem high way, and to the south upon

[**13.**] *The Possession of Will Brakenbury within the limites of Charltowne.*

One roode of grounde by estimation, more or lesse, scituate in the midle row, butting west upon the markett place, est upon the marsh by wapping dock, bounded on the north west by Mrs Ann Higginson, and on the southeast by Josseph Hills, with a dwelling house upon it, and other aptinances.

2. One wroode of grounde by estimation, more or lesse, called pspect ile, scituate in the marsh betwixt wapping dock and the midle Row.

3. Haulf an acre of grounde by estimation, more or lesse,

scituate in the east feilde butting south upon wapping streete, bounded on the north and west by Michaell Bastow, and on the west by the end of Long way. [This is sould to John March. — *Greene*.]

4. ffoure acres of earable land and swampe by estimation, more or lesse, lying in the east feilde, bounded on the southwest by Thō Coytemore, Rob Hayle and Josseph Cetcherall ; on the northwest by Rice Cole ; on the southeast by Will Stilson, and on the northeast by the swamp.

5. Milch cow com̄ones three and a haulf.

6. One acre of meaddow by estimation, more or lesse, scituate in the east feilde, butting east upon the roade, to the west upon ffrancis Willoughby, bounded on the north by the beach pointe, and on the south by the horse meaddow

7. Two acres of meaddow by estimation, more or lesse, lying in the south meade.

8. Tenn acres of land, more or lesse, scituate in the line feilde, butting north upon mistick river, south upon Edward convers ; bounded on the east by Daniell Shepheardson, and on the west by Beniamin Hubbard.

9. ffive acres of woodland by estimation, more or lesse, scituate in mistick feilde, butting west upon the drift way towards the north river, east upon the land way, bounded on the south by Rob. Rand, and on the north by Ed. Burton.

10. Six acres of meaddow by estimation, more or lesse, scituate in mistick marshes, butting west upon the north river, east upon the woodland ; bounded on the south by Josseph Hils, and on the north by Rice Cole and the woodland.

11. Two acres of meaddow by estimation, more or lesse, lying on the northwest of moūt pspect, bounded on the east by the fresh river, on the south and west by the common, and on the north by Walter Palmer.

12. ffortie and six acres of land, more or lesse, scituate in water feilde, butting northwest upon Josseph Coleman ; southeast upon John Crow and Daniell Shepheardson ; bounded on the southeast by James Pemberton, and on the northwest by Thō Lynde or the common.

——

[**14.**]   1638.   *The Possession of Thomas Lynde in Charltowne.*
1.   Thomas Lynde hath in the south feilde, one home-steede on the southwest side of the mill hill, containing haulf an acre by esteem̄ation, butting to the southwest upon Charles river, and to the northwest upon the widdow nash and Nicolas tower ther homesteade, bounded on the southeast by garden Lane allias mault lane, and on the northwest by the widdow nash ; with one dwelling house ; mault house and other outhouses upon it.

2.   Three Acres of eareable land lying in the south feilde, butting to the southeast upon Robt. Rande, his homesteed ; and to the northwest upon Josseph Hill, bounded on the west, by nicolas Stowre, and on the northeast by Edward Burton.

3.   ffoure Acres of earable land lying in the east feilde, butting to the north upon misticke river ; to the south upon George Knower ;

bounded on the east by ffrancis Willebey; and on the west by George Kōer.

4. Two Acres of earable by estemation, more or lesse, lying in the east feilde butting to the southwest upon the streete-way, and to the northeast upon the widdow nash; bounded upon the northwest and upon the southeast by Edward Mellowes.

5. Three Acres and half of earable land lyinge in the line feilde, butting to the southwest upon Cambridge line, and to the northeast upon Chalton comōn, bounded on the northwest by Rice Morrice, and on the southeast by Will Johnson.

6. Two Acres of meaddow ground and pasture by estimation, butting to the south upon Cambridge feilde, and to the north upon Gibbines river; bounded on the west by Richard Sprague, and on the east by Ralph Sprague.

7. Tenn Acres by estemation, more or lesse, of meaddow grounde, lying in misticke feilde, butting to the west upon the north river, to the east upon the comōn bounded upon the north by Abrā Palmᵉ, and on the south by Seth Sweetser.

8. Tenn Acres of woodland, lyin in mistik feilde, Nº 35, 80 pole in length and 20 in breadth, butting to the west upon the high way towards the north river, to the east upon the comōn, bounded on the north by James Browne, and on the south by George Bunker.

9. Three Acres of meaddow by estimation, more or lesse, lying on the north side of mourt prospect, butting southeast upon Edward Convers, and to the northwest upon the riverett, bounded by the comōn on the southeast (?) and northeast.

10. Eight milch cow comōn, 7 whereof fell to him in the divident, and one he bought of James Mathewes.

11. Two Acres of meaddow by estimation, more or lesse, bought by him of James mathewes, lying in misticke feilde, eastward of the east or South spring, Nº 8, butting

12. Thirtie and five Acres of woodland, lying in misticke feild, Nº 26, 100 pole in length and   in breadth, butting northeast upō will witherall and Abr Palmer, southwest upon Thō moulton and John Crow, bounded on the southeast by will Brakenbury, and on the norwest by George Hutchinson.

13. Eightie Acres of land lying in Rockefeilde,   in length and   in breadth.

14. Two Acres of eareable Land, lying in the line feilde by misticke ware, butting to the southwest upon Cambridge Line, northeast upon the bridge way, bounded on the southeast by Walter Palmer, and on the northwest by A highway.

[**15.**] *The possession of Samuell Carter in Charltowne limites.*

One dwelling house, with a yard and garden, bounded on the south by Prudence Wilkinson butting east and north upon the markett place, and east upon a comōn way.

2. Two acres of earable land by estimation, more or lesse, scituate in the east feild, butting southwest upon the bakstreete, northeast upon Capt. Sedgwick, bounded on the southeast by Ed.

Convers and will Johnson, and on the northwest by Mr Simmes, with A dwelling house upon it.

3.   ffive acres of earable land and swamp by estimation, more or lesse, lying in the east feilde, butting southwest upon Daniell Shepheardson, northeast upon walter Palmer, bounded on the southeast by Rice Cole, and on the northwest by Capt. Sedgwick. [This is sould to his father ould Thomas Cartar. — *Greene*.]

4.   Two acres of meaddow by estimation, more or lesse, scituate in the south meade, butting east upon Rob Long, west upon Rob Hayle, bounded on the south by Rice Cole, and on the northwest by Rob Long.

5.   Milch cow com̄ones, two and three quarters.

6.   ffive acres of woodland, more or lesse, scituate in mistick feilde, butting south upon the high way towards the meaddow, north upon the land way, bounded on the west by Rob Haile, and on the east by walter Palmer.

7.   Three acres of meaddow by estimation, more or lesse, lying in mistick marshes, butting west upon the north river, east upon the woodland, bounded on the south by Rice Cole, and on the north by Thō Moulton.

8.   ffive acres of woodland, more or lesse, scituate in mistick feilde, butting northeast upon John Harvard, southwest upon the reserved land, bounded on the southeast by Rich Miller, and on the northwest by John Goulde.   [This is sould to Ralph Mousall, who sould it to Peeter Tufts. — *Greene*.]

9.   ffive acres of land, more or lesse, scituate in waterfeilde, butting north west upon John berridge, southeast upon Mr Nowell, bounded on the northeast by John Goulde, and on the southwest by Richard Miller.

10.   ffifteene acres of land, more or lesse, scituate and lying in Rockfeilde.

The possession of John Penticost in Charltowne limites.

One dwelling house with a yard and garden, scituate on the west of the mill hill, bounded on the west by the widdow Nash, on the south by maultsters lane, on the east by the midle streete; long lane deviding betwixt the yard and garden.

Three acres of earable land by estimation, more or lesse, scituate in the line feilde, butting southwest upon Cambridge line, northeast upon the com̄on, bounded on the northwest by Rice Cole and on the southeast by John Brinsmeade.

[**16.**]   1638. *The Possession of John Moussell in Charlstown.*

1.   John Moussell hath in the high feilde, one home steede containing about three acres by estimation more or lesse, butting to the south upon the high way, and to the north upon the marsh towards misticke river; bounded on the east by John Brinsmeade and Ralph moussell, and on the west by Abr. Palmer. [This sould to Robert Leach. — *Greene*.]

2.   One pcell of grounde adioning to the sayd homesteede on the west side butting to the south upon the highway, to the north upon Abr. Palmer, bounded on the west by the widdow Ewer.

3. One Acre of carable land lying in the high feilde, butting to the south upon the high way, to the north upon william ffrothingam his marsh toward mistike river; bounded on the west by Richard Sprague; and on the east by James Tompsõ.

4. Two Acres of meaddow by estimation, more or lesse, lying in the high feilde marsh, butting to the south upon his owne homesteede, and Abr̄. Palmer, to the north upon Rob Carter, A Creeke deviding betwixt them, bounded on the east by George Hutchinson and on the west by Will ffrothingam.

5. One pole of grounde lying before his house, giuen him for A well yarde, the highway lying betwixt that and his house.

6. One Acre and A half by estimation, more or lesse, lying in the swampe before his house.

7. One Plott of grounde granted unto him for A houseplott, by estimation halfe a roode lying on the south east of the pounde, butting northeast upon the streete way, bounded on the southeast by John Brinsmeade.

8. Cõmones for milch cattell three and three quarters.

9. Two Acres of earable land, lying in the line feilde, butting southwest upon Cambridge lyne; to the noreast upon the highway; bounded on the   by James Tompson; and on the   by John Brinsmeade.

10. ffive Acres of woodland lying in misticke feilde Nº 21.

11. fffteene Acres of woodland lying in misticke feilde Nº 60, 100[1] butting northeast upon Ed Carrington, John Brinsmeade and Phillip drinker, south west upon Rob Rand, bounded on the norwest by five acres wast grounde and on the southeast by Rich Palgrave.

12. Sixtie Acres of land lying estimate, more or lesse, scituate in waterfeilde butting norwest upon George bunker, southeast upon Thom̄ Goble, bounded on the northeast by Ab̄ Hill and on the southwest by Thõ Richardson.

[**17.**] *The Possession of Prudence Wilkinson within Charltown limites.*

One dwelling house with a garden plott scituate on the south of the mill hill butting south upon Charles river, bounded on the north by Samuell Carter and on the east and west by the cõmon way.

2. Two acres of earable land by estimation, more or lesse, scituate in the east feilde butting southwest upon the streete way, northeast upon James Pemberton, bounded on the southeast and northwest by Seth Sweetsir.

3. One acre of meaddow by estimation, more or lesse, scituate in the south meade.

4. One milch Cow cõmon.

5. One acre of meaddow by estimation, more or lesse, scituate in mistick marshes butting southeast upon the south river, northwest upon the woodland, bounded on the northeast by Micheall Bastow and on the southwest by Sam̄ Richardson.

6. ffive acres of woodland, more or lesse, scituate in mistick feilde, butting south upon a high way betwixt it and the meadow,

---

[1] " 100 pole in length " was written and all but the " 100 " erased by the Re-corder. — ED.

north upon the land way bounded on the east by Rob. Hayle, and on the west by Rich. Ketle and Thō miner.

7. ffive acres of woodland, more or lesse, scituate in mistick feilde, butting northeast upon John Sibly, southwest upon Rice Cole; bounded on the southeast by John wolrich, and on the northwest by James Hubbard.

8. ffifteene acres of land, more or lesse, scituate in waterfeilde, butting northwest upon Mʳˢ Katherin Coytemore, southeast upon Nicolas Trerrice, bounded on the southwest by John wolrich, and on the northeast by James Hubbard.

9. Two acres of land, more or lesse, scituate in the line feilde, butting north upon mistick pond, south upon the Bridge way, bounded on the east by Ed. Carrington, and on the west by Ric. Sprague.

The Possession of Will Smith within Charltowne limites.

One dwelling house with a garden plott, scituate on the northwest of the mill hill, butting east upon midle streete, west upon crooked lane; bounded on the south by Lewis Hewlett, and on the north by Rich White.

2. ffive acres of woodland, more or lesse, scituate in mistick feilde, butting northeast upon Samuell Haule, southwest upon the woodland; bounded on the northwest by Josseph Cetcherall, and on the southeast by John Berridge.

3. Tenn acres of land, more or lesse, scituate in waterfeilde, butting northwest upon George Hutchinson, southeast upon Rich Miller; bounded on the southwest by Josseph Cetcherall, and the northeast by Jō Berridge.

[**18.**] 1638. *The Possession of Nicolas Stower in Charltowne.*

1. Nicolas Stower hath, in the south feilde, one homestead containing, by estimation, two Acres, more or lesse, butting to the east upon the mill hill, to the west upon Mʳ Josseph hille grounde, bounded on the south by the widdow Nash, and on the north by Thomas Lynde and Rob Rand, with one dwelling house and other out houses upon it.

2. Three Acres and half of earable land lying in the east feilde, butting to the south upon George Bunker, and to the north upon misticke river; bounded on the west by George Bunker, and on the east by George Hutchinson.

3. Comōn for five milch cowes and

4. Two Acres of earable lying in the line feilde, butting southwest upon Cambridge Line, to the northeast upon the high way; bounded on the northwest by Thō Caule, and on the southeast by Edward Johnson.

5. ffive Acres of woodland, lying in misticke feilde, butting to the south upon the high way towards misticke river, to the north upon the widdow nash, bounded on the east by the high way betwixt that and the meaddow, and on the west by Ralph moussell.

6. Three Acres of meaddow by estimation, more or lesse, butting to the south upon mistick river, to the north upon the

woodland; bounded on the east by walter Palmer, and on the west by Will. Lerned.

7. One Acre and haulf of meaddow by estimation, more or lesse, lying in misticke feilde; butting to the east upon the north river, to the west upon the woodland, bounded on the north by walter Palmer, and on the south by Samuell Haule.

8. One haulfe acre of meaddow by estimation, more or lesse, bought of M⁵ Ann Higinson, in misticke feilde, butting to the south east upon the north river, to the west upon the woodland; bounded on the south by Walter Palmer, and on the northeast by Thomas Brigden.

9. Two Acres of meaddow by estimation, more or lesse, lying in misticke feilde, bounded on the north by Salle path,¹ on the east and south by the fresh riverett, and on the west by Thomas Squire.

10. One Acre of meaddow by estimation, more or lesse, lying on north side of Gibbines feilde or south meade, bounded on the east by Abr. Pratt, and on the west by rice morrice; on the north by the com̅on, and on the south by Gibbins river.

11. Twentie five Acres of woodland lying in misticke feild, N° 85; 100 pole in length,   pole in breadth, butting northeast upon Edward mellow, and to the southwest upon John Brinsmeade, Phillip drinker, George felt, and rice morrice, bounded on the southeast by Rob. Cutler, and on the nowest by John Tedd.

12. Sixtie Acres of land lying in rock feild, N° 85.

[**19.**]   *The possession of Rob. Cutler within Charlstowne limites.*

One dwelling house with a garden plott scituate on the northeast side of the mill hill, butting northeast upon the streete way, southwest upō the mill hill, bounded on the southeast by mill lane, and on the northwest by Har. Garrett.

2. Two acres of earable land, by estimation, more or lesse, scituate in the east feilde.

3. One acre of meaddow by estimation, more or lesse, scituate and lying in the high feilde meade.

4. Milch cow comones one and a haulfe.

5. One acre of meaddow by estimation, more or lesse, lying in the meade at wilsones pointe, butting southeast upon mistick river, northwest upon the woodland, bounded on the

6. Tenn acres of woodland, more or lesse, scituate in mistick feilde, butting northeast upon Ed Mellowes and Will Lernett, southwest upon Joseph Tedd and M⁵ Kathorin Coytemore, bounded on the northwest by Nicolas Stower, and on the southeast by Ed. convers.

7. Sixtie and three acres of land by estimation, more or lesse, scituate and being in waterfeilde, bounded on the southeast by George Bunker, on the northwest by the com̅on, on the southwest by Rob Long, and on the northeast by walter Palmer.

The possession of John Beridge in Charlton limites.

One dwelling house with a garden plot scituate in the east feilde.

---

¹ This locality, only once referred to in the Charlestown records, is supposed to be the "Salem path," "way to Mystic" or "Salem Highway" (see pp. 5 and 7). It ran easterly from the ford at Mystic, near the present bridge in Medford Centre, to Salem. — ED.

butting southeast upon the harbour, bounded on the northeast by Will Stilson, on the northwest and southwest by Capt. Sedgwick.

2. ffoure acres of earable land by estimation, more or lesse, scituate in the line feilde butting east towards winatomyes river, northwest upon Rob Long, bounded on the northeast by Harman Garrett, and on the southwest by will witherall or John Stretton.

3. Haulf a milch Cow comon : [more twoo cows comons bought of Mʳ zachry symms. — *Greene.*]

4. ffive acres of woodland, more or lesse, scituate in mistick feilde, butting northeast upon James Tompson, southwest upon the woodland, bounded on the northwest by Will Smith and on the southeast by Henry Bullock. [This five Akers was sould to Richard Lowden.— *Greene.*]

5. fflifteene acres of land, more or lesse, situate in waterfeilde, butting north west upon George Hutchinson, southeast upon John Goulde and Samuell Carter, bounded on the northeast by Henry Bullock and on the southwest by Will Smith.

6. Two acres of meaddow, more or lesse, scituate in the meade at wilsones point.

[**20.**] 1638. *James Pemberton his possession.*

James Pemberton hath in Charlestowne Liberties

1. One pcell of grounde containing haulf A roode of grounde, by estimation, more or lesse, butting to the northeast upon the streete way ; to the south west upon the salt marsh in broad cove, bounded on both sides by the comon, being   pole in breadth, and   in length.

2. Two Acres of eareable land, lying in the east feilde, butting to the northeast upon George Bunker, to the southwest upon the widow wilkin, bounded on the northwest by the comon swampe, and on the southeast by George Bunker.

3. Two Acres of eareable land lying in the line feilde by misticke ware, butting northward upon misticke river, and southward upon the high way, bounded on the west by Samuell Haule, and on the east by Rob Long.

4. Milch cow comon, two and A halfe

5. ffive Acres of woodland, lying in misticke feilde, Nº 12, 80 pole in length, and tenn in breadth, butting to the

6. One Acre of meaddow ground, by estimation, more or lesse, lying in misticke feilde, butting to the southwest upon misticke river, to the northeast upon James Tompson ; bounded on the northwest by Samuell Haule, and on the southeast by the comon.

7. ffive Acres of woodland lying in misticke feilde Nº 28, 100 pole in length and   in breadth, butting northeast upon James mathewes and George Heborne, southwest upon Edward convers, bounded on the norwest by will Brakenbu[ry] and on the southeast by Peter Garland.

8. Thirtie two Acres of land lying in waterfeilde Nº 28, 100 pole in length and   in breadth, butting norwest upon Josseph Coleman and Thō Caule, southeast upon John Crow, bounded on the southwest by Will Brakenbu[ry] and on the northeast by Peter Garland.

[**21.**] *The Possession of Daniell Shepheardson in Charltowne limites.*

One house with a garden plotte scituate on the northeast of the mill hill, butting northeast upon the streete-way, southwest upon the mill hill, bounded on the northwest by the mill lane and on the southeast by Mr. Nowell.

2. ffive roode of earable land by estimation, more or lesse, scituate in the east feilde, butting southwest upon long way, northeast upon Sam̄ Carter; bounded on the southeast by Rice Cole, and on the northwest by Capt. Sedgewick.

3. One acre of meaddow by estimation, more or lesse, lying in the high feilde meade, butting north upon mistick river, south upon Phillip drinker: bounded one the west by Sam̄ Haule and on the east by James Hayden.

4. Cow Commones one and three quarters.

5. ffive acres of land by estimation, more or lesse, scituate in the line feilde, butting south upon Ed Convers, north upon a high way towards mistick river, bounded on the west by will Brakenbury and on the east by the high way.

6. Tenn acres of woodland, more or lesse, scituate in mistick feilde, butting northeast upon Will Batchelor, southwest upon the woodland, bounded on the southeast by John Crow and on the northwest by Seth Sweetsir.

7. Twentie and ffive acres of land, more or lesse, scituate in waterfeilde, butting northwest oupon will Brackenbury, southeast upon James Greene, bounded on the northeast by John Crow and on the southwest by Seth Sweetseir.

[**22.**] 1638. *The possession of William dade in charles Towne.*

1. One pcell of grounde lying on the east side of the mill hill containing by estimation halfe A roode, more or lesse, butting to the west upon the streete way, to the east upon the backe streete or wapping Dock; bounded on the south by George Heborne; and on the north by Thomas Coytemore: with A dwelling house upon it.

2. Two acres of eareable land by estimation lying in the east feilde, butting to the southwest upon the bake streete; to the northeast upon Daniell Shepeardson; bounded on the southeast by Edmond Hubbard; and on the northwest by Edward Convers.

3. Two Acres of eareable land, lying in the east feilde, butting to the north upon misticke river, to the south upon A swampe towards Rice Cole, bounded on the east by Ralph Sprague, and on the north by Walter Palmer.

4. Com̄on for two milch Cowes and

5. Haulfe an Acre of meaddow by estimation, more or lesse, lying in misticke feilde, butting to the north upon the north river, runing east tap; bounded on the south by George ffelch, and on the north by Thomas Squire.

6. ffive Acres of woodland, lying in misticke feilde, N° 20, butting southwest upon the south river, and northwest upon John Greene, bounded on the southwest by Rice Cole, and on the northeast by George Heborne.

7. ffive acres of woodland, lying in misticke feild, N° 51, 100 pole in length and　　　in breadth, butting northeast upon Edward Johnson, southwest upon Jo. Harvard, bounded on the norwest by John wolrich, and on the northeast by Richard Ketle.

8. Thirtie ffive Acres of land, lying in waterfeilde, N° 51, 100 pole in length and　　　in breadth, butting norwest upon Edward Johnson, southeast upon Ann Higginson and Beniamin Hubard, bounded on the southwest by John Palmer, and on the northeast by John Lewis.

[**23.**]　*The Possession of James Browne within Charltowne limites.*

X. One dwelling house with a yard and garden, containing haulfe a roode of grounde by estimation, more or lesse, scituate on the south of the mill hill, butting south upon Abr. Pratt and the wharf way, bounded on the east by Thō Brigden and ffaintnot wines, and on the east and north by the high way.

2. Two acres of earable land by estimation, more or lesse, scituate in the east feilde, butting north upon mistick river, south upon a swamp, bounded on the west by Will Baker, and on the east by Walter Palmer.

3. X. Milch cow comōnes, three and A quarter.

4. X. One acre of meaddow by estimation, more or lesse, lying in the south meade, butting east upon the great cove, west upon Thō Richardson, bounded on the south by　　　and on the north by

5. Eight acres of earable land, more or lesse, scituate in the line feilde, butting northeast upon mistick river and pond, southwest upon the bridgway, bounded on the west by Ed Johnson, and on the east by the ware high way.

6. X. ffive acres of woodland by estimation, more [or] lesse, scituate in mistick feilde, butting west upon the drift way, east upon the landway, bounded on the south by Ed Mellowes, and on the north by Thō Squire and Sarah Ewer.

7. X. Two acres of meaddow by estimation, more or lesse, lying in mistick marshes, butting north upon a creeke out of the north river, south upon the woodland, bounded on the east by Thō Ewer, and on the west by Will Baker.

8. X. ffifteene acres of woodland, more or lesse, scituate in mistick feilde, butting northeast upon Widdow Nash and Will ffrothingale, southwest upon Mr Nowell, bounded on the northwest by Thō goble, and on the southeast by Rob Haukines.

9. ffortie acres of land, more or lesse, scituate in waterfeilde, butting northwest upon Ed Burton, Thō Richardson and John Moussell, southeast upon Rob Rand and Ezecheall Richardson, bounded on the northeast by Thō Goble, and on the southwest by Rob Haukines. [The parts marked X thus above of this, is sould unto Robert Mirriam. — *Greene.*]

[**24.**]　1638.　*The possession of John Stretton in Charltowne.*

1. Two Acres of grounde by estimation, more or lesse, lying in the southfeiide, butting southeast upon the mill hill, to the north·

west upon Rob Rand, bounded on the northeast by the streete way, and on the southwest by Edward Burton.

2. ffoure Acres of meaddow grounde by estimation, more or lesse, lying in mistick feilde, butting west upon the north river, east upon the woodland, bounded on the north by

3. Comon for two milch Cowes.

4. One Acre of earable by estimation, lying in the line feilde, butting southeast upon the high way toward winotamyes river, norwest upon Rob Long, bounded on the southwest by the bridge way, and on the northeast by Harman Garrett.

5. ffifteene Acres of woodland, lying in mistick feilde, N° 64, 100 pole in length and   in breadth, butting to the northeast on George Bunker and the meadow, southwest upon Thō Lynde, bounded on the norwest by Walter Palmer, and on the southeast by Abr Palmer.

6. ffortie Acres of land by estimation, lying in waterfeilde, N° 64, 100 pole in length and   in breadth, butting to the norwest upon Walter Palmer, southeast upon John Harvard, bounded on the southwest by Abr Palmer, and on the northeast by Walter Palmer.

[**25.**]   *The Possession of Abrā Pratt in Charltowne limites.*

One dwelling house with a yard, situate on the south of the mill hill, butting south upon the wharfe way towards Charles river, bounded on the north by James Browne, on the west by Thō Brigden, and on the east by the high way.

2. One garden plott, about ffour pole of grounde, situate on the south of the mill hill.

3. One acre and haulf of earable land by estimation, more or lesse, scituate in the south feilde, butting southwest upon Charles river, northeast upon Beachers cove, bounded on the north west by Thō Brigden.

4. ffoure acres of earable land by estimation, more or lesse, situate in the east feilde, butting north upon Mistick river, south upon the widow Nash, bounded on the west by Ezecheall Richardson, and on the east by Will ffrothingale.

5. Comones for two milch cowes.

6. One acre of meadd by estimation, more or lesse, scituate in the southe meade, butting.   [This is sould to Alice Rand. — *Greene.*]

7. Two acres of meaddow by estimation, more or lesse, lying in misticke marshes.

8. ffive acres of meaddow by estimation, more or lesse, lying in mistick marshes, butting south upon a creeke of the south river to the north upon the woodland, bounded on the east by the freshett that runes from the south spring, and on the west by George Whitehand.

9. Tenn acres of land, more or lesse, scituate in mistick feilde butting northeast upon Walter Palmer, southwest upō Ed Gibbines or Mʳ Pane ; bounded on the northwest by Will Powell and on the southeast by Isaac Cole.

10. ffortie acres of land by estimation, more or lesse, scituate and lying in Rockfeilde.

[All this was given to Mr Tho: Allen and Mrs Rebeckah Trarice. — *Greene.*]

[**26.**] 1638. *The possession of Increase Nowell, Esq., within the limites of Charltowne.*

1. Two hundrethe Acres of land by estimation, more or lesse, of earable, woodland, swampe, and meaddow; scituate and being in misticke feilde, bounded on the east by the north river, on the west by M^r mathew Craddocke his farme, bounded on the south by Mr John wilson his ferme, and on the north by Capt. Robert Sedgwicke, Steven fforsdich, micheall Bastow, and ffaintenot wines, which 200 acres was given and graunted unto the s^d Increase Nowell by the Court before the boundes of the sayde towne were layde out.

2. One pcell of grounde scituate on the southeast side of the mill hill, containing one roode by estimation, more or lesse, butting to the east upon the streete way, to the west upon the mill hill, bounded on the north by Daniell Sheperdson, and on the south by the mill lane, with A dwelling house and other aptinances upon it.

3. One garden plott containing three roodes by estimation, more or lesse, scituate one the east of the saide homestead, butting to the west upon the streete way, to the east upon water lane, bounded on the south by the widdow ewer, and on the north by well lane.

4. Twelve Acres by estimation, more or lesse, of earable land, swampe and meaddow, lying in the east feilde, butting to the north upon misticke river, to the south upon the highway, bounded on the east by Seth Sweetzer, Thomas Knoerr and George Knower, and the horse meaddow, and on the west by Ralph Sprague.

5. Comones for sixe milch Cowes and one ¼ of a common bought of Will Johnson.

6. One Acre of meaddow by estimation, more or lesse, scituate and lying at the head of Gibbines' river, butting east upō the creeke, west upon the church land, bounded by Micheall Bastow and Ann Higinson.

7. Twelve Acres of meaddow by estimation, more or lesse, scituate and lying in misticke feilde, marshes, butting to the southeast upon the south river, to the northwest upon the woodland, bounded on the northeast by Rob. Long, and on the southwest by Micheall Bastow.

8. ffive Acres of woodland scituate and lying in misticke feilde; butting to the south upon Rob. Long his meaddow, to the north upon Mr Simmes, bounded on the east by Boston line and on the west by

9. Sixtie Acres of woodland, scituate and lying in misticke hundrethes, 100 pole in length, and   butting to the northeast upon Richard Sprague, southwest upon the woodland, bounded on the southeast by Mr Simmes, and on the northwest by John Greene.

10. One hundred Sixtie Acres of land by estimation, more or lesse, scituate and lying in waterfeilde, bounded on the northeast by

Mʳ Simmes and on the northwest by John Greene, Ralph moussell, Thō Carter, John Goulde, Ric Miller and Saṁ Carter, and on the south and west coṁon.

[**27.**] *The Possession of Robert Hayle within the limetes of Charltowne.*

One dwelling house with a yard and garden containing one roode of grounde by estimation, more or lesse, scituate on the southwest of the mill hill, butting south upon Charles river, north upon crooked lane, bounded on the east by Hayless lane, and on the west by Beniamin Hubbard.

2. Three acres of earable land by estimation, more or lesse, scituate in the east feilde, butting southe upon the oulde high way, north upon Will Brakenbury, bounded on the west by Thō Coytemore, and on the east by the widdow Hȧrvard.

3. Three acres of earable land by estimation, more or lesse, scituate in the line feilde, butting south upon Will Knight, north upon John Greene, bounded on the east by the church land, and on the southwest by Cambridge line.

4. Two acres of meaddow and pasture by estimation, more or lesse, scituate on the south part, butting south upon Cambridge fence, north   upon Gibbines river, bounded on the east by Ezecheall Richardson, and on the west by John Wolrich.

5. Two acres of meaddow by estimation, more or lesse, lying in the south meade, butting north upon a creeke in broad cove, south west upon   , bounded on the south by Rob Long, and on the northwest by Nicolas Davis and a creeke.

6. ffoure milch Cow coṁones.

7 Six acres of land, more or lesse, scituate in the line feilde, butting southwest upon Cambridge line, northeast upon the bridgway, bounded on the northwest by Mathew Smith, and on the southeast by the widdow Harvard.

8. ffive acres of woodland by estimation, more or lesse, scituate in mistick feilde, butting south upon the high way, north upon the woodland, bounded on the west[1] by Samuell Carter, and on the west [*sic*] by George felt.

9. ffifteene acres of woodland, more or lesse, scituate in mistick feilde, butting southwest upon George Bunker, noṛth upon the coṁon, bounded on the northwest by Thō Brigden, and on the southeast by Rob Leach.

10. ffiftie acres of land by estimation, more or lesse, scituate and lying in west rockfeilde, butting west upon the river, east upon the coṁon, bounded on the south by George Whithand, and on the north by Thō Brigden.

11. Two acres of meaddow by estimation, more or lesse, scituate in the south meade, butting south upon Samuell Richardson, bounded on the west by John Hodges, on the north by the bulls'hay, on the east by John Hodges, Ed convers and Josseph Hills.

12. Two acres of meaddow by estimation, more or lesse, scituate in the south meade, bounded on the southeast by Rob

---

[1] This should read *East*: cf. Samuel Carter's sixth lot (*ante* p. 10), and George Felt's third lot (*post* p. 58). — Eᴅ.

Long, on the west by Ed Convers, Thō Carter and Rob Long, and on the north by the creeke.

13.   Haulf an acre of meaddow by estimation, more or lesse, scituate in misticke feilde, bounded on the east by Ric. Ketle, and Goō Robines, on the south and west by the high way and on the north by the woodland.

[**28**]   1638.   *The possession of Thomas Coytemore in Chaltowne Limites.*

1.   One homestead scituate and lying in the east feilde, containing two acres of grounde by estimation, more or lesse, butting to the south east upon wapping Dock, to the norcast upon the high way, bounded on the south east by wapping streete, and on the northwest by Walter- Palmer, with A dwelling house and other aptinances upon the sayde grounde.

2.   ffoure Acres of earable land by estimation, more or lesse, scituate and lying in the east feilde, butting to the south upon a highway, north upō Will Brakenbury, bounde upō the est by Rob Hayle.   [These foure Akers was and is sould to Robert Hale. — *Greene.*]

3.   Eight Acres of earable land, scituate and lying in the line feilde by misticke ware, butting to the southwest upon Cambridge line, to the northeast upon the bridge way, bounded on the southeast by Robt Carter, and on the norwest by Ralph Sprague.

4.   Comones for foure milch Cowes.

5.   One Acre of meaddow by estimation, more or lessen scituate and lying in the high feilde maish, bounded on the north by Ed Carrington.

6.   One pcell of grounde containing haulfe A roode by estimation, more or lesse, scituate on the est side of the mill hill, butting eastward upon the back streete, to the west upon the streete way, bounded on the north by Rice Cole, and on the south by will Dade.

7.   ffoure Acres of meaddow grounde by estimation, more or lesse, lying in misticke feilde marshes, butting to the west upon the north river, to the east upon the woodland, bounded on the north by   and on the south by

8.   ffive Acres of woodland lying in misticke feilde, Nº 44, 80 pole in length and tenn in breadth, bought of Mʳ Thomas James with his house, butting to the west upon the Drift way by the north river, to the west [*sic*] upon the comōn, bounded on the north by Abr. mellowes, and on the south by Nicolas Davis.

9.   Thirtie and five acres of woodland, scituate and lying in mistik feilde, Nº 108,   length, and   in breadth, butting to the south upon the meaddow, to the north upon the common, bounded on the west by the fresh riverett, and on the east by Mʳ Hiles.

10.   Seaventie Acres of land scituate and lying

11.   One pcell of grounde scituate and being at sconce Point, butting southeast upon the harbour, southwest upon wapping Dock, bounded on the north east by Mʳ John Allin.

12.   fflfteene acres of woodland scituate in mistick feilde, bought of the asignes of John Stretton and entred in his naime.

13.   fflve acres of meaddow or five cowes grasse, lying in mistick marshes, bought of Mr Nowell, bounded by Micheall Bastow on the south, and Mr Inc. Nowell on the north.

[**29.**]   *The Possession of Edward Johnson within Charltowne limites.*

One dwelling house with a garden plott, scituate on the south of the mill hill, butting south upon Charles river, north upon crooked lane, bounded on the west by Hayles lane, and on the east by Abraham Pratt and Thō Brigden.

2.   One dwelling house with a garden plott scituate on the south of the mill hill, butting southe upon crooked lane, bounded on the north west by John Lewis, and on the north east by Josseph Hills.

3.   One acre of meaddow by estimation, more or lesse, scituate in the south meade bought of Mr. Hubbard.

4.   Milch cow comͦones fflve and a haulfe. [Three and a halfe of these comͦons are sould by Captain Johnson unto Gardy James. —*Greene.*]

5.   Two acres of land by estimation, more or lesse, scituate in the line feilde, butting southwest upon Cambridge line, northeast upon the bridgeway, bounded on the northwest by James Hubbard and on the southeast by math Smith.

6.   ffoure acres of earable land by estimation, more or lesse, scituate in the line feilde, butting southwest upon Cambridge line, northeast upon the bridge way, bounded on the northwest by Nicolas Stowers, and on the southe east by A high way.

7.   foure acres of land by estimation, more or lesse, scituate in the line feilde, butting southwest upon the bridg-way, north east upon mistick pond, bounded on the northwest by Ed Carrington and Prū wilkinson, and on the southeast by Jā Browne.

8.   Tenn acres of meaddow : swamp : and earble, by estimation, more or lesse, scituate in the line feilde, butting southwest upon Cambridge line, north upon mistick pond, bounded on the east by Thō Caule and James Hayden, and on the north west by the comͦon.

9.   Three acres of woodland by estimation, more or lesse, scituate in mistick feilde, butting west upon the drift way, east upon the land way, bounded on the north by Ed Carington.

10.   fflfteene acres of woodland, more or lesse, scituate in mistick feilde, butting northeast upon Will Johnson and James Heyden southeast upon m^r John Harvard ; bounded on the northwest by Ann Higginson, and on the southeast by Nicolas Trerrice ; [1] this was bought of m^r Hubbard.   This five acres of Robert Shorthus,[1] was also bought by Edward Johnson.

11.   ffortie acres of woodland, more or lesse, scituate in mistick feilde, butting northeast upon ffrancis Norton and Rob Long, southwest upon Ann Higginson, Nicolas Davis, John Haule, Ric. Ketle

---

[1] **Nicholas Trerrice** is written by Greene over Rob. Shorthus erased. — ED.

and John Palmer, bounded on the northwest by John Sibley and on the southeast by Will Johnson

12.   One acre of meadow by estimation, more or lesse, scituate, in mistick marshes, bought of Beñ Hubbard, butting north upon the north river, south upon the woodland, bounded on the west by Will Johnson and on the east by Thō Squire.

13.   ffive score and tenn acres of land by estimation, more or lesse, scituate in waterfeilde, butting northwest upon Henry Larrence and Will Johnson, southeast upon John Haule, Rich Ketle, John Palmer, Will Dade and John Lewis ; bounded on the northeast by John Sibley, and on the southwest by the comõn.

[**30.**]   1638.   *The possesion of Abraham Palmer in Charltowne limites.*

1.   Three Acres of land by estimation, more or lesse, scituate and lying in the high feilde, butting to the north and east upon mistick river, bounded on the south by Ralph moussell, and on the west by Josseph Hill and James Greene, with A Dwelling house and other aptinances thereunto belonging.

2.   Two Acres of land by estimation, more or lesse, lying in the high feilde, butting northward upon mistike river and to the south upon George Bunker, bounded on the west by Thomas Squire, and on the east by George Bunker.

3.   Two Acres of earable land by estimation, more or lesse, scituate and lying in the high feilde, butting to the north upon the marsh toward mistik river, to the south upon A pcell of grounde aptaining by purchase to John moussell ; bounded on the west by the widdow Ewer, and on the east by John moussell.

4.   Comõnes for foure milch cowes.

5.   ffive acres of meaddow by estimation, more or lesse, scituate and lying in mistick feilde marshes, butting to the south upon mistick river, to the east upon the south river, bounded on the north by Richard Sprague and on the west by Ralph Sprague.

6.   Sixe Acres of meaddow by estimation, more or lesse, lying in mistik feilde marshes, butting to the west upon the north river, to the east upon the woodland ; bounded on the north by George bunker, and on the south by Thomas Lynde.   A living spring in it.

7.   ffive Acres of wood land, scituate and being in misticke feilde, Nº 32, 80 pole in length and tenn in breadth, butting to the west upon the drift way toward the north river, and to the east upon the comõn or landway ; bounded on the south by Rice morice, and on the north by will Brakenbury.

8.   ffive Acres of wood land, scituate and being in mistick feilde, Nº 42, butting to the west upon the Drift way towards the north river, and to the east upon the comõn, bounded on the north by Edw Burton, and on the south by Robert Rand. [This was given in exchang for another to will Brakenbury. — *Greene.*]

9.   Twentie Acres of woodland by estimation, more or lesse, scituate and lying in mistik feilde, Nº 63, 100 pole in length and in breath, butting to the northeast upon George Bunker ; southwest upon Thō Lynde and will Brakenbury ; bounded on

the norwest by Jo Strettō, and on the southeast by James mathewes or Thō Lynde.

10.   Eightie Acres of land, scituate and lying in waterfeilde, Nº 63   in length and   in breadth ; butting to the norwest upon George Bunker ; southeast upon John Harvard ; bounded on the southwest by James mathē or Thō Lynde ; and on the northeast by John Sretton.

11.   One pcell of grounde scituate neere the oulde meeting-house, butting northeast upon the streete way, southwest upon the marsh in broad Cove, bounded on the southeast by James Pemberton, and on the norwest by highway.   [This was again resigned upon condition that it should lye in comōn. — *Greene*.]

12.   One acre of land, more or lesse, scituate in the east feilde, butting southwest upon the streeteway, bounded on the northwest by will ffrothingam, and on the southeast and northeast by Thō Ruck, with a dwelling house upon it.

13.   One acre and quarter of land by estimation, more or lesse, scituate in the east feilde, bounded on the northwest by Thō Lynde, on the southwest by Sarah Ewer and Ric Lowden, and on the southeast by will ffrothingam.

14.   And Sixe acres of land in the east feilde bought of mʳ Ruck with some oulde houseing upon it, and three Cowes grasse at wilsones point, as apears in the entry of the sale, &c.

[**31.**] *The possesion of Walter Palmer within Charltowne limites.*
Two acres of land by estimation, more or lesse, scituate in the east feilde, butting southwest upon the backstreete ; northeast upon long way ; bounded on the southeast by Thō Coytemore and on the northwest by the corne way with a dwelling house and other aptinances.

2.   ffive acres of earable land by estimation, more or lesse, scituate in the east feild, butting north upon mistick river, south upon a highway, bounded on the west by James browne, and on the east by will dade.

3.   Milch cow commones six and a quarter.

4.   ffoure acres of land, more or lesse, scituate in the line feilde, butting southwest upon Cambridg line, northeast upon the bridgway, bounded on the southeast by James Hubbard, and on the northwest by Thō Lynde.

5.   Eight acres of meadow by estimation, more or lesse, lying in mistick marshes, butting southwest upon misticke river, northeast upon the woodland, bounded on the southeast by Will ffrothingale, and on the northwest by Nicholas Stowers.

6.   ffoure acres of meadow by estimation, more or lesse, scituate in mistick meaddowes, butting south upon the north river, north upon the woodland, bounded on th east by Nicolas Stowers, and on the west by Sam. Haule.

7.   ffive acres of woodland by estimation, more or lesse, scituate in mistick feilde, butting south upon a high way towards the meaddow, north upon the land way, bounded on the east by Rob Hayle, and on the west by Jo. Palmer.

8.   ffive acres of meaddow by estimation, more or lesse, scituate

on the west of mount pspect, butting north upon George Bunker, the south and west, bounded by the comon and the freshett.

9.   Three acres of meaddow by estimation, more or lesse, scituate on the northwest of mount pspect, butting south upon will Brakenbury, north upon Ralph moussell, bounded on the east by the freshett, and on the west by the common.

10.   Thirtie acres of woodland, more or lesse, scituate in mistick feilde, in two pcells, 17 acres in one pcell, butting southwest upon long meade, northeast upon Thō Brigden and Math Smith, bounded on the southeast by George Bunker, and on the northwest by the comon; and thirteene acres in an other pcell, bounded on the north by long meade, on the southwest by Abr. Pratt, Isaac Cole, and Will Batchelor, and on the southeast by Will witherall.

11.   Eightie six acres of land by estimation, more or lesse, scituate in waterfeilde, butting southeast upon John Harvard, northwest upon the comon, bounded on the southwest by Rob Cutler, George Bunker, and Will Witherall.

––––––

[**32.**]   1638.   *The possesion of Ralph Moussell in Charletown limites.*

1.   ffoure Acres and a haulf of land by estimation, more of lesse, scituate and lying in the high feilde, butting to the south upon the highway, to the east upon misticke way, bounded on the west by George bunker and Josseph hill, and on the north by Abr. Palmer, with A dwelling house and other aptinances thereunto.

2.   ffive roodes of earable by estimation, more or lesse, scituate and being in the high feilde butting to the north upon George hutchinson's meaddow towards misticke river, to the south upon John Moussell and John Brinsmeade, bounded on the east by John Brinsmeade and on the west by John Moussell.   [This sould to Robert Leach. — *Greene.*]

3.   ffive Acres of hay grounde and pasture by estimation, more or lesse, scituate and lying in the high feilde, butting to the north upon misticke river, to the south upon henry Bullocke and James Tomson, bounded on the west by James Tomson and on the east by Thomas Squire.

4.   Comones for foure milch Cowes and A haulf.

5.   One Acre of meaddow by estimation, more or lesse, lying in the high feilde marsh, butting to the north and east upon mistick river, and south upon the great Cove, bounded on the west by

6.   ffive Acres of woodland scituate and lying in misticke feilde, butting to the south upon the meaddow toward mistick river, to the north upon John moussell, bounded on the west by the marsh and on the east by nicolas Stower and the widdow nash.   [This sold to Peter Tuft. — *Greene.*]

7.   ffiftene Acres of woodland by estimation lying in misticke feilde Nº 1, 100 pole in length and   in breadth, butting northeast upon John Harvard, southwest upon the comon, bounded on he norwest by Ric. Miller, and on the southeast by John Greene.

8.   ffiftie Acres of land scituate and lying in waterfeilde Nº 1,

100 pole in length and   in breadth, butting norwest upon Sam̄ Haule and Josseph Cetcherin, southeast upon Increase Nowell bounded on the southwest by John Greene, and on the northeast by Ric Miller.

[**33.**] *The possession of William Lernett within Charltown limites.*

Three acres of earable land and meaddow by estimation, more or lesse, scituate butting southwest upon broad cove, bounded on the northwest by James Hubbard, on the northeast by the oulde meeting house, with a dwelling house and other aptinances.

2. ffoure acres of earable land by estimation, more or lesse, scituate in the east feilde, butting north upon John Goulde, south upon the Widdow Nash, bounded on the east and west by Rich Sprague.

3. Cow commones three and three quarters.

4. Two acres of meaddow by estimation, more or lesse, scituate in mistick marshes, bounded on the east by Nicolas Stowers, on the southwest by James Tompson, and on the north by Mͬˢ Ann Harvard.

5. ffive acres of woodland by estimation, more or lesse, scituate in mistick feilde, butting south upon the high way towards the meaddow, north upon the land way, bounded on the east by and on the west by

6. ffifteene acres of woodland by estimation, more or lesse, scituate in mistick feilde, butting northeast upon the common, southwest upon Rob Long, bounded on the northwest by Ed Mellowes, and on the southeast by Sam̄ Richardson.

7. ffortie acres of land, more or lesse, scituate in Rock feilde.

The possesion of James Hubbard within Charltowne Limites.

One dwelling house with a garden plott, butting west up broade Cove, bounded on the south by Will Lernett and on the northwest by the com̄on.

2. One acre of meaddow by estimation, more or lesse, lying in the marsh at wilson Point, butting southeast upon mistick river, northwest upon   bounded on the southwest by James Garrett, and on the northeast by George Hutchinson.

3. Six acres of earable land by estimation, more or lesse, scituate in the line feilde, butting southwest upon Cambridge line, northeast upon the Bridgway, bounded on the northwest by walter Pallmer, and on the southeast by Edw Johnson.

4. Haulf a milch cow common.

5. ffive acres of woodland by estimation, more or lesse, scituate in misticke feilde, butting northeast upon Mͬˢ Coytemore, southwest upon John Hodges, bounded on the northwest by Thō Peirce, and on the southeast by Prudence Wilkinson.

6. ffifteene acres of land, more or lesse, scituate in water feilde, butting northwest upon Mͬ Coytemore, southeast upon Nicolas Tririce, bounded on the northeast by Thō Peirce, and on the southwest by Prudence Wilkinson.

[34.] 1638. *The possesion of James Tomson in Charlton Limites.*

1. Two Acres of land by estimation, more or lesse, scituate and lying in the high feilde, butting to the south upon the high way, to the north upon the meaddow towarde mistik river; bounded on the east by George Whitehand and Henry Bullocke, and on the west by Nicolas Davis, with a dwelling house and other aptinances thereunto.

2. One acre of earable by estimation, scituate and lying in the high feilde, butting to the south upon the high way, to the north upon the marsh towarde mistik river, bounded on the east by Ralph Sprague, and on the west by John moussell.

3. Two Acres of meaddow by estimation, more or lesse, lying in the high feilde marsh, butting to the south upon Nicolas Davis and Thomas Richardson, to the north upon the great Cove, bounded on the east by Ralph moussell, and on the west by Ezecheall Richardson.

4. Two Acres of earable land by estimation, more or lesse, scituate and lying in the line feilde, butting to the southwest upon Cambridge line, to the northeast upon Charlton comon; bounded on the southeast by John moussell, and on the northwest by John ffairefeilde.

5. Milch Cow Comones three and A quarter. [This qurtr sold to John Green. — *Greene.*] [one of these comons sold to John March. — *Greene.*]

6. Two Acres of meaddow by estimation, more or lesse, scituate and lying in misticke feilde, butting to the southwest upon misticke river, to the northeast upon Will Lernett, bounded on the northwest by James Pemberton and the comon, and on the southeast by A creeke.

7. ffive acres of woodland, scituate and lying in mistick feilde, N° 41, 80 pole in length and tenn in breadth, butting to the west upon the drift way towards the north river; to the east upon the land way, bounded on the south by   , and on the north by

8. ffive Acres of woodland, scituate and lying in misticke feild, No. 20, 100 pole in length and   in breadth, butting to the northeast upon long meade, southwest upon John Berridge, bounded on the norwest by Sam Haule, and on the southeast by William Powell.

9. ffortie Acres of land by estimation, more or lesse, scituate and lying in waterfeilde, N° 20, 100 pole in length and   in breadth, butting to the norwest upon Abr. Pratt and Isaac Cole; southeast upon John Greene, bounded on the southweast by Will Powell, and on the northeast by Sam Haule.

[35.] *The possession of William ffrothingale in Charletown.*
ffoure acres of earable land by estimation, more or lesse, scituate in the east feilde, butting southwest upon the streete way, north upon mistick river, bounded on the west by Ed mellowes and Abr. Pratt, and on the east by George Bunker and Thō Rucke, with a dwelling house upō it.

2. Two acres of meaddow by estimation, more or lesse, scituate in the high feilde meade, butting south upon Ralph Sprague, Jam̄ Tompson, and John Moussell, to the north upon Winthrop creeke, bounde on the east by John moussell, and on the north by Will Batchelor.

3. Two acres of earable land by estimation, more or lesse, scituate in the line feilde, butting southwest upon Cambridge line, northeast upon the com̄on, bounded on the southeast by Rice Cole, and on the northwest by Abr. Hill.

4. Cow commons three and a haulf. [more bought: of Walter Pamer, one Comon and three quarters; of Thomas Grover one Comon and a quarter; in all six comons and a halfe. — *Greene.*]

5. Six acres of meaddow by estimation, more or lesse, scituate in mistick feilde, butting south upon mistick river, north upon the woodland, bounded on the west by Walter Palmer, and on the east by Ra Sprague.

6. ffive acres of wood land by estimation, more or lesse, scituate in mistick feilde, butting west upon the drift way towards the north river, east upon the land way, bounded on the south by

7. Twentie acres of wood land, more or lesse, scituate in mistick feilde, butting northeast upon ffrancis Norton, southwest upon Rich Sprague and Thō. Goble; bounded on the northwest by Nicolas Trerrice, and on the southeast by Will Nash and Boston line. [This 20 akrs and 5 more, gott of widow nash, is sold to Mr nicolas parker of boston. — *Greene.*]

8. Sixtie acres of land by estimation, more or lesse, scituate in waterfeilde, butting northwest upon Thō Peirce, southeast upon Thō Lynde or the com̄on, bounded on the northeast by Will Nash, and on the southwest by Nicolas Trerrice. [This 60 Akars was relinquished to the towne, and in leiw thereof Granted to william ffrothingham sixty Akers of Arrable and meadow land lying and scituate at woburne, in charltowne Bounds, bounded southwest by the River (and by John March) which runs down by Thomas Graves, his farme bounded northwest by John Marches Lott, and northeast by the com̄on, and southeast butting towards Mr Graves lott. — *Greene.*]

————

The posetions of Mr nicolass parker in Charlstown limits.

1. Twenty five akers of wood land, more or less, bought of wiliam ffrothingham, as a bill of salle undr his hand testifis, baring datte the 21th 4 mo., 1648, the record of wiliam frothingham doth show the bound, folio 18.[1]

2. ffiften akers of woodland, more or less, bought of mrs Rebeckah tarice, as a bill of salle undr her hand testifis (hauing reseivd full pay), datted the 20th 6 mo, 1650, as the Record of her posetions doth show the bounds of the land, folio 40.[2]

---

[1] This reference is clearly to lot No. 7 of Frothingham's possessions, above given. — ED.

[2] This folio 40 is page [81] in this copy. — ED.

[36.] 1638. *The possesion of George Bunker within Charlton Limites.*

1. Two acres of eareable land by estimation, more or lesse, scituate in the east feilde, butting northwest upon the high way towards mistick river, bounded on the south by Ric. Sprague, and on the east by John Goulde, with a dwelling house and other aptinances.

2. Three acres of earable land, more or lesse, scituate in the east feilde, butting southwest upon Seth Sweetsir and Samuell Richardson, northeast upon   , bounded on the southeast by Ed Convers, and on the northwest by James Pemberton. [one of thes 3 Akers was sould to benia hubbard, who sold it to John March. — *Greene.*]

3. Two acres of earable land by estimation, more or lesse, scituate in the east feilde, butting north upon mistick river, south upon will ffrottlingam, bounded on the east by Nicolas Stower, and on the west by Will ffrothingam.

4. Three acres of earable land by estimation, more or lesse, scituate in the high feilde, bounded on the south by the high way, on the north by Thō Squire, Abr Palmer and Jo Hils, butting west upon the feilde way and east upon Ra. Moussell, with a dwelling house and other aptinances bought by him of the widdow Beacher, late wife of Thō Beacher of Charltowne, deceased.

5. Two acres of earable land by estimation, more or lesse, scituate in the high feilde, butting north upon the high way towards mistick river, south upon the aforsaid homesteede, bounded on the west by Abr Palmer, and on the east by Josseph Hiles.

6. ffoure acres of earable land by estimation, more or lesse, scituate in the high feilde, butting south upon the high way, north upon the meade towards mistick river, bounded on the west by Samuell Haule, and on the east by John ffairefeilde.

7. One acre of meaddow by estimation, more or lesse, scituate in the high feilde meade, butting north upon the great cove, south upon the high way, bounded on the east by Ezecheall Richardson, and on the west by

8. One acre of meaddow by estimation, more or lesse, scituate in the south meade.

9. Commones for ffifteene milch cowes.

10. Seaven acres of meaddow by estimation, more or lesse, scituate in the Line feilde, butting north upon mistick river, east upon wenatomies river, bounded on the south and west by the high way and Ed Convers meaddow.

11. Tenn acres of woodland by estimation, more or lesse, scituate in mistick feilde, butting west upon the drift way, east upon the land way, bounded on the south by Thō Knowher, and on the north by Thō Lynde.

12. ffive acres of wood land, more or lesse, scituate in mistick feilde, butting west upon the drift way, east upon the land way, bounded on the one side by Nicolas Davis, bought of

13. ffive acres of woodland, more or lesse, scituate in mistick feilde, butting west upon the drift way, west upon the land way, pᵗ. of Ed Burton tenn acres.

14. Six acres of meaddow, by estimation, more or lesse, scituate in mistick marshes ; butting west upon the north river, east upon the woodland ; bounded on the south by Abr. Palmer, and on the north by Joh Crow.

15. Three acres of meaddow by estimation, more or lesse, scituate in mistick marshes, butting west upon the north river, east upon the woodland, bounded on the

16. Tenn acres of meaddow by estimation, more or lesse, scituate in mistick marshes, bounded on the northwest by the fresh river, on the south by the north river and creeke, bounded on the east by Nicolas Davis and Ed Mellowes, and on the west by George ffelt.

17. Three acres of meaddow by estimation, more or lesse, lying on the west of mount pspect, bounded on the east by the fresh river, on the west by the woodland, and north by Ra. Spragues meade.

18. ffoure acres of meaddow by estimation, more or lesse, scituate on the northwest of mount pspect, bounded on the west by the freshett, and on the east by the comon.

19. Seaventie acres of wood land, more or lesse, scituate in mistick feilde, bounded on the southeast by George Knowhore, and on the northwest by Walter Palmer, butting southwest upon George Heborne, James mathewes, Abr. Palmer, will witherall, and long mede.

20. ffive acres of woodland scituate in mistick feilde, bought of Josseph Coleman, butting southwest upon m^r Simmes, bounded on the norwest by Thō Caule, and on the east by Boston line, a triangle.

21. One little house with a garden plott, bought of Josseph Coleman, scituate in the midle row, butting southwest upon the streete way, northeast upon the back street, bounded on the northwest by Thō Caule, and on the southeast by will knight.

22. Two Hundred and Seaventie acres of land by estimation, more or lesse, scituate in water feilde, butting northwest upon Rob. Long and Rob Cutler, southeast upon Abr. Palmer, James mathewes, Geor Hebborne, Abr. Hill, John moussell, Thō Richardson, and Ed Burton, bounded on the northeast by Walter Palmer, and on southwest by George Knowher.

————

[**37**.] *The Possesion of Sarah Ewer Late wife of Thō Ewer of Charltowne deceased.*

1. A Dwelling house with a garden plott, scituate in the midle row, butting south and west upon the markett place, southeast upon dock lane, bounded on the northeast by Mr Nowell.

2. Three roode of ground by estimation, more or lesse, scituate in the east feilde, butting southwest upon the streete way, northwest upon Ed Mellowes or Abr Palmer, bounded on the northwest by Thō Lynde, and on the southeast by Rich Lowden, with a Dwelling house and other aptinances.

3. One acre and hauf of earable land by estimation, more or lesse, scituate in the high feilde, butting south upon the highway

north upon the meaddow, bounded on the west by Ra Sprague,
and on the east by Abr Palmer.

4.   Two acres of meaddow by estimation, more or lesse, scituate
in the south meade, butting east upon broade cove, west upon
           , bounded on the south by Rob Long, and on the north
by

5.   Milch Cow comōns six and a quarter.

6.   Eight acres of earable land by estimation, more or lesse,
scituate in the line feilde butting southwest upon Cambridg line,
northeast upon the comōn, bounded on the northwest by Abr
Palmer, and southeast by Ja Greene.

7.   ffive acres of meaddow by estimation, more or lesse, scituate
in mistick marshes, butting west upon John Greene, east upon
James browne, bounded on the north by the woodland, and on the
south by a creeke against Ro Rand.

8.   ffive acres of woodland by estimation, more or lesse, scituate
in mistick feilde, butting west upon the drift way, east upon the
land way, bounded on the south by John Haule, and on the north
by Rice morris.

9.   ffive acres of woodland by estimation, more or lesse, scituate
in mistick feilde, butting west upon the drift way towards the
north river, east upon the land way, bounded on the north by Thō
Squire, and on the south by James Browne.

10.   Twentie and ffive acres of woodland by estimation, more or
lesse, scituate in mistick feilde, butting north upon the comōn,
south upon long meade, bounded on the west by The [? Widow]
Higginson, and on the east by Ra. Sprague.

11.   Sixtie acres of land by estimation, more or lesse, scituate
in Rockfeilde.

[**38.**]   1638.   *The possesion of John Wolrich in Charltowne
Limites.*

1.   Six acres of earable land and meaddow by estimation,
more or lesse, scituate on the southwest of Strawbery hill, bounded
on the east by John Sibley, on the southwest by a highway and on
the northeast by the comōn, with a dwelling house and other aptinances.

2.   Two acres of meaddow and pasture by estimation, more or
lesse, scituate in the south meade, butting south upon Cambridge
fence, north upon a creeke, bounded on the east by Rob Hayle,
and on the west by Thō Peirce.

3.   Cow commones two and and a quarter.   [these two comons
are sould with the house to georg Hodgshon. — *Greene.*]

4.   ffive acres of wood land, more or lesse, scituate in mistick
feilde, butting northeast upon John Greene,[1] southwest upon Rice
Cole and John Harvard, bounded on the northwest by Prudence
wilkinson, and on the southwest by John Lewes.   [sould to John
Greene. — *Greene.*]

5.   Thirtie and ffive acres of land by estimation, more or lesse

---

[1] Sibley erased and Greene written in by *Greene.* — ED.

scituate in watterfeilde, butting northwest upon Joh Sibley and Katharin Coytemore, southeast upon Rob Shorthus ; bounded on the northeast by widdow wilkinson, and on the southwest by John Lewes.

The posession of Thō Moulton in Charltowne Limites.

1. One dwelling house with a garden plott, scituate at sconce point, butting north upon wapping streete, south upon Henry Larrence, bounded on the west by Thō Knower.

2. One acre of earable land by estimation, more or lesse, scituate in the east feilde, butting southeast upon the marsh towards the harbour, northwest by Thō Lynde, bounded on the northeast by Thō Knowhour, and on the southwest by Thō Carter, Seniō.

3. Commones for two milch Cowes.

4. ffive acres of woodland by estimation, more or lesse, scituate in mistick feilde, butting south upon the high way towards the meaddow, north upon the land way, bounded on the east by Henry Larrence, and on the west by Thō Squire.

5. ffoure acres of meaddow by estimation, more or lesse, lying in mistick marshes, butting northwest upon a creeke that runes into the north river, southwest upon the woodland, bounded on the northeast by Rob Hayle, and on the southwest by Samuell Carter.

6. Tenn acres of wood land, more or lesse, scituate in mistick feilde, butting northeast upon Thō Lynde, southwest upon the comōn, bounded on the northwest by John Crow, and on the southeast by Ed Convers.

7. Thirtie acres of land by estimation, more or lesse, scituate in water feilde, butting northwest upon Peter Garland and Rob Rand, southeast upon Ed Convers, bounded on the northeast by Edward Convers, and on the southwest by John Crow.

[**39.**] *The possesion of Henry Larrence within Charltowne Limites.*

One dwelling house with a garden plott, scituate at sconce point, butting southeast upon the harbor, northwest upon Thō Moulton, bounded on the southwest by Steeven fforsdick.

2. ffoure acres of earable land by estimation, more or lesse, scituate in the line feilde, butting southwest upon Cambridge line, northeast upon the Bridge w[ay], bounded on the southeast by James Garrett and John martin, and on the northwest by John Tedd.

3. ffive acres of woodland by estimation, more or lesse, scituate in mistick feilde, butting south upon the high way towards the meaddow, north upon the land way, bounded on the west by Thō moulton, and on the east by Ed Joanes.

4. ffifteene acres of land by estimation, more or lesse, scituate in waterfeilde ; butting northwest and southwest upon the comōn, bounded on the northeast by Will Johnson, and on the southeast by Ed Johnson.

The possesion of Mathew Smith in Charltown limites.

One dwelling house with a garden plott, scituate on the northwest of the mill hill, bounded on the southwest by Rich white, butting northwest upon crooked lane and southeast upon the high streete, a triangle.

2. Comon for one milch Cow.

3. ffoure acres of earable land by estimation, more or lesse, scituate in the line feilde, butting southwest upon Cambridge line, northeast upon the bridgeway, bounded on the northwest by Ed Johnson, and on the southeast by Rob Hayle

4. Two acres of meaddow by estimation, more or lesse, scituate at wilsones pointe.

5. ffive acres of woodland, more or lesse, scituate in mistick feilde, butting southwest upon Walter Palmer, bounded on the southeast by Thō Brigden, northeast and northwest by the comon.

6. ffifteene acres of land by estimation, more or lesse, scituate in rockfeilde.

[**40.**] 1638. *The possesion of Edward Joanes within Charltowne limites.*

ffoure acres of land, by estimation, more or lesse, scituate in Joanes his close, bounded on the south and east by Rich Palgrave, on the north and west by the comon, with a dwelling house upon it and other aptinances.

2. Three acres of meaddow by estimation, more or lesse, scituate in the south meade, butting north upon Simmes his Creeke, south upon John Hodges ; bounded on the west by Bakers close, and on the east by Thō Squire.

3. Comones for two milch Cowes.

4. One acre of meaddow by estimation, more or lesse, scituate in mistick marshes, butting southwest upon the woodland, northeast upon the south river, bounded on the south by Ezē. Richardson, and on the west by Sam Richardson.

5. ffive acres of woodland, more or lesse, scituate in mistick feilde, butting south upon the highway towards the meaddow, north upon the woodland, bounded on the east by Mʳ Nowell, and on the west by Henry Larance or Thō wilder.

6. ffive acres of woodland, more or lesse, scituate in mistick feilde, bounded on the southwest, west and north by long meade, and on the east by Will Quick.

7. Twentie and five acres of land by estimation, more or lesse, scituate in rockfeilde.

The Possesion of John Haule in Charltowne limites.

One dwelling house with a garden plott containing hauf an acre of grounde, scituate on the south part of the comon, bounded on the west by Rich Ketle.

2. ffoure acres of earable land, more or lesse, scituate in the line feilde, butting south upon the streete way, north upon will Tutle and the comon, bounded on the east by Rob Shorthus, and on the west by Ed Burton.

3. Two acres of meaddow by estimation, more or lesse, scituate in the south meade, butting south upon Gibbines river. north upon   bounded on the east by Ed Gibbines, and on the west by   .

4. Cow comones, Two and a quarter.

5. One acre of meaddow by estimation, more or lesse, scituate in mistick marshes, at the head of the south creeke, betwixt John Goulde and ffaintnot wines.

6. ffive acres of woodland by estimation, more or lesse, scituate in mistick feilde, butting west upon the drift way towards the north river, east upon the land way, bounded on the south by spring lane, and on the north by Sarah Ewer.

7. ffive acres of woodland, more or lesse, scituate in mistick feilde, butting northeast upon Ed Johnson, southwest upon John Harvard, bounded on the northwest by Ric Ketle, and on the southeast by Nicolas Davis.

8. Twentie and eight acres of land, more or lesse, scituate in water feilde, butting northwest upon Ed Johnson, southeast upon Nicolas Davis, bounded on the northeast by Rich Ketle, and on the southwest by the comon.

[**41**.] *The Possesion of Richard Sprague in Charltowne limites.*

Three acres of earable land, by estimation, more or lesse, scituate in the east feilde, butting southwest and west upon the streete way, bounded on the southeast by gravell lane, on the northeast by will Lernett, and on the north by George Bunker, with a dwelling house and other aptinances.

2. One acre of earable land, by estimation, more or lesse, scituate in the east feilde, butting north upon Eze. Richardson, south upon the widdow nash, bounded on the east by Abr. Pratt, and on the west by Ed Mellows.

3. Two acres of land, by estimation, more or lesse, scituate in the high feilde, butting south upon the high way, bounded on the east by Jō Moussell, and on the west and northwest by the marsh way.

4. ffoure acres of meaddow by estimation, more or lesse, scituate in the south meade, butting north upon the streete way, south upon the church land, bounded on the west by Ed Mellows, and on the east by Thō Peirce.

5. Two acres of meaddow by estimation, more or lesse, lying in the south meade, butting south upon Cambridḡ fence, north upon Gibbines river, bounded on the west by Thō Brigden, and on the east by Thō Lynde.

6. Commones for three milch Cowes.

7. ffoure acres of earable land, more or lesse, scituate in the line feilde, butting northeast upon mistick pond, southwest upon the Bridḡway, bounded on the northwest by James Hayden, and on the southeast by widdow wilkinson.

8. ffive acres of meaddow by estimation, more or lesse, scituate lying in mistick marshes, butting east upon the south river, north

upon the woodland, bounded on the south by Abr Palmer, and on the north by Thō Brigden.

9.   Twentie acres of woodland, more or lesse, scituate in mistick feilde, butting northeast upon Will ffrothingam and Nicolas Trerrice, southwest upō Mʳ Nowell, bounded on the northwest by Mʳˢ Harvard, and on the southeast by Thō goble.

10.   Twentie and ffive acres of wood land, more or lesse, scituate in mistick feilde, butting north upon the Driftway towards the north river, east upon the land way, bounded on the north by Ra Sprague, and on the south by the high way.

11.   Three acres of meaddow by estimation, more or lesse, scituate on pspect meaddows, bounded on the east by the ffreshett, and on the west by the comon, bounded on the north by A swamp, and on the south by Ra Sprague.

12.   Sixtie acres of land by estimation, more or lesse, scituate in pond feilde, bounded on the one side by Ralph Sprague, on the northeast by ell pond and the river [that comes through the meaddow into Ell pond. — *Greene*], and on the northwest by the comon.

13.   ffive acres of wood land, more or lesse, scituate in mistick feilde, butting north upon the comon, south upon the meade, bounded on the east by Sarah Ewer, and on the west by Rob. Sedgwicke.

[**42.**]   1638.   *The possesion of John Brinsmeade in Charltowne Limites.*

Two acres of earable land by estimation, more or lesse, scituate in the high feilde, butting south upon the high way, north upon the meaddowes, bounded on the east by Samuell Haule, and on the west by John Moussell ; with a Dwelling house upon it.

2.   Two acres and haulf of earable land by estimation, more or lesse, scituate in the line feilde, butting southwest upon Cambridḡ line, north east upon the comon, bounded on the southeast by Thō Richardson, and on the northwest by widdow nash.

3.   One acre of meaddow by estimation, more or lesse, scituate in the south meade.

4.   One acre of meaddow by estimation, more or lesse, scituate in mistick marshes, butting west upon the north river, east upon the wood land, bounded on the south by Mʳ. Crow, and on the north by Thō Peirce.

5.   Haulf a common for a milch cow.   [sould to John March. — *Greene*.]

6.   ffive acres of woodland by estimation, more or lesse, scituate in mistick feilde, butting northeast upon Nicolas Stowers, southwest upon John Moussell, bounded on the northwest by Ed Carrington, and on the southeast by Phillip Drinker

7.   Eighteene acres of land by estimation, more or lesse, scituate in water feilde, butting northwest by ffrancis Norton, southeast upon horne pond and Ric Palgrave, bounded on the southwest by Phillip Drinker, and on the northeast by Ed Carrington.

The possesion of Phillip Drinker within Charltowne Limites.
One Dwelling house with a garden platt, scituate at the east end

of the comon. butting south upon the streeteway, north upon mistick river, bounded on the northwest by Ralph Sprague, and on the east by the comon marsh.

2. Six acres of earable land by estimation, more or lesse, scituate in the line feilde, butting southwest upon Cambridge line, northeast upon the common, bounded on the northwest by John Lewis, and on the southeast by Nicolas Davis.

3. milch cow comones two and a haulf.

4. One acre and a haulf of meaddow by estimation, more or lesse, scituate in the high feilde meade, butting south upon the high way, north upon Thō Carter and Thō Richardson, bounded on the west by Rob Cutler, and on the east by Cpt. Sedgwick.

5. Two acres of meaddow by estimation, more or lesse, scituate in mistick marshes, butting north upon the north river. east upon the woodland, bounded on the south side by Seth Sweetsir, and on the north by Ric Palgrave.

6. Tenn acres of woodland, more or less, scituate in mistick feilde, butting northeast upon Nicolas Stowers, Ric Palgrave, and John Mossell, bounded on the northwest by John Brinsmeade, and on the southeast by George ffelt.

7. Thirtie and eight arces of land by estimation, more or lesse, scituate in water feilde, butting northwest upon ffrancis nortor, southeast upon horne pond, bounded on the southwest by Georg ffelt, and on the northeast by John Brinsmeade.

[**43.**] *The Possesion of James Hayden in Charltown Limites.*
A Dwelling house with a garden plott, scituate at the east end of the comon, butting east upon the creeke, west upon the comon, bounded on the north *by the north*[1] by the streete way, and on the south by James Greene.

2. ffoure acres of earable land by estimation, more or lesse, scituate in the line feilde, butting northeast upon mistick ponds, southwest upon the bridgeway, bounded on the southeast by Ric Sprague, and on the northwest by mill river.

3. Common for one milch cow.

4. One acre and haulf of meaddow by estimation, more or lesse, lying in the high feilde meade, butting north upon mistick river, south upon   bounded on the west by Dan. Shepheardson, and on the east by Isaac Cole.

5. ffive acres of woodland, more or lesse, scituate in mistick fielde, butting west upon the Driftway towards the north river, east upon the land way, bounded on the one side by Ric Palgrave.

6. Tenn acres of wood land, more or lesse, scituate in mistick feilde, butting north east upon ffrancis Norton, south west upo Rob Shorthus and Beñ Hubbard, bounded on the northwest by will Johnson, and on the southeast by Thomas Knowhor.

7. Eighteene acres of land by estimation, more or lesse, scituate in water feilde, butting northwest upon the comon, southeast upon John Sibley and Mrs Coytemore, bounded on the southwest by will Johnson, and on the northeast by Thō Knowhor.

---

[1] The words in italics are an evident repetition. — ED.

The possesion of Seth Sweetsir, within Charltowne Limites.

Two acres of earable land by estimation, more or lesse, scituate in the east feilde, butting southwest upon the streeteway, northeast upon Long way, bounded on the southeast by Sā Richardson, and on the northwest by Prudence Wilkinson, with a Dwelling house upon it and other aptinances.

2.   Two acres of earable land by estimation, more or lesse, scituate in the east feilde, butting north upon mistick river, south upon Thō Knowher, bounded on the west by Mr Nowell, and on the east by George Knowhor.

3.   Common for one milch cow.

4.   ffive acres of meaddow by estimation, more or lesse, scituate in mistick marshes, butting west upon the north river, east upon the woodland, bounded on the south by Thō Coytemore, and on the north by Phillip Drinker.

5.   ffive acres of land by estimation, more or lesse, scituate in mistick feilde.

6.   Tenn acres of woodland, more or lesse, scituate in mistick feilde, butting northeast upon Isaac Cole and will Batchelor, southwest upon the comon, bounded on the northwest by Ed Gibbines, and on the southeast by Dan Shepherdson.

7.   Thirtie and ffive acres of land by estimation, more or lesse, scituate in waterfeilde, butting northwest upon Thō Lynde or the comon, southeast upon Rob Blott and Thō wickes, bounded on the southwest by Ed Gibbines, and on the northeast by Daniell Shepheardson.

[**44.**]   *The possesion of James Greene within Charltown Limites.*

One Dwelling house with a Garden plott, scituate at the east end of the comon, butting east upon the creeke, west upon the common, bounded on the south by Ralph Sprague, and on the north by James Hayden.

2.   Haulf a common for a milch cow.

3.   ffoure acres of earable land by estimation, more or lesse, scituate in the line feilde, butting southwest upon Cambridge line, northeast upon the common, bounded on the northwest by Sarah Ewer, and on the southeast by Thō Brigden.

4.   One acre of meaddow by estimation, more or lesse, scituate in mistick marshes, at the head of the south creeke, bounded on the east by ffaintnot wines, and on the west by John Lewis.

5.   ffive acres of woodland, more or lesse, scituate in mistick feilde, butting northeast upon Zecheill Richardson, southwest upon the comon, bounded on the northwest by John martin, and on the southeast by Rob Blott.

6.   ffiftee acres of land, more or lesse, scituate in water feilde, butting northwest upon Daniell Shepheardson, southeast upon Mr Simmes, bounded on the southwest by Rob Blott, and on the northeast by John martin.

The possesion of George Hebbourne within Charltowne limites.

One Dwelling house with a garden plott, scituate in the midle row, butting southwest upon the streeteway, northeast upon the back streete, bounded on the southeast by well lane, and on the northwest by will Dade.

2.   Haulf an acre of earable land by estimation, more or lesse, scituate in the south feilde, butting southeast upon the comor. toward Beacher's Cove, bounded on the southeast by Josseph Hills, on the southwest by Abr. Pratte, and on the northwest by Thō Brigden.

3.   One cow comon and a haulf.

4.   Two acres of earable land, more or lesse, scituate in the line feilde, butting northeast upon mistik river, southwest upon the bridge way, bounded on the southeast by Rob Long, and on the northwest by a high way.

5.   ffive acres of wood land, more or lesse, scituate in mistick feilde, butting northeast upon George Bunker, southwest upon James Pemberton and Peter Garland, bounded on the northwest by James mathewes, and on the southeast by Abr. Hill.

6.   Thirtie and six acres of land, more or lesse, scituate in water feilde, butting northwest upon George Bunker, southeast upon Rich Sprague or the comon, bounded on the northeast by James matthews,[1] and on the southwest by Abr. Hill.

7.   One pcell of swamp grounde, lying in the east feilde, bounded by will Brakenbury on the south. [this is exchanged with John march as in the sales and exchanges of lands is Recorded Page 133 [Page 148] for an Aker of Land Lying in the East feilde. — *Greene.*]

[**45.**]   *The possesion of Rob[ert] Rand within Charltowne limites.*

One dwelling house with a garden plott scituate on the west side of the mill hill, butting west upon the midle streete, east upon the high streete, bounded on the

2.   Haulf an acre of grounde by estimation, more or lesse, scituate in the south feilde, butting southeast upon crooked lane, northwest upon thō Lynde, bounded on the northeast by Ed Burton, and on the southwest by nicolas Stowers.

3.   One acre and a haulf of land by estimation, more or lesse, scituate in the south feilde, butting northeast upon the streete way, southwest upon Thō Lynde, bounded on the southeast by Ed Burton and John Stretton, and on the northwest by the comon.

4.   One acre of meaddow by estimation, more or lesse, scituate in the south meade, butting southeast upon the mouth of Gibbines river, northwest upon John Hodges, bounded on the [this is sould to m^r John Hodges. — *Greene.*]

5.   Three milch Cow comon one wherof he bought of good. Potter.

6.   Two acres of earable land, more or lesse, scituate in the line feilde, butting northeast upon mistick river, southwest upon Ed Converse, bounded on the northwest by Rob Long and on the southeast by Beniamin Hubbard.

7.   ffour acres of meaddow by estimation, more or lesse, scit-

----

[1] " Matthews " written over " Pemberton " erased. — ED.

uate in mistick marshes, butting north upon a creeke that comes out of the north river, south upon the woodland, bounded on the east by will Baker.

8.   ffive acres of woodland, more or lesse, scituate in mistick feilde, butting west upon the Drift way towards the north river, east upon the land way, bounded on the north by Abr. Palmer, and on the south by James Tomson and will ffrothingam.

9.   fffifteene acres of woodland, more or lesse, scituate in mistick feilde, butting northeast upon John moussell, southwest upon Ed Convers and John martin, bounded on the southeast by Eze. Richardson and on the southwest by Petter Garland.

10.   Thirtie and seaven acres of land by estimation, more or lesse, scituate in waterfeilde, butting northwest upon James Browne and Rob Hawkins, southeast upon Ed Convers and Thō Moulton, bounded on the northeast by Ezē. Richardson and on the southwest by Peter Garland.

The possesion of John Palmer in Charltowne Limites.

ffoure acres of land by estimation, more or lesse, scituate in the line feilde, butting northeast upon mistick ponds, southwest upon the comōn, bounded on the southeast by a swamp, and on the northwest by Thō moultō.

2.   One acre of meadow by estimation, more or lesse, scituate at Wilsons point.

3.   ffive acres of woodland, more or lesse, scituate in mistick feild, butting south upon a high way towards the meaddow, northe upon the landway, bounded on the east by Walter Palmer, and on the west by

4.   Eleven acres of land by estimation, more or lesse, scituate in waterfeilde, butting northwest upon Ed Johnson, southeast upon m^{rs} Higginson, bounded on the southwest by Rich Ketle, and on the northeast by Will Dade.

[**46.**]   1638.   *The Possesion of George Whitehand in Charltown Limites.*

Two acres of earable land by estimation, more or lesse, scituate in the high feilde, butting south upon the high way, north upon Henry Bullock, bounded on the west by James Tomson, and on the east by the high way; with a Dwelling house and other aptinances.

2.   Commones for Two milch cowes.

3.   ffive acres of woodland, more or lesse, scituate in mistick feilde, butting east upon the south river, west upon

4.   Two acres of meaddow by estimation, more or lesse, scituate in mistick marshes, butting southeast towards the head of the south creeke, northwest upon the woodland, bounded on the northeast by Abr. Pratt, and on the southwest by Ro Long.

5.   Tenn acres of woodland, more or lesse, scituate in mistick feilde, butting north upon the common, southwest upon George Bunker; bounded on the northwest by Rob Leech, and on the southwest (*sic. — Ed.*) by will Baker.

6.   Thirtie acres of land, more or lesse, scituate in Rockfeilde.

The possesion of Nicolas Davis in Charltowne Limites.

Two acres of arable land by estimation, more or lesse, scituate in the high feilde, butting south upon the high way, north upon the meade towards mistick river, bounded on the west by Thō Richardson, and on the east by James Thompson.

2.   Two acres of meaddow by estimation, more or lesse, lying in the south meade, butting northeast upon Simmes creeke, southwest from the comõn bounded on the southeast by Rob Hayle, and on the northwest by Thō Squire.

3.   Six acres of earable land by estimation, more or lesse, scituate in the line feilde, butting southwest upon Cambridge line, northeast upon the comõn ; bounded on the northwest by Phillip Drinker and on the southeast by ffaintnot Wines.

4.   Commones for Two milch cowes.

5.   One acre and a haulf of meaddow by estimation, more or lesse, scituate in Long meade, bounded on the west by Thō Squire, on the north by the fresh river, and on the south by Ed Joanes and Will Quick.

6.   Two acres of meaddow by estimation, more or lesse, lying in Long meade, bounded on the east by George Bunker, and on the west by Rob Hayle.

7.   ffive acres of woodland, more or lesse, scituate in mistick feilde, butting

8.   ffive acres of wood land, more or lesse, scituate in mistick feilde, butting northeast upon Ed Johnson, southwest upon mʳ Harvard, bounded on the northwest by John Haule and on the southeast by mʳˢ Higginson.

9.   Thirtie acres of land by estimation, morc or lesse, scituate in waterfeilde, butting northwest upon John Haule, southeast upon Abr Pratt and the common, bounded on the southwest by the comõn and the northeast by mʳˢ Higginson.

[**47.**]   *The possesion of Samuell Haule in Charltowne Limites.*

ffoure acres of earable land by estimation, more or lesse, scituate in the high feilde, butting south upon the high way, north upon the marsh towarde mistick river, bounded on the west by John Brinsmeade, and on the east by George Bunker, with a Dwelling house upon it and other aptinances.

2.   One acre of meaddow by estimation, more or lesse, lying in the high feilde marsh, butting north upon mistick river, bounded on the west by winthrope creeke, on the south by Rob Sedgwick, and on the east by a creeke.

3.   One acre of meaddow by estimation, more or lesse, lying in the south meade.

4.   Commones for two milch cowes.

5.   Six acres of earable land by estimation, more or lesse, scituate in the line feilde, butting northeast upon the high way towards mistick river, south upon the Bridgway, bounded on the northwest by Will Batchelor, and on the southeast by James Pemberton.

6.   ffive acres of woodland, more or lesse, scituat in mistick feild, butting east upon the south river, west upon

7. Two acres of meaddow by estimation, more or lesse, lying in mistick marshes, butting north upon the north river, south upon the woodland, bounded on the west by Will Batchelor, and on the east by Will Johnson.

8. Two acres of meaddow by estimation, more or lesse, lying in mistick marshes, butting east upon the north river, west upon the woodland, bounded on the north by Nicolas Stowers, and on the south by a creeke.

9. Twentie acres of land, more or lesse, scituate in mistick feilde, butting southwest upon the comon, bounded on the southeast by Josseph Cetcherall and James Tomson, and on the northwest by long meade, and with a sharp angle to the northeast.

10. ffiftie acres of land by estimation, more or lesse, scituate in waterfeilde, butting northwest upon Will Batchelor and George Hutchinson, southeast upon John Greene and Ralph moussell, bounded on the northeast by Joseph Cetcherall, and on the southwest by James Tompson.

[**48.**] 1638. *The possesion of Thō. Squire in Charltown Limites.*

Six acres of earable land and meddow by estimation, more or lesse, scituate in the high feilde, butting north upon the high way towards mistick river, south upon George Bunker, bounded on the east by Abr

2. Two acres of earable land by estimation, more or lesse, scituate in the high feilde, butting south upon the high way, north upon the meade towards mistick river, bounded on the west by John ffairfeilde, and on the east by Ezē. Richardson.

3. One acre of meaddow by estimation, more or lesse, lying in the south meade, butting northeast upon Simmes creeke, southwest upon the comon, bounded on the northwest by Ed Joanes, and on the southeast by Nicolas Davis.

4. milch cow comones three and a haulf, wherof one was bought of geor whithand, one of Josseph Coleman, and one and a haulf he had in the Devident.

5. Two acres of earable land, more or lesse, scituate in the line feilde, butting southwest upon Cambridge line, northeast upon the common, bounded on the northwest by Thō Brigden, and on the southeast by John Lewis.

6. One acre of meaddow by estimation, more or lesse, lying in mistick marshes, butting west upon the north river, east upon the woodland, bounded on the north by Rob Blott, and on the southeast by Beniamin Hubbard.

7. One acre of meaddow by estimation, more or lesse, lying at Wilsones point.

8. ffive acres of woodland, more or lesse, scituate in mistick feilde, butting west upon the Drift way towards the north river, east upon the woodland, bounded on the north by a high way, and on the south by Sarah Ewer.

9. One acre of meaddow by estimation, more or lesse, lying in mistick feilde, butting north upon the north river, bounded on the

south by Ed Joanes, on the east by Nicolas Davis, and on the west by Will Dade.

10. ffive acres of woodland, more or lesse, scituate in mistick feilde, butting south upon the high way towards the south river, north upon the comon, bounded on one side by John Lewis.

11. Tenn acres of woodland, more or lesse, scituate in mistick feilde, butting north upon the comon, bounded on the south and east by the freshett, and on the west by James Garrett.

12. Twentie acres of land by estimation, more or less, scituate in east Rockfeilde.

[**49.**] *The possesion of micheall Bastow within Charltowne limites.*

ffoure acres of earable land by estimation, more or lesse, scituate in the east feilde, butting south upon wapping streete, John martin, Will Quick and Will Brakenbury, north upon the high way, bounded on the east by Nehemiah Bourne and Will Quick, and on the west by Long way, with a dwelling house and other aptinances. [One Aker of these 4 was sould to Thomas Cartor, senior. — *Greene.*]

2. Two acres of meaddow by estimation, more or lesse, lying in the south meade, butting north upon a high way towards the creeke, south towards Cambridge fence, bounded on the west by the Church land, and on the east by A high way.

3. Two acres of meaddow by estimation, more or lesse, lying in mistick marshes, butting southeast upon the south river, northwest upon the woodland, bounded on the northeast by m^r Nowell, and on the southwest by widdow wilkinson,

4. Milch cow commones two and a haulf.

5. ffive acres of woodland, more or lesse, scituate in mistick feilde, butting south upon the high way, north upon the woodland, bounded on the west by Samuell Richardson, and on the east by Thō Squire and John Lewis.

6. Tenn acres of woodland, more or lesse, scituate in mistick feilde, in two pcells ; ffive acres, butting southwest upon ffracis Norton, bounded on the southeast by Boston line, and on the northwest by Sam Richardson (a triangle) ; the other five acres bounded on the south by m^r Nowell his farme, on the north by the high way, and on the east by Steē fforsdick.

7. Twentie and five acres of land by estimation, more or lesse, scituate in west Rockfeild, bounded on the west by the river, on the east by the comon, and the south by Sam Richardson, and on the north by Steeven fforsdick.

The possesion of John Hodges within Charltowne limites.

Tenn acres of earable land and meaddow by estimation, more or lesse, scituate in Gibbines feilde, butting south upon the river, bounded on the north and west by m^r Averie, and on the east by the meaddowes, with a Dwelling house and other aptinances.

2. Commones for two milch cowes.

3. Two acres of earable land by estimation, more or lesse, scituate in the fence feilde bought of Ed Sturges.

4. ffive acres of woodland, more or lesse, scituate in mistick feilde, butting south upon the high way towards the south river, north upon the woodland, bounded on the east by   and on the west by   .

5. ffive acres of land by estimation, more or lesse, scituate in mistick feilde, butting south and north upon the high way betwixt it and the meadow, bounded on the east by John Pane, and on the west by Seth Sweetsir.

6. Six acres of meaddow by estimation, more or lesse, scituate in mistick marshes, butting south upon the south creeke, north upon the woodland, bounded on the east by m^r Bellingham, and on the west by John Goulde.

7. ffive acres of woodland, more or lesse, scituate in mistick feilde, butting northeast upon Thō Peirce and James Hubbard, southwest upon Thō Carter, bounded on the northwest by Ezē Richardson, and on the southeast by Rice Cole.

8. ffortie and five acres of land, more or less, scituate in water feilde, butting northwest upon the comōn, southeast upon the river, bounde on the southwest by Ezē Richardson, and on the northeast by Rice Cole.

9. Eleven acres of land, more or lesse, scituate in waterfeilde, bought of Ed Sturges, butting northwest upon ffrancis norton, southeast upon Thō Peirce, bounded on the southwest by Rice morrice, and on the northeast by George ffelt.

[50.] 1638. *The possesion of Thomas Peirce within Charltowne Limites.*

ffive acres of earable land and meaddow by estimation, more or lesse, scituate in the west end, butting west upon Rich Sprague, east upon Ed Burton and the comōn, bounded on the north by the high way, and on the south by the Church land, with a Dwelling house upon it and other aptinances.

2. One acre of meaddow by estimation, more or lesse, scituate in the south meade, butting east upon the creeke, west upon the church land, bounded on the north by Ed Burton, and on the south by m^r Nowell.

3. One acre of meaddow by estimation, more or lesse, scituate in the south meade, butting south upon Cambridg fence, bounded on the east by John wolrich, and on the northwest by micheall Bastow.

4. ffoure acres of earable land by estimation, more or lesse, scituate in the line feilde, butting southwest upon Cambridge line, bounded on the southeast by Will Baker, on the northwest by a comōn swamp, and on the northeast by the brooke.

5. Commones for five milch cowes.

6. ffive acres of woodland, more or lesse, scituate in mistick feilde, butting   .

7. Three acres of meaddow by estimation, more or lesse, scituate in mistick marshes, butting west upon the north river, east upon the wood land, bounded on the north by widdow Nash, and on the south by Chubuck or John Brinsemeade.

8.   One acre of meaddow by estimation, more or lesse, lying in mistick long meaddow, bounded

9.   ffifteene acres of woodland, more or lesse, scituate in mistick feilde, butting northeast upon m^{rs} Coytemore, southwest upon Ezē. Richardson and John Hodges, bounded on the northwest by Rich Palgrave, and on the southeast by James Hubbard.

10.   Sixtie and two acres of land by estimation, more or lesse, scituate in waterfeilde, butting northwest upon Josua Tedd, Rice Morrice, John Hodges and George ffelt, southeast upon will ffrothingam, bounded on the southwest by James Hubbard, and on the northeast by Ric Palgrave.

The possesion of Augustine Walker within Charltowne Limites.

One house plott containing haulf a roode of grounde by estimation, more or lesse, scituate at sconce point, butting southeast upon the harbour, bounded on the northwest and southwest by the marsh, and on the northeast by James Garrett, reserving libertie of way sufficient for the servis of the ffort.

[**51.**]   *The Possesion of Edward Larkin within Charltowne limites.*

One Dwelling house with a garden plott, scituate on the southwest of the mill hill, butting southwest upon crooked lane, northeast upon m^r Allin, bounded on the southeast by Isaac Cole, and on the northwest by John Greene.

2.   One milch cow comon.

3.   One acre of meaddow by estimation, more or lesse, lying in the high feilde marsh, bounded on the east by Thō Carter, and on the other pts of it by a creeke.

4.   ffive acres of woodland, more or lesse, scituate in mistick feilde, butting northeast upon Ezekell Richardson, southwest upon the reserved land, bounded on the northwest by Rob Blott, and on the southeast by Thō Carter.   [Three of these Akers were sould to Edward Johnson. — *Greene.*]

5.   Tenn acres of land by estimation, more or lesse, scituate in waterfeilde, butting northwest upon Seth Sweetsir, southeast upon m^r Simmes, bounded on the southwest by Thō Carter, and on the northeast by Rob Blott or Will Stidson.

The possesion of James Garrett within Charltowne Limites.

One Dwelling house with a garden plott and yard, scituate in Sconce point, butting southeast upon the harbour, northwest upon the marsh, bounded on the northeast by Steven fforsdick, Thō Moulton, and Thō Knowhor, and on the southwest by Augustin Walker, not hindering the high way about the batterie.

2.   One milch cow common.

3.   Six acres of earable land, by estimation, more or lesse, scituate in the line feilde, butting southeast upon the high way towards winatomies river, northwest upon Henry Larrance, bounded on the southwest by Cambridg line, and on the northeast by John Martin.

4.   One acre of meaddow by estimation, more or lesse, scituate at Wilson's point, bounded on the south by mistick river, on the

northeast by James Hubbard, and on the southwest by a creeke.

5.   Tenn acres of woodland, more or lesse, scituate in mistick feilde, butting south towards the river, north upon the cõmon, bounded on the west by Ralph Sprague, and on the east by the ffresh river and Thõ Squire.

6.   acres of land by estimation, more or lesse, scituate in east rockfeilde.

[**52.**]   1638.   *The possesion of Will Johnson in Charltowne Limites.*

One Dwelling house, with a garden plott and yard, haulf a roode of grounde by estimation, more or lesse, scituate in the midle row, butting southwest upon the streete way, northeast upon the back streete, bounded on the southeast by Rice Cole, and on the northwest by Thõ Carter.

2.   Haulf an acre of land by estimation, more or lesse, scituate in the east feilde, butting southwest upon Ed Convers, northeast upon long way, bounded on the southeast by Will Dade, and on the northwest by Sammuell Carter.

3.   Cow cõmones two and a haulf.

4.   ffoure acres of earable land by estimation, more or lesse, scituate in the line feilde, butting southwest upon Cambridge line, northeast upon the common, bounded on the southeast by a common swampe, and on the northwest by Thomas Lynde.

5.   One acre of meaddow by estimation. more or lesse, scituate in mistick marshes, butting north upon the north river, south upon the woodland, bounded on the west by Samuell Haule, and on the east by Beniamin Hubbard.

6.   Haulf a roode of grounde by estimation, more or lesse, scituate in the south feilde, butting southwest upon Charls' river, northeast upon Nicolas Stowers, bounded on the southeast by Sarah nash, and on the northwest by Thõ Caule.

7.   ffive acres of woodland, more or lesse, scituate in mistick feilde, butting south upon the high way towards the south river, north upon the land way, bounded on the east by   and on the west by

8.   ffive acres of woodland, more or lesse, scituate in mistick feilde, butting northeast upon ffrancis Norton, southwest upon Beniamin Hubbard, bounded on the northwest by Edward Johnson, and on the southeast by James Hayden.

9.   Thirtie and seaven acres of Land by estimation, more or lesse, scituate in waterfeilde, butting northwest upon the common, southeast upon Edward Johnson, bounded on the southwest by Henry Larrence, and on the northeast by James Heyden.

[10.   Three Akers of Land which was Edward Larkins, scituate on mistik syde, butting   . — *Greene.*]

The possesion of Mathew Averie within Charltowne Limites.

Nine acres of earable land and meaddow, by estimation, more or lesse, scituate in Gibbines feilde, butting south upon the river, north upon the common. bounded on the east by John Hodges, and on the west by Ric. Miller, with a Dwelling house.

2. Commones for ffoure milch cowes.

3. ffive acres of meaddow by estimation, more or lesse, lying in mistick marshes, butting west upon the north river, east upon the woodland, bounded on the south by George bunker, and on the north by Thō Chubbucke or John Brinsmeade.

4. Twentie and ffive acres of woodland by estimation, more or lesse, scituate in mistick[1] feilde, butting southeast upon Thō Lynde and George Hutchinson, southeast upon the reserved land, bounded on the northwest by Daniell Shepheardson, and on the southeast by Thō Moulton.

5. ffiftie and three acres of land by estimation, more or lesse, scituate in waterfeilde, butting northwest upon will. Brakenbury and James Pemberton, southeast upon John martin and Ed Convers, bounded on the southwest by Daniell Shepheardsone, and on the northeast by Thō Moulton. Twentie acres bought of m^{rs} Higginson. Near 40 acres bought of m^{rs} Higginson.

[**53.**] *The possesion of Ralph Sprague within Charltowne Limites.*

One acre of earable land and meaddow by estimation, more or lesse, scituate at the east end of the comōn, butting south and west upon the high way, bounded on the southeast by Phillip Drinker, and on the northeast by mistick river, with a Dwelling house upon it and other aptinances.

2. Two acres of earable land by estimation, more or lesse, scituate in the east feilde, butting north upon mistick river, south upon a swamp, bounded on the east by Rob Sedgwick, and on the west by will Dade.

3. ffoure Acres of meaddow by estimation, more or lesse, scituate in the south meade, butting northwest upon the streete way, south upon Simmes his creeke, bounded on the southwest by Edward Convers, and on the northeast by James Greene.

4. Two Acres of earable land by estimation, more or lesse, scituate in the high feilde, butting north towards mistick river, bounded on the east by Abr. Palmer and Ralph Moussell, and on the west and south by George Bunker.

5. Three Acres of earable land by estimation, more or lesse, scituate in the high feilde, butting south upon the high way, north upon the meaddow, bounded on the east by Sarah Ewer, and on the west by James Tompson.

6. Commones for six milch cowes.

7. ffoure Acres of earable land by estimation, more or lesse, scituate in the Line feilde, butting southwest upon Cambridge line, northeast upon the bridgway, bounded on the northwest by John Tedd, and on the southeast by Thō Coytemore.

8. ffourteene acres of meaddow by estimation, more or lesse, scituate in mistick marshes, bounded on the north and west by the woodland, and on the east by Abr. Palmer.

9. ffive Acres of wood land by estimation, more or lesse, scituate in mistik feilde, butting west upon the Driftway towards the

---

north river, est upon the woodland, bounded on the north by James Tompson, and on the south by Ric Sprague.

10.   Thirtie and ffive Acres of Woodland by estimation, more or lesse, scituate in mistick feilde, butting south towards the north river, north upon the common, bounded on the east by James Garrett, and on the west by Sarah Ewer.

11.   ffoure Acres of meaddow by estimation, more or lesse, scituate in pspect meaddowes, bounded on the east by a freshett, on the west by the comon, on the north by Rich Sprague, and on the south by James Garett.

12.   Nintie acres of land by estimation, more or lesse, scituate and lying in Pond feilde, bounded

----

[**54.**] 1638. *The possesion of ffrancis Willoughby within Charltown Limites.*

One pcell of grounde, scituate on the south of the mill hille, butting south upon Charls river, north upon crooked lane, bounded on the west by Thō Brigden and Abr. Pratt, and on the east by a lane ; with a house upon it.

2.   Two acres of earable land by estimation, more or lesse, scituate in the east feilde, butting north upon mistick river, east upon the marsh, bounded on the west by thō Lynde.

3.   ffoure acres of earable land by estimation, more or lesse, scituate in the east feilde, butting north upon mistick river, south upon the swamp, bounded on the west by George Hutchinson, and on the east by Sam Richardson.

4.   One milch Cow common, bought of Peter Garland.

5.   ffoure acres of meaddow by estimation, more or lesse, lying in mistick marshes, bounded on the east by whithands iland, on the south and west by the creekes, and on the north by Captaine Sedgwick.

6.   ffive Acres of woodland, more or lesse, scituate in mistick feilde, butting southeast upon the high way towards the south river, northeast upon the landway, bounded on the   one side by Rob Long.

7.   Twentie acres of land by estimation, mor or lesse, scituate in waterfeilde, butting northwest upon Thō Caule and Rob Haukins, southeast upon Thō moulton, bounded on the southwest by James pemberton, and on the northeast by Rob Rand.

The possesion of Rice Morrice within Chaltowne limites.

Two acres of land by estimation, more or lesse, scituate upon the comon, butting north towards the streete way, south upon another high way, bounded on the est and west by the comon, with a Dwelling house upon it and other aptinances.

2.   Three Acres of meaddow by estimation, more or lesse, lying · in the south meade, bounded on the east by Nicolas Stowers, on the north by A high way, on the south by John Sibley and the creeke, and on the west by the Comon.

3.   Two acres of earable land by estimation, more or lesse, scituate in the line feilde, butting southwest upon Cambridge line,

northeast upon the common, bounded on the southeast by Thō Lynde, and on the northwest by Rob Haukins.

4. One milch cow common.

5. ffive acres of woodland by estimation, more or lesse, scituate in mistick feilde, butting west upon the Drift way towards the north river, east upon the land way, bounded on the north by Abr. Palmer, and on the south by John Haule.

6. ffive Acres of woodland, more or lesse, scituate in mistick feilde, butting northeast upon Nicolas Stowers, southwest upon Ric Palgrave, bounded on the northwest by Georg ffelt, and on the southeast by Josua Tedd.

7. Eighteene Acres of land by estimation, more or lesse, scituate in waterfeilde, butting northwest upon ffrances Norton, southeast upon Thō Peirce, bounded on the southwest by Josua Tedd, and on the northeast by John Hodges.

[**55.**] *The possesion of Rob Haukines within Charltowne Limites.*

Two acres of earable land by estimation, more or lesse, scituate in the south feilde, butting southwest upon Charls river, bounded on the northeast and northwest by the great cove, and on the southeast by Thō Brigden, with a Dwelling house upon it and other aptinances.

2. ffoure Acres of earable land by estimation, more or lesse, scituate in the line feilde, butting southwest upon Cambridge line, northeast upon the common, bounded on the southeast by Rice morrice, and on the northwest by Thō Carter.

3. Milch Cow commones One and three quarters. [half a comon he sould to John March. — *Greene.*]

4. Two acres of meaddow by estimation, more or lesse, scituate in pspect meade.

5. Tenn Acres of wood land, more or lesse, scituate in mistick feilde, butting northeast upon Will Nash, southwest upon mʳ Simmes, bounded on the northwest by James Browne, and on the southeast by Thō Caule.

6. Twentie and five acres of land by estimation, more or lesse, scituate in waterfeilde, butting northwest upon Ric. Palgrave, southeast upon Peter Garland and Rob Rande, bounded on the southwest by Thō Caule, and the northeast by James Browne.

The possesion of Will Baker within Charltowne limites.

Two acres of earable land by estimation, more or lesse, scituate at the west end of the comon, intirely fenced, with a Dwelling house upon it, and other aptinances.

2. Eight acres of earable land by estimation, more or lesse, scituate in the line feilde, butting southwest upon Cambridge line, southeast upon the comon, bounded on the southeast by Ed Burton, and on the northwest by Thō Peirce.

3. One acre of meaddow by estimation, more or lesse, scituate in the south meade, butting southeast towards charls river, northwest upon John Hodges, bounded on the southwest by Rob Rand, and on the northeast by James Browne.

4.   One acre of meaddow by estimation, more or lesse, scituate in the south meade, bought of Thō Knowher.

5.   Three milch cow commones [And three quarters bought of Thomas Goble. — *Greene.*]

6.   ffive acres of meaddow by estimation, more or lesse, scituate in misticke feilde marshes, butting north upon a creeke in the north river, south upon the woodland, bounded on the west by Rob Rand, and on the east by Jaṁ Browne.

7.   Two acres of meaddow and pasture by estimation, more or lesse, scituate in the south meade, bought of John wolrich and entered before in his name.

[**56.**]   1638.   *The possesion of George Hutchinson within Charltowne limites.*

Haulf an acre of grounde by estimation, more or lesse, scituate on the southwest of the mill hill, butting southwest upon Charls river, northeast upon crooked lane, bounded on the northwest by mault Lane, and on the southeast by Nic Trerrice, with a Dwelling house upon it and other aptinances.

2.   ffoure acres of earable land by estimation, more and lesse, scituate in the east feilde, butting north upon mistick river, south upon Thō Ruck, bounded on the west by Nicolas Stowers, and on the east by ffrācis Willoughbey.

3.   One acre and haulf of meaddow by estimation, more or lesse, scituate in high feilde meade, bounded on the south by John Mossell and Ralph Moussell, nor by a creeke, and on the west by John Moussell.

4.   Milch Cow commones two and a quarter.

5.   One acre of meaddow by estimation, more or lesse, scituate a Wilsones point, butting south upon mistick river, north upon the upland, bounded on the west by Nicolins Trerrice, and on the east by Rob. Cutler.

6.   One acre of meaddow by estimation, more or lesse, scituate in mistick marshes Nº 20.

7.   Haulf an acre of meaddow by estimation, more or lesse, scituate in mistick marshes, butting south upon the north river, bounded on the west by Thō Brigden, and on the northeast by the woodland.

8.   ffive acres of woodland, more or lesse, scituate in mistick feilde, butting west upon the Drift way, east upon the land way, bounded on the south by Ed Convers, and on the north by Josseph Hiles.

9.   ffive Acres of woodland, more or lesse, scituate in mistick feilde, butting northeast upon Walter Palmer, southwest upon John Crow and Math Averie, bounded on the northwest by Will Batchelor, and on the southeast by Thō Lynde.

10.   ffortie acres of land by estimation, more or lesse, scituate in waterfeilde, butting northwest upon Beñ Hubbard and Rob Shorthus, southeast upon Samuell Haule, Joss. Cetcherall, Will Smith and Joh Berridge, bounded on the southwest by Will Batchelor, and on the northeast by Thō Lynde.

The possesion of Will Stidson within Charltowne Limites.

Two acres of earable land by estimation, more or lesse, scituate in the east feilde, butting southeast upon the Harbour, northwest upon a high way, bounded on the southwest by John Berridge, and on the northeast by a high way, with a Dwelling house upon it.

2. ffoure acres and a haulf of land by estimation, more or lesse, scituate in the east feilde, butting southeast upon the high way, northwest upon will Brackenbury, bounded on the northeast by Georg Hebborne, and on the southwest by m^{rs} Harvard and Rob Hayle.

3. ffoure milch cow comones. [one of those comons sould to Augustin Lyndon. — *Greene.*]

4. Three Acres of meadow by estimation, more or lesse, lying in mistick marshes, butting west upon the north river, east upon the woodland, bounded on the south by Thō Squire, and on the north by m^{rs} Harvard.

5. ffifteene acres of wood land, more or lesse, scituate in misticke feilde, butting northeast upon Ezhiell Richardson, southwest upon the comon, bounded on the northwest by James Greene, and on the southeast by Ed Larkin.

6. Thirtie and five acres of land by estimation, more or lesse, scituate in waterfeilde, butting northwest upon Seth Sweetsir, southeast upon m^r Simes, bounded on the southwest by Ed Larkin, and on the northeast by James Greene.

[**57.**] *The possesion of Ric Palgrave within Charltowne Limites.*

ffive Acres of earable land and meaddow by estimation, more or lesse, scituate upon the comon, butting south upon the streete way, north west upon Ed Joanes, bounde on the east and west by the comon, with a Dwelling house, &c.

2. One acre and haulf of meaddow by estimation, more or lesse, lying in the south meade, butting south upon Gibbines river, north upon the comon, bounded on the east by John Sibley, and on the west by Saṁ Haule.

3. ffoure milch cow comon.

4. ffive Acres of meaddow by estimation, more or lesse, intirely enclosed, scituate in the south meade, bounded on the east by m^r. Simmes and Edward Jones, and on the other sides by the comon.

5. Two acres of earable land by estimation, more or lesse, scituate in the Line feilde, butting southwest upon Cambridge line, northeast upon the comon, bounded on the northwest by ffaintnot Wines, and on the southeast by Jā Tomson.

6. ffive Acres of woodland by estimation, more or lesse, scituate in mistick feilde, butting west upon the Drift way, east upon the land way, bounded on the north by   and on the south by

7. ffoure Acres of meaddow by estimation, more or lesse, lying in mistick marshes, butting west upon the north river, east upon the woodland, bounded on the south by Phillip Drinker, and on the north by Steeven fforsdick.

8. Twentie Acres of woodland, more or lesse, scituate in mistick feilde, butting northeast upon Phillip Drinker, Georg ffelt, Rice morrice, and Josua Tedd, southwest upon Ezē Richardson, bounded on the northwest by John moussell, and on the southeast by Thō Peirce.

9. ffiftie and six acres of land by estimation, more or lesse, scituate in waterfeilde, Devided by horn pond in three p^ts, One butting northwest upon John Brinsmeade, Ed Carington, and Georg Knowher, southeast upon Thō Caule and Rob Haukines, bounded on the southwest by the pond, and on the northeast by Ed Burton ; the second butting northwest upon Georg ffelt, southeast upon will Nash, bounded on the southwest by Thō Peirce, and on the northeast by the pond : the Third an iland on the southwest side of the pond.

10. Twentie and ffoure Acres of land by estimation, more or lesse, scituate in west Rockfeilde, butting west upon the river, east upon the comōn, bounded on the south by John Tedd, and on the north by George whitehand.

[**58.**] 1638. *The possesion of John Greene within Charltowne limites.*

Three quarters of an acre of land by estimation, more or lesse, scituate at the west end of the comōn, bounded on all sides by the common, with A dwelling house upon it and other aptinances.

2. Two Acres of meaddow by estimation, more or lesse, lying in the south meade, butting southwest upon the creeke, northeast upon the comōn, bounded on the west by Samuell Haule.

3. Eight Acres of earable land by estimation, more or lesse, scituate in the line feilde, butting west upon Thō Goble, east upon the church land, bounded on the south by Rob Hayle, and on the north by Ed Mellowes.

4. ffive commones for milch cowes.

5. ffive Acres of woodland by estimation, more or lesse, scituate in the mistick feilde, butting west upon the meaddowes, east upon Thō Peirce, bounded on the south by Will Dade, and on the north by the high way.

6. ffoure acres of meaddow by estimation more or lesse, lying in mistick marshes, bounded on the east by Sarah Ewer, on the west by bull lotte,[1] butting south upon a creeke, and north upon the woodland.

7. [more ten Acres bought of John Sybley, as apears at the sales of lands.[2] — *Greene.*] ffifteene Acres of woodland, more or lesse, scituate in mistick feilde, butting northeast upon m^rs Ann Harvard, southwest upon the comōn, bounded on the northwest by Ralph Moussell, and on the southeast by m^r Nowell.

8. Sixtie Acres of land by estimation, more or less, scituate in waterfeilde, butting northwest upon Will Powell, James Tomson, and Samuell Haule ; southeast upon Mr Nowell, bounded on the southwest by the comōn, and on the northeast by Ralph Moussell.

---

[1] " Bull lotte " written over " George Bunker " erased, in Greene's hand. — Ed.
[2] See John Sibley's sixth lot on next page. — Ed.

The possesion of Thomas Goble within Charltowne limites.

Haulfe an Acre of grounde by estimation, more or lesse, scituate at the west end of the comon, bounded on all sides by the common, with a dwelling house upon it and other aptinances.

2. ffoure Acres of earable land by estimation, more or lesse, scituate in the line feilde, butting southwest upon Cambridge line, northwest upon the streete way, bounded on the east by Ed Mellowes, Thō Brigden, and John Greene, and on the west by John Sibley.

3. Commones for milch cowes two and three quarters. [this three quarters is sould to William Baker. — *Greene.*]

4. ffifteene acres of woodland, more or lesse, scituate in mistick feilde, butting northeast upon Will ffrothingam, southwest upon Mʳ Nowell, bounded on the northwest by Ric Sprague, and on the southeast by James Browne.

5. ffiftie acres of land by estimation, more or lesse, scituate in waterfeilde, butting northwest upon John Moussell, southeast upon Ezē. Richardson, bounded on the southwest by James Browne, and on the northeast by a pcell of comon grounde.

[59.] *The possession of John Sibley within Charltowne limites.*

Two Acres of earable land by estimation, more or lesse, scituate on the south side of strawbery Hill, butting southwest upon the streete way, bounded on the north west by John wolrich, and on the other sides by the common; with a dwelling house upon it, &c.

2. ffoure acres of earable land by estimation, more or lesse, scituate in the line feilde, butting southwest upon Cambridge line, north upon the streeteway, bounded on the west by Rich. Ketle, and on the east by Thō Goble.

3. One acre of meaddow by estimation, more or lesse, lying in the south meade, butting south upon Gibbines river, north upon Rice Morrice, bounded on the east by the cove, on the west by Rich. Palgrave.

4. Milch cow commones two and one quarters.[1]

5. One Acre of meaddow and pasture by estimation, more or lesse, scituate in the south meade, on the north of Joh Hodges.

6. Tenn acres of woodland more or lesse, scituate in mistick feilde, butting northeast upon Rob. Long, southwest upon John wolrich and widdow Wilkinson, bounded on the northwest by mʳˢ Coytemore, and on the southeast by Ed. Johnson.[2] [This sould to John Greene. — *Greene.*]

7. Twentie and eight acres of land, more or lesse, scituate in waterfeilde, butting northwest upon James Hayden and Will Johnson, southeast upon John Wolrich and John Lewis, bounded on the southwest by Ed Johnson, and on the northeast by Mʳˢ Coytemore.

The possesion of Thomas Knowhor within Charltown limites.

One dwelling house with a garden plott, scituate at sconce point,

---

[1] " One " written by Greene over " three " erased. — ED.
[2] The whole of section six is erased. — ED.

butting north upon wapping streete, bounded on the east by Thō
Moulton, and on the west by

2. ffoure acres of land, more or lesse, scituate in the east
feilde, butting

3. One acre and haufe of meaddow by estimation, more or
lesse, lying in mistick marshes, betwixt will Lennett on the one
side, and James Tompson on the other side.

4. ffive acres of woodland, more or lesse, scituate in mistick
feilde, butting northeast upon Boston line, southwest upon Nicolas
Trerrice, bounded on the northwest by James Hayden, and on the
southeast by ffrancis Norton.

5. Twentie and ffive acres of land by estimation, more or lesse,
scituate in waterfeilde, butting northwest upon the common, southeast upon Mrs Coytemore and Josua Tedd, bounded on the southwest by James Hayden, and on the northeast by ffrancis Norton.

[**60.**] 1638. *The possesion of Thō. Graves within Charl-*
towne Limites.

One Dwelling house with a garden plott, scituate on the south
of the mill hill, butting south upon charles river, north upon
crooked lane, bounded on the east and west by the high wayes.

2. Commones for two milch cowes, one whereof was bought of
Mr Nowell.

3. Tenn acres of woodland, more or lesse, scituate in mistick
feilde, butting northeast upon George Bunker, southwest upon
Will Brakenbury and James Pemberton, bounded on the northwest
by Abr. Palmer, and on the southeast by George Hebbourne.

4. Thirtie and two acres of land, more or lesse, scituate in
waterfeilde, butting northwest upon George Bunker, southeast
upon a pcell of common, bounded on the southwest by George
Hebborne, and on the northeast by Abr. Palmer.

5. Three acres of earable land by estimation, more or lesse,
scituate in the east feilde, bought of Mr Nowell.

6. One acre of meaddow by estimation, more or lesse, lying
in the south meade, bought of Mr Nowell and entered before in
his name.

7. ffortie acres of land by estimation, more or lesse, scituate in
waterfeilde, bought of the assignes of John Stretton and entered
before in his name.

8. Eightie acres of land, more or lesse, scituate in waterfeilde,
bought of Abr. Palmer and entered before in his name.

9. One Hundred and twentie acres of land, more or lesse, scituate in waterfielde, bought of Mrs Harvard and entered before in
her name.

10. Eighty ackers of land lying in watterfeilde, which was
given in way of exchange for a lott att shaw sheine : this eighty
ackers is bounded on the west by the river that runs beetwin my
hundrid and twenty ackres and this eighty, and steven fosdick lying
on the east and the comon belonging to Charlstown on the north.[1]

---

[1] Lot ten is entered by Samuel Adams, Recorder. — ED.

The possesion of Eliz. Cetcherall within Charltowne Limites.

One dwelling house with a garden plott, scituate in the east feilde, butting southwest upon the back streete, northeast upon George Hebborne, bounded on the southeast by the high way, and on the northwest by Will Dade.

2. Two acres of earable land by estimation, more or lesse, scituate in the est feilde, butting southwest upon

3. Haulfe a milch cow common.

4. ffive Acres of woodland, more or lesse, scituate in mistick feilde, butting northeast upon Sam̄ Haule, southwest upon the comon, bounded on the northwest by Samuell Haule, and on the southeast by Will Smith.

5. ffifteene acres of land by estimation, more or lesse, scituate in waterfeilde, butting northwest upon George Hutchinson, southeast upon Ralph Moussell and Rich Miller, bounded on the northeast by Will Smith, and on the southwest by Samuell Haule.

[**61.**] *The possesion of Edward Carrington within Charltowne limites.*

One Dwelling house, with a garden plott Joining to the west side of the pounde, butting northeast upon the streete way, Will Bucknam.

2. Commones for two milch cowes.

3. One acre of meaddow by estimation, more or lesse, scituate in the high feilde marsh, butting east upon the great cove, west upon a high way, bounded on the south by Thō Coytemore, and on the north by Will Phillips.

4. ffoure acres of earable land by estimation, more or lesse, scituate in the line feilde, butting southwest upon the Bridgway, northeast upon mistick river, bounded on the northwest by Rob. Long, and on the southeast by Thō Goble.

5. Two acres of woodland, more or lesse, scituate in mistick feilde, butting west upon the Drift way, east upon the land way, bounded on the north by the high way, and on the south by Ed Johnson.

6. One acre of meaddow by estimation, more or lesse, lying in mistick marshes, butting west upon the woodland, east upon Rob. Long, bounded by the creeke and the woodland.

7. ffive acres of woodland, more or lesse, scituate in mistick feilde, butting northeast upon John Tedd, southwest upon John Moussell, bounded on the northwest by George Knowhor, and on the southeast by John Brinsmeade.

8. Eighteene Acres of land by estimation, more or lesse, scituate in waterfeilde, butting northwest upon ffrancis norton, southeast upon Ric. Palgrave, bounded on the southwest by John Brinsmeade, and on the northeast by George Knowhor.

The possesion of Thō Ruck within Charltowne Limites.

ffive acres of land by estimation, more or lesse, scituate in the east feilde, butting southwest upon the streete way, northeast upon Nicolas Stower and George Hutchinson, bounded on south east by Sam̄ Richardson and the hiḡ way, and on the northwest by Will ffrothingam and Abr. Palmer.

2.   One acre of land by estimation, more or lesse, scituate in the east feilde, bounded on the southeast by Ed. Convers, on the northwest by James Pemberton, on the southwest by John Goulde.

3.   Three acres of meaddow by estimation, more or lesse, scituate at Wilson Pointe, butting east upon the north river, west upon the ferme, bounded on the one side by Josseph Hiles.

4.   Twentie acres of land, more or lesse, scituate in mistick feilde, bounded on the north by the common, on the west by Josseph Hiles, and on the south east by a swamp and meade.

[**62.**]   *The possesion of Nicolas Trerrice within Charltowne limites.*

One Dwelling house with a garden plot, scituate on the south, east of the mill hill, butting southwest upon Charles, northeast upon crooked, bounded on the northwest by George Hutchinson and on the southeast by George ffelt.

2.   Commones for two milch cowes.

3.   Eight acres of earable land by estimation, more or lesse, scituate in the line feilde, butting southwest upon Cambridge line, northeast upon the bridgway, bounded on the northwest by ffrancis Norton, and on the south east by John Tedd.

4.   Two acres of meaddow by estimation, more or lesse, scituate at Wilsones point.

5.   ffifteene acres of woodland, more or lesse, scituate in mistick feilde, butting northeast upon Thō Knowhor and ffrancis Norton, southwest upon Ric. Sprague, bounded on the northwest by Rob Shorthus, and on the southeast by Will ffrothingale.

6.   ffortie and five acres of land by estimation, more or lesse, scituate in waterfeilde, butting northwest upon John Wolrich, widdow wilkinson and James Hubbard, southeast upon George Hutchinson and a pcell of com̄on, bounded on the southwest by Rob Shorthus, and on the north east by Will ffrothingam.

The landes and Tenements of Mrˢ Kathorin Coytemore within Charltowne limites.

Six acres and hauⁱf of earable land by estimation, more or lesse, scituate in the line feilde, butting southwest upon Cambridge line, northeast upon the Com̄on, bounded on the southeast by Sarah Ewer, and on the north by winotamies river.

2.   Commones for three milch cowes.

3.   Twentie acres of woodland, more or lesse, scituate in mistick feilde, butting northeast upon Rob. Long and Rob. Cutler, southwest upon Thō. Perce and James Hubbard, bounded on the northwest by Joshua Tedd, and on the southeast by John Sibley.

4.   ffiftie Acres and two of land by estimation, more or lesse, scituate in waterfeilde, butting northwest upon James Hayden and Thō Knowhor, southeast upon John wolrich, widdow Wilkinson and James Hubbard, bounded on the southwest by John Sibley, and on the northeast by Joshua Tedd.

5.   Seaven acres of land by estimation, more or lesse, scituate

In the high feilde, with a dwelling house upon it and other aptinances, bought of Abr. Palmer, and entered before in his name.

6. five acres of meaddow by estimation, more or lesse, lying in mistick marshes, bought of Abr. Palmer, and entered before in his name.

7. Two acres of meaddow by estimation, more or lesse, scituate at wilsones pointe.

[**63.**] *The possesion of ffrancis Norton within Charltowne limites.*

One dwelling house with a garden plott, scituate in the midde row, butting west upon the market place, east upon wapping Dock, bounded on the south by Will. Brakenbury, and on the north by Dock Lane.

2. Commones for two milch cowes.

3. ffoure acres of land by estimation, more or lesse, scituate in the line feilde, butting southwest upon Cambridge line, northeast upon the bridgway, bounded on the southeast by Nicolas Trerrice, and on the northwest by Mr Thō Allin.

4. Six acres of woodland by estimation, more or lesse, scituate in mistick feilde, butting southwest upon will ffrothingam and Nicolas Trerris, bounded on the northwest by Thō Knowhor, and on the east by Boston line (a triangle).

5. Ninteene acres of woodland, more or lesse, scituate in mistick feilde, butting northeast upon Micheall Bastow, southwest upon Ed Johnson, will Johnson and James Heyden, bounded on the northwest by Rob. Long, and on the east by Boston line.

6. Eightie and one acres of land by estimation, more or lesse, scituate in waterfeilde, bounded on the southeast by Josua Tedd, Rice Morrice, Ed. Sturges, George ffelt, Phillip Drinker, John Brinsmeade and Ed Carrington, on the northwest by the cōmon, on the southwest by Thō Knowhor, and on the northeast by Rob. Long.

The possesion of Beniamin Hubbard within Charltowne limites.

One dwelling house with a garden plott, scituate on the southwest of the mill hill, butting southwest upon Charls river, northeast upon crooked lane, bounded on the northwest by George ffelt, and on the southeast by Rob. Hayle.

2. ffiftie and one acres of land by estimation, more or lesse, scituate in waterfeilde, butting northwest upon Will. Dade, John Lewis and John wolrich, southeast upon will. Batchelor and George Hutchinson, bounded on the southwest by Ann Higginson, and on the northeast by Rob Shorthus.

The possesion of Thōm Wilder in Charltowne limites.

ffive acres of woodland, more or lesse, scituate in mistick feilde, butting south upon the highway towards the south river, north upon the woodland, bounded on the east by Ed. Jones, and on the west by Henry Larreice.

This he bought of Beniamin Hubbard.

[64.]   1638.   *The possesion of Edw Mellowes within Charl-towne limites.*

Three acres of land by estimation, more or lesse, scituate in the east feilde, butting southwest upon the streeteway, northeast upon will Lernett, bounded on the northwest by Rich Sprague and the high way, and on the south east by Thō Lynde and the Widdow Nash, with a dwelling house and other aptinances.

2.   Two acres of earable land by estimation, more or lesse, scituate in the east feilde, butting north upon mistick river, south upon the widdow Nash, bounded on the west by Will Learnett, and on the east by Eze. Richardson and Ric. Sprague.

3.   Tenn acres of land by estimation, more or lesse, scituate in the line feilde, butting east upon Rich. Sprague, west upon Thō Goble, bounded on the south by Thō Brigden, and on the north by the streete way.

4.   Two acres of land by estimation, more or lesse, scituate in the line feilde, butting east upon the Church land, west upon Thō. Goble, bounded on the south by John Greene, and on the north by Thom Brigden.

5.   Milch cow commones ffive and Three quarters.

6.   Seaven acres of meaddow by estimation, more or lesse, lying in mistick marshes, bounded on the west by George Bunker, on the east by Ed Pane or Ed Gibbines, and on the north and south by the woodland.   [3 of those hay lotts are sould to Peeter Tuft. — *Greene.*]

7.   ffive acres of woodland by estimation, more or lesse, scitu-ate in mistick feilde, butting west upon the Drift way, east upon the landway, bounded on the north by James Browne, and on the south by Thō Lynde.

8.   Thirtie and five **acres of** land, more or lesse, scituate in misticke feilde, butting southwest upon Nicolas Stowers, John Tedd, and Ed Convers, bounded on the southeast by Will Lernett, and on the north by the common.

9.   ffive acres of woodland, more or lesse, scituate in misticke feilde, butting

10.   Ninetie and five acres of land by estimation, more or lesse, scituate in west Rockfeilde, butting northwest upon the river, southeast upon the common, bounded on the northeast by Sam Carter, and on the southwest by Mathew Smith.

The possesion of John Martin within Charltowne limites.

One Dwelling house with a garden plot, scituate in the east feilde, butting southeast upon wapping streete, northwest upon Micheall Bastow, bounded on the southwest by will Quick, and on the northeast by Math Averie.

2.   Six acres of earable land by estimation, more or lesse, scituate in the line feilde, bounded on the southwest by James Garrett, on the northwest by Henry Larrence, and on the south-east and northeast by the high way.

3.   Tenn acres of woodland, more or lesse, scituate in mistick feilde, butting northeast upon Rob Rand, southwest upon the com-

mon, bounded on the northwest by Ed Convers, and on the southeast by James Greene.

4. Twentie acres of land by estimation, more or lesse, scituate in waterfeilde, butting northwest upon John Crow, southeast upon Mr Simmes, bounded on the southwest by James Greene, and on the northeast by Ed Convers.

[**65.**] *The possesion of Abraham Hill within Charltowne Limites.*

One Garde plott, scituate on the southwest side of the mill hill, butting west upon crookede lane, east upon midle streete, bounded on the south by John Penticost, and on the north by Josua Tedd.

2. One pcell of grounde at the south end of Rob Rands house, betwixt the said Abr. Hill and Josua Tedd.

3. Two acres and a haulf of land by estimation, more or lesse, scituate in the line feilde, butting southwest upon Cambridge line, northeast upon the common, bounded on the southeast by Thō Richardson, and on the northwest by Joh. Penticost.

4. ffive acres of woodland, more or lesse, scituate in mistick fcilde butting northeast upon John Knowhor, southwest upon Peter Garland, bounded on the northwest by George Hebborne, and on the southeast by John Moussell.

5. Seaventeene acres of land by estimation, more or lesse, scituate in water feilde, butting northwest upon George Bunker, southeast upon the common, bounded on the southwest by John moussell, and on the northeast by George Hebborne.

The possesion of John Lewis within Charltowne Limites.

One Dwelling house with a garden plott, scituate on the southwest of the mill hill, butting southwest upon crooked lane, north, east upon Josseph hills, bounded on the southeast by Ed Johnson and on the northwest by Isaac Cole.

2. One milch cow common.

3. One acre of meaddow by estimation, more or lesse, lying in mistick marshes, betwixt James Greene and James mathewes eastward of the east spring.

4. ffoure acres of earable land by estimation, more or lesse, scituate in the line feilde, butting southwest upon Cambridg line, northeast upon the comon, bounded on the southeast by Phillip Drinker, and on the northwest by Thō Squire.

5. ffive acres of woodland by estimation, more or lesse, scituate in mistick feilde, butting south upon the highway towards the south river, north upon the comon, bounded on the one side by Thō Squire.

6. Twentie and three acres of land by estimation, more or lesse, scituate in waterfeilde, butting northwest upon Ed Johnson and John Sibley, southeast upon Beñ. Hubbard, bounded on the southwest by Will Dade, and on the northeast by Jō wolrich.

[**66.**] 1638. *The possesion of Josua Tedd within Charltowne limites.*

One Dwelling house with a garden plott, scituate on the west of the mill hill, butting east upon midle streete, west upon crooked lane, bounded on the south by Abr Hill, and on the north by Lewis Hewlett.

2.   One pcell of grounde betwixt the said Josua Tedd and Abr. Hill, lying in A triangle at the south end of Rob Rands house or homestead.

3.   One milch cow common.

4.   Two acres of earable land by estimation, more or lesse, scituate in the line feilde, butting south upon Ed Convers, north upon the high way towards mistick river, bounded by Will Brakenbury and George Bunker.

5.   ffive acres of woodland by estimation, more or lesse, scituate in mistick feilde, butting northeast upon Rob Cutler, south west upon Rich. Palgrave, bounded on the northwest by Rice Morris, and on the southeast by Mrs Kathorin Coytemore.

6.   fffteene acres of land by estimation, more or lesse, scituate in waterfeilde, butting northwest upon ffrancis Norton and Thō Knowhor, southeast upon Thō Peirce, bounded on the southwest by M^{rs}. Coytemore, and on the northeast by Rice Morrice.

The possesion of George ffelt within Charltowne Limites.

One Dwelling house with a garden plott, scituate on the southwest of the mill hill, butting southwest upon Charls river, northeast upon crooked lane, bounded on the norwest by Nicolas Trerrice, and on the southeast by Beñ. Hubbard.

2.   One milch cow common.

3.   ffive acres of woodland by estimation, more or lesse, scituate in misticke feilde, butting south upon the high way towards the south river, north upon the woodland, bounded on the west by Prū Wilkinson, and on the east by Rob Hayle.

4.   Haulf an acre of meaddow by estimation, more or lesse, lying in misticke marshes, butting west towards the north river, bounded on the north by Will Dade, and on the south by George Bunker.

5.   ffive acres of woodland by estimation, more or lesse, scituate in mistick feilde, butting northeast upon Nicolas Stowers, southwest upon Ric. Palgrave, bounded on the northwest by Phillip Drinker, and on the southeast by Rice Morrice.

6.   fffteene acres of woodland, more or lesse, scituate in mistick feilde, butting northeast upon Abr. Palmer and James mathewes, southwest upon Ed Convers, bounded on the northwest by Thō Lynde, and on the southeast by James Pemberton.

7.   Thirtie and eight acres of land, more or lesse, scituate in waterfeilde, butting northwest upon ffrancis Norton, southeast upon Rich Palgrave and Thō Peirce, bounded on the southwest by Edward Sturges, and on the northeast by horne pond.

[**67.**]   *The possesion of John Tedd within Charltowne limites.*

Two acres of earable land by estimation, more or lesse, scituate in the high feilde, bounded on the south by George whitehand, on the north by Ralph Moussell, on the west by James Tompson, and on the east by the high way, with a dwelling house upon it.

2. Milch cow comones one and three quarters; the ¾ was bought of Henry Bullard.

3. One acre of meaddow by estimation, more or lesse, scituate at Wilsones Point.

4. Six acres of land by estimation, more or lesse, scituate in the line feilde, butting southwest upon Cambridge line, northeast upon the bridgway, bounded on the northwest by Nicolas Trerrice, and on the southeast by Ralph Sprague.

5. ffive acres of wood land, more or lesse, scituate in mistick feilde, butting north east upon Will Powell, south west upon the comon, bounded on the northwest by John Berridge, and on the southeast by Ed Gibbines or Ed Pane. it was bought of Hen. Bullock.

6. Twentie and ffive acres of land by estimation, more or lesse, scituate in waterfeilde, butting northwest upon the comon, southeast upon Thō Carter and John Goulde, bounded on the southwest by John Berrigge, and on the northeast by Ed Pane.

7. Tenn acres of woodland, more or lesse, scituate in mistick feilde, butting northeast upon Ed. Mellowes, southwest upon George Knowhor and Ed Carrington, bounded on the Northwest by James Convers, and on the southeast by Nicolas Stow.

8. Twentie acres of land by estimation, more or lesse, scituate in west rock feilde, butting west upon the river, east upon the common, bounded on the north by Will Baker, and on the south by Nicolas Stowers.

The Possesion of Rice Cole within Charltowne limites.

One Dwelling house with a garden plott, scituate in the midle row, butting southwest upon the streete way, northeast upon the backstreete, bounded on the northwest by Will Johnson, and on the southeast by the mill way.

2. Two acres of earable land by estimation, more or lesse, scituate in the east feilde, butting southwest upon Long way, northeast upon the swampe, bounded on the southeast by Will. Brakenbury, and on the north west by Dañ Shepherdson and Sam Carter.

3. Two acres of swamp by estimation, more or lesse, lying in the east feilde, bounded on the east by Sam Carter, on the west by Ed. Convers, on the south by Capt Rob Sedgwick, and on the north by Rob. Cutler and Walter Palmer.

4. Milch Cow comons Three and a quarter.

5. ffoure acres of earable land by estimation, more or lesse, scituate in the line feilde, butting southwest upon Cambridge line, northeast upon the comon, bounded on the southeast by John Penticost, and on the northwest by Will ffrothingam.

6. ffive acres of woodland by estimation, more or lesse, scituate in mistick feilde.

7. ffoure acres of meaddow by estimation, more or lesse, lying in mistick marshes, butting west upon the north river, east upon the woodland, bounded on the south by Will. Brakenbury, and on the north by Sam Carter.

8. Tenn acres of woodland, more or lesse, scituate in mistick

feilde, butting northeast upon John wolrich, Prū. Wilkinson, and James Hubbard, southwest upon Thō. Carter, bounded on the northwest by John Hodges, and on the southeast by Mᴿˢ Harvard.

9.   ffifetye acres of land by estimation, more or lesse, scituate in waterfeilde, bounded on the northwest by Mᴿˢ Harvard, on the east by the River, and on the southwest by John Hodges.

[**68.**]   1638.   *The posession of Richard Ketle in charltowne limites.*

One house, with a garden plott containing haulfe an acre of grounde by estimation, more or lesse, scituate on the south part of the comon, bounded on the east by John Haule.

2.   Three acres of earable land by estimation, more or lesse, scituate in the line feilde, butting north upon the streete way, bounded on the south west by Cambridge line, and on the east by John Sibley.

3.   Milch cow comon one and a haulf.

4.   ffive acres of wood land by estimation, more or lesse, scituate in mistick feilde, butting south upon the high way towards the south river, north upon the comon, bounded on the west by a high way, and on the east by goo.   Robines.

5.   ffive acres of woodland, more or lesse, scituate in mistick feilde, butting northeast upon Ed. Johnson, southwest upon Mᴿ John Harvard, bounded on the northwest by Will. Dade, and on the southeast by John Haule.

6.   Twentie acres of land by estimation, more or lesse, scituate in waterfeilde, butting northwest upon Ed. Johnson, southeast upo Mᴿˢ Higginson, bounded on the southwest by John Haule, and on the northeast by **John Palmer.**

The possesion of Marie [1] *Nash, Widdow, late wife of Will. Nash, decea:ed.*

One Dwelling house, with a garden plott, scituate in the south fcilde, butting southeast upon mault lane, bounded on the southwest by Thō. Lynde, on the northeast by John penticost, and on the northwest by Nicolas Stowers.

2.   One acre of earable land by estimation, more or lesse, scituate in the south feilde, butting southwest upon Charles river, northeast upon Nicolas stowers, bounded on the northwest by Will. Johnson, and on the southeast by Thō Lynde.

3.   Two acres of land by estimation, more or lesse, scituate in the east feilde, bounded on the northwest by Ed. Mellowes, on the southwest by Thō Lynde, on the southeast by Abr Palmer, and on the northeast by Will Lernett.

4.   Two milch Cow commones.

5.   One acre of meaddow by estimation, more or lesse, scituate in mistick marshes, butting west upon the north river, east upon the woodland, bounded on the south by Thō. Peirce, and on the north by Josseph Hills.

6.   ffive acres of woodland by estimation, more or lesse, **scituate**

---

[1] "Marie" written over "Sarah," erased. — ED.

in mistick feilde, bounded on the south by Nicolas Stower and on the west by Ralph Moussell.

7. ffive acres of woodland, more or lesse, scituate in mistick feilde, butting southwest upon James Browne and Rob. Hawkines. bounded on the northwest by Will ffrothingale, and on the east by Boston line. [This 5 akers is sold to William ffrothingam he sold it to nicolas Parker, Boston. — *Adams.*]

8. Thirtie acres of land by estimation, more or lesse, scituate in waterfeilde, butting northwest upon Ric. Palgrave, southeast upon Will. Brakenbury and comon, bounded on the southwest by Will. ffrothingham, and on the northeast by Josseph Coleman and horne Pond.

[**69.**] *The possession of Thomas Brigden within Charltowne Limites.*

One Dwelling house with a garden plott, scituate on the south of the mill hill, butting south upon Charles river, north upon ffaintnot wines, bounded on the west by a lane, and on the east by Abr. Pratt.

2. One garden plott, scituate on the south of the mill hill, bounded on the south by Abr. Pratt, on the north by crooked lane, on the east by ffrancis Willoughby, and on the west by Ed. Johnson.

3. Haulfe an acre of earable land by estimation, more or lesse, scituate in the south feilde, butting southwest upon Charles river, north east upon the cove, bounded on the north west by Rob. Haukines, and on the southeast by Abr. Pratt.

4. Three acres of meaddow by estimation, more or lesse, scituate in the south meade, butting south upon Cambridge fence, north upon Gibbines river, bounded on the east by Ric. Sprague, and on the west by Ezecheill Richardson.

5. Two acres of earable land by estimation, more or lesse, scituate in the line feilde, butting southwest upon Cambridge line, northeast upon the comon, bounded on the northwest by James Greene, and on the southeast by Thō. Squire.

6. Two acres of earable land by estimation, more or lesse, scituate in the line feilde, butting east upon the church land, west upon Thō Goble, bounded on both sides by Ed. Mellowes.

7. Milch cow commones Two and a haulf.

8. Two acres of meaddow by estimation, more or lesse, lying in mistick marshes, butting east upon the south river, west upon the woodlande, bounded on the south by Richard Sprague, and on the north by Ezecheill Richardson.

9. ffifteene acres of woodland by estimation, more or lesse, scituate in mistick feilde, butting northeast upon the comon, southwest upon George Bunker, bounded on the northwest by Mathew Smith, and on the southeast by Rob. Hayle.

10. Twentie and ffive acres of land by estimation, more or lesse, scituate in west Rockfeilde, butting west upon the river, east upon the common, bounded on the south by Rob. Hayle, and on the north by Math. Smith.

[11.] halfe an acre of medow in mistick meade.

The possession of Rob. Shorthus within Charltowne limites.

Haulfe an acre of grounde by estimation, more or lesse, scituate at the west end of the comon, bounded on the south by Will Baker, with a dwelling house upon it.

2.   ffoure acres of earable land by estimation, more or lesse, scituate in the line feilde, bounded on the south by the streete way, on the west by John Haule, and on the north and east by the comon.

3.   One milch cow common.

4.   Twentie and ffive acres of land by estimation, more or lesse, scituate in waterfeilde, butting northwest upon John Wolrich, southeast upon George Hutchinson, bounded on the southwest by Beniamin Hubbard, and on the northeast by Nicolas Trerrice.

[**70.**]   1638.   *The Possesion of Steeven fforsdick within Charltowne limites.*

One dwelling house with a garden plott, scituate at sconce pointe, butting southeast upon the harbour, bounded on the northeast by Henry Larrence, on the west by James Garrett, and on the north by Tho̅. Moulton.

2.   Two acres of meaddow by estimation, more or lesse, scituate in the high feilde marsh.

3.   Commones for two milch cowes.

4.   Seaven acres of earable land and meaddow by estimation, more or lesse, scituate in the line feilde, butting northeast upon mistick river, southeast upon the bridgeway, bounded on the west by a high way, and on the east by Rob. Long, a highway also at the end betwixt the upland and the meaddow.

5.   Haulfe an acre of meaddow by estimation, more or lesse, lying in mistick marshes, butting west upon the north river, east upon the woodland, bounded on the south by Mr Palgrave and on the north by Tho̅. Lynde.

6.   Twentie acres of woodland by estimation, more or lesse, scituate in mistick feilde, butting south upon Mr Nowells ferme, north upon the comon, bounded on the east by ffaintnot Wines, on the west by micheal Bastow and the comon.

7.   ffortie acres of land by estimation, more or lesse, scituate in west rockfeilde.

The possesion of Will. Quick within Charltowne limit s.

One Dwelling house with a garden plott, scituate in the east feilde, butting south upon wapping streete, north upon Micheall Bastow, bounded by Isaac Cole on the one side and Abr. Hill on the other.

2.   ffive acres of woodland, more or lesse, scituate in mistick feilde, bounded on the west by Ed. Joanes, on the east by Tho̅. Coytemore, on the south and north by the meaddow.

Tenn acres of land by estimation, more or lesse, scituate

The possesion of Richard Miller within Charltowne limites.

1.   Eight acres of earable land and meaddow by estimation, more or lesse, scituate in Gibbines feilde, butting south upon the

river, north upon the comõn, bounded on the west by Mr Pane, and on the east by Math. Averie, with a dwelling house upon it, &c.

2. One milch cow common.

3. ffive acres of woodland, more or lesse, scituate in mistick feilde, butting northeast upon Mr Harvard, southwest upon the comõn, bounded on the southeast by Ralph Moussell, and on the northwest by Sam̃ Carter. [This exchang^d with Ralfe Mousull and sould to Peeter Tufts. — *Greene.*]

4. fffifteene acres of land by estimation, more or lesse, scituate in waterfeilde, butting northwest upon Josseph Cetcherall and Will. Smith, southeast upon Mr Nowell, bounded on the southwest by Ralph Moussell, and on the northeast by Sam̃. Carter.

[**71.**] *The possesion of ffaintnot wines within Charltowne limites.*

One Dwelling house with a garden plott, scituate on the south of the mill hill, bounded on the south by Thõ. Brigden, on the north and east by the high way, and on the east by John Cullick.

2. One milch cow common.

3. ffoure acres of earable land by estimation, more or lesse scituate in the line feilde, butting southwest upon Cambridge line, northeast upon the comõn bounded on the northwest by Nicolas Davis.

4. Haulfe an acre of meaddow by estimation, more or lesse, scituate in mistick marshes, eastward of the south spring, betwixt John Haule and James Greene.

5. ffive Acres of woodland, more or lesse, scituate in mistick feilde, butting south upon Mr Nowell his farme, north upon the comõn, bounded on the west by Steeven fforsdick, and on the east by Josseph Hiles.

6. Tenn Acres of land by estimation, more or lesse, scituate in west Rock feilde.

The possesion of William Butchelor within Charltowne limites.

ffoure acres of earable land and meaddow by estimation, more or lesse, scituate in the high feilde, butting south upon the high way, bounded on the east by Rich Sprague, and on the northwest by Mr Winthrop, with a dwelling house upon it. [A peece of salt and fresh meadow of this sould to Robert Leach. — *Greene.*]

2. Three milch cow commones.

3. ffoure acres of earable land by estimation, more or lesse, scituate in the line feilde, butting southwest upon the Bridgway, northeast upon the highway towards mistick river, bounded on the northwest by Rob. Long, and on the south east by Sam̃. Haule.

4. One acre of meaddow by estimation, more or lesse, lying in mistick marshes, betwixt Sam̃. Haule on the one side and James Pemberton on the other side.

5. fffifteene acres of woodland, more or lesse, scituate in mistick feilde, butting northeast upon walter Palmer, southwest upon

Seth Sweetsir and Daniell Sheapearson, bounded on the northwest by Isaac Cole, and on the southeast by George Hutchinson.

6. ffortie acres of land by estimation, mor or lesse, scituate in water feilde, butting northwest upon Beniamin Hubbard, southeast upon Sam̄ Haule, bounded on the southwest by Isaac Cole, and on the northeast by Georg Hutchinson.

[72.] 1638. *The possesion of John March within Charltowne Limites.*

One Dwelling house with a garden plott bought of Rob Haukines, scituate one the north side of the Mill Hill, butting northeast upon the streeteway, southwest upon John Goulde ; bounded on the northwest by will Powell, and on the southeast by Harman Garrett.

2. Haulf a milch Cow common [more half a cows comon, bought of Thō wilder, who bought it of John Brinsmead, who had it given : more one cowes comon, bought of James Tomson, to whom it was given. In all twoo cows comons belonge to John March. — *Greene.*]

3. Two acres of earable Land by estimation, more or lesse, scituate in the Line feilde, bought of Sammuell Richardson, butting southwest upon Cambridg Line, north east upon the com̄on, bounded on the northwest by James Tompson.

4. Two acres and a haulf of earable land by estimation, more or lesse, bought of Abr. Hill, scituate in the line feilde, butting southwest upon Cambridge line, northeast upon the com̄on, bounded on the southeast by will ffrothingall.

5. [twoo akers of Arrable Land, more or less, bought of John Gould, lying in the east feild, bounded by william Brakenbury on the north, now John marches, by Robert Hale on the east, by the highway on the south, by Solomon Phips on the west.

6. Ten Akers of Arrable Land, more or less, bought of Abraham Palmer, lying in mistik feild, bounded south by Richard Harrington, and on the north by Abraham Palmer.

7. Granted by the towne in the year 1642, and ranued and confirmed by the select townsmen in the year 1649. A cows marsh lott Being one Aker, more or less, lying in mistik marshes over against charltown neck : Bounded north norwest by Ralph sprague and a great creek, and northeast by mᵣˢ Katerin Coytmore, and south and southwest by Richard Lowden. — *Greene.*]

The possesion of Robert Leach within Charltowne Limites.

One Dwelling house with a garden plott, scituate in the midle row, butting southwest upon the streete way, northeast upon the back streete, bounded on the southeast by Thō. Caule, and on the northwest by Geo: Bunkers house. [This sould to Samuell Haward. — *Greene.*]

2. Two acres of land by estimation, more or lesse, scituate in the east feilde, bounded on the southwest by mᵣ Zaccariah Simmes, on the northwest by Ed. Convers, on the northeast by Rice Cole, and on the southeast by John Allin.

3. Common for one milch cow.

The possesion of Gauddy James within Charltowne Limites.

Two acres of land by estimation, more or lesse, scituate in the east feilde, bought of William Dade, butting southwest upon the back streete, northeast upon the long way, bounded on the southeast by Edmond Hubbard, and on the northwest by Edward Convers, with a Dwelling house upon it.

2.   One acre of meaddow by estimation, more or lesse, lying in the meade at Wilson point, butting southeast upon mistick river, northwest upon the wood land, bounded on the one side by George Hutchinson.

3.   ffive acres of wood land, more or lesse, scituate in mistick feilde, bought of George ffelt, butting south upon the high way towards the south river, north upon the wood land, bounded on the west by Prudence Wilkinson, and on the east by Rob. Hayle.

[**73.**]   *The possesion of John Goulde within Chartowne Limites.*

One Dwelling house with a garden plott, scituate on the north side of the mill hill, butting west upon the high streete, south upon the mill-hill, bounded on the northeast by Rob. Cutler, Harman Garrett and John March.

2.   Common for one milch cow.

3.   ffoure acres of earable land by estimation, more or lesse, scituate in the line feilde, butting southwest upon the bridgway, northeast upon mistick river, bounded on the northwest by Ed. Carrington, and on the southeast by Rob. Sedgwick or Josseph Hills.

4.   Tenn acres of wood land by estimation, more or lesse, scituate in mistick feilde, butting northeast upon m^r John Harvard, southwest upon the common, bounded on the southeast by main. Carter, and on the northwest by Thō Carter.   [Sould to William Phillips and by him sould to Isaak Wheeler. — *Greene.*]

5.   One acre and hauIf of meaddow by estimation, more or lesse, lying in mistick marshes, butting south upon the south creeke, north upon the woodland or highway, bounded on the east by John Haule, and on the west by John Lewis.

6.   Twentie and five acres of land by estimation, more or lesse, scituate in waterfeilde, butting northwest upon John Berridge and Henry Bullock, southeast upon m^r Nowell, bounded on the southwest by Samuell Carter, and on the northeast by Thō Carter.

The possesion of Thomas Caule within Charltowne Limites.

One Dwelling house with a garden plott, scituate in the litle south feilde, butting southwest upon Charles river, northeast upon Nicolas Stowers, bounded on the northwest by Captain Sedgwick, and on the southeast by William Johnson.

2.   One garden plott, scituate in the midle row, butting southwest upon the streete way, northeast upon the back streete, bounded on the southeast by George Bunker, and on the northwest by Rob Leach.

3.   ffoure acres of earable land by estimation, more or lesse, scituate in the line feilde, butting northeast upon the Bridgway,

bounded on the west by Edward Johnson, and on the southeast by Nicolas Stowers, A triangle.

4. Common for one milch Cow.

5. ffive acres of woodland, more or lesse, scituate in mistick feilde, butting southwest upon m^r Simmes, bounded on the northwest by Rob Haukines, and on the southeast by Josseph Coleman and Boston Line.

6. fffteene acres of land by estimation, more or lesse, scituate in waterfeilde, butting northwest upon Richard Palgrave, southeast upon James Pembroke and Petter Garland, bouded on the southwest by Josseph Coleman and horne pond, and on the northeast by Rob. Haukines.

[**74** and **75**.]   Blank.

[**76**.]   1638.   *The possesion of Isaac Cole within Charltowne Limites.*

One Dwelling house with a garden plott, scituate in the east feilde, butting south upon Wapping streete, north upon Micheall Bastow, bounded on the east by William Quick, and on the west by the common.

2. One milch common.

3. One acre of meaddow by estimation, more or lesse, lying in the high feilde, butting north upon mistick river, bounded on the east by Thō Carter, and on the west by James Heyden.

4. Tenn acres of woodland, more or lesse, scituate in mistick feilde, butting northeast upon Walter Palmer, southwest upon Edward gibbines and Seth Sweetsir, bounded on the northwest by Abrā. Pratt, and on the southeast by Will Batchelor. [Sould to M^r Thō Allin. — *Greene.*]

5. Twentie and three acres of land, more or lesse, scituate in waterfeilde, butting northwest upon m^{rs} Ann Higginson, southeast upon James Tompson, bounded on the southwest by Abr. Pratt, and on the northeast by Will Batchelor.

The possesion of William Bucknam within Charltowne Limites.

One Dwelling house with a garden plott, butting northeast upon the streeteway, and bounded on the southeast by Edward Carrington.

The lands and Possesions of Peeter Tuft within charltowne lymits, which he bought of Ralph Mowsall, of Edward Mellows, of Richard Lowden, and of Thomas Wilder.[1]

Twenty and five Akers of Arrable land by Estimation, more or lesse, scituate and lying on Mistik syde, bought (and payd for) of Ralph Mowsall, which land is bounded North by the Rayles, and and south by John Greene, west by Richard Cooke, and East by another parcell of Richard Cooks land,

more, Three marsh Hay lotts by estimation, more or lesse, with about three quarters of an Aker of upland adioyning : scituate and lying in Mistik marshes, bought (and payd for) of Edward Mellows, which land is Bounded on the south by George Hutcheson,

---

[1] The possessions of Peter Tufts are all written in Greene's hand. — Ed.

and North by a great creek, Bounded on the East by John wilkison, and Northwest by a highway.

more, fifteen Akers of Arrable Land by Estimation, more or lesse, scituate and lying at the Towne of wooburn : which was James Hubbards, and is bought and payd for, which Land is bounded by Thomas Peirce, senio^r, on the East, and by Jacob Greene on the west, on the North by Katherin Coytmore, and on the south by Nicholas Trarice.

[**77.**] *The possesion of Edward Burton within Charltown Limites.*

Two acres of earable land by estimation, more or lesse, scituate in the south feilde, butting east upon crooked lane. west upon Rob Rand, bounded on the north by John Stretton, and on the south by Thō Lynde.

2.   Three acres and a haulf of earable land by estimation, more or lesse. scituate in the line feilde, butting southwest upon Cambridge line, south upon the streeteway, bounded on the north by a common swamp, and on the east by John Haule.

3.   One milch cow common.

4.   One acre of meaddow by estimation, more or lesse, lying in the south meade, bounded on the east by John Greene, and on the other sides by Thomas Peirce.

5.   ffive acres of woodland, more or lesse, scituate in mistick feilde, butting west upon the Drift way towards the north river, east upon the land way, bounded on the north by George Bunker, and on the south by William Brakenbury.

6.   Eleven acres of land by estimation, more or lesse. scituate in waterfeilde. butting northwest upon George Bunker. southeast upon James Browne, bounded on the southwest by Richard Palgrave, and on the northeast by Thō. Richardson.

WILLIAM BRAKENBURY.	INCREASE NOWELL.
ABR. PALMER.	RALPHE SPRAGUE.
THOMAS CARTER.	NICHOLAS STOWER.
	EZEKIL RICHERSON.
	WALTER PALMER.

[These names are autograph signatures. — ED.]

The posesion of Gady James.[1]

Know all men by thes presents that I, Edward Jonson, of wooburn, in the countey of midellsexe, in New england, have Bargained and sould, and Doe by thes presents writing give, grant, Bargain, and sell unto gaudy James of Charlstown, Three Cowes comons and one halfe, lying on the nearest comons to Charlstown, neare the Neck of land, to have and to hould the said Comons to him and his heiers for ever with warantise from all former guiftes,

----

[1] This entry is in Recorder Adams's hand. — ED.

grants, Bargains, sauells, morgages, Jointers, Dowrys, by him att Any Time dated or Done, and ffrom the Dower of Suzana, his now beloved and maried wife, in wittnes hear of he hath hear unto sett his hand.   Datted the 23 of the first mo. 1658.   And the said Edward Johnson Doth hearby Acknoledg̅ him selfe satisfied, and paid.

   wittnes :
WILLIAM JOHNSON.   EDWARD JOHNSON.
DANIELL D. EALIACE.   SUZAN JOHNSON.

This sale was Acknoliged the 26th i mo, 1658, before
     RICHARD RUSELL,
       Comisoner in Charlstown.

This is a trew copey of Edward Johnsons Dead of Sale, made to Gaudey James, And hear entred this first Day of 1 mo, 1659, By

       SAMUELL ADAMS,
        Recorder.

[**78.**] 1638. *The lands and Tenements of Mr Edward Pane within Charltowne Limites.*

Thirtie acres of earable land and meaddow by estimation, more or lesse, scituate at the west end, bounded on the southwest by Gibbines river, on the east by Richard Miller, and on the north-west by the common, with a Dwelling house and other aptinances.

2. ffour milch Cow commones.

3. ffive acres of earable land by estimation, more or lesse, scit-uate in mistick feilde, bounded on the west by John Hodges, and on the east: north: and south by a high way betwixt it and the meaddow.

4. Two acres and a haulf of meaddow by estimation, more or lesse, lying in mistick marshes, bounded on the west by Ed: Mel-lowes, and on the north and south by the woodland.

5. ffifteene acres of land by estimation, more or lesse, scituate in mistick feilde, butting northeast upon Abr: Pratt and Isaac Cole: southwest upon the common, bounded on the southeast by Seth Sweetsir, and on the northwest by Henry Bullock or John Tedd.

6. ffortie and ffive acres of land by estimation, more or lesse, scituate in waterfeilde, butting northwest upon Tho̅. Lynde or the common, southeast upon Tho̅. Carter, bounded on the northeast by Seth Sweetsir, and on the southwest by Henry Bullock.

The 30th of the 11th mo. Anno Dom̅. 1644.

A litle Island of meaddowing, lying on the northeast side of the Creeke by William Stidsones: bounded on the northwest with the lands of m^r Nowell: and on the other sides with the marrish grounde, that pteining to William Stidson was granted to Abraham Hau-kines by a towne act.

3ᵗʰ 3 mo. 1653.

It was granted unto Edward burtt to have a house plott on the northwest of widdow larkins house, and the front of the hous plott is to begin even with the south corner of mʳ Ralph worys house, and to be fourtene foott wide from the widow larkins line north west, and so to Rune downe to the seaw[ay?] ¹ one a strait line. this was acordingly laid out by Robert Cotter and thomas goold, who weare there unto a point by the select men of the towne, and so it is freely given unto the fore said Edward burt and his aires for ever   as his owne proper Right and in trust.

Witness in the name of the select men of Charlstown:

SAMUELL ADAMES,
Record.

[79.] ² *The Possession of Thomas Carter senior within Charl-town limitts.*

One Dwelling house with a barn and a garden of a quarter of an Aker, more or lesse, bounded Northeast by the back lane, south west by the fore street, and southeast by William Johnson, and Nortwest by Phinias Pratt.

2. One dwelling house with a parcel of ground of a quarter of an Aker, more or lesse, which he bought of Richard Robinson, adioyning to his house aforenamed.

3. Alsoe foure Akers of arrable Land, more or lesse, bought of william Learned, lying in the East feild, bounded East by Richard Sprague, West by Edward Mellows, North by Georg Bunker, South by widow Nash.

4. One Aker of arrable Land, more or lesse, bought of Richard Robinson, lying in the East feild, bounded East by John Penticost, west by John March, south by Sollomon Phips, North by Robert Chalkly.

5. Alsoe five Akers of Arrable Land, more or lesse, lying in the East feild, bought of samuel Carter, bounded North by the high-wag. East by sollomon Phips, west by widdow Cole, and southward by William Dade, and sollomon Phips.

6. Likewise one Aker of Arrable land, more or lesse, bought of Mihell Baestow, lying in the East feild, on Moltons poynt; bounded southeast by sollomon Phips, northwest by Thomas Graves; northeast by the River, and south by William Stilson.

7. Alsoe three cow lotts gras: being by estimation three Akers, more or lesse, lying in the East feild without the Neck by mistik River, whereof the one was given by the towne in the dividend, and is bounded east by the river, west by Ralph Mousall, and southwest by Robert Hale, and by the highway west.

The second Portion or cows gras, was bought of Thomas Lynde: bounded west by a Creek, east by the highway: south by Edward Larkin, and north by Thomas Lynde.

The third Portion of cows gras, was bought of William Potter,

---

¹ The houses of Larkin and Woorey were both near the ferry. — ED.
² The following records to, and including page [91] are in the handwriting of Greene. — ED.

and is lying in the corner of the feild, bounded west by **Isaac Cole**, and its bounded on all the other three sydes by the river.

8. Milch Cows Comons four and a quarter.

9. Alsoe twoo Akers of arrable Land, more or lesse : lying on mistike syde in mistik feild, bounded East, and with the river by Richard Sprague, and west by the highway, North by Richard Sprague, and south by mistresse Martha Winthrope.

The Possession of Robert Leach within Charltowne Lymmitts.

A Dwelling House with a yeard and garden, and out housing, standing and scituate in the feild without the Neck, Bounded west by the Comon, and East by Ralph Mousall, south by Sollomon Phips, and North by Mᵣˢ. Katherin Coytmore : which Robert Leach bought of John Baker.

3. twoo Akers of Arrable Land, more or less, adjoyning to the house, and bounded as the house which Robert Leach bought alsoe of John Baker.

3. One Aker of Arrable Land, more or less, lying and scituate in the same feild, bought of Ralph Mousall, Bounded Northwest by Robert Leaches owne Land, and bounded west by the Comon, North by William frothinghams marsh Lott, and southwest by Richard Sprague.

4. one Aker and a halfe of Arrable Land, more or less, bought of James Greene, lying and scituate in the same feild, Bounded Northwest by Richard Sprague, southwest by Mᵣ William Barnard, west by the Comon, and North by william frothinghams marsh Lott.

5. One peece of meadow land, part salt, part fresh, bought of william Bachelor, lying and scituate in the same feild, Bounded Northwest by a creek, south east by Richard Sprague, west by the Comon, and East by william ffrothinghams salt marsh lot.

6. One Cows Comon, bought of Abraham Palmer.

twoo Cows Comons, bought of maior Sedgwick.

one Cows Comon was given him.

[80.] 1638. *The Posession of Robert Mirriam in Charltowne Limitts.*

1. one dwelling house with a yeard and a garden, containing halfe a rood of Ground by estimation, more or less, with a store house standing thereon : all which is Bounded and butting on the south by Nicholas Trarice, and the wharfe way, bounded on the west by Thomas Brigden and faintnot winds : and on the East and North by the highwayes.

2. five Akers of woodland by Estimation, more or less, scituate in Mistik feild, Butting west upon the drift way, and East upon the Land way, and south by Edward Mellows : and North by Thomas Squire, and Sarah Ewer.

[thes five ackers of woodland is sould to James barett and recordid upon his head. — *Adams.*]

3. more fifteen Akers of woodland by estimation, more or less, scituate in Mistike feild, Butting northeast upon widow Nash : and william ffrothingham : south west upon Mᵣ Increase Nowell, and

Northwest by Thomas Goble : And South East by Robert Hawkins

[This fiften ackers of land is sould to Jams barett and recordid upon his head. — *Adams.*]

4. Alsoe twoo Akers of meadow by Estimation, more or less, lying in Mistik marshes : Butting North upon a Creek out of the North River : and south upon the woodland, East by Thomas Ewer, And west by william Baker.

[This to ackers of meadow is sould to James barett and recordid upon his head. — *Adams.*]

5. Likewise one Aker of meadow by estimation, more or lesse, lying in the south meade, Butting East upon the great cove, west upon Thomas Richeson : south by   and North by

6. Alsoe Three cows comons and a quarter, lying on the stinted comon without the Neck.

The Lands and posessions of Peeter Tuffts with in charltowne Lymits, which he bought or Ralph Mousell, of Edward Mellows, of Richard Lowden, and of Thomas wilder.

1. Imprimis : Twenty and five Akers of Arrable Land by estimation, more or less, scituate and lying on Mistik syde, bought and payd for, of Ralph Mousall, which Land is bounded south west by the rayles, and south East by John Greene, west and East by twoo parcells of Richard Cooks Land.

2. more Three marsh hay lotts by Estimation, more or less, with about three quarters of an Aker of upland adioyning : all scituate and lying in mistik marshes, bought and payd for of Edward Mellows : which Land is bounded on the south by George Hutcheson, and North by a great creeke, Bounded East by John wilkison, and North west by a highway.

3. more fifteen Akers of Arrable Land by Estimation, more or less : scituate and lying at the Towne of wooburn, which was James Hubbards, and is bought and payd for : which Land is bounded on the East by Thomas Peirce, senior, and by Jacob Greene on the west, and by M[r] Katherin Coytmore on the North, And south by Nicholas Trarice.

Wheare as Jacob Greene having erected a new end to his Dwelling house in the marsh, and the east end ther of exstends to the Towne way to M[r] Danfors warehouse : The select men, Taking notes of the same, and land on which it stands, Doe heare by aprove of the said bulding, and doe lik wise order and grant unto the fforsaid Jacob Grene that all the land on which the forsaid house stands, shall bee the forsaid Jacob grenes and his heires for ever. wittness this 28, the 6 mo., 1659, in the name of the Rest.

SAMUEL ADAMS, *Record.*

[81.] *The Lands and Posessions of M[r] Nicholas Trarice within Charltowne lymites.*

1. One dwelling House with a garden Plott, scituate on the southwest syde of the Mill Hill, Butting southwest upon Charls

river, North East upon elbowe Lane, Northwest upon George Hutcheson, And south Eeast upon ould Jones, and John Cole.

2.   Comons for twoo milch Cowes.

3.   Eaight Akers of Arrable Land by Estimation, more or lesse, scituate in the Lyne feild, Butting southwest upon Cambridge Lyne, North East upon the Bridgway, and North west upon ffrancis Norton, and south East upon John Tydd.

4.   Fifteen Akers of wood land by Estimation, more or lesse, scituate in Mistik feild, Bounded North East by Thomas Knowher, and Francis Norton, southwest by Richard Sprague : Northwest by Robert Shortas, And south East by william ffrothingham.   [This 15 ackers is sold to M^r nicolas parker of boston. — *Adams.*]

5.   Twoo Akers of marsh meadow by Estimation, more or lesse, scituate on Mistik syde at wilson's poynt, Bounded by the River on the one syde, and by the upland on the other, and by George Hutcheson on the 3^d syde, and by Mr Thomas Allen on the other syde.   [this is sould to william Dade. — *Greene.*]

6.   Forty and five Akers of Arrable Land by Estimation, more or lesse, scituate in wooburn, Boundded North west by John woolrych, widdow wilkins, and James Hubbard : and south East by George Hutcheson, and a parcell of the comon, southwest by Robert shortas, and North East by william frothingham.

The Lands and Posessions of Mr Prats: which is now Mrs Rebeckah Trarices, and her childrens: in Charltowne.

1.   One dwelling House with a yard in which it stands, scituate in Charltowne, nere the River and south of the Mill Hill, Bounded south by the wharfway, and Charls river, Bounded North by Robert Miriam, which was James Browns, west by Thomas Brigden, and East by the high way next Thomas Graves.

2.   One Garden Plott of ground, scituate in Charlstowne, being about foure pole of ground, more or lesse, lying nere the mill Hill, upon the River Syde, Bounded west by Edward Johnson, North by Thomas Brigdens Garden, East by Thomas Kimbols Garden and warehouse : and south by Charls river.

3.   One Aker and a halfe of Arrable Land by Estimation, more or lesse, scituate in the south feild, Butting southwest upon Charls River, North East upon Beechers Cove, and Northwest by Thomas Brigden.

4.   Three Akers of Arrable Land by Estimation, more or lesse, scituate in the East feild, which was Richard Spragues, and by exchang coms to bee Rebeckah Trarices, Bounded on the one syde by william stilson, on the other syde by mistik River, on the other syde by the high way, and on the fourth syde by

5.   Three Akers of marsh meadow by Estimation, more or lesse, scituate in mistik marshes, nere M^r wilsons farme. Bounded on the one syde by the upland, on another syde by the River, on the 3d syde by Edward Drinker, and on the fourth part by Mathew Smith.

6.   Forty Akers of Arrable Land by Estimation, more or lesse

scituate and lying at wooburn, Bounded west by Cambridge Lyne, East by Isaac Cole, North by Anne Higginson, and south by James Tomson and william Powell.

[**82.**] *The first Division* [1] *of Lands one Mistick syde Ten Acres to A house: wher of five were again resigned for the accomodutting of After comers.*

No: of Lot	4 :	Mr Increase Nowell	5 pt. of Thō: Hubberd.
	5 :	Edward Jones	5
	6 :	Thomas Moulten	5
	7 :	William Learned	5
	8 :	Thomas Squire	5
	9 :	George Whitehand	5
	10 :	Sam: Richeson	5
	11 :	William Baker	5
	12 :	John Hodges	5
	13 :	Peter Garland	5
	14 :	Mr Zacha: Symes	5
	15 :	Walter Palmer	5
	16 :	Robert Hale	5
	17 :	George Felch	5
	18 :	Tho: Minor	5
	19 :	John Greene	5
	20 :	William Dade	5
	21 :	Rice Cole	5
	22 :	Nicho Stower	5
	23 :		
	24 :	Thō: James	5
	25 :	Seth Switzer	5
	26 :	Edwa: Gibbons	5
	27 :	Edwa: Convers	5
	28 :	Mr Andrews	5
	29 :	Rich: Palgrave	5
	30 :	Mrs Higginson	5
	31 :	John Haule	5
	32 :	John Woolrych	5
	33 :	Will: Brakenbury	5
	34 :	Mr Eason of Hauks	5
	35 :	Abrah: Palmer	5
	36 :	James Browne	5
	37 :	Tho: Squire: Tho: Ewer 5 of Jos. Hubbe:
38 :	39 :	Mr Hough	20
	40 :	Ralph Sprague	5
	41 :	James Tomson	5
	42 :	Abra: Palmer of m$^{r.}$ Crow 5
	43 :	Edwa: Burton	5
	44 :	Tho: James	5
	45 :	m$^{rs.}$ Eason	5
		Beniamine Hubbard	5
		Henry Lawrence	5

---

[1] This division was made 6th, first month, 1637. — ED.

William Johnson	5
John Lewis	5
Samuell Haule	5
Michaell Bastowe	5
Ezekiell Richeson	5
James Pemberton	5
Robert Longe	5
Robert Sedgwick	5
John Palmer	5
Widdowe Harwode	5
Widdowe Wilkins	5
Richard Kettell	5
Thomas Peirce	5
George Hepbourn	5
John Mowsall	5
William Nash	5
Ralph Mowsall	5
Thomas Richardson .	5
Edward Sturgis	5
George Hutcheson	5
James Heyden	5
Edward Carrington	5
Thomas Ewer	5
Rice Morris	5
Thomas Knower	5
Thomas Lyne	5
Edward Mellowes	5
Richard Sprague	5
William Frothingham	5
Robert Rand	5
George Buncker	5
Abraham Mellows	5
Nicholas Davis	5

[83.]   Blank.

[84.]

At a meeting of the Sellectmen the third Day of the twelvth month, 1656. The confirmation of the Proprieties of severall Inhabitants of Charletowne in the stinted Pasture, Betwixt the Neck of land Menotomies River, and the Farmes of Meadford and Mr Winthrops — Past — By the Aprobation of the Sellectman, with Concurrence of all the Proprietors, Being, by their Generall consent Recorded and Ratified to stand Legall and vallid to their use for ever from the Date abovesayd : They Paying in Three pence each Common to the Recorder for Entring and Recording Them.

Confirmed and Entred for Thomas Lynde, senio^r — nineteen commons.

     I say to him and his heires —

JOHN GREENE, Recorder.[1]

---

[1] This phrase and confirmation are repeated after each entry of grants, but are omitted in printing. — ED.

same for Alice Mousall, twelve commons and three quarters.
"   "   George Bunker, tenn Commons.
"   "   Captaine Francis Norton, six commons.
"   "   Nicholas Davison, seaven commons.
"   "   Robert Long, eight commons.
"   "   William Dade, eight   "
"   "   John Mousall, eight   "
"   "   John March, six   "
"   "   Mr Thomas Allen, five "
"   "   widow Mary Cartar, four commons and a quarter.
"   "   Robert Leach, four commons.
"   "   Augustin Lyndon, one common.
"   "   Abraham Smith, three commons.
"   "   Katherine Coytmore, three commons.
"   "   Parnell Nowell, three   "
"   "   John Greene, three   "
"   "   William Bacheler, three   "

[85.]
same for John Roper, three commons and a halfe.
"   "   manes sallyes children, three commons.
"   "   Thomas Goble, twoo commons.
"   "   Thomas Bridgen, senio^r twoo commons and a half.
"   "   Widdow Arrold Cole, twoo   "   " a quarter.
"   "   John Penticost,   twoo   "
"   "   Edward Drinker,   twoo   "
"   "   Georg Foule   twoo   "
"   "   Randall Nicholls, twoo commons.
"   "   Gardy James,   four   "
"   "   susanna White,   twoo   "
"   "   John Cloys,   one   "
"   "   John Smith,   "   "
"   "   Mary Walker,   "   "
"   "   Aaron Ludkin,   "   "
"   "   Samuell Beadle,   "   "
"   "   George Heypbourn, "   "
"   "   ffaintnot winds,   "   "
"   "   William Stitson,   "   "   sould to Lyndon.
"   "   Powell's children   "   "
"   "   John March, six commons.
"   "   Robert Hale, five   "
"   "   widow Amy Stower, four commons.
"   "   "   Joanna Larkin,
"   "   James Cary, two com̄ons & a quarter.

[86.] Blank.

[87.] *Charletowne, the first of March, or the first moneth* ${}^{16\frac{5}{5}\frac{7}{8}}$.
It is Agreed that the first head line shal bee Meadford Farme,
that line betweene them and o^r Towne, And all other head lines to
rune Parralell with that line foure scoore poole assunder.
The first Lott distinguished by the figure one, shall begin at

the southeast corner where Mrs Nowells Farme and Meadford farme meet, And so successively according to the figures, 1, 2, 3, 4, &c., to the end of the last figure or lott. And at the end of the first Range to turne back againe in the second Range. And so to the third, &c., successively till each man have halfe his Proportion, for the first, And then the first to begin againe, 1, 2, 3, 4, &c., and successively each number to take place, in the second division, as in the first, till every man have his other half e of his Lott.

It is Agreed that the Ponds shall not be measured.

It is Agreed that he that Tarrys not in the Towne as an Inhabitant for one year next ensuing the date hereoff, upon his going out of the Towne shall lose his whole Proprietie, both off wood and commons.

It is further Agreed, That no man shall sell his wood or commons but to the Inhabitants of Charletowne, upon forfeiture of twelve pence, p. load of eyther wood or Tymber : And not to dispose of the commons to any of any other Towne, upon forfeiture of the same, And if any remove to inhabite in any other Towne, shall make no use of their commons, but shall sell it or lett it to some of the Towne of Charletown, that the commons may be reserved for ever to the use of the Inhabitants of Charletowne.

It is Agreed that each shall pay for the laying out of his wood lott within one moneth after it is layd out, upon forfeiture of his wood and commons. And the select men of Charletowne shall have heerby power to sell it to pay the survayour.

This was Agreed unto by vote of the inhabitants of Charletowne at a meeting in the meeting hous, this first off March $\frac{16 57}{16 58}$, and ordered to be Recorded in the Towne Booke.

The returne of the committee Apoynted by the Inhabitants of Charltowne for the division of the wood and commons one Mistick syde, with the Inhabitants there assent to the Articles above mentioned : Accepted, by drawing each his Lott, the Day and year above written ; And is as Followeth : —

Lotts.		Wood in Acres.	Comons.
1	Edward Carrington	0052	009
2	Christopher Goodwine	0018	003
3	Thomas Alice Rand..................	0034	006
4	Richard Sprague	0086	015
5	Edward Brazier.....................	0012	002
6	Jacob Greene	0052	009
7	Samuel Beadle	0018	003
8	George Heypbourn..................	0011	002
9	John Trumble......................	0054	009½
10	Mihell Long.......................	0023	004
	10 Families	0360	062½
11	John Clough	0008	001½
12	Josiah Wood	0008	001½
13	John Palmer	0012	002
14	Sarah Sallees Hous	0004	001

LOTTS.		WOOD IN ACRES.	COᵐONS.
15	William Bullard.....................	0019	003
16	William Clough	0016	003
17	Mʳ Winthrops Farme................	0046	008
18	Edward Wilson	0009	001½
19	John Funnell........................	0033	005½
20	Nathaniell Blancheer	0012	002
10	Families	0167	029
21	John Mirick........................	0017	003
22	Thomas Lynde	0066	011½
23	John Withman	0010	002
24	William Morris.....................	0012	002
25	John Long	0031	005
26	John Patefield.....................	0019	003
27	Randolph Nichols..................	0062	011
R			
28	Robert chalkley....end	0028	004½
29	William Jones Mason	0015	002½
30	Josuah Tydd	0025	004½
10	Families	285	049
31	John Richbell	0024	004
32	Lawrence Dous.....................	0026	004½
33	Monseiur Beluile	0017	003
34	John George.......................	0011	002
35	John Baxter........................	0007	001
36	Thomas Brigden, senioʳ.............	0018	003
37	Thomas Osborne....................	0018	003
38	Widow Gobles, Hous...............	0003	001
39	John Cloys.........................	0024	004
40	Thomas White.....................	0026	004½
10	Families	174	030
41	Robert Cutler	0056	009½
42	John Roper	0020	003½
43	Thomas Cartar.....................	0026	004½
44	John Fosdicke.....................	0014	002½
45	T. G. Drinkers hous	0005	001
46	Cap. Lushers hous	0004	001
47	ffaint winds	0010	002
48	Robert Long......................	0060	010½
49	James Broune	0029	005
50	Barnaby Davis.....................	0027	004½
10	Families	0251	044
51	Michell	....	....
52	Beniamine Wilson	0011	002
53	ould mʳ Richard Browne............	0015	002
54	Phinias Pratt	0014	002½
55	Thomas Wilder.....................	0034	006
56	Thomas Peirce	0024	004½
57	Edward Burt	0018	003
58	George Hutcheson	0027	004½
59	William Croul.....................	0013	002

LOTTS.		WOOD IN ACRES.	COMONS.
60	William Roswell...................	0016	002½
	10 Families	172	[029]

[88. 89.] Blank.

[90.]

LOTTS.		WOOD IN ACRES.	COMONS.
61	Nicholas Shapley	0028	004½
62	Elias Roe	0016	003
63	Seth Switzer	0023	004
64	Thomas Sheppy	0019	003
65	William Dade	0044	007½
R			
66	capt. John Allen ....end....	0095	017
67	Mʳˢ Nowell and Farme	0048	008½
68	mʳ Richard Russell................	0091	016
69	Isaak Cole......................	0010	002
70	Mathew Price	0028	005
	10 Families	402	069½
71	John Johnson	0014	002½
72	William Hilton	0037	006½
73	Widow Nash.....................	0003	001
74	Charletowne Mill	0057	010
75	Daniell Edmunds	0026	004½
76	William Bachelor.................	0018	003
77	Roger Spencer...................	0037	006½
78	Thomas Starr	0026	004½
79	Thomas Adams	0010	001½
80	Samuell Cartar	0045	008
	10 Families	0273	048
81	Mʳˢ Sedgwicks Ali state...........	0028	005
82	Mʳ Zachary Syms	0057	010
83	Marke Kings	0019	003
84	Mʳˢ Kempthorne	0010	001½
85	John Mansefild	0005	001
86	Peeter Nash	0008	001½
R			
87	Widow Cole...........end½........	0005	001
88	Josuah Edmunds.................	0037	006½
89	widow Cartar...................	0013	002
90	Sollomon Phips.................	0051	009
	10 Families	0233	040½
91	Widow Streeters hous............	0004	001
92	William Bicknor.................	0013	002
93	Giles Fiffeild	0015	002½
94	John Burrage...................	0025	004½
95	Captain Francis Norton...........	00s9	015½
96	Mʳ Nicholas Davison and Farme	0081	015
97	Edward Johnson.................	0022	004
98	Henery Harbert.................	0039	006½
99	John Blancheer.................	0037	006

Lotts.		Wood in Acres.	Comon.
100	John Lawrence	0014	002½
	10 Families	0339	059½
101	William Goose	0005	001
102	Phillips estate	0007	001½
103	William Stitson....................	0054	009½
104	George Blancheer	0026	004½
105	William Foster	0029	005
106	Thomas Hett	0028	005
107	Samuell Adams....................	0054	009½
R 108	Mrs Trarice ....end....	0009	001½
109	Thomas Kimball	0029	005
110	Henry C[ooker]y....................	[0009]	001½
		[0250]	[044]
111	John Mousall......................	0019	003
112	widow Frothingham	0035	006
113	Gardy James	0007	001
114	John March	0025	004½
115	Miheil Smith	0014	002½
116	Natha. Smiths hous	0003	001
117	James Heyden.....................	0019	003
118	Leift: wheelers Farme	0007	001½
119	Hadloks hous......................	0004	001
120	John Tucky	0005	001
	10 Families	0138	024½
121	Mr Willoughby's state	0023	004
122	Samuell Ward.....................	0034	006
123	William Baker	0022	003½
124	John Call	0010	002
125	Mrs Graves	0050	009
126	John Phillips.....................	0015	002½
127	John Knight......................	0018	003
128	old Pritchard	0011	002
129	widow stubbs.................	0005	001
130	Thomas Mousall....................	0032	005½
	10 Families	0220	038½
131	George Buncker	0052	009
132	Mathew Griffin	0014	002½
133	widow Stowers	0012	002
134	Henery salter	0007	001
135	william Johnson	0027	004½
136	Richard Kettle....................	0026	004½
137	Thomas Brigden, Junior.............	0016	003
138	sargt Cutters hous..................	0010	001½
139	ffaithfull Rous	0032	005½
140	John Scott ......5 Rang [e] End....	0019	003
	10 Families	0215	036½
141	James Cary	0019	003½
142	Thomas Welsh	0030	005
143	Mr Thomas Shepheard	0042	007½

LOTTS.		WOOD IN ACRES.	COMONS.
144	Richard Templar....................	0017	003
145	James Peckar	0012	002
146	John Drinker	0019	003
147	Thomas Gould......................	0054	009½
148	Robert Leach.......................	0017	003
149	Samuell Blancheer..................	0014	002½
150	Beniamine switzer	0010	002
	10 Families	0234	041
151	John Harris	0015	002½
152	Aaron Ludkin	0010	001½
153	John Smith	0024	004½
154	Walther Allen.....................	0031	005
155	John Penticost	0025	004½
156	Abraham Bell	0016	003
157	Joseph Stower.....................	0004	001
158	Beniamine Lathrop	0016	[003]
159	John Dudly	[014]	[002½]
160	Richard Lowden	[036]	[006]
	10 Families	[0191]	[033½]
[91.]			
161	Richard Austin	0007	001
162	Zachary Long	0022	003½
6 R——			
163	Steeven Fosdike.............end....	0025	004½
164	John Gould	0052	009
165	Deacon Robert Hale	0039	007
166	Mʳˢ Coytmore and hous............	0028	005
167	Jonathan wads hous................	0011	002
168	Joseph Noyes......................	0011	002
169	widow Alice Mousall	0036	006
170	Thomas Jones, Butcher	0032	005½
	10 Families	0263	045½
171	William Syms	0041	007
172	Thomas Filleborne.................	0007	001
173	Widow Larkin.....................	0012	002
174	Walter Edmonds...................	0039	007
175	Thomas Jenner....................	0009	001½
176	Mr Thomas Allens	0014	002½
177	Elder Greene......................	0028	005
178	Thomas Orton.....................	0020	003½
179	John Cutler	0025	004½
180	Roger Els	0008	001½
	10 Families	0203	035½
181	Miles Nutt........................	0012	002
7 R——			
182	Mathew Smith...............end....	0011	002
183	George Foule......................	0059	0010
184	Abraham Smith....................	0018	003
185	Richard Stowers...................	0032	005½
	5 Families	0132	022½

These following had not any Lott alowed them, but vpon due considderation, when the whole Towne mett, It was Agreed that they should have as here under sett downe, the nomber to begin wher the other left, and they Amongst themselvs to draw their lotts : —

LOTTS.		WOOD IN ACRES.	COMONS.
186	Mr Morley	0020	003½
187	John Martin........................	0010	002
188	Mathew Smith	0006	001
189	Edward Wyer	0004	001
190	Steveen Grover.....................	0004	001
191	Daniell King.......................	0004	001
192	Alexander Bow.....................	0004	001
193	John ffoskit	0004	001
194	John Hamblton	0004	001
195	James Grant........................	0004	001
196	James Davis	0004	001
197	Isaac Cole, Junio^r	0004	001
198	woorys house	0004	001
199	Trumbles hous.....................	0004	001
200	Jacoes hous	0004	001
201	Shephard Daniells hous	0004	001
202	Hercules Corser	0004	001
	17 Families	092	020½

Bainell whitemor being with the selectt men is willing to acsept of allowance in the comon.

SAMUL : T :

[This entry is recorded by S. Adams, Town Clerk. — ED.]

[92.] Whear as wee Robertt hale and Richard Lowden were apointed to lay out a peselle of Grounde unto william Johnson, the which should bee for satisfaction for a high way layd out for the Countrey through his land bought of Mr Thomas Allen. Acordingly wee have layd out a p'sill of land lying beettwine the high way that Runneth from the peney ferre to malden meting house and the marsh lott that was formerly belonging unto James Browne and is now in the posesion of James Barrett, the which land layd out to wiliam Johnson is Bounded on the south by a litell small oake marked, and so to Runn by a Right Angle from the line that Runneth by the high way. and it is boundid on the north by an oake stump that is about a Rod to the west of the high way, and ffrom the sayd stump to a mapell stump, and so by a willow tree to the bounds of James Browne, wee say all the comon ground that lyeth betwine the afforsaid south and north bownds, and the said high way and James Barretts medow aforsaid : wittnes our hands the Thirtey one day of the eleventh moneth, one thousand sixe hundreth ffiftey and eight.

ROBERT HALE
RICHARD LOWDEN.

This retorne of Robertt hale and Richard lowdens is aproved of by the selectt men the 31 : 11 : 1658, by mee Richard Rusell by order of the selectt men of Charlstown.

This is a trew copey heare, entred this twenty one day of the fifth moneth, one thousand sixe hundreth ffiftey and nine : as attest by mee.

Carry this to 652 page of this booke. SAMUELL ADDAMS,
                entered.   Record. ffor
                                        Charlstowne.

[93,94.] Blank.

[95.] Articles of Agreement made And Concluded this 15th 2nd mo : 1662, betweene the selecte men of Charlestowne, In the behalfe of the propriators of the stented Common of the one partie : And Leffttenant : Richard Sprague : of the other partie : Concerning the fencing the said Common : which lyeth betweene Cambridge And Mr Winthroups farme : And sattisfection for the same.

Imprimis the said Leffttenant Richard Sprague : is to make up and mayntayne all that fence belonging to the said Common betweene it and Mr Winthroups farme : which said fence is to begine at misticke Bridge and so Along in the Lynne betweene the said Common and Mr Winthroups farme : to A Rocke which is for A Bound marke : Aboute some : six or seven : pooles : one the south east side of Winters Brooke : where it is to meeit Mr Winthroupes farmes fence : The fence is to be made sufficiently, And so mayntayned for One And twentie Yeares Next Insueing the Date hearof, Sufficent to fence of all reasonable Cattle : and to make good all Damoges that may Arrise from any difficentse in the said fence : or any part there of : Exsepting the Gate which he the said Richard is not to mayntayne : In Consideration where of the said Leffttenant Richard Sprague is to have the use of twentie Cowe Commons the full terme of twentie one yeares A fore Exspresed : he and his Assignes : And at the end of the said Terme thay are to be Serrendered up unto the said propriators Againe.   Also he is to have free Leave And Libarty to make use of any Stones : or Brush : from of the Common : for making or repeairing the said fence : And for the true performance of every perticular Above Exspresed : the Selecte men in the behalfe of the propriatores And Richard Sprague for him selfe : his heires Executors And Administrators : Doe firmly by these ptsnts bind them selves each partie : to the other : In the Just and full summe of Two hundred Pounds : In witnes where of thay the boeth parties have heare unto Interchangably put theire hands : the day and yeare Above written : It was also Agreed upon before the signing hear of, that what the said fence shall be Ajudged worth at the end of the fore mentioned terme of one and twentie yeares : more than it is at this present : is to be payed unto the said Richard Sprague : or his Assignes :

The fence at present is Ajudged worth thirtie pounds by muttuel consent.

RICHARD SPRAGUE.[1]

Signed And Delivred In the Presents of

SOLOMON PHIPPES,
EDWARD BURTT.

[Recorded by *Burtt.* — ED.] 1662.

___

[96.] Blank.

___

[97.] This page Appointed to record the Ticketts granted out.
The 29th of December, 1662, A tickett granted to phenias Sprague for Cutting and carring fower cord of whole timber from Charlstowne Comon, on Misticke side, limited to be done whin [within — ED.] the ensuing yeere 1663.

ꝑ JAMES CARY, *recorder.*

The 29th of October, 1662, A Tickett granted to Steephen paine for Cutting fower Cord of whole timber and six trees of pine from Charlstowne Comon, on misticke, to be done whin the yeear 1663.

ꝑ JAMES CARY, *recorder.*

The 29th of October, 1662, A Tickett granted to Edward Carrington to Cutt tenn Cord fire wood and ten popler or ash Trees from Charlstown Comon, on Misticke side, within one year ensuing (63.)

ꝑ JAMES CARY, *recorder.*

The 17th of Jania*, 1662, a Tickett granted and given out to John Roy, of Charlstowne, for the Cutting and Carring of twelve cord fire wood from of the Comon, on Mistick side, by Selectmⁿˢ order.

ꝑ JAMES CARY, *Recorder.*

The 20th of ffebrua*, 1662, a Tickett granted and given out to John Rosse, of Maulden, for the Cutting and Carring of Ten Cord of firewood from of the Common, on Mistick side, p order of the Selectmen and in their name

JAMES CARY, *Recorder.*

The 20th of April, 1663, It was granted unto Jacob Greene to Cutt and Carrie of Twentie Cord fire wood for his own use by Will Greene before the last of Octob* next, from of the commo, our wood, on Mistick side.

ꝑ JAMES CARY, *Recorder.*

The 20th of Aprill, 1663, it was granted by Tickett unto Miles Nutt to Cutt and Carrie of six cord of fire wood and fencing from of our wood Interest on Maulden Comon, by Thō May before next decebr.

JAM: CARY, *Recorder.*

---

[1] The names of Sprague, Phipps and Burt are autograph signatures. — ED.

The 20 : of April '63 : granted vnto Edward Wyer by Tickett to Cutt and Carrie Six Cord of fire wood for his own use of Charlstow, wood interest on Maulden side, comon, by Sam¹ Lewis, before march next ensuing.

JAM: CARY, Recorder.

The 13 of Janua^e : '63 : Granted vnto Josias Wood to Cutt, and p Tickett Carrie Ten trees for bolts from of our wood interest on Maulden Comon, within 12 month of this Date.

JAM: CARY, Recorder.

The 15 : 11 : 63, graunted unto Peeter Tufts, of Maulden, to Cutt, and p Tickett Carrie Twentie small trees, fencing Stuffe from of our wood interest on Maulden Comon, within 12 months of this date.

JAMES CARY, Recorder.

The 15 : of Noveber, '65, granted to Mr Willowbie to Cutt and Carrie twentie cord of firewood for his use, by the hands of Peeter Tufts, within 6 months.   ⍴ Tickett.

The 8th of Janua^e, '65, granted to Capt Norton to Cut and Carrie thirtie cord of firewood of our interest, in Maulden comon, before Septeb 29 next.   ⍴ Tickett.

[98.]   Blank.

[99.]

A.[1]

Averie of Cole,	111
Averie of Higginson,	111
Allen of Cole,	115
Allen of Wade,	115
Ayre to Willson,	116
Ayre to Haule,	116
Allen to Lowden,	120
Allen to Johnson,	127
Allen to Polgrave,	127
Allen to Dade,	128
Addams of Temple,	132
Arrington to Scott,	135
Allen of Dicks,	135
Andrews to Knight,	137
Arrington to King,	138
Arrington to Drinker,	139
Addams of Hadlock,	141
Adams to Smith,	141
Addams of Cook,	145
Allen to Hale,	146

[1] This Index, pages [99–102], is in the handwriting of Nathaniel Dows. Town Clerk 1695–6 to 1719. — ED.

B.

Vide E.

C.

Vide O

G.

Grissell of Willson,	118
Gould of Hill,	118
Gove of Larkin,	121
Gould to Edmonds,	122
Green of Carter,	123
Green of Sally	123
Green of Woory,	123
Goble to Baker,	123
Green to Drinker,	123
Green to Tufts,	126
Greenland to Moulton,	129
Greenland of Martin,	129
Green to Carrington,	130
Greenland to Harris,	130
Goble to Baker,	130
Goodwin of Bridges,	130
Gibbs to Dows,	132
Gibbs to Rand,	133
Garrat to Beadle,	137
Gold to Hale,	146

H.

Higginson to Averie,	111
Haule of Ayre,	116
Hubbart to March,	116
Hodge to Richardson,	117
Hubbard to Green,	118
Hill to Gould,	118
Hall to Luddington,	118
Hodgman of Willson,	119
Hale of Pemberton,	120
Hurst to Temple,	120
Harrington of Symes,	121
Harrington of Stilson,	121
Hawkins of James,	122
Hipburn to Rand,	124
Hipburn to Dows,	124
Harbert to Carter,	128
Harris to Greenland,	130
Hayden to Knight,	133
Hepborn to March,	133
Hodges to Rand,	134
Harbard of Kilcup,	139
Hadlock to Addams,	141
Hilton to Price,	142
Hill of Cuttler,	142

J.

James to Layhorn,	118
James of Power,	119

James of Felch,   120
James of Wilder,   122
James of Roper,   122
James of Hawkins,   122
Jaquith of Barnes,   123
Johnson of Allen,   127
James of Roper,   136
Johnson to Stowell,   144
James to Wiloby,   144

H.

Halle to Foster,   143
Hamond to James,   145
Hale of Pemberton,   146
Hale of Brown,   146
Hale of Allen,   146
Hale of Gould,   146
Hale of Converse,   147, 178
Hale of Martin,   147

[100.]

D.

Davis to Fessenden,   114
Drinker of Goble,   123
Drinker of Green,   123
Drinker of Sprague,   123
Dows to Salley,   124
Dows of Hipburn,   124
Dows of Rand,   125
Dexter of Long,   125
Dows to Lynd,   126
Dade of Allen,   128
Dade of Trarice,   128
Dexter of Moulton,   132
Dows of Gibbs,   132
Dexter of Palmer,   133
Drinker to Rugg,   134
Dicks to Allen,   135
Drinker of Arrington,   139
Dows to Ells,   140

K.

Killcup of Roberts,   119
Kittle to Temple,   120
Knight of Hayden,   133
Knight to Cloyes,   136
Knight of Andrews,   137
King of Arrington,   138
Kilcup to Harbard,   139

E.

B.

F.

L.

M.

[101.]

P.

W.

R.

[102.]

[103.] Blank.

[104.] *Sale of Lands by Mr John Crow of Charlton 4th mo, 1638.*

1. Mr John Crow of Chaltowne hath soulde unto Mathew Averie the sixteenth of the fourth moneth 1638, his dwelling house with all th apurtinances thereto aptaining, with eight acres of land thereto belonging, lying in Gibbines feilde, together with all other his right and title within the limittes of the sayde towne.

2. Viz. Com̅ones for foure milch Cowes.

3. five acres by estimation, more or lesse, of meaddow scituate and lying in mistick feilde marshes, butting west upon the north river, and east upon the woodland, bounded on the south by George Bunker and on the north by Chubbuck.

4. Twentie five acres of woodland scituate and lying in mistick

feilde[1] pole in length and   in breadth, butting to the northea ·
upon Thō Lynde and Georg hutchinson, southwest upon the
reserved land, bounded on the northwest by Daniell Snepheardson,
and on the southeast by Thō Moulton.

5.   ffiftie and five acres of land, scituate and lying in water
feilde,[2] [butting] northwest upon will Brakenbury and James Pemberton, southeast upon John Martin and Ed. Convers, bounded
on the southwest by Dan. Shepheardson, and on the northeast by
Tho. Moulton. N° 12. 100 pole in length, and   in breadth.

6.   One acre of meaddow, by estimation, more or lesse, scituate
and lying before the house buting south upon gibbines river,
bounded on the west by Rich miller, and on the east by John
Hodges, bought of

The assignes of m[rs] Ann Higginson, Soulde unto Mathew Averie.
Twentie acres of land, more or lesse, scituate in mistick feilde,
butting northeast upon Ed. Johnson, southwest upon John Harvard, bounded on the southeast by Ben. Hubbard, and on the
northwest by Ric. Davis.

And ffortie and five acres of land, scituate in waterfeilde, butting northwest upon Rich. Ketle, John Palmer, and will Dade,
southeast upon Abr. Pratt and Isaac Cole, bounded on the southwest by Nicolas Davis, and on the northeast by Ben. Hubbard.[3]

Att a metting of the selectt men the 23 the 11: 1659, was
granted and Confirmed unto the Towne of Malden a parsill of land,
more or les, which pasill of land is bowndid on the west by m[r]
Joseph hills medow, and on the north by the land of michell
Smith, and so joying to the high way, And william Brankenbury
on the northeast. This p[r]sill of land Aforsaid is given to the
towne of Maldon in Consideration of ther buldin a metting house :
that this is ther Reall Actt and Deed,   wittnis in the name of the
selectt men.

SAM ADAMS, *Reco.*

[**105.**]   *Artikles of Agreement Between Mary Nash, widow,
and John Penticost, both of Charls towne, New England, made the
20th of July, 1638.*

This Indenture, made the twentieth day of July, Anno Domini
1638, Between Mary Nash, of Charles towne, widow, on the one
party, and John Penticost, of Charles towne aforesayd, Rope
maker, on the other partie, Witnesseth that the sayd Mary Nash,
for and in consideration of Eighteen pounds, payd to her by the
sayd John Penticost, hath bargained, sould, given, and granted,
And by these presents doth fully and absolutely bargaine, sell,
give, and grant unto the same John Penticost Three severall parcells of Land lying and being in the Towne and feild of Charles

---

[1] "Feilde" is written over "hundrethes N°. 12, 100" erased, in Abraham Palmer's
hand. — ED.

[2] "Waterfielde" written over "the great hundrethes butting" erased in Palmer's
hand. — ED.

[3] So much of page [104] is in writing of Palmer. — ED.

Towne afouisayd, That is to say, One smale parcell of land within the Towne, Abutting west and north upon the Land of the sayd Mary Nash, and East upon the street called Crooked Lane, and south upon the street or lane called Malt Lane. And Another parcell of land Abutting west upon the street called Crooked lane afoursayd, and North upon the Lands of Josuah Tydd, East upon the street called the middle street, and south upon the Lane or high-way called Rope-makers lane. And alsoe another parcell of Land containing three Akers, more or lesse, lying and beeing in Charletowne Comon feild called New Towne Lyne, Abutting west upon New Towne Comon, North upon the Lands of Rice Cole, East upon Charltowne Comon, and south upon Thomas Richeson : To have and to hould all and every the sayd three parcells of Land untoo the sayd John Penticost, his heires and assignes for ever. And the sayd Mary Nash doth covenant to and with the sayd John Penticost that shee is the true and Rightfull owner of all the three parcells of land before by these presents mencioned to bee bargained and sould. And that the sayd premises, and every parcell thereoff, now Bee, and so shall continew, clearly discharged and exonerated of and from all other former bargaines and contracts whatsoever. In witness whereoff the parties aforesayd have to these presents Indenture interchangably set their hands and seals the day and year above written, as apears by the originall coppy in the hands of the sayd John Penticost[1]

JOHN GREENE.

[**106.**] *Sale made by Abr. Palmer of Charltown to m^{rs} Katherin Coytemore.*[2]

Abraham Palmer of Charltowne soulde unto m^{rs} Katherin Coytemore of the same towne A Dwelling house, with one p'cell of grounde adjoining, three acres by estimation, more or lesse, scituate in the high feilde ; And two acres of ground in the same feilde, betwixt Thō. Squire and George Bunker ; And two acres of grounde in the same feilde, betwixt John moussell and Sarah ewer ; as also ffive acres of meaddow by estimation, more or lesse, in misticke marshes, at the mouth of the south river.

[**107.**] *Sale made by Sarah Ewer, Late wife of Thomas Ewer of Charltown, Deceased, Unto ffrancis Willoughby of Charltown, in the Yeare* 1639.

Sarah Ewer, Widdow : sole exequetrix of Thomas Ewer, Deceased, bargained and soulde unto ffrancis Willoughby of Charltowne, one Dwelling house, with a garden plott, scituate in the midle row, butting south and west upon the markett place.

[**108.**] [All sould to Robert Mirriam in the year 1649, as apears. — *Greene.*]

Sale made by James Browne of Charltowne unto John Cullick of the same towne the twentie fift of the fift., 1639.

James Browne of Charltowne Soulde unto John Cullicke his

---

[1] In Greene's hand. — ED.
[2] In Abraham Palmer's hand to and including page [110.] — ED.

Dwelling house and garden, with all th aptinances, scituate on the south side of the mill hill.

2.   ffive acres of woodland, scituate in mistick feilde, butting west upon the Drift way, east upon the land way, bounded on the one side by Edward mellowes.

3.   fffifteene acres of woodland by estimation, scituate in mistick feilde, butting southwest upon Increase Nowell, northeast upon Will Nash, bounded on the southeast by Rob. Haukines, and on the northwest by Thō Goble.

4.   Two acres of meaddow by estimation, more or lesse, scituate in mistick marshes, butting north upon a creeke coming out of the north river, to the south upon the woodland.

5.   One acre of meaddow by estimation, more or lesse, scituate in the south meade, butting east upon the great Cove, to the west upon Thō. Richardson, and three milch cow comͦones and a quarter.

[109.] *Sale made by Nicolas Davis, sometime of Charton, now of Woobourne, unto John ffissenden of Cambridge, glover, the twentie one of the tenth month*, 1642.

Nicolas Davis, some time of Charltowne, Planter, being lawfully possessed of six acres of earable land in the line feilde, as apeares both by the towne and Court recordes : Hath Barggained and soulde by a deede of sale, under his hand : the said six acres of land unto John ffissenden of Cambridge : Glover : To have and to houlde to him and his heires for · ever :

In the presence of
              RICH. JACKSON :
              JOHN SILL.

[110.] *Sale made by George Bunker of Charltown unto Abr. Palmer of the sayd towne, the* 21. *of the sixt mo*, 1639.

George Bunker of Charltowne soulde unto Abr. Palmer of Charltowne Tenn acres of woodland, more or lesse, scituate in misticke feilde, butting west upon the Drift way, east upon the landway, bounded on the north by Thō. Lynde.

Thomas Ruck, sometime living in Charltowne, soulde unto Abr. Palmer of Charltown six acres of land by estimation, scituate in the east feilde, together with a Dwelling house and other aptinances about it, the first of the tenth mo. Ann. 1639.   Also three acres of meaddow by estimation, scituate at Wilson poynt.

Edward Mellowes, of Charltowne, soulde unto Abr. Palmer, of the sayd towne : one acre of land with a house upon it, scituate in the east feilde, butting southwest upon the streete way, and bounded on the northwest by Will ffrothingam :

Also, one acre and hauïf of land, mor or lesse, scituate in the same feilde, betwixt Thō. Lynde and Will ffrothingame, Annͦ 1639.

[111.]   Sale made by Isaac Cole, Inhabitant in Charltowne, unto M^r. Thō Allin, of the same towne, the 25th of the 3^d Moneth, 1646:

I. Isaac Cole, of Charletowne, acknowledge by this to have sould untoo Mr Thomas Allin, of the sayd towne, A parcell of land, being ten Acres by estimation, more or less, scituate in misticke feilde. Butting North East upon Walter Pamers land, southwest upon Edward Gibbons and Seth Sweetzir, one the north-west upon Abraham Pratt, and one the south East upon William Bachelor. [5 Akers of these sould to william Dade. — *Greene*.]

JOHN GREENE.

An Acknowledgment of a guift of Land of Thomas Carter, senior, unto his son in Lawe, william Greene, lying in woeburne.

Know all men by this presents, that I, Thomas Carter, of Charle-towne, senior, doe hereby Acknowledge that I have assigned and made over halfe of my Lott which I had lying at woeburn, as well halfe that which by Lott I had given mee, as likewise halfe of all the other which I bought in the towne aforesayd. The whole Lott by estimation, more or lesse, being six score and fifteen Acres : I, the foresayd Thomas Carter, doe surrender by this, the haife of it which is threescore and seven Acres and a halfe, unto my son in law, william Greene, for him and his heires, to posses without any disturbance or molestation from mee or any of myne. In witnes wherof I, the sayd Thomas Carter, doe set to my hand this Thirtith of the first Moneth, 1647.

JOHN GREENE.

An acknowledgment by Thomas Cartar, senior, of a deed of guift of certaine land given unto his son John Cartar, by him, lying at woburne the 16 of the 2 moneth, 1648.

Know all men by these presents, that I, Thomas Cartar, senior, of Charltowne, doe hereby acknowledge that I have assigned and freely and fully given and made over the other halfe of my Lott which I had lying at woburne, untoo my son John^1 Cartar, both half my Lott which was given mee in the dividint, as alsoe half of that which I bought in the same towne, lying by the other ; the whole lott, and what was bought, being by estimation six score and fifteen Akers, more or less, which as above I have divided and given to my son william Greene, and to this my son John Cartar : And I, Thomas Cartar, doe surrender the half the foresayd land, which is three score and seven Akers and a half unto my son John Cartar, to bee his and his heigrs for ever, to posses it without lett, disturbance, or molestation from mee or myne, or any, by so much as I can hinder them : which land Arrable and meadow if any bee within the compas of the sayd half lott, this sixty and seven Akers and a halfe is bounded southeast by the land of M^r In-crease Nowell, North East by Edward Convers, Northwest by william Greene, and southwest by the Comon. In wittnes heerof I the sayd Thomas Cartar have set to my hand to a bill of the deed which is in the hands and posession of my son John Cartar, written this 20 of the 3^d Moneth, 1648.

JOHN GREENE.

[Page [111] in Greene's hand. — ED.]

---

^{1} "John" written over " Joseph " erased by Greene. — ED.

[**112.**] Jonathan Wade, sometime of Charltowne, being law-fully possesed of tenn acres of land in mistick feilde upon the long hill by mistick river: Doth by these presentes sell and hath by an act of his under his hand bargained and soulde unto m^r Thomas allin, Teacher of the Church of Christ in Charltowne: the said tenn acres of land, with all the proffites and commodities of the same: To have and to houlde: to him and his heires for ever In the yeare of our Lord one thousand six hundred thirtie and nine. — [*Palmer.*][1]

I, Martha Coytmore, widow, acknowledge that I have sould unto John Scott of Charletowne A cowe common of myne, and I am fully payd for it. witness my hand the 3^d of the 3^d moneth, 1646. JOHN GREENE.

[**113.**] *Sale of Hous and Land made by william Ayre of Charltowne, unto Richard willson of Cambridge, the 24th day of the 7th Moneth,* 1646:

Know all men by this presents, that I, william Ayre, of Charl-towne Inhabitant: for and in consideration of a sume of money, have sould: and by this testify to sell, unto Richard willson of Cambridge, Inhabitant: six Acres of Earable Land and meadowe: by estimation more or less, scituate on the southwest syde of strawberry Hill: bounded on the Easte by John sybley: one the southwest by a highway: And on the North and East by the comon: with a dwelling House upon it, and all its other appurte-nances: Alsoe Thirty and five Akers of Land, more or less, by estimation, scituate in watter feild, butting Northwest upon John sybley and Katherine Coytemore: southeast upon Robert shortas, bounded on the Northeast by Prudence wilkinson: and on the southeast by John Lewis: Alsoe twoo and on quarter Milche cowes comons on the stinted comon of Charltown without the neck: To have and to hould the sayd Howsing, Lands earrable or Med-dow, cowes comons, and the Appurtenances ther untoo belonging; by the sayd Richard willson and his heires for ever. In witnes hereof I, william Ayre, doe by this acknowledg it this 24th of the 7th Moneth, 1646:

In the presence of JOHN GREENE.

Sale of Land made by william Ayre of Charltown, unto Ralph Haule of the sayd towne, the 21th day of the 7th Moneth, 1646.

Know all men by this presents, that I, william Ayre of charl-town have sould, and by this doclare it, untoo Ralph Haul of the sayde town, five Acres of Land, more or lesse, lying and scituate in mistik feild, Butting North east upon John Green: southwest upon Rice Cole, and John Harverd, Bounded on the Northwest by Prudence Wilkeyson: and one the southwest by John Lewis: To have and to hould and enjoy the sayd five Acres of land and the Apurtenances belonging therunto: by the sayd Ralph Haule and his heires for ever, this 21th day of the 7th Moneth, 1646.

In the presence of
JOHN GREENE.

---

[1] From here to page [141] inclusive the record is in Greene's hand. — ED.

[114.] *Sale of Land made by Abraham Palmer of charl-*
towne in new England unto John March of the sayd towne, the 5ᵗʰ
day of the 12ᵗʰ Moneth, 1646.

Know all men by these presents, that I, Abraham Palmer of
Charletown, have sould unto John March of the sayd towne,
seaven Acres and a halfe of land, lying and scituate in Mistike
feilde : bounded on the south by Edward Harringtons land, and
on the North bounded by an other parcell of my owne land : To
have and to hould the sayd seaven Acres and a halfe of land and
the appurtenances theruntoo belonging : by the sayd John March
and his heires for ever, this 5ᵗʰ day of the 12ᵗʰ Moneth, 1646.

JOHN GREENE.

In the presence of
mʳ INCREASE NOWELL.

Sale of land made by Benjamin Hubbard, of charletowne, in new
Engl', unto John March, of the sayd towne, the 17 *day of the* 2ⁿᵈ
Moneth, 1644.

Know all men by these presents, That I, Beniamine Hubbard, of
Charltown, have sould unto John March, of the sayd towne, one
Acre of land lying in the East feild, which the sayd Beniamin did
lately purchas of mʳ Bunckher. To have and to hould and enioy
the sayd Acre of land and the apurtenances therunto belonging to
him, the sayd John March, and to his heighrs for ever.

In witnes wherof, I, the said Beniamin Hubbard, have to these
presents, set my hand this 17 day of the 2ᵈ Mo., Anno Domino
1644.

BENIAMIN HUBBARD.

JOHN GREENE.

More. I, John March, have bought of the foresayd Abraham
Palmer twoo Akars and a halfe of Arrable Land, more or lesse,
joyning to the aforesaid seaven Akers and a halfe of land Above
mentioned, which land in all is 10 Akers, more or lesse, is scituated
on mistik syde, and adioyning on the North syde unto the land of
James Greene, and at the west its bounded by the coṁon, at the
Easte and bounded by the land of Robert Nash : and on the south
syde by Harringtons land, the 5 of the 2ᵈ Mo., 1647.

JOHN GREENE.

[115.] *An exchange of land by mʳ John Hodges with Ezekile*
Richeson.

Know all men, That I, John Hodges, have changed with Ezekiell
Richeson, and given him my 45 Akers of land, scituated in water
feild, bounded on the North East by Rice Cole. And for the said
land Ezekiell Richeson hath given mee a lot of medow ground by
the south syde of the great Pond which lies North east from my
house. And more, he hath given mee one cow common, which did
belong to him in charls towne ; the lot was 3 Akers, more or less.

the 29ᵗʰ of the 1ˢᵗ Mo., 1647, more, I bought one half Cowes
common of Edward sturgis, with his house.

JOHN GREENE.

Sale of House and land made by George whitehand, of Charle towne, unto Richard stower, of the sayd towne, the 25 day of the 4 Mo., 1646.

Know all men by this presents, That I, Georg Whithand, of Charltowne, doe by this declare to have sould and doe sell unto Richard stower, of the sayd towne, A dwelling House, scituate without the neck one the mayne, with a Barn and shop and other out Howsing, with 2 Akers of land, more or lesse, lying and adioyning to the House, with 2 Cowes commons and one hay lot ioyning to the planting ground of Thō : Caule, on mistik syde. And I, Georg whithand, do acknowledg my self to bee fully payd and satisfyed tharfore, And I resigne all this abovsayd hous, howsing, land, and Cowes Common, to remaine and to appertaine to the sayd Richard stower, and to his heires for ever.

JOHN GREENE.

Sale of Land made by John sybly unto John Greene, the 20ᵗʰ of the 3ᵈ Mo., 1647.

Know all men by this present, That I, John sybly, of charltown, doe sell and by this declare it unto John Green, senior, ten Akers of wood land, more or lesse, scituate in Mistik feild, butting north east upon Robert Long, southwest upon John woolrich and Prudence wilkison, one the Northwest by Katherin coitmore, and on the southeast by Ed. Johnson. And I do acknowledg myself to be fully satisfied and payd therfore, the day and date above written.

JOHN GREENE.

[**116.**] *A sale of a House and the Apurtenances pertaining theruntoo of Grace Smith, Inhabitant in charle town, unto John Peerce of London, seaman, in manner and   as followeth :—*

Know all men by this presents, that I, Grace Smith, widdow : late wife of Thomas Smith of charltowne, deceased, doe acknowledg that I have sould and am fully payd for it, A House, yeard and garden, all joyning and being together, scituate in charle towne, unto John Peerce of London, Marriner : which house, yeard and garden, did formerly belong unto Isaac Cole, carpenter, of the same town, who sould it all afore named and was fully payd for it, unto Thomas Smith, above named, which house and ground is on the one syde bounded by a vacant peace of Ground wherin is a comon well on the west syde, and one the East syde by John waffes house, by the street one the south syde, and by James Brouns ground one the North syde : which House, Howsing, yeard and garden doth belong unto the sayd John Peerce, with all due appurtenances thertoo belonging, and his heighers for ever as his lawfull and due purchase, bought with his money of the sayd widdow Grace Smith, to whom it did belong, and she did and her husband buy it of Isaac Cole who first built it, whom she fully hath payed for it. This house, yerd, garden, being the sayd John Peerces and his heires to have and to hould for ever :

Acknowledged before m^r Increase Nowell, and acknowledged by Grace smith unto John Greene as by the covenant apeareth the 15th of the 5th Moneth, 1648.

JOHN GREENE.

A sale of land of Thomas Brigden untoo samuell Richison the 21th of the 11th Mo: 1647.

Know all men by this presents, that I, Thomas Brigden, of charltown, doe acknowledge that I have sould and doe sell unto samuell Richeson of woburn, A parcell of Arrable Land, being five and twenty Akers, more or lesse, lying and scituate in woeburn : bounded on the North by Samuell Richesons land, on the south by Robert Hale, on the Easte by charltown comon, And by Jones river on the west, And I acknowledge my self to be fully payd therfore, And by this I resign unto the sayd samuell all my title, right, and interest thertoo unto him and his heighrs for ever, this 21th day of the 11th Moneth, 1647.

JOHN GREENE.

A sale of a House and a garden in charltowne, By George Bunker unto Phinias Prat, the 20th of the 3^d month, 1648.

Know all men by these presents, that I, George Bunker, Inhabitant in charltowne, have sould, assigned, and set over, and by this declare that I doe sell, assigne and set over unto Phinias Prat, inhabitant, in the same towne, A House or Tenement with a garden to it adioyning : which house and garden stands and is scituate in charltowne in the great through fare street which goes from the Neck of land into the market place, this house and garden stands right over against the way that goes up to the windmill hill, and that way which goes intoo elbow lane, the house is bounded on the front by the street way or by the west, and the house and garden is bounded East by the back street which goes to the pitt where the Beasts drinke, and where the Creek begins which runs on the back syde of the maiors garden into Charls River, and it is bounded Northward by samuell Howard, and southward by Thomas Carter, senior : Alsoe, I, Georg Bunker, doe acknowledg my selfe to bee fully payd and satisfied for this sayd hous and garden, And I doe heer by resigne all my Right, Titell, and interest unto the sayd house and garden unto the sayd Phinias Prat to be his and his heigres for ever.

JOHN GREENE.

[117.] *A sale of land made by Obadiah Wood of Charltowne untoo Joseph Carter of the same towne Inhabitant, the 13 day of the 2$_d$ Mo., 1646.*

Know all men by this presents, That I, obadiah wood, inhabitant in charletown, have sould, and by this declare it; unto Joseph Carter of the sayd town, five Akers of Arrable Land, more or lesse, lying in mistike feild, Bounded on the East by Abrah : Hill, on the west by William smith, on the North by the Rayles, on the south by m^r Richard Russels 20 Akers Lott, the sayd Joseph carter to have and to hould the sayd five Akers, with all Apurtenances, for him and his heirs for ever.   JOHN GREENE.

A sale of a House in Charletowne made by Alice Hubberd of the same towne untoo John Greene, the 22ᵗʰ of the 10ᵗʰ Moneth, 1645.

Bee it knowen untoo all men by this presents, That I, Alice Hubberd, the wife of Beniamine Hubberd, inhabitant in charltowne. Doe by this Acknowledg to have sould unto John Greene, senioʳ, A House in charltown, next to william Bachelers house, for the sume of 14 pounds. And I confes my selfe to bee fully satisfied and payed for the same.

John Greene.

A sale of a house and land by Richard Wilson of Boston unto francis Grissell of charltowne, the 16 of the first Moneth, 1649.

Know all men by these presents, that I, Richard wilson of Boston, in New England, doe by this declare that I have bargained with and sould unto francis Grissell of Charltowne A dwelling house with an orchard and other housing, pertaining to the house, which is all scituate and lying at the west end of the towne, near the way to Cambridg; it is bounded by the comon on all sydes, but next to Thomas Goble on the Easte syde, and on the west by a creek.

Also two Akers of meddow land, more or lesse, bounded on the Easte by the comon, on the west by the creek, on the south by Richard Palgrave, and on the north by Thomas Peirce.

Also, eaight Akers of planting land, more or less, scituate in the feilde next Cambridg line, bounded west by Thomas Goble, Easte, by the Lower feild, and south by Thomas Goble, north by Edward Mellows.

Alsoe twoo Akars of planting land, more or less, scituate in the same feild, bounded south and North by Edward Mellows west by Thomas Goble, and Easte by the lower feild.

Also two cowes comons on the stinted comon of charltowne.

The sayd francis Grissell to have and to hould the foresayd housing, orchard, meddow, planting land, and cows comons, to him and his heigrs for ever. This all pertained unto John Greene formerly, of whom I, Richard Willson, bought it. In witness of this sale I, Richard Willson, have set to my hand to a copy hereof in the presence of mʳ Increase Nowell, the day and date above written.

John Greene.

[**118.**] *A sale of a cows comon by Abraham Hill unto John Gould, both of charltowne, the 24ᵗʰ day of the first Moneth, 1649.*

Know all men by these presents, that I, Abraham Hill of Charltown, have sould and doe sell unto John Gould, of the same towne, half a cows comon, which lyes upon the stinted comon, and which was given mee by the towne, and I acknowledge my self to be payd and fully satisfied for the same. And I doe heerby resigne up all my right, titell, and interest in the sayd half cow comon, to be the sayd John Goulds and his heigrs for ever, as apears by a bill of my hand, which I have given to the sayd John Gould the day and date above written.

John Greene.

A sale of Land by Gardy James to Rowland Layhorn, both of Charltowne, the 28ᵗʰ day of the first moneth, 1649.

Know all men by these presents, that I, Gardy James, Inhabitant in Charltown, have sould, assigned, and set over unto Rowland Layhorn, of Charltown aforesayd, A lott of five Akers of arrable Land, be there more or lesse : being half the ten Aker Lott which I, Gardy James, bought of John Power, hosier, who had it of William Mirable, and he had it of Georg. Michell, who had it of William Learned, which was the first proprietor of the sayd ten Akers, it being given him by the Towne in the first dividing of the Land of charltown on mistik syde, which five aker of Land is lying and scituate on mistike syde, among the five aker Lotts, which five akers aforesayd lyes towards the south syde of the aforesayd ten Akers ; adioyning on the North syde unto Richard Pratt, who is the owner of the other part of the ten Akers above mentioned, And it is bounded south by Thomas Brigden, East by William Johnson, west by the salt marsh meddows : which foresayd five Akers, more or lesse, I, Gardy James, confess myselfe to be fully payd and satisfied for. And I doe hereby resigne unto the sayd Rowland Layhorn all my right, Titell, and interest in the same to be his and his heigres for ever, wittnes my hand to the copy hereof in the hands of Rowland Layhorn.

JOHN GREENE.

A sale of Land by Ralph Hall unto William Luddington, both of Charletowne, the 10ᵗʰ day of the 10ᵗʰ moneth, 1649.

Know all men by these presents, That I, Ralph Hall, of Charltowne, in New England, Pipe stave maker, for a certaine valluable consideration by mee in hand Received, by which I doe acknowledge my selfe to be fully satisfied, and payed, and contented : Have bargained, sould, given, and granted, and doe by these presents Bargaine, sell, give, and grant unto william Louddington, of Charlstowne aforesayd, Weaver, Twenty Achors of Land, more or less, scituate, Lying, and Beeing in Maulden, That is to say, fifteen Acres of Land, more or less, which I, the sayd Ralph, formerly purchased at the hand of Thomas Peirce, of Charltowne, senioʳ, Bounded on the Northwest by the land of Mʳ. Palgrave, Phisition, on the Northeast by the Lands of John Sybly, on the South Easte by the Lands of James Hubbert, and on the south west by the Land of widdow Coale, And the other five Acres herein mencioned sould to the sayd William, Are five Acres, more or less, bounded on the southeast by the Land of Widdow Coale, aforesayd, on the southwest by Thomas Grover and Thomas Osborne, Northeast by the Ground of Thomas Molton, and Northwest by the forsayde fifteen Acres : which five Acres I formerly purchased of mʳ. John Hodges, of Charltowne. To Have and to hould the sayd fifteen Acres, and five Acres of Lands, with all the Appurtenances and priviledges thereoff To Him, the sayd William Luddington, his heigres and Assignes for ever : And by mee, the sayd Ralph Hall, and Mary my wiffe, to bee bargained, sould, given, and confirmed unto him, the sayd william, and his heigres and Assignes for him, and them peasable and quietly to posses, inioy, and improve to his and their owne proper use and usses for ever, and the same by us by vertue hereoff to bee warrantedtised (*sic*), mayntained, and defended from any other person or persons hereafter Laying clayme to the same by any former contract or Agreement conserning the same : In wittness wherof, I, the sayd Ralph Hall, with Mary my wiffe, for our selves, our heires, executors and Administrators, have hereuntoo sett our hands and seales. Dated this Tenth day of December, 1649.

This is Testified before the worshipfull M^r. Richard Bellingham.

JOHN GREENE.

[**119.**] *A sale of Howsing and Land by Sarah Power, unto Gardy James of charletowne, the 3^d Day of the 10th Moneth, 1645.*

Be it knowen unto all men by these presents, that I, Sarah Power, Inhabitant in New England, in the towne of Charletowne, being Authorized and ordained to make sale of my husband John Powers, howsing and lands in the aforesayd towne, as by Letter of Atturney appeareth : I the foresaid Sarah Power, hereby testify that I have bargained and soulde unto Gardy James, of the sayd towne, one dwelling House and the Appurtenances theruntoo belonging, together with five Akers of planting Land, more or lesse, lying by and adioyning to the same House : And the sayd Sarah Power in behalfe of her husband, doth covenant and Promise too and with the sayd Gardy James, his heirs, executors, administrators and assighnes, that they shall or may lawfully and quietly hould, occupy, and enioy the foresayd premises without any Interrupting off or by the sayd John Power, or any of those that have been formerly owners of the same : And further, he sayd sarah Power. in the Absence of her husband, doth hereby Acknowledg my self to bee fully satisfied and payd for all the Abovsayd bargaine and premises by the sayd Gardy James : In wittnes wherof I the sayd Sarah Power have set too my hand and seale the 3^d December, 1645.

JOHN GREENE.

An Acknowledgment of a sale by William Roberts of wapping in ould England unto William Kilcop of charltowne in new England, of A House and Land, scituate in the sayd charletowne, the 8 Moneth the 18 day, 1646.

Know all men by these presents, that I, William Roberts of wapping, in the County of Middlesexe, wine cooper, doe acknowledge myself to give unto William Kilcop, sive maker of charletowne, in new England, in the Continent of America, a generall Acquitance of the receit of all the money which was due unto Mathew Avery or his Assignes, conferming a certaine house and land scituate near to Mr Hodges his poynt, in the sayd parish of charlestowne, Hee surrendering up his receits of the payments of the sayd money being forty and eaight not being payd unto the right owner, I the sayd William Roberts being the right owner of the sayd monyes, doth fully by this free him of all trouble hereafter, conferming the payement of the sayd money, he giving mee the sayd bills that I may know how to demand my mony of them.

Againe, having receaved it by virtue of letters of atturny, witness my hand this 18th day of the 8th Moneth, 1646.

JOHN GREENE.

[**120.**] *A sale of Land by William Roberts unto Rowland Layhorn, both of charletown, the 29th of the 1st moneth, 1648.*

Know all men by this presents, that I, William Roberts, have sould and doe sell unto Rowland Langhorn five Akers of meddow by estimation, more or lesse, lying and scituate in mistik marshes, butting west upon the North River, east upon the woodland, on the south by George Bunker, and on the North by Tho. Chubbock or John Brimsmead, And alsoe I, William Roberts, doe declare by this that I doe sell unto the sayd Rowland Langhorn fifteen Akers of arrable Land, lying on mistike syde, which is A part of five and twenty Akers of myne: all which is bounded south east upon Tho. Lyne and Georg Hutcheson, south west upon the reserved land, north west by Daniell Shepherdson, and southeast by Thomas Moulton, And I, william Roberts, doe by this resighn all my right, title, and interest in the sayd medow and upland afour mentioned unto the sayd Rowland Layhorn and his heires for ever; wittness my hand to the bill in his hands this present the 29th day day of the 1st moneth, 1648.

JOHN GREENE.

A sale of house and Land by Richard Willson, Mason, of Cambridg, unto George Hodgshon of Cambridg, the House and Land lying and scituate in Charltowne, at the west end thereof, made the 8th day of the 8th Mo: 1647, As followeth:

This witnesseth that Georg Hodgshon of Cambridge hath bought of Richard willson, Mason, of Cambridg, A House and an orchard and Lots of Meadow and upland ioyning to the house, which is scituate in charltowne, at the west end therof: on the one syde bounded by John Sybley, and on the other syde by the highway and the comon. Alsoe all the priviledges apertaining thertoo, As 2 Cowes comons: also libertyes to cutt wood on the comon, to be used about the sayd hous and grounds, also the Lot on mistik syde of about 35 Akers, with what apurtenances els belongs to the sayd house and ground which the sayd Richard bough of mr Aier, who married the wife of mr John woolrych, whose house it was formerly: It is all to be and to belong unto the sayd Georg Hodgshon and his heirs for ever. And the sayd Richard hath given the sayd Georg full and lawfull possesion of all the premises. In wittnes here of both the sayd parties have set to their hands and seales the day and date above written.

JOHN GREENE.

[**121.**] *A sale of 3 Akers of Land by Georg Felch unto James Barret.*

Know all men by this presents, that I, Georg Felch, Inhabitant in Charltown, on mistike syde, doe by this acknowledge that I have sould, and am fully payd for it, unto James Barret, of the same town, three Akers of Arrable land, more or lesse, which I bought of ffrancis Mills, which sayd land lyes on mistik syde, within the rayles, bounded on the east syde by Richard Kettell, and by the cuntry high way on the west syde, bounded on the North by Edward Carrinton and on the south by A high way. And the sayd James Barret is to enioy and to hould the sayd three Akers of land for him and his heighrs for ever.

In witnes hereof, I, Georg ffelch, have set my hand to a bill of sale of the same, the 26th day of the 3d Moneth, 1648.

JOHN GREENE.

A sale of a Cows Comon by James Pemberton unto Robert Hale.

Know all men by these presents, that I, James Pemberton, inhabitant in Charltown, on mistik syde, doe hereby acknowledge that I have sould and doe sell untoo Robert Hale, of Charltown, one cow comon, of the stinted comon, without the Neck, to be his and his heighrs for ever: and I doe acknowledg my self to bee fully satisfied, and payed for the same, as dos apear by a bill I have delivered to him with my mark theruntoo, this 12th day of the 3d Moneth, 1648.

JOHN GREENE.

A sale of land betweene Georg ffelch and Gardy James.

Know all men by these presents, that I, Georg Felch, of Charltown, doe acknowledge that I have sould unto Gardy James, of the same towne, half my Ten Aker Lott, lying on mistik syde, the other halfe of which Lott my mother wilkinson occupieth and enioyeth, And I doe hereby acknowledge my self to be fully payed and satisfied therfore, And I doe heerby resign over all my right, titell, and interest in the sayd half ten Aker Lott, unto the sayd Gardy James, to bee his and his heigres for ever.

witnes my hand, this 1st day of the 2d Mo., 1649.

JOHN GREENE.

[**122.**] *A sale of a marsh Lott by Edward Hurst vnto Richard Temple, both of charltowne.*

Know all men by these presents, that I, Edward Hurst, doe by this declare that I have sould unto Richard Temple A marsh hay lott, being twoo Akers, more or less; scituate on charltown stinted comon: bounded on the west by Powell's farme, on the East by Rice Morris, on the south by the River, and on the North by the comon. And I, Edward Hurst, doe acknowledg my self to be payed and fully satisfied for the same, and hereby testify that I doe surrender all the forementioned Lott unto Richard Temple, to be his and his heighrs for ever, without let or molestation from mee or any of myne for ever. written the 2d of the 12th Moneth, 1648.

JOHN GREENE.

A sale of a dwelling house and 3 Akers of land by Richard Kettell unto Richard Temple, both of charltowne.

Know all men by this presents, That I, Richard Kettell, doe by this declare that I have sould unto Richard Temple one dwelling

house, with a garden plott of half an Aker about it, scituatt on
the stinted comon of charltowne: Richard Palgraves meddow
nearest to it on one syde, and Rice Morris his house one the other
syde.   Powells farme on the North syde and the comon on the
south syde: Also, 3 Akers more or less, lying at the upper end of
the great feild over the creek: butting south easte towards the high
way to cambridg, southwest to cambridg line, and east to John
Sybley: And I, Richard Kettell, doe hereby acknowledg my self to
bee payd and fully satisfied for the same, and doe surrender to
Richard Temple all my right and Title thertoo unto him to bee his
and his heighrs for ever, without let or molestation from mee or
any of myne: written the 2ᵈ day of the 12ᵗʰ Moneth, 1648.

JOHN GREENE.

---

*A sale of a house, garden and barne, by Peircis Bridges, widdow
of william Bridges: unto Richard Temple, both of charltowne.*

Know all men by these presents, that I, Peircis Bridges,
doe heerby declare to have sould unto Richard Temple, one dwelling house and a Barn, And half an Aker of ground, more or less,
scituate on the stinted comon of Charltowne: being between
Richard Kettell, and mʳ Palgraves meddow, and Powells farme on
the North syde: being round encompassed by the comon: And I,
Peircis Bridges, doe hereby acknowledg my self to be fully payd
and satisfied therfore, And I hereby doe surrender unto Richard
Temple all my right and title thertoo unto him to bee his and his
heighrs for ever, without lett or molestation from mee or any of
myne: written the 2ᵈ day of the 12ᵗʰ Moneth, 1648.

JOHN GREENE.

---

*A sale of three Cows Comons by Mʳ Thomas Allen untoo Richard
Lowden.*

Know all men by these presents, that I, Thomas Allen, of charltown, doe hereby declare to have sould, and I am fully payd for
them, untoo Richard Lowden, 3 cows comons scituate on the stinted
Comon of Charltowne: which did formerly belong to mʳ Pratt,
deseased, which 3 cows comons I doe by this surrender to be the
sayd Richard Lowdens, and his heigrs for ever: written the 24ᵗʰ
day of the 12ᵗʰ Moneth, 1648.

JOHN GREENE.

[**123.**]   *A sale of twoo cow comons by Mʳ Zachary Syms to
John Burrage, the 24ᵗʰ day of the first Moneth*, 1649.

Know all men by these presents, that I, Zechary symms, of Charltown, have sould, and by this declare it, untoo John Burrage, of
the same town, twoo cows comons, lying and scituate on the
stinted comon, without the Neck, which were given mee in the
divident of that comon; and I acknowledg my self to be fully
payd and satisfied for them, And I doe hereby resigne all my
right, titlle, and interest in the sayd twoo comons to be John
Burrage and his heigres for ever, as I have written under my owne
hand which he hath.

JOHN GREENE.

A sale of a house a yeard and garden, of Edward Larkin, Turner, of Charltowne, unto John Gove of the sayd towne, the 29ᵗʰ of September, 1647.

Bee it known unto all men by these presents, that I, Edward Larkin, of Charltowne, Turner, for and in consideration of Tenn pounds in hand received, have bargained and sould unto John Gove, of the Towne aforesayd, one Tennement or dwelling house, with all the Appurtenences as yeard, garden, and fences belonging to the same, To have and to hould the sayd house and Land, with the Appurtenance therunto belonging, to the sayd John Gove, his heire and Assignes for ever: And the sayd Edward Larkin, being the true and right owner of the same, doe covenant, and promise That the premises, and every parcell therof, now bee and soe shall continue cleerly discharged and exonerated of and from all other former bargaines what soever: And the sayd Edward Larkin doth covenant to give the sayd John Gove, or his assigne, full and free possession upon the first of March next ensueing the date hereof. In wittnes wherof I have set too my hand and seale as appeareth in the coppy of the sale, this 29ᵗʰ of September, 1647.

Acknowledged before mʳ Increase Nowell, the 28ᵗʰ of the 2ᵈ Moneth, 1649.

JOHN GREENE.

the bill of sale was sealed and delivered in the presence of us,

EDWARD MELLOWES,
SAMUELL CARTTER.

A sale of a cow comon by Mʳ Zachary Symms unto Richard Harrington, the 2ᵈ of the 7ᵗʰ Mo., 1648.

I, Zachary Symms, doe heerby certifye all to whom it may consern: that I have sould untoo Richard Harrington one of my cow comons, which was given mee in the divident of the comon: and I am fully payd and satisfied therfore, as apears under my hand which he hath, And I doe heerby resigne all my right, titell, and interest in the same cow comon unto the sayd Richard Harrington, to bee his and his heigres for ever: written the 21ᵗʰ day of the 3ᵈ Moneth, 1649.

JOHN GREENE.

[**124.**] *A sale of twenty Akers of Arrable Land, by mʳ ffrancis Willoughby, unto william Bucknam, the seaventeenth day of the third moneth, 1649.*

Know all men by these presents, That I, ffrancis willoughby, Inhabitant in Charltowne, doe by this Acknowledge that I have sould, and I am fully satisfied for it, unto william Bucknam, of the same town, Inhabitant, A parcell of Land Arrable: of twenty Akers, more or lesse, lying and being scituate on mistike syde: Bounded on the south by mʳ. Thomas Allen, on the North by william Phillips: and on the west by mʳ. Richard Russell: and on the East by william Sargeant: and I, ffrancis willoughby, doe heerby Resigne all my Right, Tytell, and Interest in the foresayd twenty Akers of Land untoo william Bucknam, to bee his and his Heighrs for ever : As appears by a coppy of this sale delivered unto william Bucknam with my owne hand thertoo.

JOHN GREENE.

A sale of twoo march lotts by william stilson, of Charltown, unto Richard Harrington, of the same towne, the 22th of the 3d Moneth, 1649.

Know all men by these presents, that I, William stilson, Inhabitant of Charltowne, in New England, doe by this acknowledge that I have sould unto Richard Harrington, of the same towne, twoo Akers of meddow, more or lesse (which I bought of Samuell Richeson), which is lying and scituate in mistik marshes, Bounded west by the upland, East by Edward Jones, south by the upland, and North by the widdow Wilkins :

And I, william stilson, doe declare that I am fully payd and satisfied for the same : and I doe hereby Resigne all my Right, Titell, and Interest in the foresayd twoo Akers, more or lesse, unto the sayd Richard Harrington, to be his and his heigres for ever.

Wittnes my hand to a writting the day and date above written.

More there is sould by mee, William stillson, at the same tyme, unto the sayd Richard Harrington, A peece of upland ground lying at Hadlock's poynt, at high-watter marke, being five pole in the front at high water on the south syde, and one the North syde three pole, and alsoe on the east and west sydes three poles ; it lies between Robert Long, senio[rs], meadow, and william stillson's owne upland.

And I, william stilson, doe acknowledge my self, to be fully satisfied therefore, and hereby resigne all my Right, Titell, and Interest in the sayd Land unto Richard Harrington, to be his and his heigres for ever, wittness my hand to a writting he has the day and date above written. JOHN GREENE.

A sale by Robert Cole, Marriner, unto Arrold Cole, widow, his mother, both of Charltowne, in New England, the 12th of the 8th month, 1649.

Know all men by these presents, that I, Robert Cole, marriner, Inhabitant in Charltowne, New England, doe hereby declare that I have Resigned, and doe resigne unto my mother, Arrold Cole, all my part off and all my Right, Titell, and Interest In. the twoo Akers of meadow Land, and one cow com̄on, which did ioyntly belong unto us both, which meadow Land lyes and is scituate in the Valey of the Easte feild, at the head of the swamp, Bounded one the Easte by Robert Cutler and A highway, on the west by william Bacheler, on the North by Thomas Lynde, and one the south by Thomas Carter, And I hereby resigne it all unto my sayd mother, to bee hers and her heires for Ever. In witness heer off, I, with my wiffe, Philip Cole, have sett to our hand, this twelvth day of the eaighth moneth, A thousand six hundred forty nine.

This was Testified before M[r]. Increase Nowell, Magistrate, the day above written.

JOHN GREENE.

[125.] *A sale of House and Barne, with Garden or Ground pertayning therunto, by John Gould, Inhabitant in Charltowne, unto Gualter Edmonds of the same towne, this tenth of the 3 mo., 1649.*

Know all men by these presents, That I, John Gould, Inhabitant in Charltowne, for and in the consideration of a certain sume of money, have sould and by this declare that I doe sell, unto Gualter Edmonds, of the same towne, one dwelling-house with a Barne and a Garden, Being half an Aker of Ground, more or lesse, whereon the sayd House, and Barn are scituated, which House, Barn, and Land, stands, lies, and is scituated within Charltown, and nere the windmill hill of the said towne; And this House, Barn, and Garden Ground, is Bounded on the North by the mill Hill, on the west by the high street, and on the south by the mill hill, and on the Northeast By Robert Cutler, Harman Garret, and John March.

More, I, John Gould have sould, and doe sell, unto the sayd Gualter Edmonds one cows comon (which was given mee in the dividend) and one halfe cows comon, which I bought of Abraham Hill, both lying and scituate on the stinted comon without charltowne Neck, &c.[1]

JOHN GREENE.

Arrold Cole, widow, and her son, Robert Cole: land within charlestown Neck unto Richard Lowdon, of the same towne, the 19th of the 8th moneth, 1649.

Know all men by these presents, that wee, Arrold Cole, widow, And Robert Cole, marriner, both Inhabitants in charletowne, doe hereby declare that we have sold and doe sell unto Richard Lowden, of the same towne, Halfe of the twoo Akers of meadow land belonging unto us, lying in the valey of the East feild at the head of the swamp: which Land is Bounded on the East by Robert Cutler and a highway: and on the west by William Bacheler, and on the North by Thomas Lyne, and on the south by Thomas Carter. &c., &c.

JOHN GREENE.

A Resignation of sertaine Land within charletowne Neck by Robert Cole, marriner, unto his mother, Arrold Cole, both of charletowne, the 19 of the 8 moneth, 1649.

Know all men by these presents, That I, Robert Cole, marriner, Inhabitant in charltowne doo hereby declare That I have resigned, and doe resigne, unto my mother Arrold Cole, all my part off: And all my Right, Titell, and interests in the twoo Akers of meadow land and one cow comon, which did ioyntly belong unto us both, which meadow Land Lies and is scituate in the valey of the East feild at the head of the swamp, Bounded on the East by Robert Cutler and a highway, on the west by william Bachelor, on the North by Thomas Lyne, and on the south by Thomas Carter. And I, Robert Cole, doe resigne it unto my mother, Arrold Cole, to bee hers and her heigrs for ever.

JOHN GREENE.

---

[1] In order to save space, the following deeds have been abbreviated by omitting the merely formal portions, the *habendum* and warranty clauses, etc. The titles are also condensed. — ED.

[126.] *Thomas wilder unto Gardy James, the 15 of the 8ᵗʰ month, 1647. 6 of these.*

Know all men by these presents, That I, Thomas wilder, of Charltowne have sould, and by this declare it, unto Gardy James, of the same towne, one hay lott, lying and scituate in the high marshes, which lotts bounds up to Mʳ winthrops orchard : And I, Thomas wilder, doe acknowledg my selfe to be satisfied and fully payd therfore.

Also I, Thomas Wilder, have sould unto Gardy James halfe a fresh meaddow lott, lying at the west end of charltowne, and its fenced out of the comon. And I, Thomas wilder, doe acknowledg my selfe to be fully payd and satisfied for the same, And I doe hereby resigne all my titles, Rights, and Interests in the sayd hay lott, and in the sayd halfe fresh meadow lott unto the sayd Gardy James, to bee his and his heigres for ever. Wittnes my hand to the coppy of the sale the day and date above writen.

JOHN GREENE.

John Roper untoo Gardy James, the 4 day of the 11ᵗʰ month, 1649.

Know all men by these presents, that I, John Roper, Carpenter Inhabitant in charltown, doo acknowledg to have sould untoo Gardy James of the same towne, Twoo Akers and a halfe of meadow and broken up land, more or lesse, lying in the feild without the Neck, bounded North east upon mistik ferry and River) and south upon the stinted Comon, for which twoo Akers and a halfe of Land I. John Roper, doe acknowledg my Selfe to bee fully satisfied and payd. And I doe hereby Resigne all my Rights, Tittells and Interests therein unto the sayd Gardy James and his heigres for ever, wittness my hand to the paper of the sale hereof :

JOHN GREENE.

Robert Haukins unto Gardy James, 28ᵗʰ of the second month, 1646.

Know all men by these presents, that I, Robert Haukins, Inhabitant in charltowne, have sould, and by this declare, that I am fully satisfied and payd therefore : four cows comons, lying on the stinted Comon in charletowne, without the Neck, And I doe hereby Resigne all my Rights, Tittells, and Interests in the same 4 cows comons, unto the sayd Gardy James, to bee his and his heigrs for ever : wittnes my hand to the paper of the sale hereof, the day and date hereabove written, all not p.

JOHN GREENE.
6 of them.

Know all men by these presents, that wheras there was A grant by the select townsmen, in the year 1642, unto Richard Lowdon, of a cows marsh Lott, being an Aker more or lesse, which Lott is lying and scituate one mistik marshes, over Against Charltowne

Neck: It being bounded on the North norwest by a great Creek, and on the Northeast by John March, And its bounded south and East by mistik River: This graunt was renued and confirmed to him and his heigrs for ever By the Select Townsmen of charltown the 10ᵗʰ day of the 10ᵗʰ month, 1649.

JOHN GREENE.

[**127.**]   *Mrˢ· Alice Barnard, the wife of Mʳ william Barnard, unto Abraham Jaquith, both of Charletowne, the 23ᵗʰ of the twelfth moneth,* 1648.

Know all men by these presents, that I, Alice Barnard. the wife of Mʳ· William Barnard, of Charltowne, doe acknowledg that I have sould, and am fully payed therefore. unto Abraham Jaquith, one house, scituate without the Neck, which once pertained to Ezekiell Richeson, with a parcell of land lying within and between the upper corner post of the house, and runing with a straight line to the Garden of the aforesayd Abraham Jaquith, which house, land and all the Apurtenances thertoo pertaining, I, Alice Barnard, with the consent and in the behalfe of my husband, Mʳ William Barnard, doe hereby Resigne all my Right, titles and Interests, and my husband's, or any from us, unto the sayd Abraham Jaquith, to be his and his heigrs for ever.

As apeareth by my hand set to the paper of the sale. in the presence of Mʳ Increase Nowel, the 17ᵗʰ of the 10ᵗʰ moneth, 1649.

JOHN GREENE.

Joseph Cartar unto Jacob Greene, 19ᵗʰ day of the 11ᵗʰ moneth, 1649

Know all men by these presents, that I, Joseph Cartar, of Charltowne, in New England, have sould, and by this declare that I doe sell unto Jacob Greene of the same towne, five Akers of planting Land, more or lesse, lying and scituate in mistik feild: Bounded on the East by Abraham Hill, and on the west by william smith, which now is Jacob Greenes land, on the North by the ould raile fence that was, and one the south by mʳ· Richard Russell, And I, Joseph cartar, doe acknowledge my self to bee fully satisfied and payed therefore, And I resigne all my Rights, titells, and Interests in the sayd Land, unto the sayd Jacob Greene, to bee his and his heigres for ever: as apeareth by my hand to the paper of the sale wherunto my hand or mark is sett in the presence of Mʳ· Increase Nowell.

JOHN GREENE.

Manis Sally unto Jacob Greene, both of Charlestown the 19ᵗʰ day of the 11ᵗʰ moneth, 1649.

Know all men by these presents, that I, Manis Sally, have sould for a certaine sume considerable, and by this declare that I doe sell unto Jacob Greene (A parcell of Arrable Land which I formerly bought of william Mirrable), scituate and lying on mistike syde, Being ten Akers more or lesse, Bounded North by Thomas Graves, south by Jacob Greenes owne Land which he bought of

Joseph Cartar, East by the ould fence that was or Railes, and John Wilkeson, and west by m^r· Richard Russell, And I, Manis Sally, doe acknowledge my selfe to bee fully payd and satisfied for the same, and I doe hereby resigne over unto the sayd Jacob Greene all my Rights, titells, and interests in the sayd parcell of land to bee his and his heigres for ever, As apeareth by my hand to the paper of the sale, wherunto my mark is sett in the presence of m^r· Increase Nowell.

JOHN GREENE.

Ralph woory unto Jacob Greene, 7th of the 4th mo: 1649.
Know all men by these presents, that I, Ralph woory, Inhabitant in Charltown, have sould and doe by this declare it, A House, yeard and the apurtenances, standing in charltown, unto Jacob Greene, for the sume of twenty and five pounds, which House stands nere the Comon fery, bounded by the sayd Ralph woory on twoo syds, and by william smith on another syde, And I, Ralph woory, doe confes I am fully payd and satisfied by the sayd Jacob Greene for the same, And doe hereby Resigne all my Rights, Titells, and Interests in the same, to bee the sayd Jacob Greenes and his heigrs for ever. As witnesseth a bill of my hand, which M^r· Increase Nowell hath seene and set to his hand as wittness thereunto, the seventh of the fourth moneth, 1649.

JOHN GREENE.

[**128.**] *John Trumble unto Joseph Cartar, the eaighteenth day of the 11th moneth, 1649.*
Know all men by these presents, that I, John Trumble of charltowne, marriner, doe by this acknowledg that I have sould and doe sell unto Joseph Cartar, currier, of the same towne, one halfe Aker of Plow land, more or lesse, lying in the great feild nere to the Towne: which ground is bounded with the Lands of John Scott on the south east: And with the highway on the North east, and with the Lands of John Trumble, which were Mr William Barnards on the south west, &c., &c.

JOHN GREENE.

A Resignation and guift of certaine Land: by Thomas Cartar senio^r unto John Cartar, his son, of wooburn: 20th of the 12th month, 1649.
Know all men by these presents, that I, Thomas Cartar, Black smith, Inhabitant in charltowne, have resigned, and by this doe declare it, that I doe resigne and freely give over unto my son John Cartar of wooburn, all my Rights, Titells: and Interests: from my self, my heigrs, executors or assignes: In A certaine parcell of Land Arrable or meadow amounting to the number of three score and seaven Akers and a halfe, which was halfe of my Lott and purchase which was given mee, and which I have bought and payd for: all which Land Arrable or meadow lyes and is scituate within the presincts of the towne of wooburn: all which land is Bounded: southeast by Mr Increase Nowell's Land: and North

East by Edward Convers Land: Northwest by william Greenes Land, which was the other halfe of my given and purchased Land: and on the southwest it is bounded by the comon:

JOHN GREENE.

Thomas Goble unto william Baker the 11th of the 1st month, 1650.

Know all men by these presents, that I, Thomas Goble of charltown, have sould, and am payd for it, three quarters of a cows comon, lying on the stinted comon, unto william Baker of the same towne, &c.

JOHN GREENE.

James Green unto Edward Drinker, the 2^d of the 12th moneth, 1647.

Know all men by these presents, That I, James Greene, Inhabitant of charltown, have sould, and am payd for it: and by this declare it, unto Edward Drinker of the same towne, five Akers of Arrable Land, more or less, lying and scituate on mistik syde, it is Bounded from the southwest unto the Northwest by the marsh: and north East by Georg Hutcheson, and Edward Carrington, &c.

JOHN GREENE.

Richard Sprague unto Edward Drinker, the 8th of the 4th month, 1649.

Know all men by these presents, that I, Richard Sprague, of charltowne, Yeoman, have sould unto Edward Drinker of the same towne, one half Aker of Land, more or less, with a barn standing upon the same with all the appurtenances therunto belonging: which housing and Land did belong unto Ralph Sprague of charltown, and is scituatt and lying nere to the Neck ioyning to the comon: and is Bounded north west by william Bridges, and southeast by Edward Drinker, and north east by Richard Sprague, &c.

JOHN GREENE.

[**129.**] *m^r ffrancis willoughby unto Edward Larkin, the 26th of the 11th month, 1649.*

Know all men by these presents, That I, ffrancis willoughby of charltowne, have sould, and am payd for it, unto Edward Larkin of the same towne, A parcell of Ground, bounded on the south east syde by James Miriks house and ground, bounded on the south syde by Charls River: and on the 3^d syde, bounded by the highway next M^r woorys, and on the fourth syde which is the front which lyes to the Northeast, the ground going not further than the forefront of the house.

JOHN GREENE.

An exchange of land between sollomon Phips and Joseph Carter, both of Charltowne the 9th of the 2^d month. 1650.

Wheras, there was and is an exchange of some ground between us, Joseph Carter and sollomon Phips, It is mutually agreed between us, that Joseph Carter shall have a yeard or three foot of ground in breadth and about six pole in length of ground which did appertaine and belong unto Alice Rand, and which sollomon Phips bought of her for Joseph Cartar, it being measured a Yeard or three foot wide at the upper and lower ends of the fence which was between the sayd Joseph Cartars house and Alice Rands planting ground between him and Robert chalklys. And this is to bee the sayd Joseph cartars and his heigrs for ever : without lett or molestation from Alice Rand or sollomon Phips, or any from them, And in exchang and leiwe of the foresayd ground The sayd sollomon Phips is to have a Yeard or three foot of ground in breadth, and about six pole in length of the ground which did appertaine and belong unto the sayd Joseph Cartar, which lies and is scituate between sollomon Phips, his house and Joseph cartars house : out of the sayd Joseph cartars garden, it being measured a Yeard or three foot wide at the upper and lower ends of the garden fence, which is between them, and about six pole in length : moreover it is agreed between them, first that sollomon Phips shall at his owne charge and cost, take up and remove the garden fence that is now between them, and set it down again, as is before mentioned, three foot into Joseph Cartars ground, and then Joseph Cartar is to maintaine a pole and a halfe of that fence at the lower end of the garden for ever. And sollomon Phips is to maintain all the rest of that fence up to their housen for ever, And the three foot or Yeard of ground out of Joseph Cartar's garden fore mentioned to bee and remaine unto the sayd sollomon Phips and his heigrs for ever, without lett or molestation from the sayd Joseph Cartar or any from him : Also it is mutually agreed between them That the well that is before sollomon Phips his house, which was equally digd and made by them both, shall remain ioyntly between them, both to have A full, a free, and an equall right therto, and use therof without lett or molestation by the one or other of them, or any from them to the other : Alsoe, they are to bee at equall charge and cost about the repayring and maintaining therof : as also in the compassing or covering therof : And they shall not, none of them nor any from them, make or set upp any buildings before eyther of their houses upon enny pretence whatsoever to the lett or molestation or grievance one of another.

JOHN GREENE.

Alice Rand unto Joseph cartar, the 18th *day of the* 2^d *month,* 1650.

Know all men by these presents, that I, Alice Rand, of charltowne, widdow, acknowledg that I doe sell, and am payd for it, unto Joseph cartar, currier, fourteen foot and a half of my Land, which belonged unto me in dividends, at the front, and 6 pole at the length, which runs backward from the street, which did belong unto mee, Alice Rand, and which was next to Joseph cartars house and garden, where he now dwelleth : the which fourteen foot and a half wide of ground in front and 6 pole in length.

[**130.**] *william Luddington [his wife " Ellin " joining in the deed] to Joseph Cartar, the 17th day of September,* 1649.

Know all men by these presents, that I, william Luddington, of charltowne Inhabitant, dwelling on that part of the towne which is comonly called Mistik syde, in the county of midlesex, weavar: have, for and in consideration of nine pounds ten shillings, already received in good marchantable payment, given, graunted, bargaind, sould, and confirmed: and by these presents doth fully, absolutely, give, graunt, bargain, sell, and confirme unto Joseph Cartar of the sayd Towne and County: currier: one messuage or tenement, with all the Land tilled or untilled belonging to the same, that is to say five Acres of Land, more or less, as it was aunciently layd out to william Dade: with all the fences, Timber, and appurtenances therunto lying and belonging, scituate lying and being on mistike syde, Bounded on the east by Georg Hutcheson, and Peeter Tuft, and on the North west by Manis sally: and south by william Dade, To have and to hould, &c.

John Greene.

Georg Heipbourn unto Alice Rand, the 25th *day of the* 2d *month,* 1650.

Know all men by these presents, That I, Georg Hepbourn. Inhabitant in charltowne, doe acknowledg to have sould and I doe sell unto Alice Rand, widow, of the same towne, three quarters of an Aker of Arrable Land lying in the great feild within the Neck, and its bounded west by Robert cutler, east by George Bunker, north by the River, and south by george hepbourne, &c.

John Greene.

A sale of and exchang of certaine housing and Land and meadow ground, between Laurence Dous and Manis Sally: the 26th *day of the* 11th *month,* 1649.

Know all men by these presents, That I, Laurence Dous, Inhabitant in charltowne, upon and in consideration of certaine housing and Land lying on Mistik Syde, nere the ferry, which was sould unto Alice Rand by Manis sally, to the full vallew and worth of twenty and seaven pounds and ten shillings: towards the payment of which sume I, Laurence Dous, doe resigne and deliver all my Rights, Tittells, and interests in a certaine parcell of marsh Land, which belongs unto mee, for Five pounds of the same money, unto the sayd Manis sally, to be his and his heigrs for ever, which parcell of marsh land is lying on mistike syde nere the River, and bounded by it on the west syde, and on the Northeast by william Johnson: and on the north by another parcell of mr. Laurence Douses land, and by william Mirable on the southeast.

John Greene.

A sale of an Island of Arrable Land by Georg Hepbourne, lying on mistike syde, unto Laurence Dous, the 26th *day of the* 11th *month,* 1649.

Know all men by these presents, that I, Georg Hepbourn, Inhabi-

tant in charltowne. have sould and doe by this declare that I
doe sell and am fully payd for it, unto Laurence Dous, of the sayd
Towne, A certaine Iland of Arrable Land, being one Akar, more
or less : which Land is lying and scituate on mistik syde, in the
marshes opposite to the Neck of charltowne, on the other syde of
the River, this Iland is bounded by manis sally south east and
west, and on the North by william Johnson : And I, George Heipbourn, doe hereby resign unto the sayd Laurence Dous all my
Rights, Titells, and interests, unto the sayd Iland to bee his and
his heighrs for ever.

JOHN GREENE.

[**131.**] *Alice Rand to Lawrence Dows, the 26ᵗʰ of the 11ᵗʰ month,*
1649.

Know all men by these presents, that I, Alice Rand, widow, Inhabitant in charle towne, doe acknowledg that I have sould unto
Laurence Dous, of the same towne, certaine parcells of Land
meadow and Arrable, of the same towne, certaine parcells of Land
meadow and Arrable, lying on mistik syde, the meadow land being
all that I bought of manis sally, which was half of that which
manis sally and Aron Ludkin bought of Ralph mousell.

Alsoe, three Akers of Arrable Land, in one parcell, and one
Aker and a half Arrable Land in another parcells. All which
parcells of meadow and arrable Land lyes and are bounded as followeth, viz. : the meadow land lyes in the marshes one mistik syde,
Bounded with the creek where the Dock is, and Bounded by Aron
Ludkin on another part, and by william mirable one another
part.

The three Akers of Arrable Land lyes on the upland above the
marshes, Bounded south by Joseph Cartar, north by mee Alice Rand,
west by Aron Ludkin, and east by the marsh.

The Aker and a half of Arrable Land lyes and is bounded by
the marshes on the north, and south by Richard Stower, west by
Aron Ludkin, East by Richard Lowden.

Alsoe, a peece of Land of about half an Aker of Arrable Land,
more or less, being scituate near charltown hill, towards the branch
of the River of charltown, which runs towards mʳ Houghs and mʳ
Hodges poynt, which ground is bounded south by widow Stower,
and west and North by Thomas Lynde, and east by the highway.
All which Land and parcells thereof, both Arrable and meadow, as
well that on mistik syde as that on charltowne, I confess I am payd
ror all, &c.

JOHN GREENE

manis sally unto Alice Rand, both of charltowne, the 26ᵗʰ of the
11ᵗʰ month, 1649.

Know all men by these presents, that I, manis sally, inhabitant
in charl towne, have sould and by this declare it that I doe sell
unto Alice Rand, widow, inhabitant in the sayd towne, a parcell
of Land Arrable, and meadow, with half a barn which stands on
the same land, and half the enclosed yeard wherin the Barn stands.
The Arrable Land being eleven Akars, more or less, by estimation.

Alsoe, one half of all the meadow which manis sally bought of Ralph mousell, and half the Dock at the Creek, with the priveledges thertoo belonging : all which I, manis sally, doe acknowledg my self hereby to bee fully satisfied and payed for. And I doe hereby resigne both myne and my wives and heigrs Titells, Rights, and Interests therin, to bee the sayd Alice Rands and her heigrs for ever.

JOHN GREENE.

Mr *Robert Long, senio*^r, *Sells myne and my wives interests unto Richard Dexter, the 14*th *of the 3*^d *month,* 1650 :

Know all men by these presents, That I, Robert Long, of Charltowne, have sould, and declare by this that I doe sell unto Richard Dexter of the same towne : (and I am payd for them :) five marsh Lotts and a halfe, which I bought of m^{rs} Anne Higginson : they being scituate and lying on mistik syde, in mistik marshes, Beeing Bounded on the south by a creek which runs out of wilkison's creek to the south springe, on the North syde it butts unto three five Aker Lotts of Richard Dexter's and John Pamer's, which was comon and butted upon James Pemberton's : And it Butts west upon william Bucknam's which was m^r Nowell's.

Alsoe I, Robert Long, have sould and declare by this that I doe sell unto the sayd Richard Dexter, one five Aker Lott, which was m^r Symms, of upland ground, scituate and lying on mistike syde, which I am also payd for : which ground is bounded on the west by John Pamer's three five Aker Lotts, and East by a five Aker Lott of Richard Dexter's which hee bought of John Pamer, and it is bounded North by william Sargeant and south by the marsh Lotts which Richard Dexter bought of mee.

Alsoe I, Robert Long, have sould and declare by this that I doe sell unto the sayd Richard Dexter one five Aker Lott of upland ground, situate on mistik syde, and I am payd for it, which five Akers was given mee in the divident, And it is bounded on the East by the Land which belongs to the children of Isaak wheeler which is in Richard Cook's hands, And it is bounded west by a five Aker Lott, which Richard Dexter bought of John Pamer, on the North it is bounded by william sargeant, and on the south by James Pemberton's marsh and Richard Dexter's marsh Lotts, etc.

JOHN GREENE.

[**132.**] *Francis Chickering and Sarah, his wife, both of Dedham, unto William Meads, of Gloster, the 22*th *of the 4*th *month,* 1650.

This Indenture witnesseth that we, francis Chickering and Sarah, my wife, of Dedham, in the County of suffolk, yeoman, for and in consideration of the sume of Seaven and fifty pounds and ten shillings : Twenty pounds therof being in hand payd by William Meads, of Gloster, in the County of Essex, Husbandman, Have and by these presents doe fully and absolutely bargaine, sell, and assigne, set over and confirme unto the sayd William Meads, One Messuage, or Tennement, with a Barne, Cow house, and all the appurtenances thereunto belonging, and two Akers of land, more or less, thereunto adjoyning, And allsoe four Akers of land lying and beeing in the west feild of charltowne, alsoe twoo Akers in the same feild lying next the bridge going intoo the hither part of the sayd feild, and alsoe on hay Lott lying by A Cove, which is called Maggotten Cove: bee it more or less in the severall Akers: And alsoe the comonage for twoo Cowes and a quarter, and alsoe all the corne now standing, growing, and being upon the sayd Land or any part or parcell theroff, with the fences and priviledges theruntoo belonging, All lying and being in Charltowne, late in the occupation of John Sybly, deceased, — To have and to hould the sayd Messuage or Tennement, Barne or other edifices therunto belonging with the severall peeces and parcells, and benefits as before expressed in Land, with the priviledges thereuntoo belonging untoo the sayd William Meads, his heires and assignes for ever, to his and their only proper use and behoofe, Provided, that if the sayd William Meads, his heires, executors or Assignes, shall not pay or cause to be payd unto us the sayd ffrancis Chickering and Sarah, his wife, or to their heires, executors or Assignes, in Charltowne, the sume of seaven and thirty pounds and ten shillings, being the remainder of the sayd sume abovesayd to bee payd in wheat, Pease, and Barley, good and marchantable, and at marchantable price at the day of payment: or in Cattell, as they, or twoo men Indifferantly chosen by them, shall agree: Twenty pounds theroff to bee payd in corne or cattell as aforesayd, in and upon the first day of November, in the yeare one thousand six hundred and fifty and one, and for none payment thereof, at the day aforesayd, this present bargaine and sale shalbe voyd and of no effect, And Alsoe the last seaventeen pounds and ten shillings, being in full payment to bee paid as aforesayd upon the first day of November, one thousand six hundred fifty and twoo: otherwise for non payment therof, this present bargaine, sale and convayance to bee utterly voyd and of none effect, But shall return againe to the sayd francis and his Assignes, with all the priviledges theroff, In witnesse wherof, wee have eyther to other to these present Indentures of sale set to our hands and seals, Dated as above the two and twentyeth day of June, one thousand six hundred and fifty.

JOHN GREENE.

Henery Evans and Hester his wife of Boston, yeoman unto Richard Palgrave, Phisition, and Anna his wife, this fifth of the fifth 1650.

This Indenture wittnesseth that wee, Henery Evans and Hester Evans, my wife, of Boston, in the County of Suffolk, yeoman, for and in the consideration of the sume of fifty pounds, Have bargained, sould, given, granted; and doe by these presents fully, clearly and absolutely Bargaine, sell, give, and grant unto Richard Palgrave, Phisition, and Anna Palgrave his wife: both of Charltowne in the County of Middlesex in New England, one Messuage Tennement or House with a Barne, Cowhouse, and all the appurtenances thereunto belonging: with twoo Akers of Arrable Land, more or less: all standing together, and are scituate upon the comon of

charltowne, at the west end of the Towne : all which house and
Land is fenced round, and is butting North towards the street way,
and south upon a high way, And East and west butting on the
comon : Alsoe three Akers, more or less, of meadow land lying in
the south meade behinde the house, bounded East by Nicholas
Stower : north by a high way, south by John Sybly and the Creek,
and west by the Comon : Likewise four Akers of Arrable Land,
more or less, bought of William Phillips, lying and scituate in the
upper feild over the Creek, Bounded South west by Cambridg Lyne,
and west by some of Cambridg towne Lotts, bounded East by the
ends of Thomas Goble, and Thomas Peirces Lotts, and North alsoe,
by Thomas Gobles other Lott, Alsoe, four Cows Comons lying on
the stinted Comon without charltown Neck : All the sayd particulers
before mentioned with all the priviledges thertoo appertayning doe
wee Henery Evans and Hester my wife, resigne and freely and fully
deliver up unto the sayd Richard and Anna Palgrave and theire
heires, to have and to hould to his and their only proper use and
behoof forever : In witness wherof wee have both to a writing of
the sale hereof set to o^r hands this present day being the fifth of
the fifth month, 1650.

JOHN GREENE.

[**133.**] *Michaell Long unto John Smith, the sixth day of the
ninth month one thousand six hundred and fifty.*

Know all men by these presents, that I, Michaell Long, Inhabitant in Charltowne, have sould, and by this declare that I doe sell
unto John Smith of the same towne, A certaine plott or peece of
ground (which was given mee by the Townsmen) which peece of
ground lies and is scituate at the upper corner above the Spring
next John Peerces house, and between his house and william
Brakenburies peece of ground, which foresayd plott of ground is
fifteen foot one way and twelve foot annother way : And I confes
my selfe to bee fully payd and satisfied for it, etc.

JOHN GREENE.

---

*James Greene unto Peeter Tuft, and Peeter Tuft [myne and my
Wives Interest,] unto Thomas Sawyer, the sixth day of the tenth
month,*1650.

Wheras, formerly, I, James Greene, Inhabitant in charltowne,
have sould, and am fully satisfied and payd for it, unto Peeter Tuft
of the same towne, A House and a garden with a peece of marsh
lying behinde it, all beeing an Aker and a halfe of land, more or
less : which house, garden, and marsh, is lying and scituate without charltowne Neck, and is bounded East by the house which was
Philip Drinkers, and west by the marsh Lott of Ralph Sprague,
and North by the Comon, and south by a Creek which I resigne up
to the sayd Peeter Tuft, to bee his and his heigrs for ever.

Alsoe, *know all men by these presents*, That I, Peeter Tuft, now
Inhabitant in the towne of Malden, doe by these acknowledge that
I have sould, and doe sell the same house, garden, and peece
of marsh, of an Aker and a halfe of ground, more or lesse unto
Thomas Sawyer, of charltowne, with all the due appurtenances
therunto belonging, etc.   JOHN GREENE.

Mr Robert Sedgwick unto ffaithful Rouse, the 2^d day of the first Month, A. 1650.

Know all men by these presents, that I, Robert Sedgewick of charletowne, Inhabitant, Doe declare and acknowledge that I have sould and doe sell unto ffaithful Rouse, Inhabitant of the same towne —

A dwelling house with a yeard, and a garden: alsoe, one ould house with the ground it stands upon (though at present it stands most in my garden) unto ffaithfull Rouse : All which Housing, house, yeard, and garden stands and is scituate on the East syde of the market place of charletowne, and its bounded west or street syde by the market place, and East by Mr Robert Sedgwicks garden, likewise on the south by another part of that Garden and m^r Sedgwicks house, and North by william Bacheler, It is all fully payd for, And is to remaine to the said ffaithfull Rouse and his heigrs for ever.

JOHN GREENE.

[**134.**] *Know all men by these presents*, that I, John March, have given mee by the towne 4 Akers of Arrable Land, more or less, which I desired to have recorded, And it lies on mistick syde at the head of the five Akers in the middle range, Bounded south by Richard Rusell, east by Thomas Graves, north by Thomas molton and Georg Knower, and west by the five Aker Lotts.

JOHN GREENE.

more fifty and five Akers of Arrable and meadow by estimation more or lesse, scituate and lying at woeburne, in charltowne bounds, which is bounded southeast by william ffrothingham, and North alsoe by william ffrothingham, and North east by the Comon, and southwest by the River which runs by Thomas Graves.

John Baker [myne and my wives interests] unto Thomas Lynd, the 17th day of the 12th month, 1650.

Be it knowen unto all men by these presents, That I, John Baker, Taylor, inhabitant in charltowne, have sould and by this declare that I doe sell unto Thomas Lynde, senio^r, inhabitant of the same Towne, all that parcell of ground lying and scituate between the ground of Gwalter Allen on the southeast syde, And the ground of mee, the aforesayd John Baker, on the Northwest; alsoe it is bounded by another parcell of myne, Thomas Lynde's, land on the southwest, and it is bounded on the Northeast by the street syde or the comon high way : for all the which parcell of land I, the sayd John Baker, doe acknowledge myselfe to bee fully satisfied and payed, &c.

JOHN GREENE.

Lawrence Dous unto Thomas Lynde, senio^r, the 13th of the 12th month, 1650.

Be it knowen unto all men by these presents, That I, Lawrence
Dows, of charletowne, have sould and doe sell unto Thomas Lynde
of the same Towne, one littell close, containing by estimation halfe
an Aker of ground, more or lesse, it lying and being scituate next
and adioning to the house and orchard of widow Stowers, on the
southeast syde, and bounded by the ground of mee, Thomas Lynde,
on the North East syde, as alsoe bounded on the Northwest by
another part of the ground of mee, Thomas Lynde, alsoe it is butting on the East syde by the comon high way: And I, Lawrence
Dows, doe acknowledg that I have received of the sayd Thomas
Lynde, the sume of nine pounds in full satisfaction for the same
close, &c.

John Greene.

[**135.**] *Maior Robert Sedgwick unto Thomas Lynde, senio*ᵣ,
the 10ᵗʰ of the 10ᵗʰ month, 1650.

Bee it knowen unto all men by these presents, that I, Maior Robert
Sedgwick, of Charltowne, for and in consideration of thirty and
four pounds to mee in hand payed, have sould unto Thomas Lynde
of the same Towne, all that five Acres of Land, bee it more or
less, belonging unto mee, lying in the south feild butting upon
Charls River, and the Land late mᵣ Pratt's on the East and west:
And alsoe seaven Cows Comons, lying on the stinted Comon in
Charltowne, between Menotomies and Charltowne; And alsoe I
doe promice to save him harmless from anys claiming any right in
the sayd premisses from by or under mee, in wittnes hereof I have
sett to my hand the day and date above written, as in the evidence
is aparent.

John Greene.

---

*mᵣˢ Hanna Mellows unto Richard Lowden, both of charltowne the
third of the first month,* 1651.

Know all men by these presents, that I, Hanna Mellows, late wife
of Edward Mellows, of Charltowne, deceased, for and in consideration of a certaine sume of mony to mee in hand payed, and
to bee payd: have bargained and sould, and doe by these presents
bargaine and sell unto Richard Lowden, of Charltowne aforesayd:
A Dwelling House, scituate and being on charltowne Neck, over
against the pound, with the home lott upon which it standeth,
containing two acres of land, more or lesse, Bounded on the
North by Mathew Gibbs, his ground, on the south by the Lands
of Thomas Lynde and the widow Nash, on the East by the
Land of Thomas Cartar, and on the west by the highway: Alsoe
two acres of Land, more or less, in the same feild, bounded
on the North by the Lands of Thomas Cartar and George
Buncker: on the south by the Lands of Richard Sprague and
George Buncker, on the west by the Lands of widow Nash, and on
the East by Mistik River, As alsoe one milch Cow Comon, and
three-quarters of the stinted common of Charltowne, &c.: in
witnes wherof, I have set my hand and seale unto the evidence of
the sale the 13ᵗʰ of the ninth month, 1650.

John Greene.

Bee it knowen unto all men by these presents, that I, Thomas Lynde, of Charltowne, seniour : have sould unto John March of the same towne, seniour, Twoo Akers of Land, lying in the great feild, A highway on the Northeast, and the highway on the south-east, and the Land of Robert Chalkly on the Northwest, and the Land of the sayd Thomas Lynde on the southwest, for the which sayd twoo Akers of Land I doe acknowledge myself to be fully satisfied and payed, &c. : In witness hereof I have sett to my hand to the originall coppy before m^r Increase Nowell, the seaventeenth day of the twelveth month, A thowsand six hundred and fifty.

THOMAS LYNDE.

JOHN GREENE.

[**136.**] *Samuell Richeson unto Ezekiell Richeson, both of the Towne of wooburne, the 27th of the first month*, 1651.

Know all men by these presents, That I, Samuell Richeson, In-habitant in wooburne, having formerly sould unto Ezekiell Riche-son, my brother (who is since deceased), forty Akers of Arrable and meadow Land by Estimation, bee it more or lesse : which Land is lying and scituate in the Towne of wooburn on that syde of the Towne towards Reading : This sayd Land is bounded on the south by some Land of myne, samuell Richesons, It is bound North by some Land of Thomas Richeson our brother : It is bounded westerly by a Runing Brook : And it is bounded Easterly by the Comon, &c. : And as I formerly have done so I doe heerby Resigne up all myne, my wives, and heires Rights, Titells, and Interests in the sayd Land unto my sister, Susanna Brooks (who was the wife of my deceased brother, Ezekiell Richeson) for her life tyme, to enioy it without Lett or molestation from any : And after her decease then it all to bee my cousen Theophilus Richesons : and his heires forever : But if he should decease be-fore he come to Age to poses the same, then it to bee davided equally between the surviving children of the foresayd Ezekiell and Susana Richeson : And that this is both our full entents and meanings wee have Joyntly sett to our hands to the coppy hereof, which is in the hands of Susanna Brooks.

JOHN GREENE.

---

m^r *Thomas Allen* [*for "myselfe and my wife"*] *untoo william Johnson, the 18th day of the 8th month*, 1651.

Know all men by these presents, that I, Thomas Allen, of Charl-towne, have sould, and by this doe declare, that I doe sell untoo william Johnson, inhabitant in the same Towne, Twenty Akers of Arrable Land, by estimation being more or less, which Land lies and is scituate on mistik syde, within the bounds and limitts of Charle Towne : And it is bounded northeast by the Lands of william Sargeant, and southwest by the Lands of Edward Carrinton, And south East by the Lands of John Pamer : and northwest by the Lands of william Buckman. &c.

m^r Thomas Allen ["*for myselfe and my wife*"] *untoo m^r Richard Palgrave, the 18th day of the 8th month,* 1651.

Know all men by these presents, That I, Thomes Allen, of Charltowne, have formerly sould (and by this I declare it) untoo m^r Richard Palgrave, deceased, late inhabitant in the sayd Towne, A cows hay Lott, part of salt and part of fresh marsh meadow: which Land lies and is scituate in the marsh of charltowne, in the meadows over against the mill, which hay Lott or Land is bounded on the one syde by the River of the mill dam: on the other syde by the Land of william Kilcop: on another syde by a parcell of Land which Richard Palgrave bought of Edward Jones: and on the other syde by another parcell of meadow of the sayd Richard Palgrave, &c.: And I Resigne up unto m^{rs} Anne Palgrave the widow of m^r Richard Palgrave late deceased &c.

[137.] *m^r Thomas Allen untoo william Dade this seaventeenth day of the eaight month,* 1651.

Know all men by these presents, That I, Thomas Allen, of charltowne, have sould, and by this declare that I doe sell untoo william Dade of the same Towne, four Hay Cowe Lotts of salt marsh meadow, by estimation more or lesse, lying and scituate in mistik marshes, over against m^r wilsons farme, butting and bounded on three sydes by the River of mistik, and on the East syde bounded by twoo hay Lotts of william Dades, which he bought of mistress Trarice: all which four Hay Lotts are within the Bounds and lymitts of charltowne.

more. 3 cow Lotts and a halfe of salt and fresh marsh by estimation more or lesse, scituate on mistik syde within charltowne limitts: which Hay Lotts are bounded on the south by the south River or south spring: west by a part of James Pembertons Lands, and on the North by the Lands of James Pemberton, Richard Cook, and Richard Dexter: and on the East its bounded by A creek.

more. 5 Akers by estimation, more or lesse, of Arrable Land, lying and scituate in a Neck of Lande on mistik syde within charltowne Lymitts: which Land is bounded North west by the Lands off Arrold Cole, and Richard Stower: and south East by a parcell of Land of 5 Akers of Seth Switzer, which hee bought of mee, Thomas Allen, And the twoo ends of the Land is bounded by twoo highwayes.

more. one cow hay Lott and a halfe of salt marsh (by estimation more or lesse) lying and scituate on mistik syde within charltowne Lymitts, bounded on the one syde by the Land of seth switzer, on another syde by the Land of Richard Harrinton, on another syde by the River, and on the other syde by the upland.

more. 7 cows cõmons Lying and scituate on the stinted cõmon without charltowne Neck, wherof one of the 7 comons doth belong untoo m^r John Allen, &c.

A sale of a parcell of Land lying and scituate on mistik syde By m^r Richard Palgrave untoo Ralph Shepheard: the 19th day of the 1st month, 1650 : – 51.

Know all men by these presents, that I, Richard Palgrave, of charltowne, in the county of Midlesexe, Phisition, with the consent and Assent of Anne my wife, have sould unto Ralph Shepheard of Maldon, in the county aforesayd Taylor : my Lott of upland, lying by the North springe on Mistik syde, containing five Ackers : to bee compleat : Alsoe, my four cow Lotts, as they are granted mee from the Towne. To the sayd Ralph to have and to hould to him and his Heirs for Ever, without any molestation from mee or my heigrs, Execcutors, or Administrators. In witnes wherof wee have to the originall coppy put our hands the day and date above written.

---

*m*rs *Rebeckah Trarice untoo william Dade, both of charltowne, the 9th of the 10th month: 1651.*

Know all men by these presents, That I, Rebeckah Trarice, of charltowne, By and with the will and consent of my husband Nicholas Trarice, have sould, and by this declare that I doe sell, untoo william Dade of the same Towne, inhabitant, Twoo hay Lotts of marsh meadow, by estimation more or less, which Land is scituate on mistik syde at willsons poynt, which twoo Hay Lotts are bounded on the one end by the River, on the other end by the upland, and on the one syde by the Land of George Hutcheson, and on the other syde by the land of mr Thomas Allen, &c.

JOHN GREENE.

[**138.**] *Hennery Harbard and Ellinor his wife, both of Charlstowne untoo John Cartar of woburn, the 12th day of the 7th month, 1651.*

Know all men by these presents, that wee, Henery Harbard, and Ellinor my wife, doe acknowledge that wee have sould, and by this declare that wee doe sell unto John Cartar of woburn, fifteen Akers of Arrable Land, by estimation more or less : which Land lies and is scituate in woburn, on the south east syde of the Towne : which Land is bounded on the southeast by the Land of mr Increase Nowell : it is bounded southwest by a parcell of Land which Ralph Mousell sould to John Cartar : it is bounded northeast by the Land which was samuell Cartars, and sould by him to John Cartar, and it is bounded northwest by the Land which was william Smiths, and which he sould to Edward Convers, &c.

JOHN GREENE.

A Sale of a parcell of Ground scituate by the sea syde in the place called wapping, in charltowne: sould by James Browne, Glazier, Inhabitant in charltowne, untoo Captaine Nicholas Shapley, Marriner, of the same Towne, the 20th of the 9th mo: 1651.

Know all men by these presents, that I, James Browne of charltowne, Glazier, have sould, and by these doe declare that I doe sell [for £33] untoo Captaine Nicholas Shapley, of the same towne, To have and to hould, to him and to his heires for ever. To say, one smale peace of ground paled in, wherupon somtyme stood my dwelling House, lying and being in charltowne, nere the sea syde, and fronting to the southeast toward the sea, and on the Northwest bounded by the highway, and on the southwest bounded by the

Hous and Garden ground of the aforesayd Nicholas Shapley : And so being scituate Triangular.

more over, I doe acknowledge to have alsoe sould unto the sayd Nicholas Shapley, all that Ground which lieth upon the sea Bank or Beach, and fronteth square with the aforesayd ground, as alsoe that Ground wherupon somtyme stood Richard Russells warehous, excepting the highway, one pole, 16 foote and ½ of Ground which lyeth between the one parcell of ground and the other above mentioned.

JOHN GREENE.

Ralph woorey untoo John Penticost, The 6ᵗʰ of the 9ᵗʰ month, 1651.

Know all men by these presents, that I, Ralph woorey of charltown, in New England, have sould for eleven pounds five shillings : untoo John Penticost of charltown, aforenamed, three Akers and a halfe of Arrable ground, more or lesse, lying in the east feild, Bounded by the highway on the hill syde, on the southwest ; by Thomas Lyne on the North west, by william Bachelor and william Dade on the Northeast, And southeast by Thomas Cartar and Daniell Shepheardson : To have and to hould to him and his heigres, in witness wherof I have hereunto set to my hand.

the 6ᵗʰ day of the 9ᵗʰ month, 1651.

JOHN GREENE

[**139.**] *mʳ Robert Cook. Apothecary* [*"myne and my wives interest,"*] *unto Roger Spencer, marchant, the 7ᵗʰ day of the 8ᵗʰ month, 1651.*

Know all men by these presents, That I, Robert Cook, Apothecary, inhabitant in charlstowne, have sould, and by this declare that I doe sell unto Roger Spencer, marchant, of the same towne, A dwelling Hous with a garden and a Yeard therunto belonging, containing by estimation a quarter of an Aker of ground, more or less : which Hous, garden and Yeard is all fenced about, and it stands and is scituate in charletowne in the market place, being fronted by the market place on the south, and its bounded on the East by the Dwelling Hous of mʳ ffrancis Norton, and its bounded on the west by the Land called Puddle Lane, and its bounded on the North by the comon ground that lies towards the cattells well, and I, Robert Cook, doe acknowledg that I have received one full fourth part of the sume I am to have for the sayd Hous, Yeard and garden, of the sayd Roger Spencer, and I have receaved 3 bills for the other 3 parts of the payment, &c., &c.

JOHN GREENE.

A mutuall exchanging of certaine parcells of Land lying on mistik syde : Between John Greenland, Carpenter, and Thomas Molton, Planter, both Inhabitants on mistik syde, the one in Charltowne, the other in Maldon, the 20ᵗʰ of the 7ᵗʰ month, 1650.

Know all men by these presents, that wee, John Greenland and Thomas Molton, both Inhabitants on mistik syde, in New England : Have agreed, and doe agree, and by this declare it, To exchange each with other certaine parcells of Arrable Land, all lying and scituate on mistik syde, the one parcell within charltowne Bounds, and the other parcell within Maldon bounds ; Our Agreement being in manner and forme following : That is, that I, Thomas Molton, Planter, doe give up and Resigne unto John Greenland, Carpenter, All my Rights, Titells, and Intercsts in a certaine parcell of Arrable Land, Being five Akers by estimation, more or lesse, which five Akers lies and is scituate within the bounds of charltowne, on mistik syde, in a place called molton's Iland, which sayd parcell of five Akers is bounded East by a high way, and west northwest by the Lands of Georg ffelch, and so runs so bounded compas to the Lands of Robert Burden, which is south of the sayd five Akers : And for and in consideration heerof, I, John Greenland, carpenter, doe give up and resigne unto the foresayd Thomas Molton, Planter, all my Rights, Titells, and Interests in ten Akers of Arrable Land, more or lesse, which I bought of John Martin, ship carpenter, of charltowne, which Ten Akers lies and is scituate within the Bounds of the Town of Maldon. The sayd ten Akers is bounded northeast by the Lands of Robert Rand, and southwest by the comon, Northwest by Edward Convers, and southeast by the Lands of James Greene. And to declare that we both are reciprocally agreed and contented with this exchange wee both have enterchangably set to our hands to bothe originalls of this wrighting the day and date above written.

JOHN GREENE.

Augustine walker, marriner, [and wife Mary] unto steeven ffosdik, the 31ˢᵗ of the 3ᵈ month, 1652.

Know all men by these presents, That I, Augustine Walker, marriner, inhabitant in charltowne, New England, Have sould and by this declare that I doe sell unto steeven ffosdik, carpenter, inhabitant in the same Towne, A marsh Lott by estimation as it was given to Robert Cutler in the Devident, which marsh Lott lyes and is scituate on mistik syde at wilsons poynt, within charltowne bounds, which marsh lott is bounded by and butting south east upon mistik River, northwest upon the woodland, west and by south bounded by George Hutcheson, and East and by north by Joseph Cartar, And I, Augustine walker, doe acknowledge for my self, my wife and my heires, to bee fully satisfied and payed by the sayd steeven ffosdik for the sayd marsh Lott. And I, Augustine Walker and my wife Mary, doe, &c.

JOHN GREENE.

[**140.**] *John Martin, shipwright, [and wife Sarah] unto John Greenland, hous carpenter, this twentieth day of the seaventh month, 1650.*

Know all men by these presents, That I, John Martin, shipwright, Inhabitant in charltowne, in New England, have sould and by this declare that I doe sell unto John Greenland, carpenter, of the sayd charltown Inhabitant, Ten Akers of Arrabell Land, by Estimation more or less, which Land lies and is scituate on mistik syde, within the bounds of the Towne of Malden, the sayd Land is

bounded North east by Robert Rands Lands : and southwest by
the coṁon, North west by Edward Convers Lands, and south East
by the Lands of James Green, &c., &c.

John Greene.

*John Martin, shipwright, and Sarah his wife, unto m^r Thomas
Breeden, The third day of the second month, A thousand six hundred and fifty twoo.*

Know all men by these presents, that I, John Martin, shipwright,
Inhabitant of charltowne, And sarah my wife, for and in consideration of fifty pounds, in good payments made : Have given, granted,
bargained, sould, and confirmed : And by these presents do fully,
absolutely, Give, grant, bargaine, sell, and confirme : (unto m^r
Thomas Breeden, marchant, and of the same Towne inhabitant)
My now dwelling House with all the out Housing about it, and all
the ground belonging to it, with all the Railes, pailes, posts, and
fencings, belonging to the sayd Hous and ground ; And all the
Appurtenances therof : being by estimation an Aker of Ground. It
is bounded on the southwest by James Brown, on the Northwest
by Robert Hale in the East feild, it is Bounded on the North East
by Randoll Nichols : and on the front towards Charls River being
nine pole and a halfe broad, with all proprieties and priviledges on
the front to the low watter marke belonging to mee or the ground,
(the high way excepted), &c., &c.

John Greene.

Augustine walker [*and wife Mary*] *unto Edward Carrinton, the
5th day of the fourth month, A thousand six hundred and fifty two.*

John Greene.

Know all men by these presents, that I, Augustine walker, marriner, Inhabitant in charltowne, and Mary my wife, for and in consideration of the sume of three pounds, so prised by Robert Hale,
which is payed, Have given, granted, bargained, sould, and confirmed, And by these presents Doe fully absolutely Give, grant,
bargaine, sell, and confirme unto Edward Carrinton of Charltowne,
a certaine parcell of upland scituate in Maldon, being four Akers
by estimation, more or lesse, which Land is bounded East by the
Land of william Stitson, which was Richard Russells, bounded on
the west by a highway which borders John Uphams Land, bounded
on the North by the land of John March, and on the south by
william Bucknams land, which was John Martins, &c., &c.

John Greene.

[**141.**]   *John Greene untoo Edward Carrinton, the seaventeenth
day of the fourth month,* 1652.

Know all men by these presents, That I, John Greene, Inhabitant
in charltowne, for and in consideration of the sume of twenty
pounds in good payments being payd, Have Given, granted, bargained, sould, and confirmed, And by these presents, Doe Give,
grant, Bargaine, sell, and confirme : unto Edward Carrinton, of the

same towne, twoo parcells of Land, scituate on mistik syde. The parcell being of salt marsh meadow, with some upland annexd to it, lying nere the pound. It all being bounded by william sargeant on the East syde, and on the North west by bull lotts, and on the upland syde by Edward Drinker: and on the other Ende by a Creek: which parcell of meadow was and is accounted four Akers and a halfe, or four cow hay Lotts and a halfe by Estimation, more or less: The other parcell of Land Is fifteen Akers of upland or Arrable Land by Estimation, more or less, which lyes and is scituate in Maldon, and nere Charltowne Lyne, And is bounded on the South by Mr Increase Nowell, on the North by Peter Tuft, which was Ralph Mousalls, on the East by Turky Hill, And A path: And on the west by sollomon Phips and John Lawrence, And I, John Greene, Doe acknowledge for my selfe, my wife and my Heirs To bee fully satisfied and payed by the said Edward Carrinton for both the foresayd parcells of Land, &c., &c.

JOHN GREENE.

William Harris untoo John Greenland, land on Mistic syde the twelfth day of the fourth month, A thousand six hundred and fifty twoo.

Know all men By these presents, that I, william Harris, yeoman, Inhabitant in charltowne, and Edee, my wife, for and in consideration of sixteen pounds In good payments payed, Have, Given, Granted, Bargained, sould, and confirmed, And by these presents, Doe fully, absolutely, Give, grant, Bargaine, sell, and confirme, unto John Greenland, carpenter, and of the same towne, Inhabitant, A certaine parcell of Land lying and scituate with in the bounds of the Towne of Malden, the which I bought of my father william stitson, unto whom it was given by the Towne, which Land is valewed by Estimation to bee fifteen Akers, more or less: And it is bounded on the south by Elias Maverick, and on the west by william sargeant, on the North by Thomas Caule, and on the East by Thomas Grover, &c., &c.

JOHN GREENE.

Thomas Goble unto william Baker, the 22th of the 10th mo.: 1653.

I, Thomas Goble, of Charltowne, doe hereby Acknowledge the sale of three quarters of A A Cows Comon, upon the stinted comon of charltowne, without the Neck, unto william Baker of the sayd charltowne, for the which I, Thomas Goble, Acknowledge I have received full satisfaction, and am fully payd therfore. As witness my hand to the bill of sale this 22th of the tenth month, 1653: this is testified untoo by Mr Increase Nowell, magistrate, under his hand, the day and date afore written.

JOHN GREENE.[1]

[142.] *Sale of a house and garden without Charlstowne Neck, 6 day the 3 mo. 1653.*

Know all men by these preasants, that wheare as I, peircis bridges,

---

[1] Here ends Greene's writing. — ED.

formerly the widow of william bridges, deceased, but now the wife of John harrison, of boston, Ropemaker, had sould and by this declarr that I doe sell unto christopher goodwinge, Bricklayer, Inhabitant in charlstown, with the consent of my husband John harrison, my house and garden, being by estematyon halfe an aker of land, more or lesse, and wee, John and percis, doo by this declare that wee are fuly satisfied and paid therefore by the sayd Christopher goodwing, the said house and garden beinge bownded by the grownd of Edward Drinker one the one side and by the way to the ferrey, on the other syde allso by the comon beefore and by a smale parcell of medow of Richard Spragues behind, and who ever enjoys the lands, and to make good and maintaine the fence betwine Richard Sprague and them, and also thes are to ackno'i lg and testifie that wee, percice and John harrison, have have likewise sould and doe Confirm unto christover goodwing to cow comons on the stinted comon in charlstown, and wee, john and peircis harison, doe both heare by Resigne up all our Right and all the Right of the heires of executors and administrators of the said william Bridges, Deceased, with all titells, claims, and intrists in the said house and grownd, and all the partes therof, with all Dew apurtenancis ther unto belonging : unto the said Christopher goodwing, to bee his and his heires for ever, and we, john and percis harrison, for our selves and the heires of william bridges, doe bind our selves to save the said christover goodwing and his heirs free from all claims and pretencis that may bee made to the said house and grownd by any person ore person what so ever, and in wittness there unto wee have sett to our hands this present sixth day of the third mō., 1653, as a bill of sale undr our hands given and acknoligid before Mr. Increce nowell, testifies.

Samuell Adams, Clarke.

Know all men, that I, Iohn smith, of charlstown, have solde and doe heare by confirme unto francise litlefeild one dweling house, with all the land belonging there unto, now setewate in charlstown which land is bowndid up on the north west up waping creecke, on the south east by charlstown river, and also all the timber and bords there to belonging, all which house and land and timber the forsaid John Smith, with Sarah, his wife, doe sell and have sold unto francis littellfeild, and doe heare by give up all our right and intrest unto the aforsaid francis and his aires for ever, as a bill of salle under our hands, datted the 22 the 5 mo., 1653, testifieth.

Samuell Adams.

[**143.**]   *Robertt miriam of concord, to James Barett of charlstown in the year* 1653.

Know all men By thes presents, that I, Robertt meryam of Concord, in new england, have sould unto James Barett of Charlstown, twenty-to ackers of woodland and medow, lying in Charlstown bounds, all which all which land is bounded and lying in thre severall parsills that is five ackers of woodland, more or less, lying in mystake feild. Buting west up on the drift way, and east up on the land way and south by Edward melows, and north by thomas squier and sarah ewer. The second parsill is fiften ackers[1] of woodland, by estematyon, more or less, setewate in mistake feild, butting north east upon widow nash and wiliam frothingham, and south west up on m^r Increace nowell, and north west by thomas goble, and south east by Robertt haukins. The third parsill is to ackers of medow by estematyon more or less, lying in mistake marshis, Butting north up on a Creeke coming out of the north river, and south up on the woodland, and east by Thomas ewer, and west by william Barker : all which parsils of land and evry one of them, I, Robert miryam, have sould unto Jams Barett aforsayd, and have Received full satisfactyon for the same. and thes are further to declare that I doe with my wife, mary meriam give, &c., &c., &c.

as wittness our hands and sealls this twentyth day of the eight moneth, one thousand sixe hundred fifty and thre. this is a trew ded of salle, which was   ROBERTT MERIAM.
Sealled and delivred   And recordid by
in the presence of   SAMUELL ADDAMS,
     SAMUELL ADDAMES,   *Clarke.*
     JOHN SWETT,

[144.] *James Baretts Deed of Salle to Peter Tuffts.*

Know all men by thes p^rsence, that I, James Barrett, of charlstown, in the countey of medellsex, plantor, with the assent and consent of hannah my wife, have alinated, sould, Asseighned and sett over and doe by these p^rsents alienate, Bargain and sell unto petter Tuffts of malden, in the county Aforsayd, plantor, fiftenne Accers of land sumtins the lott of James Browne, Bounded or lying Betwine the lotts of mr. Increase nowell, Thomas goble, Robertt Hawkins, widow nash and william ffrothingame, with all the timber, wood, profits and Imunitys, ther to Bee longing, to have and to hold, &c. ; and, further, I doe p'mis That I will with in one yeare from the date hear of acknoledg the sall hear of Beefore Athority, That in all points it may stand firme and bee enroled acording to order of law, allso, I doe acknoledg my selfe fully payd and content for the Aforsaid ffiften accers of land, namely by the recipt of fiften pounds and tenn shilings before the sealing hearof, and doe by thes p^rsents, Acquit and discharge the said petter, his heirs, executors, and Administrators from evry parte and parcell therof, in witness whear of I have hear unto putt hand and seall this second day of the Third mo., on thousand sixe hundrid fifty and three.   This Deed of sall was acknoliged by James barett and
Sighned, sealed, and Delivered his wife hanah, Beefore mr.
  in the pesents of   Increase nowell, the 22 of the
     THOMAS HETT,   9 mo. 1653, as under his hand
     THOMAS OSBORN,   Testifieth, and is by order of
     JOHN MOULTEN.   both ptys Recordid By
                 SAMUELL ADDAMS,
                    Clarke.

---

[1] This fiften ackers is sold to Peter tufts. — *Side note on ms.* in Adams' hand. — ED.

[**145.**] [1] *To all Peeple to whom this present writing shall come to be seen or read, know yee*, that I, Richard Temple of Charles Towne, in New England, husbandman, for and in consideration of Thirty and twoo pounds and ten shillings, to mee in hand payed by Edward Brazier of the same Towne, husbandman, to my full content and satisfaction before the ensealing and delivery heerof, Have Bargained, sould, Given and Granted, &c., unto the sayd Edward Brazier, his Heyres, Execcutors, Administrators, and Assignes, one Messuage or Tennement, scituate, lying, and Being in the aforenamed Towne of Charlstowne, Late my owne mansion place, Conteyning one Dwelling House, without Houses, orchard, and Land Adioyning, about one Aker and halfe, more or Lesse, Being surrounded with Charls Towne Comon : part whereof I purchased of Richard Kettell, and the other part of William Bridges. Alsoe four Akers of Land broken upp, bee it Less or more, Lying in Charltownes westerly planting feild, being Bounded with Cambridge Lyne on the Northwest, alsoe a Hay Lott, by mee purchased of m[r] Hurst, being Bounded by m[r] Palgrave on the west, and m[r] Davison's marsh on the East, with all the Apurtenances or priviledges to all or any part therof belonging or in any wise Apertaining, To Have and to hould the sayd Messuage or Tenement with all and singular the priviledges and Appurtenences that was Richard Kettels, or by any other wayes or means thertoo appertaining or in any wise belonging, unto the same Edward Brazier, his heigres and Assignes, to his and their only proper use and behoofe, and proper goods and Lands forever, &c., &c.

In wittnesse whereof, wee, the above named Richard Temple and Joanna Temple, my wife : have hearunto put our hands and seales this thirtieth day of the fourth month, Called in the year of our Lord God, One thousand six hundred fifty and four.

Know all men by these presents, that wheras william **Mead** of Charletowne, had bought of ffrances Chickering of Dedam, A Hous, a Barne, and other howsing, and all apurtenances thertoo belonging, and twoo Akers of Land therto adioyning, and alsoe four Akers of Land lying in the west feild, and twoo Akers lying in the same feild, nere the Bridg, and A Hay Lott nere mayotten Cove, and twoo Cowes Comons and A quarter, with all the fencing and priviledges thertoo belonging, all formerly belonging unto John sybly, deceased.

Know all men by these presents, that wee, william and Rebeckah Mead have and doe by these presents declare and testifye that wee both doe ioyntly Resigne up all our Rights, Titles, and Interests, in all and each of the perticulers aforementioncd from us and our heigres unto Thomas welsh of charltowne, who has payd us therfore, unto the sayd Thomas to bee his and his heigres for ever. As is to bee seen under our hands upon the paper of the sale with M[r] Nowell's hand to it.

written the 5th of the 6th month, 1654.

JOHN GREENE.

---

[1] The record again begins in the hand-writing of Greene.— ED.

[**146.**] *Know all men by these p'sents*, that I, Richard Temple and Johanna Temple, my wiffe, both off Charletowne, in New England, Inhabitants, Have sould, and wee doe heerby confirme unto Samuell Adams, Inhabitant of the same towne, Forty Akers of upland, bee it more or lesse, which Land was formerly given unto Harman Garrett, smith, by Charltowne, As the Records of the Towne sheweth : which Land is Bounded on the North syde by m^r zachary Symms his farme, and on the south by Meadford farme, and on the southwest by m^r James Garretts Land, And on the North East it is bounded by the com̄on ; And alsoe, more, twoo Akers of Land lying in the west feild in Charltowne, next Cambridge, Bounded North by Richard Sprague, &c., and west by Richard Kettell, and south by a highway, &c.

wittnesse our hands and seals this sixth day of the sixth moneth, A thousand six hundred fifty and four.

JOHN GREENE.

Know all men by these presents, that I, Thomas Molton, of Maldon, Planter : have sould, and by this declare it, unto Richard Dexter, of Charltowne, Planter : A five Aker Lott of upland by estimation, more or less, which Thomas Molten formerly bought of Walter Pamer. It is scituate on mistik syde nere the south springe. It is Bounded on the Easte by Georg Felt, on the south by William Dade, on the West by James Pemberton, and on the North by William Sargeant.

Alsoe, a parcell of salt marsh meadowe, likewise scittuate on mistike syde, Bounded Easte by Molton's Iland, and west by wilkinsons creek, and North, part with a Creek which goes to the south spring, and part by Georg felt, and it is Bounded South by the south River which goes up to Molten's Iland. Those Parcells of meadowe was sould by mee Thomas Molton unto Richard Dexter, alsoe it was parted equally by Lott unto Isaak Wheeler, Richard Dexter, and John Greenland : to each of them in four parcells : after they had enioyed it a year ; And I Thomas Molton Doe for myselfe my wiffe &c.

In witness hereof I have hereunto set to my hand this twoo and twentieth day of the seaventh month, A thousand six hundred fifty and four : This sale was made and delivered ten years agoe though writings being lost they were by these Renewed.

JOHN GREENE.

Know all men by these presents, that I, mathew Gibs, Planter, Inhabitant in charltown, New England, have sould and by this declare it that I doe sell unto Lawrence Dous, of the same towne, four Akers of upland and meadow by estimation, more or less : which land I bought of Anna ffrothingham of the same towne, which Land is scituate at Cambridge Lyne, it is bounded East by charltown com̄on, and west by Cambridg ware, North by m^rs Catherin Coytomore, and south by william Johnson ; All which wee Mathew and Mary Gibs doe &c.

In wittness hereoff wee have sett our hands to the original coppy in Lawrence Dous hands.

JOHN GREENE.

[**147.**] *Know all men by these p'sents*, That I, Mathew Gibs, Planter, Inhabitant in charltowne, in New England, Have sould and by this declare that I doe sell unto Lawrence Dous and Thomas Rand, both Inhabitants in the sayd towne, A Hous and A Garden, with a peece of marsh adioyning to it, with all the fencing and due Apurtenances therunto belonging, which is all standing and scituate nere the Neck of Charltowne. Alsoe three quarters of an Aker of upland by estimation, more or less, it is lying in the Easte feild over against the Hous, and its bounded South by Richard Lowden and Thomas Cartars Land, and west by the street way which runs between the Hous and it, and North by Richard Sprague and a highway at one end : Likewise a Cowes Comon. All which Hous ; &c., wee Mathew Gibs and Mary Gibs, my wiffe, Doe, &c., Resigne up, &c. In witnes hereoff wee have hereunto sett to our hands the twelfth day of the eighth month, A thousand six hundred fifty and four.

JOHN GREENE.

Know all men by these presents, that I, James Heyden, Inhabitant in Charltowne, have sould, and by this declare that I doe sell unto John Knight, senior, Planter, Inhabitant in woeburn, A certaine parcell of Land which was my Lott given mee by the towne in the divident, it being eighteen Akers of Land by estimation, more or less, scituate and Lying in woeburn, nere Captain Johnsons : And it is bounded northwest upon the comon, and south easte by John sybly, and m^{rs} Katherine Coytemore's Lands, and south west by william Johnsons Lands, and one the north east by Thomas Knowher's Lands ; and I Doe for my selfe, and my wiffe &c. In witness hereunto I have sett to my hand to the originall coppy : which is subscribed by m^r nowell's hand, the 9th day of the 8th month, 1654.

JOHN GREENE.

[**148.**] *John Palmer, Planter, unto Richard Dexter, alsoe Planter, both Inhabitants in Charltowne, New England, the 20th day of the twelveth month*, 1654.

Know all men by these presents, That I, John Palmer, Inhabitant in Charltowne, have sould, and by this declare it unto Richard Dexter, of the said Charltowne, Inhabitant, five Akers of Arrable Land, being by Estimation more or less, and its lying and scituate on mistik syde, within Charltowne bounds, nere to the south Creeke, which five Akers, I, John Palmer, formerly bought and payed for it off maior Robert Sedgwick, who was alsoe an Inhabitant in the sayd Charletowne. This five Akers of Arrable Land is Bounded east and west by Parcells of Richard Dexters Lands, it is Bounded North by william sargeants Land, and on the south by another parcell of Richard Dexters Lands : &c.

JOHN GREENE.

A mutuall Exchanging of Parcells of Land, scituate within charltowne neck in the Easte feild : Between Georg Heypbourn, Glover : and John March, Husbandman, Both Inhabitants in the sayd charltowne in New England, the sixth day of the first month, 1655.

Know all men by these presents, that wee, George Heypbourn and John March, both Inhabitants in charltowne, in New England, Have Agreed, and doe Agree : and by this declare it. To Exchange one with the other each A parcell of Land, George Heypbourn's parcell is an Aker and a halfe of Land by Estimation, being more or less : the Land Lyes and is scituate in the Easte feild, within the Necke : It is bounded on the south in part by william stitson : and in part by Thomas Caule, the successor of Daniell Shepherdson : it is bounded on the North by a parcell of Ralph Sprague's Land, and which was formerly maister Trarice's : it is bounded on the west by william Dade's Land : and its bounded on the Easte by a parcell of m^r Increase Nowell's Land.

John Marche's Parcell Is one Aker of Arrable Land, scituate and lying likewise in the Easte feild within the Neck : it is bounded on the Easte By Robert Hale's Land : and its bounded on the west by sollomon Phips' Land ; it is bounded on the south by the Trayning place : and it is bounded on the north by another parcell of Land of the sayd John Marches, &c.[1]

JOHN GREENE.

[**149.**] *A sale of A Hous and Garden Plott, with other Lands by John Drinker, inhabitant in Charltowne, unto John Rugg, inhabitant in Lancaster, both Towns in New England, the tenth day of the first month A thousand six hundred fifty-five.*

Know all men by these presents, That I, John Drinker, ship carpenter, Inhabitant in charltowne, New England, with the consent of Elizabeth Drinker, my wiffe, Have sould (and by this declare it) unto John Rugg, Planter, inhabitant in Lancaster, in the sayd New England, A certaine Hous or Tenement, with A Garden by it.

And alsoe A peece of marsh belonging to the Hous : and lying behynde the Hous : Being the iust halfe of that marsh which was given by the Towne unto Phillip Drinker and James Greene, the other halfe being now in william Bicknor's hands.

The Hous, Garden, and marsh are standing, lying, and scituate, at the Easte end of the stinted comon : Butting easte upon a littell creek : west upon the comon : North upon the street way : and South by william Bicknor.

Alsoe A cowe comon Lying on the stinted comon, without the Neck : Likewise twoo Akers of marsh meadow by estimation, more or lesse, scituate in mistick marshes : Butting west upon the North River : Easte upon the upland, and Running up into the woodland, so farr as other marsh Lotts doe Runn up, and were layd out by the Townes apoyntment. It is bounded South by Seth Switzer : And North by Richard Palgrave, now Ralph Shepheards, &c.

JOHN GREENE.

A sale of Lands Lying on Mistick syde, by Ezekiall and susanna Richeson : untoo Thomas Molton and John Greenland, both of Charltowne, New England.

Know all men by these presents, That whareas Ezekiell Richeson, Planter, formerly Inhabitant in the Towne of woeburn, in New

---

[1] Hepburne and March both conveyed their own and their wives' interests. — ED.

England, and since Deceased : having some eaight years past for and in consideration of a A certaine sūme to mee in hand payd, having bargained and sould unto Thomas Molton and John Greenland certaine Land Lying and scituate on mistike syde : being thirty and five Akers of Arrable Land, by Estimation more or lesse, which Land is bounded south west by Robert Rand's Land : and its bounded south Easte by the Lands of John Hodges : and its bounded Easte near and by the great Swampe ; And wee Ezekiell and Sussanna Richeson my wiffe, &c. And I Susanna Richeson now Brooks, formerly the wiffe of Ezekiell Richeson doe bynde myselfe, &c. In witness hereuntoo I have sett to my hand and seale untoo the evidencee of this sale the three and twentieth day of the first month A thousand six hundred fifty and five.

JOHN GREENE.

[**150.**] *A sale of Land by Thomas Molton and ffrancis wheeler, alias Cook, unto John Greenland, all of Charltowne, Inhabitants: written the ninth day of the first month A thousand six hundred fifty and five.*

*K*now all men by these presents, That wheras Thomas Molton, Planter, Inhabitant in Charltowne, New England : and Isaac wheeler, taylor, alsoe Inhabitant in Charltowne aforenamed : and since deceased, Having some ten years past for and in consideration of a A certaine sume to us in hand payed : wee having bargained and sould : And wee Thomas Molton and ffrancis Cook (formerly the wiffe of Isaac wheeler aforenamed), doe for my selfe and my children, the heires of the sayd Isaac wheeler, Wee do now by these presents renewe to Bargain, sell, And doe Resigne unto John Greenland, Planter, of the sayd charltowne, Inhabitant, Ceartaine Parcells of Meadowe Lands : Lying and scituate on mistik side by and nere the South River.

A first Parcell of the sayd meadow, containing ten Akers, by estimation more or less : which meadow ground Is Bounded Easte by some upland of Robert Burdens, lying on the Neck of Thomas Molton's Land : it is bounded west and in the middell by a parcell of John Greenlands Land : It is bounded North by the meadow of Richard Cook : And it is bounded south by the Lands of Richard Dexter.

A second Parcell of meadow which wee forenamed, sould unto the sayd John Greenland, containing Three Akers, by estimation more or less : Is lying and scituate alsoe on mistike syde, By and nere the South River, It is Bounded by a part of the South River where it divides, and it is Bounded Northwest by the Lands of Richard Dexters, alsoe it is Bounded North Easte by the Lands of Richard Cooke.

A Third Parcell of Meadow, which wee forenamed, sould unto the sayd John Greenland, contayning one Aker of Land, by estimation, more or less, which is Lying and scituate likewise on mistik syde, in the forenamed meadows : and it is Bounded North by the land of Richard Cook, and it is Bounded south by the Land of Richard Dexter : It is Bounded Easte by another Parcell of the Lands of Richard Cook. Alsoe it is Bounded west by A Creek, and another Parcell of the Lands of Richard Dexter : the whole suṁe of these meadows John Greenland hath bought and payed for all : of Thomas Molton and Isaac wheelars Heyres, &c.

written the tenth day of the second moneth A thousand six hundred fifty and five.

JOHN GREENE.

Artickles of Agreement Between m^r *John Hodges: and widdow Alice Rand, both Inhabitants in Charltowne, The tenth day of the Eighth moneth A thousand six hundred fifty and foure.*

Know all men by these presents, That I, John Hodges, Marriner, inhabitant in Charltowne, New England, Have Exchanged. And I, Alice Rand, widow, inhabitant therein, have exchanged alsoe with m^r John Hodges : certaine parcells of Land, as followeth, That is to say : I, John Hodges, have delivered, and doe by this deliver, unto Alice Rand a parcell of salt marsh meadow, scituate nere my Hous and Land, which is bounded by a parcell of meadow which I bought of Ezekiell Richeson on the south : and on the North its bounded by Robert Halle ; and west by the Bull Lott; and North Easte by Richard Kettell : This land I bought of m^r Abraham Prat.

And I Alice Rand doe exchange for the forenamed Land, with m^r John Hodges, A parcell of Land, or a hay Lott of marshe meadow of myne, scituate nere m^r Hodges Hous and Land, which was given my husband : And it is bounded next the water syde south : and north by Edward Sturgis : and west and Easte by the Lands of m^r Hodges : All which parcells of Lands wee forenamed doe willingly exchange one with the other, etc. In wittnes heerunto wee have enterchangably sett to our hands to the originall coppy, with m^r Increase Nowells hand thertoo : the 2^d of the 3^d moneth, 1655.

JOHN GREENE.

[**151.**] *A Sale of Lands by Richard Arrington and Elizabeth his wiffe: unto John Scott, all Inhabitants in charltowne, The twentieth day of the second month, A Thousand six hundred fifty and five.*

Know all men by these presents, That I, Richard Arrington and Elizabeth my wiffe, Inhabitants in charletowne (for the suṁe of eight pounds currant, which suṁe wee have all Receaved at present), wee have sould, and by this declare, that wee doe sell unto John scott of the sayd Charletown likewise Inhabitant, A certaine parcell of salt marsh meadow, with some upland adioyning untoo it, Being all of it by Estimation twoo Akers, more or less. It is Lying and scituate on mistike syde, within Charltowne bounds, it is lying nere the South river Creek, This Land was in the divident given unto Nicholas Davis, and by him sould unto Ezekiell Richeson, who sould it to william Stitson, of whom I, Richard Arrington, bought it, and payd him for it : This marsh and upland is bounded west and south by the upland : north by John wilkins, and East by william Dade, A poplar tree being within 3 or 4 foot of the stake, or bound mark of this Ground, &c.

JOHN GREENE.

A Testimoniall of a sale of a Hous and ground standing and scituate in Charletowne, by Anthony Dicks, carpenter, then resident in charletowne, untoo Gualter Allen, Hatter, alsoe resident in Charletowne.

Memorandume, That I, Harman Garret, inhabitant in Boston, New England, doe Testifye and wittness That Antony Dicks did sell a Hous and Ground unto Walter Allen, which Hous and Ground was the hous and Ground of m^r Phillips, that now keeps the ship taverne in Boston: Hee bought it, and Dwelt in it, and sould it tu the sayd Antony Dicks: Which Hous and Ground is in Charletowne, and stands at the cross lane as wee goe up to Deacon Lynds hous: and it butts upon the street way going towards Cambridge: I testify that there was a full Bargaine, and my hand was to the Bargaine writing: This was taken upon oath the thirtieth day of september, 1652.

Alsoe James Broune, Glazier, Inhabitant in Charletowne, did Testify the same the eleaventh day of October, 1652. Both Testified this above written before m^r Increase Nowell, Magistrate.

JOHN GREENE.

A sale of a Hous and Ground by m^r Increase Nowell and Parneli his wiffe, unto Richard Pritchard, both Inhabitants in charltowne, New Enyland, the 12th day of the 12th month, 1652. And Recorded the 10th day of the 11th moneth, 1655.

Know all men by these presents, that I, Increase Nowell, esquire, Inhabitant in Charletowne, New England, Doe sell unto Richard Pritchard, of the Towne, shoemaker, The Hous of myne which was Edward Yeomens, by my Orchard, for thirty twoo pounds: to be payd Ten pounds between this and the sixteenth of the third month next, In currant silver, barley, or wheat: sweet, Dry, cleane, and marchantable, at the price currant, at my dwelling Hous: And ten pounds by the twenty-ninth of the seaventh-month next, of the like pay, at the same place: And the last pay to bee the twenty ninth of the seaventh moneth, 1654, in the like pay, at the same place: And, if any payment be not payd at the tyme he is to alowe after eaight per cent for the tyme: He is to keep all the fence that I may not be anoyed by any defect therin: And if he sell the Hous, He is to let mee have it, if I will, at the price it shall then be adiudged valuable-worth. In witnes whereoff I have heerunto set my hand, by mee   INCREASE NOWELL.

PARNELL NOWELL.

I acknowledge to have Received twenty pounds for the two first payments the seaventeenth day of the eaight-month, 1653.

Receaved in full payment of the purchas twelve pounds, the fifteenth day of the sixth moneth, 1655.

By mee,   INCREASE NOWELL.

Signed and delivered in the presence of us.

GEORG HEPBURNE.
AARON LUDKIN.

[**152.**] *A sale of A Hous and Garden, standing and scituate in Charletowne, New England, by John Peirce, Marriner, now Resident in Charltowne, unto Ralfe Mowsall, Carpenter: Inhabitant in the sayd Charltowne, the 27ᵗʰ of the 6ᵗʰ mo., 1655.*

Know all men by these presents, That I, John Peirce, Marriner, now Resident in Charletowne, in and for the consideration of thirty pounds in good payments to bee payd, the one half being fifteen pounds to bee payd at present: and the other fifeteen pounds to bee payd the 27ᵗʰ day of August, 1656. I have, therfore, Given, Granted, Bargained, sould and confirmed, And by these presents I Doe fully, absolutely, Give, Grant, Bargain, sell, and confirme unto Ralph Mousall, Carpinter, of the sayd Charltowne, inhabitant, my dwelling Hous, in the sayd Charletowne, standing and scituate eastward therin, or towards the Easte end of the towne, in the place called wapping Rowe: with all the out housing about it, and the yeard and garden ground belonging to it: with all the Rails, Poles, Posts, and fencings belonging to the sayd hous and ground, alsoe all due apurtenances belonging to it. This hous and ground is bounded south by the street way: North by Thomas Mousall, Easte by Abraham Bell, and west by Thomas Mousall, and a peece of Ground common to the Towne.

Alsoe, A quarter of a cows comon, lying on the stinted comon, without Charletowne Neck, which I bought of my sister, widdow Peirces Bridges, which I have payd her for.

Likewise a Hay Lott, lying and scituate in the west feild, Bounded on the Easte by the Creek, on the south by catherine Graves, on the North by Thomas Peirce, and on the west by Thomas Brigden and Thomas welsh.

And I, John Peirce, Marriner, Doe for my selfe, my wiffe, &c.

JOHN GREENE.

A sale of a Hous and Garden, standing and scituate in Charltowne, New England: By Ralph Mousall, Carpenter, Inhabitant in the sayd Charltowne, untoo William Hilton, Marriner, Inhabitant alsoe of Charltowne, the nine and twentieth day of September, A thousand six hundred fifty and five.

Know all men by these presents, That I, Ralph Mousall, Carpenter, Inhabitant in Charltowne, New England, in and for the consideration of a certaine sume of money in good payments to bee payd unto mee or my Assignes at twoo severall tymes: I have, therfore, Given, Granted, Bargained, sould and confirmed: And by these presents I doe fully, Absolutely, Give, Grant, Bargaine, sell, and confirme, unto william Hilton, Aforementioned, Marriner, Inhabitant in Charltowne, A Dwelling House of myne standing and scituate in a place of Charltowne called wapping Roe: Eastward in the sayd Towne, or towards the East end ther off: with all the out Housing about it, with the yeard and Garden ground belonging to it, and all the Rayls, Payls, Posts, and fencings about it, and pertayning Justly to the sayd House and Ground. Likewise all due appurtenances belonging to the same: The House and ground is Bounded south by the street way, North by Thomas Mousall,

East by Abraham Bell: and west by Thomas Mousall, And a peece of Ground coṁon to the Towne.

And I, Ralph Mousall, Doe hereby for my selfe, my wiffe, &c.

John Greene.

[**153.**]   *Bee it knowen by these presents*, that I, Christian Lawrence, widdow, and John Lawrence, the son of Christian Aforesayd, Both of Charltowne: for good and valuable Consideration by us in hand receaved: Have Given, granted, bargained and sould, And by these presents Doe Give, grant, bargain and sell, untoo Nicholas shaply, of Charletowne, Marriner, one dwelling hous and a garden Lott thereuntoo belonging, Now layd out to the sayd Nicholas: by us Christian: and John: aforesayd, scituate at the sconce-Poynt, Bounded upon the south Easte by the Harbour, North West upon John Lawrence: And south west Bounded on Christian Lawrence. To Hould the sayd Hous and Land to Him and his Heires for Ever.

In witness whereoff wee have sett to our hands and seals the twoo and twentieth day of July, A thousand six hundred forty and six.

Christian Lawrence,
John Lawrence.

Sealed, signed and delivered in the presence of us.

    Randoll Nickolls,
    Nicholas Lawrence.

Acknowledged by John Lawrence, the twenty sixth of the twelveth month, A thousand six hundred forty eaight, before mr Increase Nowell.

Recorded the third of the first month, A thousand six hundred forty eaight.

By William Aspinall,
Recorder.

John Greene.

The fifth day of the Eleaventh, A thousand six hundred fifty and five. It was Granted by the selectmen of Charltowne, New England, unto the sayd Nicholas shaply, Marriner: (The street way being Reserved.) The frount of the sayd Ground, before the sayd House and Garden of Christian Lawrence, widdow, and John Lawrence, her son (above mentioned), Downe to Lowe watter marke, The sayd Ground being full fifty foot wide in ffront.

John Greene.

A sale of five Acres of Land by michall Bastowe, of wattertowne, unto steeven ffosdik of Charletowne.

Know all men by these presents, that I, Michall Bastowe, of wattertown, have sould unto steeven ffosdik, of Charltowne (both in the country of Middellsex, in New England), five Acres of Land by estimation, more or less, lying on mistik syde, this Land is butted on the South against mr Increase Nowells Lands, and upon the East its Bounded by steeven fosdiks Lands: And upon the North its bounded Against the Comon, And upon the west its bounded by Maldon Comon. This was on the orriginall subscribed by mʳ Increase Nowell, magistrate, the fourteenth day of the fifth moneth, A thousand six hundred fifty and five, and its subscribed by Michall Bastows owne hand.

JOHN GREENE.

[**154.**] *A sale of a Hous and a Barn, and A cow comon, and A peece of marsh meadowe, all standing, scituate and Being at present in Charltowne, near and within the Neck: By Phillip Knight, Planter, and Margerite Knight his wiffe, both Inhabitants in Charltown, unto John Cloys, Marriner, of the sayd Charltowne, Inhabitant, the fifteenth Day of the second month, A thousand six hundred fifty and six.*

Know all men by these presents, that I, Phillip Knight, Planter, Inhabitant in Charltown, and Margerite Knight, my wiffe, both of the County of Midlesex : weę have for and in consideration of thirty and six pounds and eaighteen shillings, of which sume I have received thirteen pounds in hand in good marchantable payment, given, granted, bargained, sould and confirmed, And by these presents Doe fully, absolutely, give, grant, bargaine, sell and confirme unto John Cloys, marriner, of the sayd Towne and county, Inhabitant, A Mesuage or House and all the housing appertaining therunto, with A Barne and A Garden, and all the fencings belonging therunto.

Alsoe, A cow comon, being on the stinted pasture without the Neck. Likewise a half Akar of marsh meadow by estimation, more or less, with all the due appurtenances belonging to all and each of the same, which House, Barne, garden and meadow stands, lyes and is scituate in Charltown, near the Neck, and all is Bounded North by the Pound, south by Lawrence Dous : Easte by the street way, and west by a Creek. &c., In the presence of Mʳ John Endicott the Governor &c.

JOHN GREENE,
Secretary.

A sale of Housing and Lands by John Roper, Carpenter, unto Gardy James, Planter, both Inhabitants in Charltowne, in the County off Midlesex, in New England, the 25ᵗʰ of the 3ᵈ month, 1656.

Know all men by these presents, That I, John Roper, of Charltown, Carpenter, have bargained and sould unto Gardy James, of the sayd town, Planter, A Tenement or Dwelling House I now dwell in, bought of Thomas Lynd, which was mʳ Hauls, alsoe A Tenement or dwelling Hous, scituate in charltown, with the edifices and apurtenances therunto belonging, together with the planting Lands and medoweing adioyning therunto adioyning, formerly bought of Thomas Squire, and he is payd for all the upland and meadowe. All being by estimation seaven Akers, more or lesse, and all stands, lyes and is scituate in the East feild, without the Neck, only one Aker and three Roode of this Land is sould to

William Jones, the forenamed is bounded on the south west with the Lands of Ralph Mousall, on the Easte with the Lands of m^{rs} Catherine Coytmore. Likewise Three Cowe Comons and a half, lying on the stinted Comon with out the Neck, with all Apurtenances belonging unto them, alsoe twoo Akers of planting Land, more or less, and a Littell spott of meadowe lying at the end of the sayd twoo Akers, All Bounded on the west by the Lands of Walter Palmer, and on the East by the Lands of m^r Barnards, north by the medows next mistik river, and south by the Comon.

All these afore mentioned housing Lands and parcels of uplands and meadows, only excepted the one Aker and three rood, sould to William Jones, have I, John Roper, sould and doe sell with the three cowe comons and a halfe unto the sayd Gardy James, to have and to hould unto him and his heires for ever, without any Reservation, And I Acknowledg my self to be fully satisfied and payd therefor, And I, John Roper, doe hereby for my selfe, my heirs, executors and Assignes, Resigne up all our Rights, Titles and Interest in sayd particulers before specified to bee the sayd Gardy James and his heires for Ever, And that this is my full entent and meaning.

[**155.**] *A sale of A House and Lands standing and scituate in charltowne: By Grace Palmer, widow: unto Anne frothingham, widow: both Inhabitants in Charltowne, New England the eleaventh day of the sixth mo: 1656.*

Know all men by these presents. That I, Grace Palmer, widdow, Inhabitant in Charltowne, in the County of Midlesex, in New England : Have (for and in the consideration of a Certaine sūme of money and Goods to mee in hand Payd) Given, granted, bargained, sould and confirmed : And by these presents ; doth fully, Absolutely : Give, grant, bargaine, sell and confirme ; unto Anne ffrothingham, widow, likewise Inhabitant in the sayd charltowne, of the County of Middlesex, in New England : My dwelling Hous, with all the out housing about it, with A yeard and orchard close by it, and likewise five Akers of pasture land, by estimation, more or less, adioyning to it the House and orchard, with all the fencings, as posts, Railes, pales round about the sayd House, yeard, orchard, and pasture-Lands, and with all due Apurtenances belonging to all and each of the forementioned parcells ; with one cows common on the stinted common, without the Neck of Charltowne : and all its due Apurtenances ; All the sayd House, Howsing yeard, orchard, and Pasture ground Is standing, lying, and scituate within Charletown Neck, towards the Towne ; all being Bounded on the west by the Lands of Anne ffrothingham, and its bounded on the East by seth switzers Lands, and on the south by the Highway to the Towne, and on the North by the Lands of George Hutcheson, and Anne ffrothingham : To Have and to Hould, etc.

This Deed of sale was acknowledged by m^{rs} Grace Palmer, the tenth of september, 1656.

Before maior Simon Willard,
Magistrate.

A sale of a Hous and ground by James Garret, marriñer, inhabitant in wapping, near London, unto Samuell Beadle, Planter, inhabitant in Charltowne, New England, the tenth day of the fifth moneth, 1656.

Know all men by these presents, That I, James Garrett, marriner, at present resident in charltown, in the county of midlesex, new England, for and in the consideration of thirty six pounds to be payd in three severall payments, alowing three years day of payment from the date hereof, I, James Garrett, Have therfore given, granted, bargained, sould, and confirmed, and by these presents I doe fully, absolutely give, graunt, bargaine, sell, and confirme unto Samuell Beadle, of the sayd Charltown, Planter ; my posession within Charltown limits, that is my former dwelling hous, with A garden and yeard anexed to it, standing and scituate at sconse poynt, Bounded northwest by the highway, northeast by widow Hadlocke and steeven fosdike, south east by the beach and battery, limited forty feet from the corner post of the battery, and so strait up by the Lyne of m^r Augustine walker, now by m^r Trumble, with A plott of ground given to m^r Garrett in the marsh to cutt a creek with convenientcy of Landing about it, alowing and not hindring free passage in the highway that goes between my Lott and m^r John Trumbles, upon any occation about the battery. Likewise a cow comon on the stinted pasture, without the Neck. Also a hay Lott of an Aker of meadow, by estimation, more or less, lying at Wilson's poynt on mistik syde, bounded south by mistik River, North East by James Hubberd, and Northwest by A Creek : with A milch cow now in his possession : All and each of this possessions perticulerly aforementioned, with all due apurtenances belonging to them, I, James Garret, Doe for my selfe, my wife, &c.

And I, samuell Beadle, doe promise and bynde myself and my heires. To pay or cause to be payd to the sayd James Garrett or his Assignes, the sume of thirty-six pounds within three years from the date hereoff, that it is to say Twelve pounds each yeare eyther in money or comodities : the payments heer in charletown, at the tymes prefixed to the content of the sayd James Garrett or his Assinges. But if it be not payd in charltown, Then the sayd Samuell Beadle, his heires or Assignes, are bound and engaged hereby to send comodities into England to the sayd James Garrett, or his heires at the least to the vallewe of twelve pounds by the year yearly, for the three years, James Garrett being to stand to the Adventures of the sea : and samuell Beadle is to stand to the vallew of the mony the goods he sends shal bee sould for, witness our hands this seaventeenth day of the eaight month, 1656.

the originall was testified before m^r Richard Bellingham, Deputy Governor, the 20 of 8 mo., 1656.

[156.] *Know all men by these presents,* That I, John Andrews, of Boston, in the County of Sussex, in New England, Cooper, Have sould, and by this declare it, unto John Knight, of Charltowne, in the County of Middelsex, in the sayd New England, Cooper, for a certaine sume to mee in hand payed to my full content and satisfaction. And I, John Andrewes, doe hereby acquitt and discharge the sayd John Knight, his heires, execcutors, and Administrators, And every of them, from the sayd payment for ever. And I, John Andrews, doe hereby give, grant, bargaine, sell, enfeoff, and confirme unto the sayd John Knight, his heires and assignes, for ever, A certain House, ground and wharfe therunto belonging and adioyning, all standing and being scituate in charltowne aforenamed, all standing, lying, and being bounded by John Mirick on the south syde, and bounded by widdow Jone Larkin on the north syde, Bounded and butting on charltowne River, westerly : And facing or fronting to the streetway going towards the wharfe Easterly : with all and singular the prēmises thereunto belonging ; All which aforenamed I, John Andrews, formerly bought of James· Mirick Cooper, and Margerite his wiffe, the former right owners and possessours thereoff, whom I have fully payed and satisfied for all the same : To have and to hould, &c. In witnes wheroff, wee, the sayd John Andrews and Hannah his wiffe, have to the originall coppy sett to our hands and seales the thirtieth day of the second-month, A thousand six hundred fifty and seaven.

This sale was acknowledged by John Andrews the 13th of the third month, 1657.

Before Captain Daniell Gookin, Magistrate.

John Greene.

A Record of a certain Hous and out Housing and an orchard of about halfe an Aker of Land, sould by m^r william Barnard to Gardy James.

Know all men by these presents, That m^r william Barnard, gentleman, inhabitant in charletowne : having formerly sould to Gardy James, Planter, of the sayd Charltown Inhabitant, A certaine Hous, with some out housing by it, and an orchard of Land of half an Aker by estimation, more or less, all which belonged to James Tomson formerly, of whom m^r Barnard bought it and payd him for it, All which Hous, housing, and Land is standing and scituate in the East feild, without the Neck : Bounded north west by william Jones, south east by John Mousall south by the highway, and alsoe butting toward mistik River by John Mousall, All being now in the Posession of Gardy James, who hath payed fully for it. Written this fourth day of the 5th month, 1657.

John Greene.

[**157.**] *A sale of a peece of Land by Thomas Lynde unto John March, both Inhabitants in Charltown, New England, the eaighteenth day of the fourth month,* 1657.

Know all men by these presents, That I, Thomas Lynde, Malster, Inhabitant in Charletowne, in the County of Middlesex, in New England, Doe sell unto John March, Planter, Inhabitant in the sayd Charletowne, for a certaine payment to mee in hand payed, an Aker of Arrable Land, being by estimation, more or less, which Aker lyes and is scituate in the easte feild, which is within charltowne Neck. This ground aforenamed is bounded on the Northwest by John Penticost: it is bounded south easte by the cars highway in the middle of the feild on the topp of the Hill: it is bounded North Easte by John March: and it is bounded south-west by maister Bates Land.

And I, Thomas Lynde Doe hereby, for my selfe, my wiffe, &c. In witness hereoff I, Thomas Lynde and my wiffe Margerite have sett to our hands and seals to the originall coppy hereoff, Before m^r Richard Russell, Comissioner, this eighteenth day of the fourth month A Thousand six hundred fifty and seaven.

JOHN GREENE,
Secretary.

A mutual exchanging of a Hous and certaine parcells of Land, standing and scituate within Charltowne Neck, in the east feilde, between John March, Planter, and Thomas Lynde, Malster, both inhabitants in Charletowne, in the County of Middlesex, in New England the 18th day of the 4th mo. 1657.

Know all men by these presents, That wee, John March and Thomas Lynde, both Inhabitants in Charletowne, New England, Have agreed, and doe agree, and by this declare it: To exchange one with the other some parcells of Land with a Hous.

John Marches being a Hous, a garden, and a peece of meadowe, being all by estimation an Aker of ground, more or less: which Hous and land is standing and scituate between Charletowne Neck, and the towne in the midle of the high way from the towne: All being Bounded East northeast by the street-way: and its bounded northwest by Lands of Thomas Lynde, and its bounded South and on the other parts by the Lands of Anne ffrothingham, widdow: All the forenamed being, standing, lying, and scituate in the east feild, within the Neck off Charletowne.

Thomas Lynde exchanges with John March for all the forenamed A Peece or Parcell of Land of his, Being twoo Akers of Planting Land by estimation, more or less: and it is lying and scituate in the easte feild, within the Neck of Charltowne, which twoo Akers are Bounded south west by John Penticosts land, north east by Arrold Coles land, southeast by William Dades land, and Northwest by Thomas Lynds Land, which formerly was william Bachelers land. And which twoo Akers of Land wee, william and Rachell Bacheler, my wiffe, doe fully and freely resigne up unto Thomas Lynde aforenamed, to bee his and his heires for ever, Our agreements Being in manner as followeth, That is to say, That I, John March, doe Resigne and give up unto the sayd Thomas Lynde all myne, my wives, and my heires, execcutors, administrators and Assignes, Rights, Titells, and interest in all the sayd Hous garden and meadow above mentioned, with all Due Apurtenances therunto belonging, to bee the sayd Thomas Lynds and his heires for Ever.

Likewise I, Thomas Lynde, Doe give and resigne up unto the sayd John March all myne, my wives, and my heires, execcutors, administrators, and assignes, Rights, Tittells, and interests in all the sayd two Akers of Land above mentioned, with all due apurtenances thertoo belonging, to be the sayd John Marches and his heires for Ever : Alsoe I, Thomas Lynde, have granted and hereby I doe grant a highway to the said John March for a cart or a plough from the great highway to goe to his Land I have sould Him, with free egress and regress, as the sayd John March or his heires, execcutors, or assignes, shall have occasion : And to declare That wee both are reciprocally agreed and contented with this exchange, wee have enterchangably sett to our hands and seals to the orriginall coppy hereoff in the presence of m^r Richard Russell, Comissioner, this present being the eaighteenth day of the fourth month, A thousand six hundred fifty and seaven.

JOHN GREENE,
Secretary.

[**158.**] *A sale of a Hous and ground by Richard Arrington, lime burner, inhabitant in Charltowne, unto Marke Kings, Marriner, Inhabitant in the sayd Towne, the twoo and twentieth day of the fifth Month, A thousand six hundred fifty and seaven.*

Know all men by these presents, That I, Richard Arrington, Inhabitant in Charletown, in the County of Middelsex, in New Eng. land, for and in the consideration of seaventy pounds to be payd in twoo severall payments, allowing one years day of payment from the date here for the last payment, I, Richard Arrington, Have therefore Given, granted, bargained, sould and confirmed ; And by these presents I doe fully, absolutely, give, grant, bargaine, sell and confirme unto Marke Kings, of the sayd charletowne, Marriner : My Posession within Charletowne lymitts, that is my present dwelling Hous, with a garden and grounds annexed to it, All standing and scituate in wapping Roe, The grounds all Being about the eaight part of an Aker of Land by Estimation, more or less : with all the fencings as Posts, Railes, Pails, and all other due Apurtenances thereunto belonging : which Hous, housing and grounds are Bounded East and North by Edward Willson, west by Edward Drinker, and South by the streetway, All and each of the perticulers aforenamed I, Richard Arrington, Doe for my self and my wife, my heires, execcutors, administrators, and Assignes, freely and fully Resigne up all our Rights, Titells, and interests in all the sayd parcells aforementioned, To bee the sayd Marke Kings and his heires for Ever.

And I, Marke Kings, Doe promise to pay unto the sayd Richard Arrington, the sume of thirty and five pounds presently upon the sealing and delivery of this wrighting, and the hous and grounds above mentioned : five pounds wherof to bee payd in money and endigo : and alsoe twoo hogsheads of sugar and five or six pounds in goods at shopps : And I, Mark Kings, promise and bynd my selfe to pay or caus to bee payd to the sayd Richard Arrington, or his Assignes, the other thirty and five pounds Between this and the twoo and twentieth day of the fifth moneth, one thousand six hundred fifty and eaight, in Charletowne aforesayd, To pay it In wheat, sugar, cotton, wooll, or the like, As Mark Kings shall provide : and all at price currant and marchantable as then : and I, Richard Arrington, doe bynd and engage my selfe by these to send a sufficient security over from England hither to secure the sayd Mark

Kings, his heires and execcutors from all claimes what ever may be pretended to all aforenamed and by whom soever, and that this is both our entents and meanings.

witnes our hands and seals to this originall copy of this copy in the hands of Mark Kings, confirmed by m^r Richard Russell, the 1st day of August, 1657.

JOHN GREENE,
Recorder

A sale of a Cowe Common on the stinted Pasture by Richard Arrington unto John Smith, both Inhabitants in Charletowne, the 28th Day of the sixth moneth, 1657.

Know all men by these presents, That I, Richard Arrington, Inhabitant in Charltown, of the County of Middelsex, in New England, doe by this declare that I doe sell A Cow Comon (which I bought of m^r zachary symms, to whom it was given in the devident) unto John Smith of the sayd Charletown, inhabitant : And I confes I am fully payed for it, as apears by my hand and seale to the orriginall hereoff, And I, Richard Arrington, doe hereby Resigne up all myne, my wives, and my heires Rights, Tytells, and interests in the sayd cow common unto the sayd John Smith, to bee his and his heires for Ever.

Wittness my hand and seale to the orriginall, The Day and date above written :

as is testified by m^r Richard Russell, Comissioners, hand to it the 30th day of the 6 month, 1657.

[**159.**] *Know all men by these presents*, that I, Richard Harrington, inhabitant in charltowne, in the County of Middellsex, in New England, for and in the consideration of twenty and six pounds currant, which I have receaved to my full satisfaction, I Richard Harrington, and Elizabeth, my wife (since deceased), Have therfore Given, granted, bargained, sould and confirmed, And by these presents I doe fully, absolutely, Give, grant, bargaine, sell and confirme unto Edward Drinker, inhabitant of the sayd Charletowne, Potter. A Hous or warehous and the ground it stands on, and halfe a well between Mary Walkers hous and this hous, and the garden in which it stands, which once belonged unto James Allison, and all is standing and scituate in Charltown lymitts, in A place called wapping Roe, the fore named being bounded east and north by Marke Kings, and due north by Robert Hale, two Railes length : west by Mary Walker, and south by the street way, All and each of the perticulers aforenamed I, Richard Harrington, Doe for my selfe, and my wiffe, &c.

this sale was made and delivered the year 1655. And I, Richard Harrington, for my selfe, my heires, execcutors, administrators, and Assignes, in wittnes hereunto have sett to my hand and seale to the orriginall copy heeroff, this twenty and eaighth day of the sixth month, one thousand six hundred fifty and seaven, this sale was confirmed before m^r Richard Russell, Comissioner, for charltown, the 31th day of August, 1657.

JOHN GREENE,
Recorder.

Know all men by these presents, that I, Tymothy Wheeler, yeoman, Inhabitant in Concord, in the County of Middlesex, in New England, Have (for and in the consideration off a certaine sume to mee in hand payd) Given, granted, bairganed, sould and confirmed, And by these presents Doe fully, absolutely, Give, grant, bargaine, sell and confirme unto Samuell Warde, yeoman, Inhabitant in charletowne, in the sayd County, A certain Parcell of fresh meadow land, being three Akers and A halfe by estimation, more or less, which Land is scituate and lying near the south mead, And it is bounded south by the stinted Pasture, and North by a peece of meadow of myne, Tymothy Wheelers, it is also bounded west by the stinted Pasture, And East by the Land of Robert Hale : And Samuell Warde doth bynde and engage himself by these presents to keep and maintaine a sufficient fence to keep out great Cattell between his sayd meadow and the meadow belonging unto Tymothy Wheeler on the North of this meadow : And I, Tymothy Wheeler, Doe for my selfe, my wife, &c.

And that this is my entent and meaning without fraude or guile, I have hereunto sett to my hand and seale to the orriginall coppy in m^r wards hands, the ninth day of the seaventh month, one thousand six hundred fifty and seaven.

JOHN GREENE,
Recorder.

[160.] To all Christian People to whom these presents shall come, William Kilcupp, of Charletowne, New England, Sivemaker, sendeth greeting. Know yee, that I, the sayd William Killcupp for divers good and valuable causes and considerations me thereunto moving, and especially for, and in consideration of the sum of threescore and twelve pounds starling, to me in hand payd by Henry Harbour of the same, Planter, at the ensealing and delivery hereoff, wherwith I do acknowleg myself fully satisfied, contented, and payd, and theroff and of every part and parcell therof doe exonerate, acquitt, and discharg the sayd Henry Harbour, his Heires, execcutors, administrators, and every of them for ever by these presents, Have given, granted, bargained, sold, enfeoffed, and confirmed, And by these presents Doe give, grant, bargaine, sell, enefeoffe, and confirme unto the sayd Henry Harbour, his Heires and Assignes, for ever, All that my dwelling Hous, out Houses, barnes, buildings, stables, cowhouses, orchards, gardens, with Tenn Acres of upland and meaddow therunto belonging, lying upon the poynt of Lands and near the Hous of m^r John Hodges in Charletowne aforesayd, and lying and being betwixt the Lands of John Hodges on the East syde, and the Lands of the said Henry Harbour on the West, and betwixt the River Southerly, and the Commons Northerly, And the meadow lying upon the milldame, And four cows commons, upon the commons of Charletowne, with all His Right, Title, and Interest of and into the sayd bargained premises, with all and singular their Appurtenances, and every part and parcell theroff, To Have and to Hould, &c. in free and common Soccage and not in capite nor by Knights service &c.

In wittness wheroff the sayd william Kilcupp hath set his hand

and seale to the orriginall writting hereoff, the five and twentieth day of May, one thousand six hundred fifty and three. And Grace Killcupp, wiffe of the sayd william Killcupp doth alsoe fully and freely give and yeild up all her Right, title, Dowr, and interest of and into the above written premises, unto the sayd Henry Harbour, his heires and Assignes for Ever, in wittness wheroff the sayd Grace hath sett to her hand and seale the fifth day of may, one thousand six hundred fifty and five, in the presence of Richard Cook, Henry Powning, Nathaniell Sowther.

This was by them both William Killcupp and Grace Killcupp acknowledged the same day before m^r Richard Bellingham, Governour.

By John Greene, Recorded this 21th day of september, 1657.

[**161.**] *A mutuall exchange of Lands now being within the Bounds of Maldon, formerly in Charltown Bounds, between Edward Carrinton and Job Lane, both Planters.*

Know all men by these presents, That wee, Edward Carrinton and Job Lane Have Agreed and doe Agree, and by these presents declare it, To exchange mutually one with another each a parcell of Land : Edward Carrintons parcell being Ten Akers of Arrable Land by estimation, more or less, which Land lies now and is scituate in Maldon bounds, which I bought of John Greene : likewise twoo Akers and a halfe of Arrable land by estimation, more or less, scituate nere the Ten Akers, which twoo Akers and a halfe I bought of Robert Burden, which was formerly m^r Increase Nowells, the sayd twelve Akers and a halfe are all Bounded North East by Robert Long, and south east by m^r Increase Nowell, North west by Peeter Tuft, which was Ralph Mousalls, and south west bounded by a highway.

Job Lanes Parcell is Ten Akers of upland by estimation, more or less ; it is now scituate in Maldon, but was formerly in charltown ; it once belonged unto Isaack wheeler now deceased, which I, Job Lane, bought and have payd for it, of francis wheeler, Isack wheelers wife : which Land is bounded south by Peeter Tufft, north by Thomas Grover, east by James Barrett and Robert Long, west by John Greenland. Our Agreements being in manner as followeth, That is to say : —

That I, Edward Carrinton, doe hereby give and Resigne up unto the sayd Job Lane, All myne, my wives, my heires, executors, and Administrators Rights, Tytells, and Interests, in all the sayd twelve Akers and a half of Lands above mentioned, and all due Apurtenances therunto belonging to bee the sayd Job Lanes and his heires for ever.

Likewise I, Job Lane, doe hereby give and resigne up unto the sayd Edward Carrinton, All myne, my wives, my heires, exeecutors, and Administrators Rights, Tittells, and Interests in all the sayd Ten Akers of Lands above mentioned, and all due Apurtenances therunto belonging, to bee the sayd Edward Carrintons and his heires for ever, &c., &c.

In witness hereof, we have enterchangably sett to our hands and

seals to the originall hereoff in the presence of m^r Humphry Atharton, magistrate.

JOHN GREENE,
Recorder.

*Know all people to whom this writing shall come to be seen or
Read,* That I, ffrancis Cook, formerly Wheeler, now the wife of
Richard Cook, yeoman, resident in Maldon, in the County of middlesex, in New England, for and in consideration of a certaine
sume to me in hand payd to my full satisfaction, by Job Lane, of
the same town, Carpenter, before the ensealing and delivery hereoff, Have bargained, sould, given, and granted : And by these
presents, for mee, my heires, execcutors, and Administrators, Doe
fully, clerely, and absolutely Bargain, sell, give, grant, Alien, enfeoff, and confirm unto the sayd Job Lane and his heires, execcutors, administrators, and Assignes, A certain parcell of arrable
Land, scituate and Lying in Maldon bound : Being Ten Akers by
estimation more or less, which is bounded north east by Robert Long,
south east by m^r Increase Nowell, south west by a highway, and
north west by Peeter Tuft, which was Ralph Mousalls, with all the
Apurtenances and priviledges to all and any part theroff, belonging or in any wise apertayning. To have and to hould, &c. In
witnes wherof wee, Richard and francis Cook have to the originall hereoff set to our hands and seales this 20th of the eaight
month, 1657, in the presence of m^r Humphry Atharton, magistrate.

JOHN GREENE,
Recorder.

[**162.**] *Know all People to whom this present writing shall
come to be seen or read,* That I, Richard Cook, yeoman, dwelling
in Maldon town, in the County of Midellsex, in New England, for
and in consideration of A certaine sume to mee in hand payd, to
my full satisfaction, by Job Lane, of the same towne, Carpenter,
before the ensealing and delivery hereoff, Have Bargained, sould,
given, granted, and by these presents, for mee, my heires,
execcutors, and Administrators, Doe full, cleerly, and absolutely
Bargain, sell, give, grant, alien, enfcoff, and confirm unto the sayd
Job Lane and his heires, execcutors, administrators, and Assignes,
A certain Parcell of Arrable Land, scituate and lying now in the
bounds of Maldon ; being forty and five Akers by estimation, more
or less, which Land is bounded south west by Lands firstly —
apertaining to m^r John Greene, and bounded north west by Ten
Akers firstly apertaining to m^r John Harvard, and sould by his
heires unto Thomas Mugg. It is bounded East by m^r John Avery
and Richard Kettell, and by five Akers of Land of Job Lanes,
sould to him by John Burden, which he had of m^r Robert Long :
and this Land is encompassed (by the Lands of Richard Sprague),
with all the Apurtenances and Priviledges, to all and any part
therof belonging or in any wise Appertaining : To Have and to
hould, etc. In witness heerunto I, Richard Cook and francis my
wife, have to the originall coppy assented, and I, Richard Cook,

have sett my hand and seale this twentieth of the eight month, one thousand six hundred, fifty seaven, in the presence of m^r Humphry Atharton, magistrate.

JOHN GREENE.
Recorder.

A sale of a Hous and garden, standing and scituate nere the Neck in charletowne: By Lawrence Dous To Roger Els, both Inhabitants in charletowne, the five and twentieth day of the tenth moneth, one thousand six hundred fifty and seaven.

Know all men by these presents, that I, Lawrence Dous, Planter, inhabitant in charletowne, in the county of Midlesex, in New England, Have sould, and by this declare that I do sell, unto Roger Else, weaver, inhabitant in the said charletowne, A Hous and a Garden, with all the fencing and due Appurtenances, all being nere the Neck of Land of Charletowne, which Hous and garden, fencing, and all due Appurtenances, I, Lawrence Dous and Margery my wiffe, Doe, for ourselve and our heires, execcutors, administrators, and Assignes, freely and fully Resigne up all our Rights, Tytles, and Interests in the sayd perticulers unto the sayd Roger Else, to be his and his heires for ever: confessinge our selves to be fully payd and satisfied therefore: But Lawrence Dous and his heires are to make and maintaine the one halfe of the fence next his meadow: Alsoe, wee, Lawrence Dous and Margery my wiffe, doe hereby engage and bynde our selues, and our heires, execcutors, administrators, and Assignes, to save the sayd Roger Else and his wiffe, and their heires, free from all uniust claimes and molestations about the sayd Hous and Garden, as from us or ours, or any person or persons, as by our means whatsoever. In witness hereof we have to the originall coppy hereoff sett to our hands the 25th of the 10th month, 1657, before m^r Richard Russell, Commissioner.

JOHN GREENE,[1]
Recorder.

[163.] *Know all men,* that I, James Hadlock, of wenham, in New England, for divers good and valewable causes and considerations, me ther unto moving and espetialy for and in consideration of the sum of sixe pounds to me in hand paid before the ensealing hearof by Samuell Adams, of Charlstown, wheare with I doe Acknowleg my selfe to bee fuly satisfied, contented and paid, and ther of and of every partt and parsil ther of Doe Aquitt and Discharge the said Samuell Adams, his heires, exsecutors, Administrators and Asighns, and every of them by these p^{e}sents for ever, and by thes p^{e}sents have given, granted, barganed, sould, enffefed and confirme, and by thes p^{e}sents doe give, grant, bargaine, sell, enfefe and confirme unto the said Samuell Adams, his heirs and Asighns, all that persill of land or house lott lying and being in Charlstown, which was formerly the house lott of Thomas ffosdick, and in the marsh, bounded on the west by mr Coytmors creek, and on North

-----

[1] End of Greene's writing. — ED.

by the Town Streat, and east by the Comon lands, and south by
mr James Garrett, with all and singular the apurtenanses therto
belonging, and all my Right, titell and intrest of and in the same,
To have and to hould, &c.

In wittnes whear of I, James hadlock, have heare unto sett my
hand and seall this Twenty Ninth day of July, in the yeare of our
lord one Thousand sixe hundred fifty and four : 1654.

JAMES HADLUCK,
his hand and seall.

Sealed and dilivered in the p^esents of
> THOMAS SHEPY,
> JOHN P PATTFEILD,
> his marke.

This is Attrew Copey heare entred And taken outt of the
originall as Attest.

SAMUELL ADAMS,
Reco.

Know all men by thes p^esents, that I, Samuell Adams, of charlstown doe heare by sell and Assighne and put over all my Right
and titell unto that p^esill of land Above spesified that I bought of
James hadluck, I Doe sell and Asighn over my titell unto the same
unto John Smith, of charlstown, his heires and asighns for ever.

wittnes my hand this 6 day of the 7 mo., 1654.

SAMUELL ADAMS.

JOHN ALBY,
KATHREN GRAUES.

[**164.**] *Know all men*, that martha Coytmor, of Charlstowne,
widow, upon due consideration and for Divers Reasons moving
mee ther unto, have sould and Doe heare by confirme unto John
wafe, of charlstown, his heires and executors for ever, that is one
Dweling house and one quarter of an Aker of land, bee it more or
les, sitewatte in charlstowne, being bounded by Isack Koall on the
north west, and mr John Gwine on the east, and on the south the
towne streat, and on the North east the land of James browne, in
consideration whear of I Doe Acknolige my selfe fuly satisfied and
Doe hear by give up all my Right and intrest unto the forsaid John
wafe and his heires for ever.

wittnes my hand this third day of the tenth moneth, one thousand
sixe hundred fourty foure.

MARTHA COYTEMORE.

Wittnes,
SAM ADAMS.

This is a trew Copey of Martha Coytemors Dead of salle to John
wafe, and is heare entred out of the originall By mee.

SAMUELL ADAMES.
Recor.

[**165.**] To all Christian peopell to whome thes p^esents shal
Com, greting, know ye that I, william hilton, of Charlstown, in the

County of midelsex, in New England, mariner, ffor valuable considerations to mee well and trewly paid by mathew price, of Charlstown, in New England Afore said, the Receipt wheer of I Doe by thes p^esents Acknoleg and ther with to be fully satisfied and paid, and of every parte and parsill therof Doe fully, clearly, Absolutely, Acquitt and discharge the said Mathew price, his heirs, executors, Administrators and Asighns for ever, by thes p^esents have granted, barganed and sould, Alinated, enffeffed and Confirmed and by thes p^esents doe fully, clearly and Abselutely grante, Bargain and sell, Alien, enfeffe and confirme unto the sayd mathew price, his heires, executors, Administrators and Asighns for ever, one Dweling house, with the yeard, garden, ground belonging unto it, and all out housing, fensing, frute treese and other Apurtenanses or towne grants to the same Apertaining or in any wise belonging, which is sitewate, lying and being in Charlstown before named, formerly being in the posetion of Ralph mousall, deseased, and is Bounded on the North by Thomas mousall, south by the Towne streatt, east by Abraham Bell, his house and land. west by Thomas mousall partly and partly by a pece of land Comon to the Towne, to have And to hould the sayd house, Land and other Apurtenances therto Belonging unto the sayd mathew price, his heires and Asighns for ever, to his and ther only proper use and Behoofe, and I, the sayd william hilton, doe Covenant, promis and grant for me, my executors, my heires, and Administrators and assighns, to and with the sayd mathew price his heires, executors, Administrators and Asighns, by thes presents that hee. the sayd mathew price, his heires and Asighns, shall and may att all times and from time to time for ever hear After, have and hold, occupie, poses and In Joy the sayd Bargained and asighned p^emises, and every parte and persill ther of, Acording to the trew intent and meaning of thes p^esents, with out the lawfull lett, trobell, sute, molestation, contradiction, or deniall of mee, of mee, the sayd william hilton, or of any of my heires, executors, Administrators or Asighns, or of any other person whome soever claming and having any Right, titell or Interest therin, from, by or under me.

In wittnes whearof I, the sayd william hilton, have hear unto putt my hand and sealle, this twenty sixt day of the sixt moneth, caled Agust, in the year of our lord God one Thousand sixe hundreth fiftey and Nine.

WILLIAM HILTON,
his seale.

Sighned, sealed, And dilivered In the p^esints of
BENIAMIN LAITHROP,
THOMAS MOUSALL,
EDWARD BURTT.

This sale was Acknowledged the 29th of the 6 month, 1659, Before me.
RICHARD RUSELL.

Enterd and Recorded att Cambrig, in midlesexe, 29th, 6th, 1659, in the 2 Book of Deeds and conveyences, page 85, as Attest:
THOMAS DANFORTH,
R.

This is a trew Copy of mathew price, his dead of salle from william hilton, as Attest

Samuell Adams,
Record.

[**166.**] I,[1] John Cutler, of Charlstowne, for valewable consid-erations, payd by Thomas heett, of said Charltown, do fully, clearly, &c., grante, &c., " unto sayd Thomas hett, his heires and Assighnes for ever, one dweling house, with a garden plott adioyning therunto sitewate, lying, and being in charlstowne before named, being formerly in the posetions of mr Richard Rus-ell of the forsaid charlstowne, and is boundid on the North with the towne streat; on the south with the house and Garden of mr Tarrice; on the east with the house and lande of Richard tempeller; and on the west the land of ffaintnott wines, to have and to hould the said house, land, ffensing, and all other Apurtenances ther to belonging, or any wise apertaining unto him, the sayd Thomas hett, his heires and Asighns for ever to his and there only proper use. " His wife, Anna Cutler, joining herein, this Twenty fifth day of the eleventh moneth, Called Janewary, in the year of our lord god one thousand six hundred fiftey and nine.

John Cutler And Anna Cutler.
There Sealles.

Sighned, sealed, and diliuered In the p[e]sents of us
mathew Griffine.
Edward Burtt.

This Deed of Sale, Acording to the trew intent and meaning ther of, was leagaly Acknowleged by John Cutler and Anna Cut-ler, his wife being exsamined apartt, to bee ther owne free actt and Deed this 21 Day of February, 1659.

Before me,   Richard Rusell.

This is a trew Copey of John Cutlers Dead of sale to Thomas hett as is hear Above: Recorded by me 23th 12 mo. 1659.

Samuell Adams,
Record.

[**167.**] Blank.

[**168.**] I, John halle, of Charlestown, for valewabell consid-erations payd by william ffoster, of sayd Charlestcwn, doe fully, clearly, &c., Acquitt, &c., " unto the said willham ffoster, his heires, executors, Administrators, and Assignes for ever, one p[e]sill of land, lying and beeing in Charlstown Adioyning unto the River — caled Charlse River, being, by estemation. one Roode of land, more or lesse, and is bounded on the North east with the Comon high way: and on the south east with the seaw or River bee-fore mentioned, and on the North west with the land and Creeke

---

[1] The original, of which this is **an abstract**, is in the same general form as that used in the preceding deed. — Ed.

belonging to Jacob greene, and on the south west with the land of John Smith, which sayd p^{e}sill of land was formerly in the posotion of my ffather, Robertt halle, late of charlstown, deseased, and by him purchased of Cap̄. John Allen, which sayd land, with all privileges and apurtenanses ther to belonging, ore in any wise apertaining unto him, the sayd william ffoster, his heires, executors, Administrators, and Asignes for ever."

Dated "this tenth Day of the fifth month, caled July, in the year of our lord god one thousand sixe hundreth and sixty.

JOHN HALLE,
his seale.

Sighned, sealed, and dilivered in the p^{e}sents of
> RICHARD MILES,
> EDWARD BURTT.

Imprimas, it was Agread up on before the sighñg and sealing of thes presents, that the plott of land mentioned in this dead is eighten foott in bredth fronting against the river, and fifty seaven foott broad att the head next to the creke belonging to Jacob grene.

RICHARD MILES,
EDWARD BURTT.

This salle was Acknowleged the first of the 7th moth, 1660, beefore me,

RICHARD RUSELL.

This is a trew Copey heare entred the 25 : 7 mo., *1660*, by me,
SAM̄ ADAMS,"
Rec.

[169.] I, Edward Johnson, of Charlstown, for valiable Consideration paid by John ffownell, of said Charlstown, do fully, clearly, &c., Discharge "the sayd John ffownell, his heires, executors, Administrators, and Assigns for ever, One Cowe Common, lying and being in the first stinted Common of Charlstowne, and is bounded North by the farme of M^r. John winthrop, and South and south west by Cambridg town lands. To have and to hould the sayd Cow Comon, with all Rights and privileges ther to belonging unto him, the sayd John ffownell, and his heires & Asignes for ever to his and ther proper use and behofe," &c.

his wife, Kathren, also joins "this fourth day of the twelfth moneth, caled ffebuary, in the yeare of our lord God one thousand sixe hundreth and sixty."

The sealls of
EDWARD JOHNSON and
KATHREN JOHNSON.

Sighned, sealed, and dilivered In the p^{e}sents of us,
> SARAH LONG,
> EDWARD BURTT.

This salle of the Comon, spesified by the p'ties above spesified, was acknowleged and Confirmed the 20ᵗʰ of ffebuary, 1660.   Before me,

RICHARD RUSELL.

This is a trew copey hear entred this 28ᵗʰ 12mo, 1660, by mee,

SAMUELL ADAMS,

Record.

[**170.**] *Know all men by these p'sents*, That of Gawdy James, late of Boston, in New England, beyond the seas, and now of winfarthing, in the Countie of Norfolk, in old England, husband man, for and consideration of a certaine competent sume of lawfull mony of England to mee by Fran : Willoughby, of London, Esq., in hand paid the Receipt whearof I Dow hear by acknowledg and to bee thear by fully satisfied, contented, and paid, have granted, bargained, alienated, and sould, and by thes p'sents Doe fully, freely, and abselutly, grante, bargain, alinate, & sell unto the sayd ffrān. willoughby, his heires, executors, Adminestrators, & Asignes, the Gate of three Cowes and a halfe, or three cow comons and a halfe, so caled, situoated, lying and being upon the Comon of Charlstown, in New england aforsaid, late in the possesiou of Captain Edward Johnson, of woodborn, in new england aforsaid, and now in the possession of the said Gaudy James, or his Assignes, Together with all the estate, right, titell, Intrest, claime, and demand, whatsoever which the [said] Gaudy James now have, or which my heires, executors, or Administrators might or may have or claim of in or to the p'mises aforesaid, or any pt ther of, of, for or by any wais or means what so ever, And I, the said Gaudy James, Doth hearby for myselfe, my heires, executors, Admʳ, covenant, p'mise, and graunt to and with the said ffrān willoughby, his heires, executors, Admʳˢ, and Assighns, that I, the said Gaudy James, my Executors or Admʳ shall, and will up on reasonable Demands made by the said ffrān willoughby, his heirs, Executors, Admʳˢ, or Assighnes, give and yield up to the said ffran willoughby, his heirs, executors, Admʳˢ, or Assighnes, full and peaceable possession of the premises aforsaid, and every pt ther of, and further Doe and execute all other legall act or acts, thing and things, whatsoever as shall bee reasonally advised or desired by the said ffrān willoughby, his heires, executors, Admʳᵃ, or Assignes, for the more ampell and full conveyance of the premises acording to the trew intent and mening of these p'sentes.   In wittness whereof, I, the said Gaudy James, have theare unto sett my hand and seale, the 22 febry, 1659.

The marke of

GAUDY ⏐◟ JAMES.

Sealed and dilivered in the p'sents of

DANIELL GOOKIN,

WM COOLING.

This is a trew copey of the original, as wittnes

JOHN PEIRCE.

This coppy above was heare entred the 28th 12 mo, 1660, by mee,
SAM ADAMS, *R.*

See the next Page which is : 145 : Page[1]

[**171.**] *Know all men by thes prsents*, That I, Nicholas Davison, have Bargained and sould, and by thes p^esents doe Bargain and sell all my Right, titell, and interest in and to one house and yard which I bought of mr Robertt Cooke, and was som times the said Cookes Stabell, and since made a slafter[2] house : unto Thomas Adams of the same Towne for the said Thomas and his heires to injoy for ever, and doe Acknowledg to have Received satisfaction for the same by a bill of Twenty and two pounds str^ll to bee paid mee baring date by this p^esents in wittnes of the truth I have heare unto sett my hand and seall this Ninth day of Aprill, one Thousand sixe hundred ffiftey and eight, 1658.

NICHOLAS DAVISON,
his sealle.

. Signed, sealed, and dilevrid in the p^esents of
JOHN DUDLY,
RICHARD TROTT.

Mrs Joan Davison Apearing before mee the 23 of ffebry, 1660, did Acknowledge her full consent, and did together with her husband ratifie and confirme the salle above expresed unto the above sayd Tho. Adams.

Before mee RICHARD RUSELL.

This is a trew copey as Above entred, this 15^the 10 : 1661, by me,
SAMUELL ADAMS, *R.*

[**172.**] On the 18th, 4th mo : 1662 : Mr Larance Hamon, Attorney unto M^r ffrancis Willoughby, Appeared with Gady James, of Boston, at the records of Charlestowne : And the said Larence hamon did then and there serender unto the said Gady James the possesion, title & Intereste of three cowes commons & ½, formerly soulld by the sd. James unto the said M^r ffrancis willoughby : as by A certaine Deed upon record in the 144 pa : of this booke may Appeare, which is Now, By the said Larance Hamon made void And standeth firme to the said Gady James and his heires for Ever : and entered Accordingly the Day & Date Above written.

p^e me EDWARD BURTT,
Recorder.
1662.

[**173.**] I, James Pemberton, Doe Acknowledge by These p^esents that I have sould And Doe sell unto Robert hale of. Charlestowne, one Cowe Common of the stented Common, without the Neck, & I Doe Acknowledge my selfe to be fully sattisfied & payed therefore :

---

[1] That is, page [171] by our marginal reckoning. — ED.
[2] Presumably a slaughter-house. — ED.

Wittness my hand: this p^e^sent: the 12th of the 3^d^ mo., 1648.

the marke ✕ of JAMES PEMBERTON.

MATTHEW BARNAT,
EZEKIELL WODWARD,
RICHARD STOWERS.

This above written is A true Coppy of the oridginall Bill of sale, compared word by word this 26th June, 1662:

p^r^ me EDWARD BURTT,

Recorder.

1662.

A sale of Land, Lying & scituate in Charllstowne, by James Browne: glazier, unto Robert hale: Carpenter, both Inhabitants in Charllstowne: the 19th of the 4th month: 1652:

Know all men by These p^e^sents, that I, James Browne, Glazier, Inhabitant in Charllstowne, And Sarah, my wife, for And In Consideration of Twentie & Eight Pounds in good Payments to be Payed, have given, granted, bargained, sould, & confirmed, & by these p^e^sents, Doe fully, absolutly, give, grant, bargaine, sell, & confirme, unto Robart hale, carpenter, And of the same Towne, Inhabitant, A certaine Parcell of Land, being & Lying in Charllstowne, In the East end of the Towne, in A Place called Wapping Roe, the said Land being two Acres & A Quarter of ground by estimation, more or Lesse. And it is bounded one the North side by the East feild: And one the East by Thomas Breedon: A long peece of the same ground Joyning to the fore said Acres one the South East corner being sixtene foot & A halfe broad and runs butting Downe towards the River one the South: is bounded by Richard Harrington, on the west side, & bye Thomas Breeden on the East: the other part of the ground fore mentioned is bounded on the south by Richard Harrington, Augustin Walker, Abraham Bell, John Peirce and the springe: and west by William ffoster and William harris: all which parcell And parcells of Land A fore mentioned, with all the payles, gates, posts, rayles And Trees, with all other rights, Priviledgs and Appurtenances, unto Low watter marke or else where there unto belonging: and I, James Browne, and Sarah, my wife, Doe hearby, &c.

In Witness heareof we booth have sett to o^r^ hands, being the

JAMES BROWNE.

Witnesse	I Sarah Browne Do freely
JOHN GREENE.	consent heare unto:
	SARAH BROWNE.

Acknowledged the first of the 5th mo: *52,* before me,

INCREASE NOWELL.

This Above written is A trew coppy of the oridginall compared word by word, this 26th June *1662:*

p^e^ me EDW. BURTT,

Recorder.

[174.] *A sale of Land lying And Scituat within Charlls-*
towne Lymitts By Mr *Tho. Allen unto Robert hale, both Inhabi-*
tants in Charllstowne, Written the 22^d *of the 30*th *mo : 1651.*

Know all men by These p^s*ents* that I, Thomas Allen of Charllstowne, have sould and by this Declare it : unto Robart hale,
Inhabitant in the same towne, three Acres of Arrabell Land and a
halfe, by estimation more or Lesse, which Land Lyeth and is scituate with in Charllstowne Neck in the East feild, which four Acres
and a halfe is bounded on the East sid by A Parcell of Land belonging unto Robart Hale A fore Named : it is bounded on the
South East sid by A high way : And its bounded on the North East
by the land of William Stitson : for all which four Acres And A
halfe I Thomas Allen Doe Acknowledge my selfe to be fully sattisfied And Payed for by the said Robart hale, &c., &c.

JOHN GREENE.   THO. ALLEN.

This Above written is a Trew Coppy of the oridginall Bill of
sale, Compared word by word this 26th June *1662.*

p^r me EDWARD BURTT,
Recorder,
1662.

Know all men by these p^r*sents*, that I, John Gould of Charllstowne have sould unto Robert Hale, of Charllstowne A foresaid,
two Acres of Land, more or lesse, butting upon the Land of William Stiddson on the North, and upon the said Robart hales Land
on the East, and upon the high way one the south, and upon John
March And William Breakenbury on the west, And I Doe hereby
Bind my selfe, that the said Robart hale and his heires shall
Quietly Injoy the said Land for ever without Disturbance from any
that shall Lay claime there to.

In Witnes whereof I the said John Gould : have sett to my
hand the 17th, 12th mo : *1648.*

JOHN GOULD.

Acknowledged this before me,

INCREASE NOWELL.
the marke ✕ of
JOHN MARCH.

This Above written is A true Coppy of the oridginall bill of
sale, compared word by word this 26th June *1662.*

p^r me EDWARD BURTT,
Recorder,
1662.

[175.] Upon An Arbitration between Robert Hale And Edward Converse, concerning Meddow Land overfflowed by the Mill
of the said Edward, It is agreed By us whose names are under
written, that the said Edward Converse shall pay for full sattis-
faction the sume of seven pounds to the said Robart Hale, and this
in Current Money or in Corne, or in Cattle, at A valluable consid-

eration, provided Notwithstanding, that If any part of the said meddowe be recovered out of the watter, it shall be Lawfull for the said Robert Hale to repossese the same : paying to the said Edward Converse twentie shillings An Acor for so much as he shall think fitt to make use of Againe. And further, If the whole shall be recovered, then the said Robert Hale shall Pay Backe Againe the whole sume of seven Pounds, and untell the mony be repaid as is Above Expressed, it shall be used by the said Edward Converse. Dated the said sume of seven Pounds to be paid by Edward month 1649. The payment of the said sume of seven Pounds to be paid by Edward Converse to Robart hale, shall be by the twentieth of the Ninth month Next Insueing the Date heare of

JOHN MOUSALL,

EDWARD JOHNSON,
MILES NUTT,

JOHN WRIGHT,

SAMUEL RICHARDSON,
× mark
JAMES TOMPSON,
T. mark

This Above Written Is A true Copy of the oridginall Writting, compared word by word this : Last Day June *1662.*

pᵉ me EDWARD BURTT,
Recorder,
1662.

[176.] *Know all men By these p'sents*, that I, John Martin, Late of Charllstowne, Shipwrite, Doe sell unto Robart hale of Charllstowne, Carpenter, and by These p'sents Doe Declare to have sould unto him Above said my six Acors of Land Lying in wotomies feild in Charllstowne, the which parcell of Land I Bought of Capᵗ Edward Johnson, inhabitant of Wooborne, the which Land is bounded by Mʳ Simes'on the East, And by Mʳ James Gareitt on the south, and by John Beridge on the North, &c. In witness heareof I have here unto set my hand : And seale this second Day of September 1654.

JOHN MARTIN,
Seale.

Memorandum before the sealing hereof ; it is Acknowledged that there was A few words written in a Booke of Robert hales, from the said Martin Exspresing the sale of the said Land above mentioned which being Not to be found as wel as Not Athenticke : which if it be heare after found is Not in any measur to be made use of Against the said Martin his heires or Assignes, to his Predidice.

Signed, Sealed, And Delived
In the Presents of us,
JOHN GREENE,
THO : HALE.

Acknowledged before mee the 2^d Day of September 1654.
DANIEL GOOKIN,
Magistrate.

This Above Written Is A true Coppy of the oridginall Deed, Compared word by word, this Last June 1662.

p^e me EDWARD BURTT,
Recorder.
1662.

[**177.**] *These Presents witnesseth* that I Richard Russell of Charllstowne have some three yeares since sould unto Robart hale of the same Place, one Quarter of one Cowe Common in the first stinted Common of Charllstowne, & Doe heerby Acknowledge my selfe fully sattisfied for the same; witness my hand this first Day of July: 1662:

[Petter Nash with Mr John Mansfild, booth of Charlestowne, Appeared at the Records & there the said Petter Did Acknowledge to have sould unto the said John mansfild, his grant of his wood Lott in booth Deuisions, & it is on misticke sid, to him the said John mansfild and his heires for ever, in whoes prescence he causd this record to be entred and put to his hand this 26 July *1662:* also Acknowledged him selfe to be fully Sattisfied & payd for the same.

PETER NASH.¹

Witnes
FFRANSIS NUCOM.

EDWARD BURTT,
1662.]

[**178.**] *Know all men by these p'sents* that I John Cutler of Charlestowne in the Countie of Midlesex, Smith, for and in Consideration of seaven pounds in hand by me received of and from Barnabie Davis of Charlstowne aforesaid, husbandman, &c., &c., Have granted, bargained and sould, Aliened, enfeofed and confirmed unto the said Barnabie Davis his heires and assigns for ever one small peece of Land or ground Contayning about three quarters of an Aker of Land, more or Lesse, sittuate. Lying and being on the side of Bunker hill in the East feild in Charlstowne aforesaid, bounded on the southeast by the Land of Richard Lowden, and on the southwest by the highway through the feild, and on the northwest by the Land of Nathainell Hutcheson, and on the northeast by the Land of the said Barnabie Davis; provided allwaies that the said John Cutler Doth reserve this privelidge to himselfe and unto his, that he shall and will save a way by Cart for him not only through the Land now sould, but also through a smale part of the said Davis his ground on the southeast side, or

---

¹ This is a copy made on this page by Mr. Henry H. Edes, from the original record coutained in Vol. 1 of the Treasury Series, old page 41. — ED.

the neerest way into the said John Cutlers other ground. To have and to hould, &c., &c. In wittnesse whereof I the said John Cutter have hereunto sett my hand and seale the twentieth day of march Ann⁰· 1665.

JOHN CUTLER A [𝕃 𝕊] ¹ seale.

Signed, sealed, and Dilivered
 in the pᵉsence of us,
  JAMES CARY,
  SOLOMON PHIPPS.

This is a true Coppie of the originall Deede, Attested by James Cary, Recorder. Entred heere and Recorded the 28ᵗʰ of December 1665.

[179.] Blank.

[180.] *Know all men by these pᵉsents*, That George Hepborne of Charlstowne in the Countie of Midlesex, Glover, for and in consideration of a vallewable sum in hand unto him paid before the sealing and diliverie of these pᵉsents by Thomas Rand of Charlstowne aforesaid, husbandman, &c., Doth fully, cleerely and absolutly grant, bargaine, sell, aliene, enfeofe and confirme unto the said Thomas Rand, his heires and assignes for ever one peece of Land Contayning one Aker, more or lesse, lying and being sittuate in the east fielde within the neck of Charlstow: and bounded as followeth, that is to say, on the north west bounded by the Land of John Cutler, and on the north east bounded by Mistik river, and on the southeast bounded by the Land of the aforesaid John Cutler, and on the south west bounded by the Land of Richard Lowden, To have and to hould, &c. In wittnesse thereof the George Hepborne hath heerunto sett and firmed his hand and seale the first day of Januarie one thousand sixe hundred sixtie and five — 1665.

       GEORG HEPBORNE [𝕃 𝕊]
        and a seale

Signed, sealed, and Dilivered in the pᵉsents of and the words (these, said, said may, out) interlined before sealing. wittnesse
  JAMES CARY,
  ARON LUDKIN,
  JOSIAS WOOD.

This is a true Coppie of the originall Deede.
    Attested By JAMES CARY,
      Recorder.

This sale included in this Deede was Acknowledged the 6ᵗʰ of Januerie 1665 byy George Hepborne to be his Legall Acte.
  Entred Jannaᵉ 17ᵗʰ By me RICHARD RUSSELL.

---

¹ We use this character arbitrarily to represent a drawing in the original representing a seal. — ED.

[181.] Blank.

[182.] John March, husbandman, and his wife, Anna March, for and in consideration of the sum of ffortie pounds paid by Thomas Rand, husbandman, both of Charlstowne, "Two Akers of Land, more or lesse, Lying and being sittuate in the eastfeilde within the neck of Land of Charlstowne, and bounded on the northwest by the Land of John Penticost and Robert Chalkley, and on the northest by the highway going through the feilde, and on the southeast by the highway also through the feilde, and on the southwest by the Land of Mᵣ Bates, now in the occupation of Robert Chalkly. And also the said John March and Anna his wife, for and in consideration of the abovesaid sum, selleth unto the said Thomas Rand Three Cows Commons, Lying and being within the stinted pasture without the neck of Charlstowne, the said comons to be unto him and his heires also for ever. To have and to hold, &c., &c.

[183.] Dated the first day of Januarie one thousand six hundred sixtie five — *1665.*

the mark
of
JOHN ✕ MARCH. a seale.
the mark
of
ANNA ✕ MARCH. a seale.

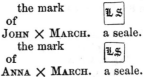

Signed, sealed, and Dilivered in the pᵉsents of us, the worde Intent and wife Interlined befor sealing.

    JOHN CUTLER,
    JOSEPH KETTLE.

This above written with that also on the other side of this leafe, is the true Coppie of the originall Deed of sale.

Attested By JAMES CARY,
Recorder.

Entred heere and Recorded Januᵣ 17ᵗʰ 1665.

Anna March, relict of John March, did Acknowledge the Legall sale of the two Akers of Land and three Cow Comons heerein owned, with the aprobation of Richard Kettle and John Cutler, overseers of the will of John March, the 6ᵗʰ of Januᵣ *1665.*

before me RICHARD RUSSELL."

[184.] *Be it known unto all men by these pᵉsents,* That I, Michaell Smith, of Maulden, in new England, in the Countie of Midlesex, planter, have made and assigned, ordained and put my wife Joana Smith in full strenth to hould all such lands, goods and chattles as I now have, to hould the full terme and time of my Jorney without any molestation, and moreover to receive all such Debts and Dues as did belong to me, I now give to my wife Joana

Smith to receive for hir use and mine; and if I never retorne, then to goe to my wife, Joana Smith, and hir assignes for ever. Giving and by these p^{e}sents granting unto my said Attorney, full power and Autheretie for me and in my name and to my only use, to sue, arreste, implead, Condemne and imprison everie of my Debters, and att hir lybertie and pleasure such p^{r}sons, and p^{r}sons out of prison to Diliver or Cause to be Dilivered, and upon the receipt of any sum or sums of money to my use to be received of any p^{r}son or p^{r}sones, acquitances or other lawfull Discharges for the same for me and in my name and stead to make, seale and diliver as my deede or deeds; and one attorney or more under hir to make or substitute, and att hir pleasure againe to revoke. And all and every other thing and all things which shalbe needfull and necessarie to be Done in or about the p^{e}mises the same to Doe, as fully and wholy as I my selfe might Doe, If I were there p^{e}sonally my selfe p^{e}sent; houlding firme and stable all and whatsoever my said Attorney shall Doe or Cause to be Done, in or about the p^{e}mises.

In Wittnesse heerof I have sett to my hand and seale nov̄ber the 8th day, 1664.

MICHAELL SMITH & a [L S]

Signed, sealed, & dilivered in the
      p^{e}sents of us all.
   JAMES CARY,
   JOHN CARY.

This is a true Coppie of the Orignalle Letter heere recorded August 23 : 1666.

Attested by
JAMES CARY,
SOLOMON PHIPPES.

[185.] Blank.

[186.] *Know all men by these presents*, That I John Coles and Ursula, my wife, of Charlstowne, for and in Consideratio of six pounds sterling to me in hand well and truly paid, by John Buridge of Charlstow, ferriman, Have bargained and sold, assigned, enfeoft and confirmed unto him the said John Buridge his heires, executors, Admistrators, and Assignes for ever, one stinted Common Lying between Charlstow neck of land and menotemies river, To have and to hould, &c. &c.

Wittnes our hands and seales this Twentyeighth day of Januarie, one thousand six hundred sixtie six, 1666.

JOHN COLLES and a [L S]

The mark of URSULA COLLS [L S]

Signed, sealed, and delivered
   in the p^{e}sents of us.
   SIMOND LYNDE,
   JOHN WOODMANSEY.

John Cole Acknowledged the sale of the Cow Comon contayned in this instrumt. Decēber 25, 1667.

before me THOMAS DANFORTH,
Assist.

Recorded heere the twentieth day of ffebrau^e: 1667,

By JAMES CARY,
Record^r.

This deede of sale was Acknowledged by Ursula Cole, as also by a letter of Attorney Left with her, bearing date Mch. the 6th, 65 ; shee doth confirme her husbands sale heerein this 18th of the 4th month, *1667*, before me,

SIMON WILLARD,
Assist.

[187.] Blank.

[188.] *To all Christian people before whome these presents shall come,*—Hugh Williams of Boston in County of Suffolk, in the Massatusetts Collonie in New England, and Hatter by Trade, with Sarah his wife, Sendeth greeting in o^r Lord god everlasting: Knowe yee that for divers good causes and considerations us thereunto moveing, especially for and in consideration of the full and just sum of Twelve pounds sterling to us in hand well and truly contented and paid, whereof we doe hereby Acknowledge to have received of John Buridge of Charlstow, ferriman, &c., Have bargained, sold, given, granted, enfeofed and confirmed unto the said John Buridge his heires, executors, Admistrators and Assignes, a certaine Tracht of Land or peece of marsh or meadow ground being Two Acres, more or less, which formerly was in the proper Tenure and possession of Mrs Catherine Coytmore, deceased, and by her as a Legacie given unto the said Sarah, the wife of the said Hugh William , being sittuate in the bounds of Charlstow, aforesaid, as it now Lyeth at Willsones Point on Mistick side, bounded by the land of George Blanchet on the northwest and by north side, and by Abraham Hills Land northeast and by east, and by the Land of the said John Buridge southerly, and the other side to the northward lyeth southeast and by East, and butteth on the north river, &c., &c., to have and to hold to him and his heires Executors, Admistrators and Assignes, &c.

[189.] In Wittness whereof wee, the said Hugh Williams and Sarah my wife, have heereunto putt our hands and seales Joyntly and severally this two and twentieth day of Aprill in the yeare o^r Lord god Everlasting one thousand six hundred sixtie and two.

HUGH ✕ WILLIAMS,
his mark and a [L S]

SARAH WILLIAMS,
and a [L S]

Signed, sealed, and dilivered
in the presents of us.
JOHN SANFORD,
RICHARD STANES.

This Deed was Acknowledged to be the Legall Act and deed of Hugh Williams and Sarah his wife the 20th of June 1663.

Before me RICHARD RUSSELL.

Recorded heere the 20th 12mo 67.

p JAM: CARY,

Record^r.

[190.] At a Legall meeting of the proprietors of the East feild, this 24th of ffebrua^r 1667, the maio^r part of them did then make choice of Lif^t Richard Sprague, William Dadie, Thomas Rand, and John Cutler, to ioyne with the overseers of the feild, Nathanell Hutcheson and Peeter ffrodingham, to settle the proportio of Each mans fence in that feild, the place where it shall stand, and that the fence sett by them shall continew for seven yeares from the date heereof. And the proprietors doe engage themselves to make and maintayne their fence, sufficent according to the towne order; that fence that the comittie above mentioned shall sett or marke unto them. In wittnes thereof we have heereunto sett our hands this 24 : 12 : *1667.*

RICHARD SPRAGUE,	NATHA^{LL} HUTCHESON,
WILL ✕ DADE's m^rke,	PEETER FFRODINHAM,
THOMAS RANDE,	BARNABIE DAVIS,
ARON LUDKIN,	JOHN CUTLER,
JOSEPH LYNDE,	RICHARD LOWDEN,
LAWRENCE DOWSE,	THOMAS CARTER,
JOHN BURIDGE,	JOHN PENTECOST,
RICH: R.K. KETTLS m^rke,	JONATHAN BUNKER.

Wee, who were appointed and chosen by the proprietors of the East feild in Charlstow̄, to measure the fence of the feild and to sett the proportion of each mans fence according to the proportiō of land that they have in that feild, we doe agree as followeth: That he that fences in the front of the feild and at the end of it shall fence fower pole and two feate for every Acre, and he that fences on the backside of the feild next to the river, shall sett up and maintaine six pole and two feate for an acre, and so p^oportionable as hee hath quantetie of Land in the said feild, more or Lesse. Jonathā Bunker is to make and maintayne the Gate at the northend of Left. Richard Spragues barne, and a fence to Drinkers Creek, and a fence against Misticke river against all his owne Land; Nathainell Hutcheson to begin his fence next to Jonathan Bunkers enclosuer to run by the river ten poles and an halfe, Joseph Stowers twelve poles and a quarter, Barnabie Davis eleven pole and a quarter, Jonathan Bunker six pole against the river and against his owne Land, and then next to him Mr Bateses Land fiftie one pole and an halfe against the river and his owne Land : next John Cutler eleven pole and an halfe, next Thomas Rand five polles, next John Cutler tenn pole and a halfe, next John Buridge five pole and three quarteres, next William Dadie nine pole and a quarter, next John ffosdick for Deacon Lynds Land nine pole and three quarters, which reaches the corner of this gener^{ll}

feild. Thomas Rand to fence seven pole at the end of the feild against Nathanell Rands close, and a pole and a halfe against Deacon William Stitson; John ffosdick more for Decon Lynds land for pole and a halfe, next John Buridge two pole; Mr Bateses Land to bear seven pole against Decon Will: Stitson; Lift. Richard Sprague to make two pole four feate betwixt Mr Chickerin and Mr Hales Land, to begin there in the line next the fence, and next Barnabie Davis three pole and a half, next John Smith five pole and two foote and a halfe, next Widow March nine pole and four foote, Joseph Lynde seven pole and three foote, Thomas Carter eight pole and four foote, next William Dadie nine pole and three foote, which reaches to the trayning close. Will: Johnson against Aron Ludkins Land two pole, Richard Kettle four pole and two foote, Aron Ludkin to make the rest of the fence to the Gate, and Will: Dadie to mayntaine the gate and the bars about the gate. [191.] John Cutler six pole and Miles Nutt two pole against Mr Trumbles Inclosure and then to begin at Mistres Longs gate into the inclosure, shee to beare eight pole and four foote; next Thomas Carter thirtie pole and fourteene foote, next Mr Zacharie Sims paster, eight poles and four foote; John Pentecost to mayntaine the gate next Robert Chalkleies and two barrs about it; next Mr Bates his land seventeene pole, Josias Wood four pole and two foote, next Samuel Carter four pole and two foote, next Seni^r and Junio^r Solomon Phipps eight pole and four foot; Beniamin Sweetsir thirty one poles, Lawerence Dowse seven pole and three foote and a halfe, widow ffrodingam twenty six pole and twelve foote and a halfe, peeter ffrodingam sixteene pole and eight foote, Nathaniell ffrodingam ten pole and five foote, Nathaniell Hutcheson twenty eight pole and a halfe against his owne land; Richard Lowden twenti six pole and thirteene foote, next Lift. Richard Sprague three pole ag^st Rich: Lowdens Land, next Thomas Rand four pole and two foote; Natha^ll Hutcheson to mayntaine the Gate and what belongs to it; Lif^t Sprague twentie three pole and three foote, which reaches to the corner of Lif^t Spragues barne by Jonath: Bunkers gate; this fencing to be made and mayntained by the proprietores mentioned suffitiently for seven yeares.

This 5th day of december, 1655, I John Gove, doe promise to pay 50^s to my Brother Edward Gove, for my father in law Mansfeild, and my mother, in full payment of his portion due to Edward from them. And that neither he nor I will ever trouble my father and mother, for any more debts or house, from the beginning of the world to this same day. And where upon I have receeved in full satisfaction a hogg and a pige. Wittnes my hand the same day above mentioned.

JOHN GOVE.

Wittnes,
HANAS SALTER hir ✕ marke,
the marke ✕ of JOHN MANSFIELD,
JOHN PENTECOST.

2 (2) called Aprill, *1630.*   Also to Mr John Mansfield, having served his brother, Mr Robert Keayne, to have a house plott.

HEZEKIAH USHER, Senio^r, *Record^r.*

[**192.**]   *Be it known unto all men by these presents,* That I, Edward Larkin of Charlestowne, Turner, for and in consideration of Tenn pounds in hand receved, Have bargained and sold unto John Gove of the Towne aforsaid one Tenement or dwelling house, with all the appertenances, as yeards, garden and ffences belonging to the same, To have and to hold, &c.   In wittness whereof I have sett my hand and seale this 29th of September, 1647.

EDWARD LARKIN and a seal.

Sealed and delivered in
the p^rsents of us
EDWARD MELLOWES,
SAMUELL CARTER.

Acknowledged the 28th 2^d m^o 1649,
before me INCREASE NOWELL.

[**193.**]   Blank.

[**194.**]   *Know all men by these p^esents,* That I, William Stetson of Charlstowne, in the Countie of Midlesex, yeoman, for and in consideration of a valleuable sum to me in hand paid before the ensealing and deliverie of these p^esents by Thomas Rand of Charlstowne and Countie aforesaid, husbandman, &c., Hath given, granted, bargained and sold, &c., ffive hay lotts and an halfe, According to the usuall Custome of hay lotts in Charlstowne, contayning more or lesse in quantetie, lying and being sittuate neere unto the North River on Mistick side, being bounded as followeth, vizt : bounded on the West by Misticke river, and on the north bounded by Richard Kettles land, and on the East bounded by Richard Stowers pasture land, and on the south bounded by Aron Ludkins Meadow, the said hay lotts lying at p^esent within the bounds of Charlstowne, To Have and to Hould, &c.   In witnes whereof I, the abovesaid William Stitson and my wife Marie Stitson, have heereunto sett our hands and seales the first day of october, in the yeare one thousand six hundred seventy one.

WILLIAM STITSON,

MARIE STITSON,

Signed, sealed, and dilivered
in the p^esents of
JAMES CARY,
RANDALE NICKELS,
JOHN NICKELLS.

This deed was Legally Acknowledged the 20th of ffebrūē *1671*, by William and Marie Stitson before me,

RICHARD RUSSELL,
Assistant.

Recorded ffebru^e 24¹ : 1671.

p JAMES CARY,
Record^{er}.

[195.] Blank.

[196.] *The Testimonie of James Tomson & John Mousall.* Memorand^a upon serious Enquiries the 6th of April, *1664.* James Tompson living in the time of these Transactiones, and John Mousell mentioned, an Acter in these things, did positively affirme that the proprietors of the land at new towne line, now Called Cambridge line, had their said land on this Condition that both the fences Inward and outward of the said feild, should be maintayned by the said proprietors Charge, and theire heires and successors for ever; thō it were then omitted to be recorded when it was first granted — for William Brackenburies deposition before a Maiestrate Concerning this thing, taken the 22^d of xi month, 1659, on the 69 page of the new Transcript.

Taken out of the new Transcript,

As atests JAMES CARY,
Recorder.

Taken upon oath by James Tomson this 7th day of June, 1672,
Before DANIELL GOOKIN.

[197.] Blank.

[198.] Blank.

[199.] *Know all men by these p^esents,* That I, George Mudge, of Charlestowne, Saylor, in the Countie Midlesex, for and in consideration of the sum of ffourteene pounds mony of new England to me in hand paid before the ensealing and Diliverie of these p^esents By William Wellsted of Charlstowne, Mariner, &c., Have given, granted, bargained and sold, &c., unto the abovesaid William Wellsted, his heires and Assignes, One peece or platt of ground lying and being sittuate in Charlstowne aforesaid, the which I bought of John Cole, it sometime being a part of the said Cole's orchard, contayning in the front next the land or back street runing by a line on the front fence, sixtie four foote in length, and on the Southeast side runing up towards the house, ffiftie two foote on a line; and on the Southwest side next the house, And on the northwest on a line ffiftie four foote, And is bounded on the southeast by the land of Thomas Smith, and on the Southwest bounded by the uper part of the said Cole's orchard, and on the northwest bounded by the land of William

Johnson: the said platt of ground lying in a certaine place, **or** called the backstreet, leading from the Creek or little bridge towards the neck of land, the said back streete northeast bounding the said peece of ground or land.   To have And to hold, &c. In witness whereof I the aboves^d George Mudg have heereunto sett my hand and seall the twenty-third day of december, one thousand six hundred seventy two.

GEORGE **C M** MUDG   ⊔ §

his marke

Signed, sealed and delivered
   in the p^esents of
    NATHANIEL CARY
       and
    JONATHAN CARY.

This is a true Coppe of the original deed,

as Atest JAM: CARY,
Recor°.
Janua° 7th 1672.

This deede was Legally Acknowledged to be Signed, sealed, and dilivered by Georg Mudge as his Legall Convayance to William Wellsted the 25th of December, 1672,

Before m̄e RICHARD RUSSELL,
Assistant.

[200.]   Blank.

[201.]   *Know all men by these presents*, that wheras Samuel Ballat, John Heyman, James Russell, John Phillips, Samuel Heyman, James Elson, Nathan Heyman, and John Cutlar, Juni^r, all of Charlestowne in New England, haveing lately purchased a peice of Marish land of Beniamin Lathrop, Senr, In Charlestowne, as may appeare more at large in a deed of the same to us made and delivered, to which this Instrument hath a Speciall reference, doe for our selves, our heires, Executors, Administrators and Assignes, Covenant to, and with the said Lathrop and his heires for ever, that hee himselfe, his heires and Assignes for ever, shall have free egresse, ingresse and Regress, to the Wharfe there intended to bee made, to laud, lay, import or transport whatsoever wood, timber, wares, or whatsoever lumber or trade for his and his heires or Assignes particuler improvement, In such quantity, manner and times, as may not bee to the damage, detriment or disappointment of all or any of the proprietors, as is provided in the fore mentioned deed of sale, without any the least let, hindrance, contradiction or opposition of them the abovesaid proprietors, or their heires or Assignes for ever.   In wittness wherunto the said Samuel Ballat In the name and with the Consent, and in the presence of the rest, hath hereunto set his hand and seale this fiifteenth day of September, Anno Dom. One thousand six hundred seventy Seven Annoq̄ Regni Regis Carolj Secundi **XXIX.**

SAMUEL BALLAT. 〔L S〕

JO^N HAYMAN, 〔L $〕

JOHN CUTLER, 〔L S〕

In the name of the Rest.

Signed, sealed, and delivered
    in presence of us,
   JOHN LONG,
   BENJAMIN TOMPSON,

This is A true Coppy of the Originall Agreement.
And Recorded here July 15th 1686.

                Attest JN^o : NEWELL,
                         Record^e.

The Bounds of the Land sold the Owners of the dry Dock: A plat of Marsh Land scittuate before the said Lathrops Doore, in Charlstown Already staked out, Containing in the front Ninety foot in width, No. Westerly Towards the great Street, running thence bakward to the Creek, between Two parralell Lines, haveing the Land of John Heyman on the East, the Land of John Blany being in quantity more or Less, Together with A high way of Ten foot in Breadth, to run through the Remainder of the said Lathrops Land, from the purchased said Land to the Street Close to the said Heymans Land with all the priviledges and appurtenances therunto belonging, And the said Lathrop reserving the priviledges abovesaid.
    Aprile 16th, *1700.*

              Entre^d by NATH^{LL} DOWS,
                        Town Clerk.

[202.] Blank.[1]

[203.] This Indenture made the Twenty Fift day of Janewary in the fourth year of her maj^{ties} Reigne anno Domini one thousand seven hundred and five^{six}, Between Charles Chambers, merch^t, Eleizer Phillips, victular, Jonathan Dows, Shipwright, Ebenezer Austin, Sadler, John Tuffs, yeoman, Robert Wyer, Inholder, and Eleizer Bateman, house Wright, all of Charlstowne in the County of Midd^{sx}, within her maj^{ties} Provinc of the Massachusetts bay in New England, Committe for the said Towne of Charlstown of the one part: and John Wesson, of Reding, in the County aforsaid, yeoman, of the other part: witnesseth, That the

----

[1] The following note is made by Mr. Edes in the original : —
   " The fourteen following folios were brought to this volume from the end of Town Records, Vol. VI." — ED.

said Charls Chambers, Eleizer Phillips, Jonathan Dows, Ebenezer
Austin, John Tuffs, Robert Wyer and Eleizer Bateman, for the
only use, benifit and behoofe of the Inhabitants of Charlstown,
aforesaid, For and in Consideration of the Rents and Covenants
herafter in and by these presents reserved and conteined, which
on the part of the said John Weson are to be paid, done, and
performed, Have demised, Granted, betaken, and to farm Letten,
And, by vertue of A power, to them derived from the Inhabitants
of Charlstown, at their Legall and Generall meeting the 25th Day
of December, Anno Domini one thousand seven hundred and four,
by these presents doth demise, grant, betake, and to farm Lett,
unto the said John Wesson, one Certaine messuage or Tenement,
Scittuate, Lying, and being within the Limitts and bounds of said
Town of Charlstowne, and belonging to said Town; conteining
one Dwelling house, Twenty Two foot Long, Eighteen foot wide,
Twelve foot stud, with a seller under it, and good Chimneys in it,
and one barn, Twenty Eight foot Long, Twenty Foot wide, and A
Leanto at the end, and Land adjoyning Containing one hundred
and sixteen acres, be the same more or Less, and an orchard of
Fruit Trees aboute Two acres, fenced intire, the whole Tract being
butted and bounded as foloweth : vizt, easterly by Grays Land,
northerly by Reding Line, Southerly by the Towns Farm, Lett
said Wesson Last year, and Westerly partly by the Country Rode
and partly by the Town Farm Lett to Williams : or howsoever
the same is otherwise butted and bounded, as it is sett forth in A
plat of the same : With all the Rights, Wayes, profitts, Commodities and Apurtenances thereunto belonging, Reserving only
aboute Eight acres of medow in said Tract, which is allready
Leased to Williams, To Have and To Hold the said Messuage or
Tenement and all other the above demised premises, unto the said
John Wesson, his heirs and assigns, from the first day of March
next ensuing the date herof, unto the full End and Term of
Twenty years from Thence next Ensuing, and fully to be Compleat
and ended. Yeilding and paying therfor unto Nathaniell Dows,
Treasurer of said Towne of Charlestowne, or to his successors in
said trust and office, for the only benifit of said Town, the yearly
Rent of seven pounds p^r year in Current Money of New england,
at, on or before the first day of march yearly, and every year,
during said Term of Twenty years. And the said John Wesson,
for himself, his Heirs, Execut^rs, adm^rs and Assigns, doth hereby
covenant, promise and grant to and with the said Charls Chambers, Eleizer Phillips, Jonathan Dows, Ebenezer Austin, John
Tuffs, Robert Wyer, and Eleizer Bateman, their heirs, Execut^rs,
adm^r and Assigns, in manner and form following : (that is to say) :
that he, the said John Wesson, his heirs, Execut^rs, Admin^rs or Assigns, or some of them, shall and Will Well and truly pay or
Cause to be paid the yearly Rent in manner and Form as aforsaid. And also shall and will Well and suficently (at his or their
Cost and charge) Support, maintaine, repair the said house, barn,
fencis, with all the needfull and nessesary repairations and Amendments, during this Term aforsaid [204.] and Keep the said
orchard fenced intire during said Term with a Good sufficent fence,

either stone wall or good posts and rails, and the said Dwelling
house, barn and fencis aboute all the land he shall improve Well
and sufficiently Repaired and Amended: So as to make it every
way Tenantable at the end of said Term of Twenty years. Shall
and will peaceably and quietly Leave, yeild up and Surrender the
same unto the said Comitte, their heirs, &c., or to the Town
Treasurer for the Time being, for the only use, benefit and behoofe
of the Towne of Charlstowne. Finally, the said Charls Chambers,
Eliezer Phillips, Jonathan Dows, Ebenezer Austin, John Tuffs,
Robert Wyer and Eleizer Bateman, doth herby Covenant, promise
and grant to and with the said John Wesson, his heirs and Assigns, that he or they paying the Rents and preforming the Covenants and agreements above mentioned, shall and may Lawfully,
peaceably and quietly have, hold, use, occupy, possess and enjoy the
said messuage or Tenement and all other the above granted premises for and during the term of Twenty years as abovesaid, with-
oute the Lett, deniall, trouble or disturbance of the said Comitte,
or their heirs, or the Inhabitants of Charlstowne, as aforesaid. In
witnes wherof the parties above named to these Indentures have
Interchangably sett their hands and seals the day and year first
above written — Before signing it is agreed that the money for
Rent above mentioned is to be paid in such money as to the
Weight therof as shall be passable commonly among the merch^{ts}
and Inhabitants Comonly in this province — the words and Reserving only Eight acres of medow in said Tract which is allredey
Lett to Williams, is found not to be in said Tract, and therfore
this Lease is not to have any referance to said words:

Enter^d befor signing —

Signed, sealed and DD in
   the present of us.

[**205.**] *This Indenture*, made the Twenty Sixt day of January, Anno Domini one thousand seven hundred and four f^{ive} in
the third year of her Maj^{ties} Reigne, Between Charls chambers,
March^t, Eleizer Phillips, Victilar, Jonathan Dows, Shipwright,
Ebenezer Austin, Sadler, John Tuffs, yeoman, Robert Wyer, Inholder, and Eleizer Bateman, Yeoman, all of Charlstowne in the
County of Midd^{sx} within her Maj^{ties} Province of the massachusetts
bay in New England, Committee for the said Town of Charlstowne,
of the one part, and John Wesson, of Charlstowne, aforesaid, yeoman, of the other part, Witneseth, &c., by these presents, Doth
demise, grant, betake and to farm Lett unto the said John Wesson, one Certain Tract or parcel of Land, scituate, lying and
being within the Limitts and bounds of Charlstowne aforesaid, and
belonging to said Towne, Conteining ninety-one acres and one-
half: be the same more or less, being butted and bounded as
followeth, vizt: northerly, by the Towns farm, now in the Tenour
and occupation of said John Wesson; westerly, partly by Timothy
Baldwin, and partly by the high way; southerly, by the said
Towns Land, and easterly by the Gray's Land; or, howsoever, the
same is otherwise butted and bounded as it is sett forth in A Platt
of the same, with all the rights, wayes, profitts, Comodities and

Apurtenances therunto belonging, Reserving Ten acres in said Tract for wood Land which the said Wesson is hereby prohibited Cutting any wood or Timber standing and growing theron, which said Ten acres for wood Land is to lye when said Committe and said Wesson shall agree it shall be in said Tract, To Have and To Hold [for 21 years from March 1st next, paying a rent of 12^d per year for the first ten years, and £5 per year for the other eleven years,] &c., &c. And also shall and will Erect, Build and finish upon said Land, A Dwelling house which shall be Twenty foot Long, and Eighteen foot wide, nine foot stud [**206.**] Between Joynts and A Leanto at the End, Twelve foot Long, the width of the house, six foot stud, and shall Digg and sufficiently ston a Conveinent seller under said house, and shall build and carry up A Double Stack of Brick Chimneys to A Convenient height above the house, and shall lay Two good floors in said house, and shall fill the walles Between the studds and ceile them with plained boards or Lime morter, and shall make Conveinent stairs, and shall board or clabboard the outside of said house, and board and Shingle the Roofe to make it every Way thite, and make Conveinent Lights in said house and Glaze them. And shall erect and build on said Land A Good barn, thirty foot Long and Twenty foot Wide, and Cover the same on the Sids, Ends, and Roofe to make it thite. And : at his own proper cost and charge Suport, maintain, Repair, and Amend the said house and barn with all needfull repairations and Amendments During said Term. And shall also plant Two acres of said Land with Good fruit Trees for an orchard, the trees to be planted thirty-three foot Assunder, and Fence said orchard intire with A Good sufficient fence aboote the same : and make and maintaine A Good sufficent fence, ston Wale or posts and Rails aboute what Land he improves. And the said Land, together with all the buildings theron that shall be erected theron as afforsaid, So well and Sufficiently repaired and Amended, With the orchard well fenced intire, and all the Land he shall Improve sufficiently fenced as aforsaid, at the end of said Term of Twenty-one years shall and will peaceably and quietly yeild up and Surrender the same unto the said Committe, their heir, &c., or to the Town Treasurer for the time being, for the only use, benifit, and behoofe of s^d Towne of Charlstowne. &c., &c .

In witnes wherof the parties above named to these Indentures have interchanebly sett their hands and seals the day and year first first above written.

Signed, sealed, and D.D. in the
    presents of us   JOHN WESSON.
       JOSEPH LEMMONS,
       BENJ^A SWEETSIR.

[**207.**] *A Copey of the Lease of Lovils Island.*
This Indenture, made the third day of August, in the year of our Lord one thousand Six hundred ninety and six, and in the eight yeare of the Reigne of our Sovereigne Lord William the third,

King of England, &c., Between James Russel, of charlstowne, in the county of midd^{sx}, within the province of the massachusetts bay in Newengland, Esqr one of the Selectmen of the aforsaid Towne, of the one part, and George Worthylake, of Boston, in the county of Suffolk, within the province afforsaid, Planter, of the other part, Witneseth, That the said James Russel, with the consent of the rest of the Selectmen of the said Town, etc., Hath demised, granted, betaken and to farm letten, &c., unto the said George Worthylake, all That, the Island commonly called and Known By the name of Lovels Island, Lying, Situate and being between the broad and the Ship channel, within the Limits and bounds of Boston aforsaid, with all the Lands, profits, priveledges, rights, commodities, Buildings, and appurtanances whatsoever theirunto belonging (Reserving Liberty for the making and drying of Fish upon the Shoar of the said Island, next the watter, as in the grant of the General court is provided, which said Island doth of right belong and appertaine unto the aforsaid Town of Charlstown, and now in the tenure and occupation of the said George Worthylake, To Have and To Hold the said Iland, &c., for the term of Twenty six years from thence Nex ensuing, yeilding and pay therfor, &c., the yearly Rent or sum of Ten pounds Current money of New England, by two even and equall portions or payments in the year; that is to say, Five pounds on the first Day of November, and five pounds on the first day of may, yearly.

And the said George Worthylake, for himself, &c., doth hereby covenant, &c., that he, the said George Worthylake, his heirs, ex$\bar{c}$cut^{rs} and ad$\bar{m}$istrat^{rs}, or Asigns, or some of them, shall and will erect, build and finish A Dwelling house upon the said Island which shall be Twenty foot Long, Sixteen foot wide, and eleven foot stud; and shall digg and well and sufficently stone A good convenient Celler under the said house, and shall Build and cary up a good Strong Stack of chimneys, to Be built with Stone from the foundation to the mantletree, and from the mantletree upward with good bricks, to A convenient height above the roofe of the house, and Shall Lay two good floores in the said house, and shall fill the Walls between the studds and ceile them with good plained boords; and shall make two paire of stairs, one pair down into the Celler, and the other pair up into the Chamber; and shall board the Walls of the said house, and board and well Shingle the roofe so as to make it every way thite; and Shall make convenient Lights in the said House and well Glaze the same; and shall at his and theire owne proper Cost and Charge from time to time, and at all Times During the aforsaid Term, when and often as need shall Require, Well and Sufficiently repair, [**208.**] support, maintaine, and Amend the said Dwelling house and the barne Now Standing one the said Iland, With all needfull and necessary repairations whatsoever, etc.

In Wittness wherof the parties above named to these Indentures have interchangably sett their hands and Seals the Day and year first above written.

Signed, Sealed, and D.D. in the
    presents of us.

[209.] Blank.

[210.] Blank.

[211.] This Indenture, made the Twenty third Day of February, in the Third year of her Maj^ties Reigne, Anno Domini one thousand seven hundred and Four^five, Between Charles Chambers, march^t, Eleizzer [Phillips], Victular, Jonathan Dows, Shipwright, Ebenezer Austin, Sadler, John Tuffs, yeoman, Robert Wyer, Inholder, and Eleizer Bateman, yeoman, all of Charlstowne, in the County of midd^sx, within her maj^ties province of the massachusetts bay, in new england, Committee for the said Towne of Charlstowne, of the one part, and Stephen Williams, of Wobourn, in the County aforsaid, yeoman, of the other part, Witnesseth that the said Charls Chambers, &c., &c., " lets unto the said Stephen Williams one Certaine Track or parcel of Land Scittuate, Lying and being within," &c., " Containing Two hundred acres, be the same more or Less, being butted and bounded as foloweth, vizt : South East by the high Way Leading from Reding to Charlstowne, Northerly by Redding Line, Westerly by Wobourn Line, and Easterly by the Town of Charlstowne Land, or howsoever the same is butted and bounded as it is Sett forth in a platt of the same : and also one piece of meddow Land lying and being within the Towns Farm, now in the Tennour of John Wesson, With all the Wayes, rights, profitts, privilidges, Commodities and Appurtenances therunto belonging : Reserving Eighty acres of said Tract for Wood Land, which the said Williams is Prohibited Cutting any Wood or Timber, Standing or Growing theron ; which said Eighty acres of Wood Land is to Lye Where said Comitte and said Williams shall Agree it shall be in said Tract : To Have and To Hold the said Tract or parcel of Land and meddow Land Containing aboute Eight acres, and all other the above Demised premises unto him the said Stephen Williams, his heirs, Execut^r, Adm^rs, and Assigns, from the first day of March, next ensuing the Date herof unto the full end and Terme of Twenty one years from thence next Following, and fully to be compleat and ended. Yielding and paying therfor yearly, &c., and for the first Ten years of the said Term, the Rent of Twelve pence p^r year, in current money of New england : at, on, or before the first Day of March yearly ; and for the other eleven years of said Term of Twenty one years, the full and just sum of five pounds Ten shillings p^r year, in current money as aforsaid, at, on, or before the first Day of March, yearly, and every year During said Term of Eleven years : and the said Stephen Williams," &c., &c.

[212.] " And also shall and will erect, build and finish upon said Land A Dwelling house wich shall be Twenty Two foot Long and Eighteen foot wide, nine foot studd between joints, and a Leanto at the end of said house Twelve foot Long, the bredth of the house, six foot stud, and shall Dig and sufficienty stone A Convenient Seller under said House, and shall build and cary up a Double stack of Brick Chimneys to A Convenient height above the house, and shall Lay two floors in said house, and Leanto and fill the Walles Between the Studs and Ceile them with Plained boards or Lime morter on the inside, and shall make Convenient Stairs, and shall board or Clabord the outside of said house, and board and Shingle the Roofe, to make it every Where Thite, and make Convenient Lights in said house, and Glaze the same : And shall also erect and build A barn upon said Land Thirty foot Long and Twenty foot wide, and Cover the same on the Sides, Ends and Roofe, to make it thite ; and at his owne proper Cost and charges suport, maintaine, Repair and Amend the said house and barn with all needfull Repairations and Amendments during said Term. And shall also plant Two acres of said Land with Good fruit Trees, for an Orchard, the Trees to be planted thirty Two foot asunder, and Fence said orchard intire With A Good sufficent fence aboute the same, and make and maintaine A Good sufficent fence stone Wall, or posts and Railes, aboute What Land he Improves ; and the said Land, medow, house, barn and fences erected and sett up on said Land as above said, so well and sufficiently repaired and Amended : with the orchard sufficiently fenced intire, and as above expressed, all the improved Land so fenced : as above said at the end of said Term of Twenty one years, shall and will Leave, &c. In witness wherof the parties above named have to these Indentures interchangably sett their hands and seals the day and year first above Written.

Signed, sealed, and D.D. in
the presents of us.

[213.] Blank.

[214.] This Indenture made the fourteenth day of August, &c., &c., Between Charls Chambers & others, committee, &c., of the one part, and Thomas Goold, husbandman, and Daniel Goold, Cordwainer, both of Charlstowne, Witneseth, &c., doth demise, grant, betake and to farm Lett unto them, the said Thomas Goold and Daniel Gould one certaine Tract or parcel of Land, Scituate, Lying and being within the Limitts and bounds of charlstowne Aforsaid, and belonging to said Towne, Containing one hundred and Ten Acres, be the same more or less, being butted and bounded as foloweth, vizt : northerly by Land in the possession of Timothy Baldwin, Easterly by Land now Lett to John Wesson, Southerly by Land of Kendall Parker, and Westerly by Land of Peter Heys : as it is sett forth in A Platt of the same, Together with all the wayes, profitts, privilidges and Apurtanances therunto belonging, Reserving fifteen acres in said Tract for Wood Land, which the said Goolds are herby prohibited Cutting any wood or Timber Standing or Growing theron, which said fifteene acres of Wood Land is to Lye ware said Committee and said Thomas Goold and Daniel Gould shall agree it shall be in said Tract. To Have and To Hold, &c., from the first day of March Last past unto the full end and Term of Twenty one years, &c., yeilding and paying therfor yearly and for the first Ten years of said Term, &c., the rent of Twelve pence p^r year in Current money of

new england at, on or befor the first day of March yearly, and for
the other eleven years of said Term of Twenty one years the full
and just sum of five pounds p^r year in current money, as aforsaid, at, on or before the first day of March yearly, and every year
During said Term of eleven [years].   And the said Thomas Goold
and Daniel Goold, &c., doth herby promise, bargayne and agree
to and with the said Charles Chambers, &c. that they the said
Thomas Goold and Daniel Goold, &c., shall and will well and
truly pay, or cause to be paid, — the yearly rent in manner and
Form as aforsaid.   And also Shall and Will erect, build and
finish upon said Land A Dwelling house [of the same dimensions,
&c., as in the previous indenture. — ED.]   [**215.**]   and build
A barn upon said Land [on same terms as preceding indenture. —
ED.]   And shall also within Two years fence in Two acres
of said land, for An orchard, and plant it [same terms as the
preceding. — ED.]   In witness whereof the parties above named
have to these Indentures Interchangably sett their hands and seals
the Day and year first above written.

THOMAS GOOLD.
DANIEL GOOLD.

Signed, sealed, & D.D. in
   the presents of us,
  STEPHEN KIDDER,
  THOMAS LORD,
  JOHN EDMANDS.

[**216.**]   Blank.

[**217.**]   This Indenture, made the Twenty sixt day of January,
Anno Domini one thousand seven hundred and four^{five}, and in the
third year of the Reigne of our Soveraigne Lady Ann, Queen of
England, &c., Between Charls Chambers, &c., &c., Committe for
the Towne of Charlstowne: of the one part, And Timothy Baldwin, of charlstown, aforsaid, yeoman, of the other part, Witneseth
That the said Charls Chambers, &c., Hath demised, granted, betaken, and To farm, Letten, &c., unto the said Timothy Baldwin,
on Certain Tract or parcel of Land Scittuate, Lying and being in
the limitts and bounds of Charlstowne, and being the Land of said
Towne, Conteining Eighty six acres and four pole, be the same
more or less, being butted and bounded as followeth, vizt: South,
erly partly on Said Timothy Baldwin and partly by Andrew Beard-
Northerly by the County Rode Leading from Reding to Wobourn,
and Easterly by the Towns Land, or howsoever the same is otherwise butted and bounded so as it is sett forth in A plat of the
Same, with all the wayes, profitts, privilidges, Rights, Commodities and Apurtenances therunto belonging, reserving fifteen acres
for wood land which is to be laid out ware the said Committe shall
apoint, which said fifteen acres of wood land Said Baldwin is
herby prohibited Cutting wood or Timber growing theron, butt may
fence it in for pastures, To have and To Hold the said Tract or
parcel of Lands and all other the above demised premises unto the
said Timothy Baldwin, &c., from the first day of march next ensue-

ing the date herof, unto the full end and Term of Twenty one years from thence next following and fully to be Compleat and ended, Yeilding and paying therfor yearly, &c., the yearly Rent of Four pounds Ten shillings p^r year in Current money of New england, at, on, or before the first day of March, yearly and every year, during said Term of Twenty one years. And the said Timothy Baldwin, &c., hereby Covnant, promise and grant, in manner and form following (that is to say) that he, the said Timothy Baldwin, his heirs, execut^r, or Adm^{rs}, or Assigns, or some of them, shall and will Well and truly pay, or cause to be paid, the said yearly rent in manner and Form as aforsaid. And also shall and will at his own cost and charges make, maintaine, repair and uphold all the fencing needfull for all and so [218.] much of said Land he shall Improve of said Tract, and the said Land with all the fencing that shall be sett up above what Land he shall improv, well and sufficently repaired and Amended at the end of said Term of Twenty one years shall and will peacably and quietly leave, &c.

In Witnes wherof the parties above named to these Indentures have Interchangably sett their hands and Seals the Day and year first above written.

Signed, Sealed & DD. in the   TIMOTHY BALDWIN,   [L S]
presence of us.
    THOMAS FROTHINGHAM,
    NATH^L DOWS.

[219.]   Blank.

[220.] This Indenture made the Seventh day of October in the first yeare of the Reigne of our Soveraigne Lady Ann, Queen of England, &c., Anno Domini one thousand Seven hundred and Two, Between Nathaniel Dows, of Charlstowne in the County of Midd^{sx}, within her Maj^{ties} province of the massachusetts bay in new England, Treasurer of said Towne of the one part, and Eleizer Bateman, of charlstown Aforesaid, yeoman, of the other part, Witnesseth That the said Nathaniel Dows, with the Consent of the Selectmen of said Towne by power derived from the vote of the Inhabitants of said Town the Second Day of March, Anno Domi. 1701–2 as by Towne Records doth Appear, For the only use and benifit of the Inhabitants of said Town, For and in consideration of the Rents and Covenants hereafter expressed, Hath demised, granted, betaken, and to Farm Letten, &c., unto the said Eleizer Bateman fourty five acres of Land, be the same more or Less, Scituate, Lying and being within the Limitts and bounds of Charlstowne aforesaid in the Second Division of wood lotts on Mistick side Which Land is the Draught of Richard Russel. Esqr, dec^d, numbered (68) and by him Given to his Son, Mr Daniel. Russel, Who gave said Land to the Town of Charlstowne aforsaid, To Have and To Hold, &c., from the first Day of December next ensuing the Date herof unto the full end and Term of Twenty years from thence next ensuing, &c., Yeilding and paying yearly, &c., the yearly Rent of Twenty five shillings in money or merchantable corn at money price yearly and every year During said

Term. And also said Eleizer Bateman, &c., doth herby Covenant, &c., that he, &c., will well and Truly pay, &c., the said yearly Rent in maner and form as aforsaid. And also to pay all publick Taxes To Town, Church and province said Land shall be Assessed on or for said Lands. And also Leave A good and sufficient fence aboute what and so much of said Land he hath or shall break up and further doth oblige himself, his heirs, &c, not to fell nor permitt to be felled any of the wood or Timber growing on said Land No otherwise than for fencing And Clearing such land as he shall Improve by breaking up & howing, &c. Finally, the said Nathaneell Dows, &c., doth herby Covenant, &c., [that said Bateman] shall and may Lawfully, peacably and quietly have, hold, use, occupy, posses and enjoy the said land and premises aforsaid, &c.

In witnes wherof the parties above named have hereunto Interchangably Sett their hands and Seals the Day and year first above written.

Signed, Sealed, and DD. in the   Eleazer Bateman, [L⅊]
presence of us
    Samuel Griffen
    Thᵒ Lord, Junᴿ.

[221.] Blank.

[222.] This Indenture made this Twentieth day of May, in the thirteenth year of her majᵗⁱᵉˢ Reigne Anno Domini one thou- sand seven hundred and fourteen, Between Nathaniel Dows of Charlestown, Treasurer, &c., and John Gowin of Lynn in the County of Essex, husbandman, of the other part, witnesseth, that the said Nathaniel Dows, Treasʳ, by ordʳ of the selectmen of Charlestowne, aforesaid, and with their consent psuant to the vote of the Inhabitants of the said Town at their Generall meeting the 1ˢᵗ of Marche Anno Dominj one thousand seven hundred and thir- teen, as in their 6ᵗʰ book of Reccords, page 108, doth apear, &c., hath demised, granted and to ffarm Letten, &c., unto the said John Gowin all that their ffarm appertaining to the poor of the said Town of Charlestown : Conteining Ninety acres, be the same more or Less, Scituate, Lying and being at Bever Dam̄, within the Limitts and bounds of said Lynn in the County of Essex, Together with all the fencings, privilidges and appurtanances therunto belonging or apperteining. To Have and to Hold, &c.. from the 1ˢᵗ day of May Last past unto the full end and term of seven years from thence next ensuing, &c., yeilding and paying therfor for the first year five pounds, and yearly during said term afterwards five pounds Tenn shillings p. annum in Current money yearly, &c. And the said John Gowin for himself, his heirs, Executʳˢ, admʳˢ and Assigns, Do herby Covenant, promise and grant, bind and oblige themselves, &c., That is to say, that the said John Gowin or his heires, executʳˢ, &c., shall and will well and truly pay or cause to be paid unto the said Nathaniel Dows, Treasurʳ, or to his successors in said Trust, the yearly rent in manner as aforesaid, and at their own cost and charge Support, amend and repair all the fence belonging therunto, and at the end of said term to surrender and peacably and Quitily Deliver up said ffarm, well and sufficenly fenced, with a good post and rail fence aboute all said ffarm [**223.**] unto Nathaniel Dows, &c., and the said Nathaniel Dows, &c., doth covenant, &c., [that the lessees] shall and may Law-fully, peacably and Quietly have, hold, use, occupie, possess and enjoy the said ffarm, &c. In witness wherof the parties above named have to these Indentures Interchangably sett their hands and seales the day and Year first above written.

JOHN GOWING
and seal   [𝔏 𝔰]

Signed, Sealed, & Deliver^d
    in the p'sence of us,
    RICH. HILTON,
    BENJ^A Dows, Junr.

———

[**224.**] This Indenture made this Sixteenth day of ffebuary in the Eleventh yeer of the reigne of our Sovereigne Lady Anne, Queen of England, &c., Anno Domini One thousand seven hundred and twelve-thirteen.

Between Nathaniel Dows of Charlestown in the Countie of Midd^x, within her maj^{ties} province of the massachusetts bay in New england, Treasurer for the said Town on the one part, & John Underwood of Charlestown aforesaid, yeoman, of the other part, *Witnesseth That* the said Nathaniel Dows, with the Consent of the Select men of the said Town, by power Derived from the Select men to him, persuant to the vote of the Inhabitants of Charles-towne may the 21th *1712*, &c., *Hath* demised, granted and to ffarm letten, &c., unto the said John Underwood, *all* that peice or parcel of said Townes meadow lying in Spott pond meadow, with some upland adjoyning therto, running upon a strait line from the sluce to the southermost end of the Northeast part of Carringtons necke of land bordering theron next the pond, lying and being within the limitts and bound of Charlestown aforesaid, To Have and To Hold the said peice or parcel of meadow and Upland from the first day of march next ensuing the date herof, unto the full end and term of Ten years from thence next ensuing, &c., paying Therfor the yearly rent of Sixteen Shillings p. year, and for every year during said Terme, at or before the first day of March yearly, unto the said Nathaniel Dows, &c. And the said Jno Underwood for himself, his heirs, Execut^s, Adm^s and assignes, doth herby Cov-enant, &c., to pay, or cause to be paid, unto Nathaniel Dows or his sucess^{rs} in said trust and office, the yearly rent in manner and form as aforesaid, and also leave a tennentable ffence upon that part of the land at the end of the said Term that he shall Improve by ffencing. Finally the said Nathaniel Dows, &c. [Covenant for quiet possession. — ED.] [**225.**] In witnes wherof the parties abovenamed have to these Indentures = Interchangably sett their hands and seales the day and year first above written.

    Signed, Sealed, and Deliv^d :
        in the presence of us :

JOHN TUFTS,	Memō agreed upon by Lessor and
THEOP: IVORY.	Lessee before Signing and Sealing,
	that the Lessee at the Expiration of

said Term shall peacably and quietly yield up and surrender all the 10 ffarme Lotts p'mises, with the appurtenances as afforesaid, unto the Lessor or to his success'* in said office, for the propper use and benifett of said Town of Charlestown.

JOHN UNDERWOOD & seal.

This Indenture the twenty eight day of may, Anno Domini 1713 and in the Twelfth year of her maj^{ties} reigne, Between Jn° Brintnall of Charlestown, in the County of Midd^x in New England, Tanner of the one part: and Nathaniel Dows, Treasur^r of the said Town in the name and by order of the selectmen of the said Town on the other part, Witneseth: That Whereas their is a Small slip of Land belonging to the said Town partly inclosed in and with the lands of the said Brintnall, at or near to a place called South Spring at Mistick side, extending forty foot in the front at the high-way and so running Down towards the marsh ten poles & a half to a stake and so to a point; the line between the said Brintnall's Land and the said slip of Towns land to run parrelell and strait with the said Brintnals land or house lott over the way: and the said slip of land being Convenient for the said John Brintnall, Now therfore for and in consideration of the yearly rent and acknowledgement of two Shillings yearly and each year to be paid by the said Brintnall, his heires, &c., unto Nathaniel Dows, Town treas^r, or his successors in his said office, for the use of the said Towne, Thes said Nathaniel Dows, treas^r as aforesaid, and by order of the select men of said Town as aforesaid, Doth by these presence lett and Grant to the said John Brintnall, his heires, &c., the said slip of Land: and also the Libberty or privilidge of the watter wch shall run through the said slip of Townsland from south Spring: for and During the Term of Twenty yeares from hence next ensuing to be Compleat and Ended. And I, the said Jn° Brintnall, Do by these presents for myself, my heires, execut^rs, and Adm^rs, promise and engage to pay the said yearly rent and Acknowledgements of Two shillings to the said Nathaniel Dows, Treas^er or his successors in said office for the use of the Town yearly and each year during the said Term, and at the end of the said Term to yield up and surrend^r the said slip of Land to the possession of the said town. In witncss wherof the said Jn° Brintnall and Nath. Dows, Treas^r have herunto Interchangably sett our hands and seales the day and year above written.

Signed, Sealed, & Deliv^d in p'ence
of us   JOHN BRINTNALL,
 EDW^D LARKIN,   & seal.
 ELEAZ^R DOWS.

[226.] This Indenture made the Twenty eight day of May, Anno Dom: 1713, and in the twelfth year of her maj^{ties} reigne, between Samuel Stower of Charlestown, in the County of Midd^sx in Newengland, yeoman on the one part, and Nathaniel Dows,

Treas^r. of the s^d Town on the other part, Witneseth That Wheras there is a small peice or corner of land: belonging to the said Town Enclosed in and with the land of the said Stowers at or near a place Called South Spring at mistick side Extending Sixty and three foot in the front at the highway: and running Down aboute ten poles and a half on a line to Brintnals and Mellowes lowermost stake: and there to run across the meadow in Spring gutter twenty four foot to an other stake against the said Stowers land: and thence up to a stake by the said Stowers upland and Orchard: and so up to a stake in Spring Gutter at the ffront in the fence Lying between a slip of the Towns land Lett to Mr Jno Brintnall and the said Stower's own land: and the said small corner of the Towns land lying and being Convenient for the said Stowers: Now therefore, for and in Consideration of the yearly rent and Acknowledgement of three shillings and six pence yearly and each year to be paid by the said Stowers, his heires, &c, unto Nathaniel Dows, Treas^{er}, or his successors in this said office, for the use of the said Town: The said Nathaniel Dows, Treas^r as aforesaid and by order of the selectmen of said Town as aforesaid, Doth by these presents grant and Lett to the said Samuel Stowers, his heires, &c., the said Corner or peice of land for and During the term of twenty yeares from hence next Ensuing to be Compleated and Ended, and the said Stowers shall not stop the passage of the Watter in the said land Coming out of South Spring: nor alter or turn it out of the Natturall course: And I, the said Samuel Stowers, do by these presents, for myself, my heires, execut^{rs}, & Adm^{rs}, promise and engage to pay the said yearly rent and Acknowledgements of three shillings & six pence to the said Nathaniel Dows, Treas^r, or his successors in said office for the use of the Town yearly: and each year during the said term: and at the end of the said to yeild up and surrender the piece and Corner of land to the possession of the said Town. In Witnes wherof we, the said Samuel Stowers and Nath^{ll} Dows, treasurer, have herunto Interchangably sett their hands and seals the day and year above written.

Signed, Sealed, & Deliver^d in the
    presence of us   SAMUEL STOWERS
      JOSEPH LAMPSON,   & seal.
      JOSEPH WHITTEMORE.

[**227.** Charlestowne, ffebruary the 27th, 1713–4.
Psuant to the vote of said Town at their gennerall meeting, may 1713, In Answare to the motion of John Slaughter, of lynn, for hireing a small bitt of land belonging to said Charlestown in the bound of lynn, it was then Voted by the Inhabitants to leave it with the Selectmen to lett the said bitt or peice of Land for a term not Exceeding seven years: and the select men of said Charlestown having some of them been on the said land and making report to the others of them: the select men think it reasonable, and Accordingly have granted and to ffarme letten to the said Jno Slafter one Certaine peice of the said Land containing about Two acres

and a half being Swamp ground bordering on the said John
Slaughters own land, lying and Extending from the said Slafters
land to the brow or pitch of the Hill in the said lott, being one of
the lotts laid out to said Charlestown ffarm in the Township of lynn :
the said Slaughter to keep up and Carfully maintaine the bounds
of the said lott and to pay or cause to be paid annually the yearly
rent of eight shillings and six pence p. year during the said term
of seven yeares to the treasurer of the said Town for the use of the
said Town : in all amounting to the sum of Two pounds nineteen
shillings and six pence : — for the true performance wherof I, the
said John Slaughter bind and oblige myself, my heires, execut^rs,
administrat^rs by these presents. In Witnes Wherof I have herunto sett my hand and seal the twenty seventh day of ffebruary,
one thousand Seven hundred and thirteen – fourteen and in the
twelf year of her majesties reigne.

Signed, Sealed, & Deliver^d in the   his
    presence of   JOHN 8 SLAFTER,   ⎍ℒ𝒮⎍
    JOHN BROWN,   mark.
    JOSEPH SIBLE.

[228.] This Indenture made the fifteenth day of July, in the
thirteenth year of his maj^ties reigne, Anno Domini one thousand
seven hundred and fourteen, Between m^rs mary Edmands of Charlstown, in the County of midd^x, in new england, widow, of the one
part, and Nathaniel Dows, Treas^r of said Town of Charlestown of
the other part, Witnesseth that the said mary Edmands For and in
Consideration of the yearly rents and Covenants in these presents
here after Expressed, Hath demized, granted and to ffarm letten :
and by these presents doth demize, grant and to ffarme letten unto
him, the said Nathaniel Dows, Town treas^r as aforesaid and to his
success^rs in said Trust and office for the only use of the said Town,
One Dwelling house, out housen and Land adjoyning, scittuate,
lying and being in Charlestown aforesaid, late the possession of
Capt Richd Sprague, decee^d, To Have and To Hold the said Dwelling house and housing and Land adjoyning from the day of the
date herof for and during the term of the natturall life of the said
Mary Edmands, Yeilding and paying therfor the yearly rent of
Eight pound ten shillings p. year and every year during said
term of her natturall life, and for every part of a year that she
shall Live proportionably to the rent above mentioned, at, on, or
before the fifteenth day of July annually. And the said Nathaniel
Dows, treasurer, for himself and success^rs in said trust and office, by
order of the select men of the said Town of Charlstown, persuant
to the vote of the Inhabitants at their generall meeting the 1st of
may, in 1714, 1713–4, and at their general meeting the 18th of
May, 1714, doth Covenant, promise, bargaine, and Agree, bind
and oblige himself and his success^rs in said trust and office as
Treas^r on account of the said Town of Charlestown, well and truly
to pay the rent and rents as above written : and if the said house
should happen to be burnt, or by any Extroordinary providence

should be lost, yett not withstanding the said rent to be paid unto
the said mary Edmands in manner and form aforesaid. And
Finally, the said Mr Mary Edmands for herself, her heires, doth
herby Covenant and promise, bargaine and Agree, bind and oblige
themselves to and with the said Nathaniel Dows, Treas^r, and his
successors in said trust and office, paying the rents as above
written, shall and may Lawfully, peacably and quietly have, hold,
use, Occupie, possess and enjoy the said Dwelling house with the
appurtenances for the only use, benifett and behoof of the Town
of Charlestown for and during the term of the naturall life of the
said mary Edmands without the Lett, trouble, denial or Contradiction of her, the said mary Edmands, or any by, from or under
her. In Witnes wherof the parties above named have to these
Indentures Interchangably sett their hands and seales the day and
year first above written.

Signed, Sealed, and D^d in the   MARY EDMANDS,
   presence of us   & seal.   [L S]
   THO^s LORD,
   ROBERT CUTLER.

[229.] This Indenture made this first day of December in
the first year of the reigne of our Sovereigne lord King of great
Brittaine, &c., Anno Domini one thousand seven hundred and
fourteen-fifteen between Mr Mary Edmands of Charlestown in the
County of Midd^x within his maj^ties province of the Massachusetts
bay in New england, widow, of the one part, and Nathaniel Dows,
Treasurer of said Town of Charlestown, of the other part, Witnesseth that the said mary Edmands For and in Consideration of
the yearly rents and Covenants in these presents herafter Expressed, Hath demized, granted and to ffarm letten : And by
these presents doth demize, grant and to ffarm lett unto the said
Nathaniel Dows, Town treas^er as aforesaid, or to his successors in
the said trust and office, for the only use of the said Town : One
Dwelling house, out housings and Land Adjoyning Scittuate, lying
and being in Charlestown aforesaid, now in the possession of M^r
Simon Bradstreet of Charlestown aforesaid, To Have and to Hold
the said dwelling house, housing and Land adjoyning from the
day of the date herof for and during the term of the naturall life
of the said Mary Edmands : yeilding and paying therfor the
yearly rent of six pounds p. year and every year during said term
of her nattural life, and for every part of a year that she shall live
proportionable to the rent above mentioned at, on, or before the
sixth day of March annually, and the said Nathaniel Dows treas :
for himself and successors in said town and office (by order of the
select men of the said Town of Charlestown psuant to the vote of
the Inhabitants at their gennerall meeting) doth Covvenant, promise,
bargaine and Agree, bind and oblige himself and his Successors in
said Trust and office as treasurer on account of said Town of
Charlestown, well and truly to pay the rent and rents as above
written, And if the said house should happen to be burnt, or by
any extriordinary providence should be lost, yett notwithstanding

the said rent to be paid unto the said Mary Edmands in manner and form as aforesaid. *And* Finally the said Mary Edmands for herself, her heires, &c., doth herby cov^t, promise, bargaine and agree, bind and oblige themselves to and with the said Nathaniel Dows, Treas^r, and his successors in the said Trust and office, paying the rents as above written, shall and may lawfully, peaceably and quietly have, hold, use, occupie, possess and enjoy the said Dwelling house and Appurtanances for the only use, benifett and behoofe of the Town of Charlestown for and during the term of, naturall life of the said Mary Edmands, or any, by, from or under her. In Witnes wherof the parties above named have to these Indentures Interchangably sett their hands and seales the day and year first above written.

MARY EDMANDS

Signed, Sealed, & D^d in   & seal   𝕃 𝕊
     the presence of
     SAMUEL BURR,
     BENJ^A DOWS.

[The following leaf (pp. 230 and 231) was brought to this place by Mr. Henry H. Edes, from the front cover of Town Records, vol. II., Greene's Transcript. — ED.]

[**230.**] This Indenture, made this third day of June Annoq̄ Domini One thousand seven hundred and Seventeen, in the third year of his maj^{tie} reigne, between Nathaniel Dows, Town treasurer of Charlestown, of the one part, and Richard Boyleston of Charlestown, aforesaid, Cordwainer, of the other part witnesseth as followeth: That the said Nathaniel Dows, town treasurer as aforesaid, by vertue of A power to him derived from the Selectmen of said Town, June the third (*1717*), For and in consideration of the rents and Covenants in these presents herafter expressed, Hath demized, granted and to ffarm letten, and by these presents doth demize, grant and to ffarm Lett unto the said Richd Boyleston, his heires, &c., One certaine peice or parcel of marsh land comonly known by the name of the horse pasture, belonging to the said Town, lying and being in said Town at Moulton's point, To Have and To Hold the said marsh unto him the said Richard Boyleston, his heires, &c., from the day of the date herof for and during the full end and term of seven yeares from hence next Ensuing, and fully to be Compleat and ended: he *Yeilding* and paying therfor unto the said Nathaniel Dows, town treas^r, or to his successors in said trust and office, the yearly rent of fifteen shillings yearly and every year during the said Terme, at, on, or before the third day of June. And the said Nathaniel Dows for himself and successors in said trust and office, doth Covenant to and with the said Richd Boyleston, that he paying the rents and performing the Covenants as above said, shall and may Lawfully, peacably and quietly have, hold, use, Occupie, possess and enjoy the said marsh and appurtanances therof without the Lett, denial or contradiction of him, the said Nathaniel

Dows, Treasurer, or his successors in said office, as treasurer for during the term of seven yeares, as aforesaid. In witnes wherof the parties above named have to these Indentures Interchangably sett their hands and seales, the day and year first above written.

RICH^D BOYLESTON
& seale.

Signed, sealed, & Deliver^d,
in the presents of us,
NATHAN^{LL} WILSON,
BENJ^A PHILLIPS.

[**231.**]   Blank.

[It appears from a note by Mr. Edes that the remaining folios in this book originally constituted the final part of Town Records, Vol. II. (Greene's Transcript), being 36 leaves, or 72 pages. These are original records, and begin with the Survey of the town highwayes made in 1670. The original reports of the Surveys of 1767 and 1802 are also preserved in the City Clerk's office, and vary somewhat in some details. These now printed are, however, the formal and attested record, and it has not seemed necessary to collate them with any earlier drafts. —ED.]

CHARLESTOWN STREETS IN 1670.

[232.] In pursuance of an order from the Selectmen, bearing date February 20th 1670; Impowering Sergt Richd Kettle. William Dady & Sergt Lawrence Dowse, to measure the breadth of the Highwayes in this Towne: This following Returne was made to the Selectmen by the said persons, viz.

FISH–STREET. — From the Ferry-way unto the corner of Capt. Allen's pales, from thence over to Samuel Carter's shop, is thirty eight feet.

BROAD–STREETE. — From Mr. Shepards House unto the extent of Mr. Hilton's Land, the breadth from Mr. Shepards over to Mr. Chickerings, is Thirty five feet: from Mr. Hiltons over to Capt. Spragues is Twenty-four foot & a halfe.

HEPBURNES LANE. — From the House formerly Mr. Hepburnes, downe to the Bridge, the way at ye upper end is Eighteene foot, at the lower end twenty four foot.

WAPPIN STREET. — From the Bridge unto Deacon Stitsons is Thirty three foot, as farre as Mr. Kings and from thence to Deacon Stitsons is Twenty eight foot, at Mr. Kings it is nineteene foot.

There is a way to a Dock (wch Issues out of this street) betweene Tho. Brigden & Jno Smith, the breadth whereof is twenty four foot & a halfe.

There is a way to Low-water mark, on the East side of Mr. Blackmore's Land, wch is Three pole wide, at least.

There is a way to Low-water mark, Issuing out of Fish-street, & passeth on betweene John Larkin, & the shop Improv'd by Jno. Mirick, downe by Joshua Ted's Salt house — the way betweene Mirick & Larkin is thirty seven foot, & betweene the Salthouse & the Wharfe is twelve foot.

From Deacon Stitson's to the Barres at Mr. Nowel's pasture is sixteene foot.

MOULTONS POINT. — From Tho. Shepie's gate to Moultons point is Sixteene foot & a halfe.

From the aforesaid Barres, thorow Deacon Stitson's pasture to the great field, & thorow that downe to the gate by Serg^t Lowdon's, is all the way sixteene foot & a halfe.

From the aforesaid gate, knowne by the name of Chalkly's gate, up into the afore-said field Highway, is sixteene foot & a halfe, except in the middle of theLane between M^r. Greene and M^r. Symmes pasture, where it is Twenty three foot.

From Thomas Rand's ground unto Laur. Dows's ground, lying from the way betweene M^r. Greene's & Jno. Penticost, leading streight downe to Benj^a. Sweetsir's ground, the breadth where of is twelve foot.

The way betweene M^r. Trumbal's & John Drinkers unto the Fort is fourteene foot.

The way from M^r. Trumbal's into Wappin-street, by Jno Smith's new house, at Jno. Smith's Twenty foot, at M^r. Trumbal's Eighteene foot.

SHEPIE'S LANE. — From Jo^o. Candage unto Tho. Shepie's by Candage is thirty one foot, by Shepie is Twenty-five foot, in the middle Twenty one foot.

From Shepie into the Training field, the way is Eleven foot.

SMITH-STREET. — From Aaron Ludkins to Nathaniel Kettle's corner, at Ludkins Twenty six foot, at Kettle's fifty one foot, in the middle forty seven foot.

BACK STREET. — From the Bridge by William Clough's to the field gate by Goodm̄ Chalky's is Thirty seven foot, at Solomon Phipps, Senior, his Barne, it is Twenty five foot.

COLE'S LANE. — From Tho. Smith's down to Back streete, at the upper end Thirty three foot, at the Lower end Thirty seven foot.

From Back streete into the Training field, by John Scots, is Twenty foot.

HILL STREET. — From Thomas Lord's up to the Town house hill is Twelve foot.

GRAVEL LANE. — From Town house Hill into Broadstreete, by M^r. Shepard's, at the upper end is five foot, at the Lower end is six foot & a halfe.

STREETER'S LANE. — From the Market-place downe to Tho. Adams, at the upper end ten foot, at the Lower end by Adams, nineteene foot.

From M^r. Symmes lower corner, over against Tho. Chadwels, the way leading to the Meeting House is Twenty six foot.

SCHOOL-LANE. — From Nathaniel Kettle's, to M^r. Willoughby's, and Kettle's Twenty two foot, at M^r. Willoughby's fifteene foot.

[**233.**] HIGH STREET. — From M^r. Willoughby's downe to Jno. Whitman's shop, at the upper end fifteene foot, at Tho. Peachee's Thirty foot, at Jno. Whitman's Twenty foot.

GRAVE STREET. — From Templar's to Mrs Graves, at Templar's Twenty foot, at Mrs Graves Twenty three foot.

PRAT'S LANE. — From Grave-streete to Tho. Brigden, senior, is six foot.

BOW–STREETE. — From Faintnot Wines to Henry Balcom, at Wines Twenty one foot, at Tho. Orton's Twenty six foot from Jn° Penticost to Henry Balcom Thirty three foot.

BRIGDEN'S–LANE — From Bow-streete to the River is Twelve foot.

HALE–STREETE. — From Bow-street to Edw⁴ Johnson, Senior, is sixteene foot.

MIDDLE–GATE. — From Thomas Rands to Math. Smiths, at Rands Thirty eight foot, at Smiths Thirty two foot.

ROPEMAKER'S LANE. — From the Town-House-Hill to Jn° Penticost, at the upper end Twenty five foot, at the Lower end Twenty two foot.

MALT–STREETE. — From Jn° Penticost to the River, at the upper end Twenty foot, at the lower-end by Deacon Lyndes Thirty foot.

WAS–STREETE. — From Henry Balcom's to the Causway at Neck of Land, at Balcom's sixty foot, at Solomon Phipps fifty foure foot, at Serg⁴ Lowden's Thirty Nine foot.

Entred per order of the Select men,

per LAUR : HAMMOND, *Record'*.

[DOINGS OF THE PROPRIETORS OF THE STINTED PASTURE. 1680–1686.]

[**234.**   Charles Town, 1680 : ffebuary : 14ᵗʰ.

Att a meeting of the proprieto'rs of the Stinted Common, as to a laying out a part of it, Then was put to Vote these ffollowing proposalls, & all of them past In the affirmative : —

1.   That there should be one Acre & a halfe layd out to a Common.

2.   Where they would have this Land layd out, it was Voted & past for the neer' or hither part of the Comon.

3.   Whether this Land should be for ever or for year', It past for a good Inheritance in ffee Simple.

4.   That a Comitte may be Chosen for the heareing & proveing & confirmjng of the Title' of Clajmer' to the respective Commons.

5.   The Committee were then Chosen by Vote, & are viz.

M' Joseph Lynde   ⎰ Capt. Ric⁴ Sprague ⎱
James Russell Esq' ⎱ Leiu⁴ Jn° Cuttler   ⎰ Capt Lar : Hammond

6.   That Serg⁴ Ric⁴ Lowden, Josiah Wood, Sn', and Tho : White be Impow'd to gether Up the Rent due to yᵉ proprieto'rs, wch mony is to be delivered to sd Comitte for defraying of Charges that arise by Surveying, Laying out & Clearing of, &c.

7.   That the Common be measured by the Care of ye Committee so that ye numb' of Acres thereon may be known.

8.   That it be left wth ye Comitte wch are Empowered to raise mony proportionable from Each Common to defray yᵉ Charge that may arise on the aforesd worke of the Comon.

9.   That the highwayes betwixt yᵉ ranges be Twenty four ffoott wide.

Voted by the above said, Xᵇʳ 19th, 1681.

1.   That the foresd highwayes be made & maintained by the proprieto'rs In Common.

2.   That a liberty be given to those y⁴ please to draw their proportion' in one Lott.

As Attest, JOHN NEWELL, *Record'*

[235.] Charles Town, 1681. Wee, the Comitte chosen and Impowerd by the Proprietors of the Stinted Comon⁸, in Charles Towne, on this Side Mistick river, for to Examine the claime⁸ of the Sever¹¹ proprietors, and to allow of Such as wee judged right, And also to lay out one Acre & a halfe of Land for each Comon, And doe accordingly allow of these ffollowing Three hundred Thirty and one Comons to belong to these ffollowing p^rson⁸, & have Laid out to them according to ord^r, one acre & a halfe, Excepting Some few that did compound with sd comitte for less land then their proportion in regard of their owne convenience, wch p^rmises was agreed unto and Confirmed by A Unanimous Vote of the sd Proprieto^rs at a Legall meeting, January the Second, 1681.

Attest : JN^o. NEWELL, *Record^r*.

To Sergt. Richard Lowden, six Common⁸	6
To Nathaniel Huchison, five Comon⁸ & three quarters .	5¾
To Sergt. Thomas Welch, six Comon⁸ & a quarter . .	6¼
To Sergt. Jno. Cuttler, Two Commons	2
To John Goodwin, Two Common⁸	2
To Thomas Jone⁸, bu^ch^r, his Estate, one Common . .	1
To John ffowle, ffour Common⁸	4
To Petter Fowle, ffive Commons	5
To the children of Deacō Rob^rt. Hale, dec^sd., five Commons	5
To George ffowle, Three Common⁸	3
To W^m. Johnsons⁸ Estate, Three Common⁸ and a halfe, wch . halfe Comon is but for Tho. March life, wch ended, it is Jno. March	3½
To Solomon Phipps, Three Common⁸ and a halfe . .	3½
To Jonathan Kettle, Two Common⁸	2
To Samuel Bicknell, Two Common⁸	2
To Samuel Kettle, Two Common⁸	2
To Joseph Kettle, one Common and a quarter . . .	1¼
To Nathaniel Kettle, one Common	1
To Thomas Joan⁸, mason, his Estate, Two Common⁸ . .	2
To Petter ffrothengham, Three Common⁸	3
To Nathaniel ffrothengham, Two Common⁸. . . .	2
To Samuel ffrothengham, one Common	1
To Thoma⁸ White, Three Comon⁸ & a halfe . . .	3½
To Thomas Rand, Senr, Seven Common⁸ and a halfe . .	7½
To Ensigh Jno. Call, one Comon and Three quart^rs . .	1¾
	76

Each one of these above sd Common⁸ Attested to

By JOHN NEWELL, *Record^r*.

[236.] To Samuel Lord, Two Common⁸ & three quarter⁸ Comon 2¾

To Thomas Welch, jun^r., one Common and three Eights Comon 1⅜

To Thomas Moussall, Three Common⁸, & in 4th book, one Comon, 4

To Deacō Aaron Ludkin, one Common	1
To James Miller, jun^r., Seven Common^s and halfe Cōmon.	7½
To Elias Rowe, Six Common^s	6
To Widow Pratt and her son Joseph Pratt, one Common	1
To Goble^s Estate, Two Cōmon^s, wch are possessed by Tho. Cresswell, who says hee did purchase them wth the other lands of Goble	2
To Samue Ward, ffour Common^s and a halfe Common	4½
To Capt. Rich^d. Sprague, Eleven Common^s	11
To Deacon John Cuttler, Two Common^s	2
To Daniel Davison, ffour Common^s	4
To Barnabas Davis, Two Common^s	2
To John Penticost, Three Common^s	3
To James Russell, Esqr., ffour Common^s and halfe Common,	4½
To M^r. Dan^{ll}. Russell, Estate, one Common	1
To M^{rs}. Elizabeth Graves, one Common	1
To M^{rs}. Prudence Russell, Estate, one Common	1
To Ensign Thomas Lynde, Three Commons	3
To the Church of Charles Town, ffour Common^s.	4
To John Smith, Two Common^s and a halfe, wch halfe Cōmon is but for Theo: March^s life, wch ended, it is his son Jno. March^s .	2½
To M^{rs}. Parnell Nowell, Three Commons	3
To Thomas Adam^s, sen^r, one Common	1
To M^r. Joseph Lynde, ffourteen Common^s	14
To Capt. Thomas Brattle, Three Common^s	3
To Susanna White, ffour Common^s	4
To William Bullerd, ffour Common^s and a quarter Cōmon	4¼
To the widow of Samuel Pearce, Eight Common^s	8
To Joseph Bachlor, one Common and a quarter Cōmon	1¼
To Thomas Carter, Senr, ffive common^s	5
To Widow Gold, Three Comon^s and three quarters Cōmo	3¾
To Benjamin Sweetser, one Common	1
To Samuel Carter^s Estate, Two Common^s and a halfe Cōmon	2½
To M^r. John Long, ffive Common^s	5
To M^{rs}. Anna Shepherd, Two Common^s	2

125⅞

Each one of these above sd Cōmon^s Attested
By John Newell, *Record^r*.

[237.]   Charles Town, 1681.

To Robert Leach ffour Common^s	4
To John Moussall, Sixteen Common^s and one Eighth of a Cōmon .	16⅛
To William Powell^s Estate, Two Common^s possessed by John ffoskitt .	2
To Laurance Dowse, Six Common^s	6
To Timothy Cuttler, one Common	1
To Abraham Smith, ffour Common^s	4
To Nathaniel Rand, ffour Common^s	4
To the heires of George or Jonath. Bunker, Ten Commons^s	10

To Thoma' Jenner, Two Common'	2
To Samuell Lynde Estate, Two Common' . . .	2
To Joʌn Burrage, Two Common'	2
To Sergt. John ffosdike, ffour Common and halfe a Common,	4½
To Thomas Dean' heires, one Common	2
To Josiah Wood, Sen'., ffour Commons	4
To Xopher Goodwin, Sen'., Two Commons . . .	2
To ffrancis Willoughbuy, Esq'., his estate, fflve Common' ⎫ and a halfe Common wch is in Capt. Lar. Hammond ⎬ possession . . . . ⎭	5½
To the Estate of Deacō Tho. Lynde, possessed by his widow, Rebecah Lynde, Two Common'	2
To John Blaney, Two Common'	2
To the widow of Capt. Wᵐ. Hudson, One Common . .	1
To Jacob Green, Sen'., Two Common' yᵗ were Eldʳ Green',	2
To Jnᵒ. Roy, One Commō	1
To Mʳ. Samuel Phipp', one Common	1
To widow Phipps and her son Joseph Phipps, Three Coᵐon', ¾	3¾
To Capt. Timothy Wheeler, Eight Common' . . .	8
To Zechariah Brigden, One Common	1
To Mʳ. John : Phillips, One Common	1
To William Dawdy, Seven Common'	7
To Thomas Lord, one Common	1
To John Joan', Two Common'	2
To Leiuᵗ. Randale Nichole, Two Common' . . .	2
To George ffelch, one Commō : improved by Ensign Tho Lynde	1
To John Kent, one Common	1
To the heires of Mʳ John Checkrin Estate, ffour Common'.	4
To Ebenezur Astin, one Common	1
To Mʳˢ. Sarah Allen, one Common	1
To John Trumble, Seⁿ., Two Common'	2
	114⅞

Each one of these abovesd Common' Attested by Jnᵒ. Newell,
    Recorᵈʳ.
[238.] Blank.
[239.] Blank.
[240.]

To the wor. Thomas Danforth, Esqʳ., ffour Commons .	4
To Mʳˢ. Kathrine Graves, one Common	1
To John Whitemore, Snʳ., One Common	1
To William Burage, one Common	1
To the Estate of Mʳ. Zech. Symes, Senʳ., Two Commons .	2
To Mʳ. James Cary Estate, Two Common' and quarter Coᵐon	2¼
To Jnᵒ. Heyman, one Common	1
To the·Estate of Timothy Symes, One Common . .	1
To Thomas Sheppie, One Common	1
	14¼

Attestt   Jnᵒ. NEWELL, Recordʳ.

Charles Town, Decemb^r. 15th, 1681.

The Committe Appointed to Oversee & manage Sundry matters relateing to the Stinted Pasture, Usually Called the Common, Lying without the neck of Land in this Town, doe Signifie to the proprieto^rs as ffollowth.

First, that wee have wth much paines & Care, examined ye Sundry Claims that have been made by any persons unto A propriety in the Sd Comon, or Stinted pasture; And doe find the respective proprieties, or numbe^r of Common^s mentioned in A Lis herewth presented; to be the clear & Honest rights of the persons respectively named in the Sd List. All wch doe Amount unto the Numbr of Three hundred Thirty one Common^s.

Secondly, that the proportions of Commons of right belonging to each p^rson as in the Aforesd List are Expressed, Shall be Confirmed by the proprietors, may be Recorded in the Town book, to Stand as their proper Estate to them And their heires for Ever, the Charge of recording to be paid by the proprieto^rs: This wee propose as necessary for the future Settlement of the right of each proprieto^r; for the prevention of all after disputes relateing there Unto.

Thirdly, Wee conceive it necessary that one Acre & A halfe of Land to A Common (According to the Vote of the proprietor^s), be Laid out at the hither end of the Comon, Excluding all necessary Highwayes, both publicke and private.

Fourthly, Wee propose that the peice of Land lying next the Towne, Viz.: from Jno. Mousall^s gate, Upon A line Over to the lower Corner of Thomas Crasswell^s Land, all y^t Land wthin that line Unto the neck of Land, be Left in Common for publick Military Exercises, &c.

Fifthly, It will be necessary y^t the laying out of the proportions of Land to Each Commoner, or proprietor, be referred Unto A Committe of meet p^rsons to be chosen together with the Artist, who are to Regulate the Same, According to their best discretions, in the most Equitable manner; the proprietors Voted the first Committe to manage this 5th Article.

Sixthly, y^t Lotts be made by the sd Committe, & Numbred according to the Number of the proprieto^r, who, upon timely notice given, shall meet & draw their Lotts, and according as the Number of their Lotts shalbe So, Shall their proportions of Land be Laid out neer or further off, the Line to begin at Jno Moussall^s.

Seventhly, That the Remainder of the Common wch lies Undivided, bee cleered of brush & Superfluous Trees; y^t it may be renderd fitt for pasturage, & y^t it be referred to the Committe to contrive the most Expedient wayes to Effect it.

[241.] Eighthly, That it be likewise referred to the Committe to Order the fencing of the Common Against M^r. Ledgits ffarme, as may be according to their best discrestion^s most Accomodable to ye poprietor^s.

9ly, that Each range be forty poles in Length: And that the land on the South Side of Cambridge Road butting to the marshes, of this side of Tho. Crasswell brook, may be Left to the Committe for to Agree with the proprieto^{rs} of the Sd marsh for Sd Land, on as profitable Terms for the proprieto^{rs} of the Common as they Can.

10ly, That a range of Lotts begin at Widow Peirces (by the Country road, of ffour poles wide) and So to Abraham Smith & so on the Westrly side of the highway Successively Unto Patrick Marks, Untill that Land is Laid out: All these foregoeing Ten Votes past in the Affirmative the day before s^d by y^e Proprieto^{rs}.

Attest: J$^{N^o}$. NEWELL, *Record^r*.

The Committe proposed to the proprietors of the Stinted Common as Foll: 2^d Janvary, 1681.

1ly, To propose the Conveniency of proceeding as farr as Johnson^s Lott from Patrick Marks, in Laying out Land to those who Adjoyn to it, and shall desire it, Leaveing open sufficient watering places.

2ly, That Such Proprieto^{rs} As shall not Improve their Land, but Suffer itt to lye Unfenced, Shall have no benifitt of feed in the Comon thereby, more then by right of Commons they now have.

3ly, Thomas Peirce moves y^t A triangle of Land lying on the upper Side the highway before his Land & under the Land of Father Bullard may be granted to him, in part of his proportion, wch the Committe Judges reasonable, & noe damage to the proprietor^s.

4ly, Thomas Welch moves y^t he takeing Six Acres of bad Land lying before his house below the highway, he may have allowed him three Acres of Land above the highway, Adjoyning to his Land, for wch he is willing to Allow Three quarter^s of an Acre.

This Third & fourth Vote Left to the Committe.

5ly, The high way Above the ffourth Range to be Three pole wide, it being A road y^t wilbe much in Use, It begining between ffoskitts & Huchison^s Land, & run^s Cross over to Welch^{es}.

6ly, That what Land is Already Laid out to perticuler person^s by ye Approbation of the Committe, by Vertue of A power given them by the proprietors, be now Confirmed to the sd person^s as their Estate, to them their heyres & Assignes for ever: Provided y^t the rest of the proprietors have their proportions in the remainder of the land to be divided, be accordingly Confirmed.

7ly, That noe person shall have his Land Laid out after he hath drawn his Lott, Untill he hath A Certificate Under the hand of the Record^r, Signifying the Numb^r of Acres to be Laid out to him.

8ly, That the land y^t is not to be laid out in this divission, but remain^s In Common, Shall not be Charged with any ffence Against the Land y^t is now to be Laid out.

These Eight Abovesd Votes were past in the Affirmative by y^e proprieto^{rs} at their meeting the day Abovesd.

Attest: J$^{N^o}$. NEWELL, *Record^r*.

[242.] A Record of the Land^s Laid out unto such person^s proprieto^{rs} in the Stinted Comon, who drew no Lots for Said Lands, but by agreem^t wth the Committe had their Lands laid to them so as might best suit their particular convenience, the same not lying wthin the range' for wch Lots were drawn, the said Committe being Impowered by the proprieto'rs. to Act therein according to their best discretion', as Appear' in the fifth Article Voted the 15th day of December *1681* in fo : 75.

To Cap' Richard Sprague on the Left hand as you goe to Cambridge Three quart'' of an Acre, more or less, Adjoyning to Jn°. Bickn''ˢ.

To Mʳ. Joseph Lynde Two parcell' viz. three quart'' of an Acre more or less next Cap' Sprague & Eighteen Acre' by Edward Brazier', wch is bounded by the way to James Miller' & by Cambridge road — sd Eighteen Acres to stand be it more or Less.   - -

To Jn° ffoule next Mʳ. Jo Lynde Three quar'' of an Acre, be it more or less.

To Thomas Lord next Jn°. ffoule halfe an Acre, & next Eliza Sym' halfe an Acre, be sd parcells more or Less.

To Elizabeth Sym' one Acre & halfe more or less Lying between the Lands of Thomas Lord.

To Solomon Phipps next Tho Lord, ffive Acres, be it more or Less.

To Jame' Miller in Two parcells, Nine Acres, more or Less, wch Lyes nigh Solomon Phipps.   -   -   -   -   -   -

To Mʳ Samuel Ward & to Mʳ Tho Graves six Acre' one quarter, be it more or Less.   -   -   -   -   -   -   -   -

To the bull Lot Three quarter' of An Acre more or Less, wch lye' between Sam¹ Ward & James Miller his mowing Land, & the bull Lot, a high way lying through Sd Lot to the meadow'.   -   -

To Thomas Welch Senʳ in two parcell' Nine Acre' one quarter, more or Less, Cambridge road passing betwixt them.

To John Kent before his house one Acre, more or less.

To the widow of Samuel Pearce in three parcell' Eleven Acre' more or less, Two : of the parcells by her house & the Third betweē Mʳ James Russell' Land & the watering place & Land of Tho Danforth E'qʳ.

To Abraham Smith one quarter of an Acre, more or less, by his house.

To Mʳ James Russell five Acres & one quarter more or less — on the right hand goeing to Cambridge & ioyning to Susana White : more in right of Cap' Ric Sprague : Mʳ Dan¹ Russell, Mʳˢ Eliza Grave', MʳˢPrudence Russell and himselfe Twenty-one Acres & A halfe Acre Adioyning to sd White South East : the brook South West, Widow Pearce North West, & by the four pole high way North East, that sᵈ high way begining at Widow Pearce' house & so runeth between the Lots & Issueth out by the Land of Ben¹. Bowers.

To Susana White Six Acre', more or less, lying between Mʳ Russell his Land.

There is A watering place (Lying between the Lands of Widow Pearce & Tho Danforth Esqʳ) Contayning Three quarter' of A acre more or less.

To Thomas Danforth Esqʳ Eleven Acre' & A halfe measured to him, Lying by that Land Comonly called Johnson' Lot, of wch parcell Six Acres was laid out to him in right of four Comon[s] & five Acres & A halfe he designed them to buy, which was purchast by him 7[br] : 29 : 1684, as may be seen in 4th Book, fo. 35.

[**243**.] Charles Towne, *1681*. Then here followeth the names of the proprieto[rs] wch did draw Lotts, and According to the Number drawn, Each one of their proportion[s] are recorded, viz. :

N[o]		Acres	N[o]		Acres
1	John Whetemoor . . .	1½	26	Thomas Rand . . .	11
2	Laur Douse	9	27	John Mousall. . . .	24
3	Samuel Phipps & company,		28	Sarah Allen	1½
	M[r] Jn[o] Phillips &c.		29	Isack Johnson . . .	4½
4	Tho. White & Companj,viz.		30	Wido. Mary Gold . .	7⅛
	Peter: Nath[l]. & Sam[l].		31	M[r] Jn[o] Long	7½
	Frothengham[s]. Jos. Sam[l]		32	Jn[o]. Smith	3
	Nath[l] & Jonath. Ketles,		33	Tho. Creswell & Goble .	3
	Geo ffoule, Mary Hudson.		34	Xoph[r] Goodwin . . .	3
5	Tho. Mousall	4½	35	Cap[t] Laur Hamond . .	8½
6	Tho Carter	7½	36	Zech Brigden	1½
7	M[r] Tho Brattle . . .	4½	37	William Daudy . . .	10½
8	Jn[o] Foskit	9	38	Jonath. Crouch ⅌	
9	Solomon Phipp[s] . . .	4½		Tho Joan[s] Estate . }	3
	M[r] Tho Jenner . . .	3	26	Jn[o] Penticost	4½
	M[rs] Rebecca: Lynd[e] Sn[r].	3	40	Cap[t] Tim[o] Wheeler .	12
	Rebeccah Lynde jun[r] .	3	41	Dan[l] Davison . . .	6
10	Edward Wilson, &c.. .	7½	42	Richrd Lowden . . .	9
11	Nath[l] Huchison . . .	8⅝	43	Tho. Welch	2
12	The Church	6	44	Jn[o]. Cutler	3
13	Tho Adams	1½	45	Ebenez[r] Astin . . .	1½
14	Jos Bacholer	1½	46	M[rs] Parnell Nowell . .	4½
15	Jn[o] Goodwin & S Bick[nll].	6	47	Sam[l]. Carter[s] Estate .	3¾
16	Major Savage	3	48	Elias Row	9
17	Randal Nichole . . .	3	49	Jn[o] Joanes	3
	Aaron Ludkin	1½	50	Samuel Lord . . .	4⅛
	Deaco Jn[o] Cutler . . .	5	51	W[m] Bullerd	3⅜
18	Nath[l]. Rand	6	52	Jn[o]. Foule	4¾
19	Jn[o] Trumbell . . .	3	53	Abram Smith	5½
20	Jn[o] Poor	1½	54	Peter Foule	7½
21	Barnabas Davis . . .	3	55	Geo Buncker	15
22	Thomas Lynde . . .	6	56	Jn[o] Checkrin	6
23	Jn[o] March	1½	57	W[m]. Burage &c. . . .	4
24	Josiah Wood	6	58	Han : Shepherd . . .	3
25	Jn[o] Fosdick	6¾	59	Jn[o] Blany	3
	To Carey Under . . }	3⅜			
	N[o] 24 . . . . . }				

Attest, Jn[o] NEWELL,
Recorder.

Charles Towne, 1685. A record of the Land[s] Laid out in Charles Towne bounds on this Side Menotamies River (being called the Stinted Pasture) Unto the proprieto[rs] thereof (Accord-

ing Unto A Vote of theirs past, when Conveened together March
Tenth 1684–5) which was Effected and performed by their Committee (Chosen and Confirmed by the Said proprieto^{rs} March 27th
1685), who haveing finished the said worke, The Selectmen of Said
Towne being Sattisfied therewith, Ordered it, y^t each man^s proprietie in the Said Land According to the platt of Ensigne David
ffiske the Surveyo^r, (According to Law) be recorded in the Town^s
booke of record^s, to be their propper right, and Estate.

Nathaniel Huchison Two Acres One Quart^r bounded by his owne
Land South Easterly, by the high way North westerly.

Jno Mousall, Nine Acres Abuting to his owne Land.

Richard Lowden Eight Acres Adjoyning to his owne land.   More
to sd Lowden Three Acres bounded North Easterly by the Country
rode, North Westerly by the Land of John Cutler jun^r, and west
South^{r}ly by the Land of Tho. Welch jun^r.

Thomas Welch jun^r Seven Acres one halfe & twenty pole (wch
jncludes his N° 43 Above named) bound North East^{r}ly & East
South^{r}ly by Ric^d. Lowden, South Westerly by form^r divident, West
north^{r}ly by Land of Jno. Cutler jun^r.

John Cutler, jun^r : ffifteen Acres, bounded North Easterly by y^e
Country rode.   East South^{r}ly by Ric Lowden, Tho Welch, jun^r &
his own Land.   South Westerly by Mr Elias Row, & west North^{r}ly
by the Alias range way two pole wide Land of Mr Ward & Tho
Adams.

[244.]   Mr Elias Row, Twenty Eight Acres bounded north^{r}ly
by Jno. Cutler, Easterly by his form^r division, South^{r}ly by A highway wch Comes Over Long hill so Cald, and west north^{r}ly by the
range highway Two pole wide.

Thomas Adams Senr, three Acres one halfe, bounded North
East^{r}ly by the County high way, South East^{r}ly by the range way
two pole broad.   South West^{r}ly by Mr Ward^s Land, West north^{r}ly
by the land of Jonath. Buncker^s heyres.

Mr Saml Ward^s Land ffifteen Acres & A halfe, bounded north
East^{r}ly by Thomas Adams, South East^{r}ly by the range highway
Two pole wide, South west^{r}ly by James Miller, West North^{r}ly by
Thomas Lynde & Buncker^s heyr^s.

James Miller, Twenty Six Acres Three quarter^s, bounded North
East by Saml Ward, South East by the range way two pole breadth,
South west by Thomas Rand, West North^{r}ly by Laur Douse,
Widow Hudson, & Thomas Lynde.

Thomas Rand, Twenty Six Acres one quarter, bounded North
East by James Miller, South East by the range highway Two pole
broad, South west^{r}ly by the highway, West North^{r}ly by Saml Lord
and Laur. Dowse.

Samuel Lord Nine Acres One quart^r & Twenty pole, North East
by Laur Dowse, South East by Thomas Rand, Alias One Acre of
Land left for A Quarry, Southwest by the highway, West north^{r}ly
by the range high way Two rod wide.

Laur Dowse Twenty One Acres bounded North East by Widow
Hudson, South by James Miller & Tho. Rand, South west^{r}ly by

Sam¹ Lord, West north'ly by Josiah Wood & Samuel Lynde, otherwise the Two rod high way.

Widow Mary Hudson three Acres & one halfe Acre, bounded North west by the high way two rod wide, North East by Tho. Lynde, South East by James Miller & South west by Laur Dowse.

Thomas Lynde, Twenty One Acres, bounded north west by the range way two rod broad, Nor East by Jonathan Buncker⁸ heyres, South East by Sam¹ Ward & James Miller, Southwest'ly by Wido Hudson.

Jonathan Buncker⁸ heyres, Thirty five Acres & one quarter, bounded North East by the Country rode, South East by Thomas Adam⁸ & Sam¹ Ward, South west by Tho. Lynde & Widow Smith, nor west by Mʳ Brattle, Mʳ Mary Long & Deacō Aaron Ludkin, the range way divideing sᵈ Bunck'ˢ Lot: as 16¼: & 19.

Widow Smith, Ten Acres One halfe (bounded) oth'wise fourteen acre⁸) north East by Buncker, South East by the range way two rod wide, South west by Sam¹ Lynde, West north'ly by Mʳ Checkrin and Mʳ Brattle.

Sam¹ Lynde, Seven Acres bound Nor East by Widow Smith, South East by the range way Two pole wide, South west by Josiah Wood & Nor west by March & Mʳ Chickrin.

Josiah Wood, Twenty one Acres & Twenty four pole, bounded South East by the range way two rod wide, Southwest by Sergt. Tho Welch, West North'ly by sᵈ welch, John ffoskit, Wᵐ Johnson & March, North East'ly by Sam¹ Lynde.

Sergt. Thomas Welch, Twenty one Acres, bounded Northwest by alias A two pole way, Mʳ Joseph Lynde, North East by John ffoskit & Josiah Wood, South East by Sam¹ Lord, South West'ly by the highway. Minde there is wthin these bounds of Welch one quarter of A acre left for A Common Quarry.

John Foskitt, Seven Acre⁸, bounded North-wést'ly by A two pole highway, Mʳ Joseph Lynde, North East by William Johnson, South East by Josia Wood, South West'ly by Sergt Thomas Welch.

[**245.**] Charles Towne, 1685. To the heyre⁸ of William Johnson, viz., Son Isack, Seven Acres bounded Nor west by Alias A two pole way, Joseph Lynde, North East by March, South East by Josiah Wood, And South west'ly by Sergᵗ Welch.

To March Three Acre⁸ And a halfe, bounded Norwest by Alias A two pole way, Mʳ Lynde, northeast by Mʳ Chickrin, South east by Sam¹ Lynde & Josia Wood, And Sow West by Wᵐ Johnson.

To Jnº Chickrin ffourteen Acres, bounded Nor West by Alias A two pole way Mʳ Lynde, north-east by Mʳ Brattle, South East by widow Smith & Sam¹ Lynde and South west by march.

To Mʳ Brattle Ten Acres & A halfe, bounded Nor West by Alias A two pole way, Mʳ Lynde, north East by Mʳˢ Mary Long, South East by Bunckʳ & widow Smith, and South west by Mʳ Chickrin.

To Mʳˢ Mary Long ffourteen Acre⁸, bounded Nor west by Alias A two pole way Mʳ Lynde and Mʳ Davison, North East by Aaron Ludkin, South East by Jona. Bunck'ˢ heyrs And South west by Mʳ Brattle.

To Deacō Aaron Ludkin Three Acre° one halfe, bound North East by the Country rode to Notamies, the two rod way Comejng through s^d land. South East by Buncker, Sow West by Mrs Long and Mr Danl Davison, Norwest by Jacob Green & Widow Syms.

To Mr Daniel Davison Fourteen Acres, bound South East by the two pole high way, South west by Mr Joseph Lynde, Nor west by Capt Ric. Sprague & Jacob Green And N^{or} East by Aaron Ludkin.

To Mr Joseph Lynde fforty nine Acres, bounded South East by A two pole high way, South west by A highway, North west by A two pole high way And by Mr Jenner & Capt Sprague, And north East by Mr Davison.

To Mr Tho Jenner Seven Acres, bounded northwest by A two pole way, North East by Capt Ric Sprague, South East by Mr Lynde & South west by s^d Lynde.

To Capt Richard Sprague Thirty Eight Acres & A halfe Acre, bounded nor west by A two rod wide high way, North East by Jacob Green, South east by Mr Davison & Mr Lynde And South west by Mr Jenner.

To M^r. Jacob Green Three Acres And a halfe, bounded Nor west by a two pole highway, North East by Eliza Syms, South East by Aaron Ludkin and Danl Davison & Sow West by Capt. Sprague.

To M^{rs}. Eliza Syms Three Acres & halfe acre, the two pole way pasing through the Same, bounded North east by the Country rode to notamies, South East by Aaron Ludkin, South west by Jacob Green and Ensign Call, And Nor west by Ric Lowden.

To Ensigne Call & Company (Viz. Tho White, Nathl ffrothenghā Saml Kettell, Jonath. Kettell, Nathl Kettell, Joseph Kettell, And Ruth ffrothengham), Fifty four Acres & one quar^{tr} Acre, bounded north East by Eliza Sym°, South East by A two pole way, South west, And west by the highway. Likewise North^{rly} by Mr Willis.

To Mr Willis Seven Acres, bounded West North^{rly} by the highway, North East^{rly} by Tho. Carter, East South^{rly} & Southwest^{rly} by Ensigne Call.

To Thomas Carter, Senr, Seventeen Acres one halfe, bounded west north^{rly} by the highway, North East by Ric. Lowden, East South^{rly} by Ensign Call, Southwest by Mr Willis.

To Richard Lowden Nine Acres One quart^r Acre, bounded West no^{rly} and North East^{rly} by the high way, East South^{rly} by Eliza Syms and Ensigne Call, and Southwest by Tho. Carter.

To Edward Wilson A Triangle of Land Cont. Three Acres & halfe, bounded South West by Notamies Rode, west north^{rly} by the way to Cambridge, Nor East by the farme, & East South^{rly} Ditto.

[246.] To A Quarry place Cont bounded north East^{rly} by the Country rode to Menotamies, North East'ly, by Richard Lowden & Thomas Carter, Alias the high way to Cambridge, west South'ly : by John Mousall West South'ly. Minde Cambridge rode is South west'ly.

[Aprill 9, 1690 Edward Wilson Acknowledgd this peice of Land or one Cows pasture, to be the . . as the right . .
attest : JOHN NEWELL, *Recorder*.]

To John Mousall fforty Eight Acres one quarter & Ten pole, being bounded North'ly by menotamy rode, East'ly by the quarrie place or Comon Land, South'ly by Cambridge rode & Edward Wilson. South west by newton Line, And west North'ly by Sam¹ Bickner & Jn° Goodwin.

To Edward Wilson Seven Acres bounded North'ly by Jn° Mousall, South'ly by Richard Lowden, East'ly by Cambridge rode.

To Ric Lowden Three quarters of an Acre, bounded North'ly by Cambridge rode.

To Sam¹ Bicknor & Jn° Goodwin ffourteen Acres. bounded North East by menotamies Rode, South East by Jn° Mousall, South west by newton line, North west by Burrage.

To John & William Burage Twelve Acres one quart', bounded northeast by Menotames rode, East South'ly by Bickn' & Goodwin, South west'ly by the Line, About Nor west by Randale Nicholes. Minde there are two high ways Laid through this Lot, viz. to M' Brattles, Russells and Dickonson' Lands ; for wch wayes Land was Allowed to sd Burrages.

To Lieut. Randale Nicholes Seven Acres, bounded North East by menotamies rode, South East by Burage', South west by the Line and North west'ly nigh the river.

On the North Side of Menotamies rode.

To Timothy Cutler Three Acres and A halfe, bounded Southw'ly by menotamies rode, West north'ly by marsh or the river, North East'ly by Jn° Cutler, Sen', East South'ly by the range way.

To Lieut. Jn° Cutler Seventeen Acres and A halfe Acre, bounded South East'ly by the range way, West South'ly by Timothy Cutler, north west'ly by the meadows, East North'ly by Nath¹ Rand. there is Alowance for two ways through this Land, Unto the meadows.

To Serg' Nath¹ Rand fourteen Acres, bounded South west by Jn° Cutler, nor west by the meadows, north East'ly by Tho. Lord, East South'ly by the range way.

To Thomas Lord Three Acres & one halfe Acre, bounded west north'ly by the meadow, North East'ly by Jn° Blany, East South'ly by the range way, & South west'ly by Nath¹ Rand.

To John Blany Seven Acres, bounded west north'ly by the meadow, north East'ly by A high way to Dickson' Land, East South'ly by the range way, South west'ly by Tho. Lord.

To Susana White Ten Acre & one halfe acre, bounded nor west by the meadow, &c., nor East by Joseph ffrost, South East by the range way, & South west'ly by the way to Dickson' Land.

To Joseph Frost Three Acres and halfe acre, bounded by meadow & river, Nor west by a Comon watering place, North East by the range way, East South'ly & South West by Susana White.

A watring place lying between Joseph Frost & Mr Thomas Graves.

To Mr Thomas Graves Three Acres & halfe acre, bounded West north'ly & north East'ly by the river, East South'ly by the range way South west'ly by the watering place.

To Mrs Prudence Russell Three Acres & halfe Acre, bounded nor west And north East'ly by the river, South East by Anna Shepherd & Wm Bullerd, Southwest by Benj. Sweetser, & Norwest [^{er}]ly by the range way.

[**247.**]   Charles Towne, 1685.   To Beniamin Sweetsir Three Acres & halfe, bounded by A range way which reach^s to the river Nor west, by Mrs Prudence Russell nor East, by Wm Bullerd South east, & by Peter Tufts Souwest.

To Peter Tufts Seven Acres, bounded by the rangeway norwest by Beniamin Sweetser, North East, South East by Wm Bullerd & Capt Wheeler, South west by John Peirce.

To John Peirce Seven Acres, bounded nor west by the range way, Nor East by Peter Tufts, South East by Capt Tim^o Wheeler, Sou West by Jonathan Peirce.

To Jonathan Peirce Ten Acres & halfe Acre, bounded North west by the range way, Nor East by John Peirce, South East by Capt Wheeler, And South west by Thomas Peirce.

To Thomas Peirce thirteen Acres three quarters & Twenty pole, bounded Nor west by the range way, North East by Jonath. Peirce, South East by Capt Wheeler And the Cary^s, South west by Tho Mousall.

To Thomas Mousall ffourteen Acres, bounded Nor west by the range way, Nor East by Tho Peirce, South East by the Cary^s & Tho Danforth Esqr, Southwest by Jno Kent.

To John Kent nine Acres one halfe & Twenty pole, more or less, bounded Norwest by the range way, North East by Tho Mousall, South East by Tho Danforth, Esqr, & South west by Tho Dean^s heyrs.

To Thomas Dean^s Estate three Acre$_s$ & A halfe, bounded Nor west by the range way, nor East by Jno Kent, South East by Tho Danforth, Esq$_r$. & South west by Saml Carter^s heyres.

To the heyres of Samuel Carter, dec., Eight Acres Three quarters bounded Nor west by the range way, Nor East by Dean^s heyrs — and Thomas Danforth, Esqr, South East by A range way, And South west'ly by Menotamie rode.

To Thomas Danforth, Esqr, Twenty Nine Acres Three quarters, bounded South East by the range way, South west by Carter, nor west by s^d Carter, Dean, Kent, & Tho Mousall, nor East by the Cary^s.

To Nathan^l Cary, &c., Seven Acres $\frac{3}{4}$, 20 pole, bounded South east by the range way, South west by Mr Danforth, Nor west by Tho Mousall and Tho Peirce, Nor East by Capt Tim^o Wheeler.

To Capt Timothy Wheeler Twenty Eight Acres, bounded Sou East by the range way, South west by the Cary^s, Nor west by Tho peirce. Jonath. Peirce, Jno Peirce and Peter Tufts, And Nor East by Wm Bullerd.

To William Bullerd Seven Acres three quart^{rs} & twenty pole, bounded South East by the range way, South west by Capt Wheeler, Nor west by Peter Tufts, Benj Sweetser, & Prudence Russell, Nor East by Mrs Anna Shepherd.

To Mrs Anna Shepherd Seven Acres, bounded by Mistick river North East^{r}ly, by Xopher Goodwin East South^{r}ly, by John Penticost South west^{r}ly. Likewise by the range way passing through middle of s^d Land (to the river) South East^{r}ly, by Wm Bullerd South westl^{r}y, and by Mrs Prudn^c Russell west north^{r}ly.

To John Penticost Ten Acres & A halfe Acre, bounded Nor west by the range way, North East by Mrs Anna Shepherd, East South^{r}ly by Peter Frothengham, And South west^{r}ly by Widow Daudy.

To Widow Daudy Twenty four Acres and A halfe, bounded nor west by the range way, Nor East by Jno Penticost, East South^{r}ly by peter Froth'gham & Solomon phip^s, And South west^{r}ly by Ro^{brt} Leech.

[248.] To Robert Leech Fourteen Acres. bounded North west by the range way, nor East by Widow Daudy, East South^{r}ly by Solomon Phipps draught, Sovthwest^{r}ly by Tho: Joan^s.

To Thomas Joan^s his estate Seven Acres, bounded Norwest by the range way, Nor East by Robert Leech, South East^{r}ly by Solomon Phipp^s draught, Southwest^{r}ly by the Lot belonging to the Church.

To Charles Town Church ffourteen Acres, bounded Norwest by the rangeway, North East by Thomas Joan^s, Sow East^{r}ly by Solomon phipps draught and Mr James Russell, South west^{r}ly by Mr Jno Herbert.

To Mr John Herbert Three Acres & halfe acre, bounded norwest by the rangeway, Nor East by Charles Town Church, South East^{r}ly by Mr James Russell, And South west^{r}ly by Mr James Russell.

To Mr James Russell Thirty one Acres & halfe acre, bounded North west by the range way, North East^{r}ly by Mr Jno Herbert & Solomon Phipps draught, South East by A range Way, & South west^{r}ly by Menotamies rode.

To Solomon Phipps & Company (viz. Saml phipps, Mr Hale, Lieut Phillip^s, Jno Roy & Joseph phipps) Fifty three Acres & halfe acre, bounded South East by the range way, North East^{r}ly by Peter Frothengham, West north^{r}ly by Widow Daudy, Robert Leech, Tho Joan^s & Charles Town Church & Southwest^{r}ly by Mr James Russell.

To Peter Frothingham Ten Acres & halfe, bounded Nor west by Jno Penticost, Nor East^{r}ly by Xopher Goodwin, South East by the range way, South west^{r}ly by Solomon Phipps, &c.

To Christopher Goodwin Seven Acres, bounded West north^{r}ly by Mrs Anna Shepherd, North by mistick river & A high way to the fford from the Country rode, East South^{r}ly by the rangeway, South west^{r}ly by Peter ffrothengham.

To One halfe Acre for A gravel place & one halfe acre for a landing place.

To John ffoule, Fourteen Acres through wch is layd out A high way to the ford, And A high way by the Upper Side of the bridge to the river; S^d Land bounded West north'ly & north East'ly by mistick river, East South'ly by the highway and ffarme, South west'ly by Ebenez' Astin, & west north'ly by a range way.

To Ebenez' Astin Three Acres one halfe, bounded west north^[r]ly by the range way, North East'ly by Jn° ffoule, South East by the ffarme, South west by Mary Trumbell.

To Mary Trumbell, in right of Jn° Trumbell, Sen', Seven Acres, bounded West north'ly by the range way, North East'ly by Ebenez' Astin, East South'ly by the ffarme, South West'ly by Peter Foule.

To Peter Foule Seventeen Acres & halfe acre bounded N^{or} west'ly by the range way, north East'ly by Mary Trumbell, East South'ly by the ffarme, South west'ly by Lidia Marshall & Abraham Foule.

To Abraham ffoule Ten Acres & halfe Acre, bounded north west'ly by the range way, north by his bro peter ffoule, East South'ly by Lidia Marshall & Barnabas Davis, South westward by Tho Marable.

To Thomas Marable Three Acres & halfe acre, bounded norwest'ly by the range way, north east'ly by Abram Foule, East South'ly by Barnabas Davis, South westward by Jn° ffosdicke.

To Sergt John Fosdick fffteen Acres three quarters Acre & Eighteen pole, bounded nor west'ly by the range way, north East'ly by Tho Marable, East South'ly by barnabas Davis, Tho Creswell & Jn° Smith, south westward by Nathl Huchison.

[249.]   Charles Towne, 1685 : To Nathaniel Hutchison Eighteen Acres & Seventy three pole, bounded nor west'ly by the range way, north East'ly by Jn° Fosdike and Jn° Smith, East Southward by Sd Smith & Jn° Wheteemor, South westard by the Country rode.

To John Whetemor Three Acres three quart^{rs} bounded South by the highway, nor East by John Smith, And norwest by Nathl Huchison.

To John Smith Seven acres bounded South east ward by the high way, South west ward by Jn° Whetemoor, west northard by Natha^l Huchison and Jn° Fosdike, & north East'ly by Tho Creswell.

To Tho Creswell Eight Acres & twenty pole bound^d East South'ly by a two pole way, from the highway by Jn° Smiths, South west'ly by Sd Smith, west north'ly by Jn° Fosdick, & north East'ly by Barnabas Davis.

To Barnabas Davis three Acres One halfe acre, bounded East Southard by the two pole way, South westard by Tho Cresswell, west northard by Jn° Fosdike, Tho Marable & Abraham Fould, & north East ward by Lidia Marshall.

To Lydia Marshall three Acres & halfe acre, bounded East Southard by a two pole way, wch Extends to Peter Foules Lot, South westward by Barnabas Davis, west northward by Abram ffoule, & north Eastward by Peter Foule.

By ord' of Selectmen & Comitte.
pr. JOHN NEWELL, Record'.

Att a meeting of the Select men, January : 5th 1685–6.

Wee the Aforesd by Vertue of a vote of the inhabitants of this Towne bareing date Aprill 15th last past Empowering us to make Sale of the wood on the Stinted pasture (to the proprietors of the Said Land) for the Use of Charlestowne : Have Sold Unto these persons after named that parcell of wood on his or their Lot (for prices as ffolloweth) wch was Layd out by Ord^r of the Committe, Chosen by the proprieto^rs of the Sd Land, And Confirmed by them (the 27th of last March) for the laying out Sd Land, the divission whereof was Voted the 10th day of March, 1684–5.

Viz Unto Jn° Cuttler jun^r his wood for Six Shill mony.
Unto Mr Danl Davison his wood for ffive Shill.
Unto Mr Joseph Lynde his wood for Twenty Shill.
Unto Deacon Jn° Cutler his wood on 5 Comons for Ten Shill.
Unto Thomas Lord his wood for ffive Shill.
Unto Mr Elias Row his wood for Ten Shill.
Unto Mr Thomas Graves his wood for Two Shill.
Unto Mr James Russell his wood for Twenty ffive Shill.

Jani. 18.

Laur Dowse his wood for five Shillings.
Nathl Rand.
Lieut Randale Nicholes his wood for three Shill.
Unto Thomas Pearce his wood for Seven Shill.
Unto Thomas Rand his wood for Six Shill.
Unto Sergt Lowden his wood for Eight Shill.
Unto Geo Buncker^s heyrs.
Unto James Miller his wood for nine Shill.
Unto Mr Wm Brattle the wood on three Comons for Six Shill.
Unto Nathl Huchison his wood for Ten Shill.
Unto Jn° ffoule his wood for five Shill.
Unto Eleaz^r Phillip^s per T : A, his wood for One Shill.
Unto M^r Jn° Herbert his wood for ffive Shill.
Unto Ebenezer Astin his wood for ffive Shill.
[250.] Unto Timothy Cutler his wood for Three Shill.
Unto M^r Jn° Trumbull per daugh^{tr} Mary, his wood for Six Shill.

Jany. 25.

Unto Thomas Danforth Esqr his wood for Twenty Shill.
Unto Samuel Lord his wood for Three Shill.

Febu'y. 2.

Unto Mrs Mary Long her wood, for Three Shill.
Unto John Mousall his wood for Three pounds ffive Shill.
Unto Jn° Newell the wood of Jn° Penticost for two Shill.
Unto Susanna White.
Unto Sergt Jn° Fosdik his wood for twelve Shill.
Unto Marke Athy the wood of Abram Smith^s heyrs for Three Shill.
Unto Sergt Tho Welch his wood for ten Shill.
Unto Jn° Whetemoor Senr his wood for two Shill.
Unto Tho Cresswell his wood for Six Shillings.

Att A meeting of the Committe for the Stinted Pasture, March 6th, 1685–6.

Then they Orderd this return to be recorded, wch should have bin Entered in the page 77[1], And So have preceeded this Last divission of the Stinted pasture.

Charlestowne, Aprill the 16[th] & 17[th] dayes, 1685.

　I david ffisk then Layd out those Severall nooke[s] & Corner[s] of Land found within the former divident to the Severall p[r]son[s] Und[r] mentioned by Ord[r] of the Committe for the Stinted Co͞mon, & with their helpe and Assistance, two of them Carrying the Chaine, namely, Ensign John Call & James Lowden : On the East Side of the high way leading to menotamies, viz., to Nath[l] Huchi-on two parcell[s], one fifteen pole, & the Other thirty pole. To Tho ffoskitt two parcell[s], one two pole[s] & A halfe, the other twenty Seven poles. —— the Land in the Cow pen by Bullard[s] to Serg[t] Tho Welch one Acre & A quarter & Seven pole. To Tho Creswell on his front halfe An acre & fourteen pole ; And one his back side, & A Small Slip on the west side of his Orchard A Joynjng to a high way Laid out one Acre three quarter[s] & Eight pole[s]. To John Kent Sen[r], on his back side three quarter[s] of an Acre by A pole high way wch goes downe betwixt Creswell & Kent, wch high way goes at bottome of Creswell & Welch[s] Land A Cross To Tho Peirce ten poles by the Corner of the high way Leading to the feild bridge. To M[r] James Russell in A highway to Marke[s] house halfe an Acre. These Seven p[r]sons above named was p[r]sent when I Laid this Land out to Each of them, And Each of them did helpe therein. And Accepted of their Sever[l] peice[s] of Land Except Tho Welch jun[r].

　　　　Attest by mee.

　　　　　　　　DAVID FISKE, *Surveyo[r]*.

Furth[r] I do declare yt the first day that I began to lay out Lots I layd out the Land to make Up the Last whole range in the first divident to m[r] Elias Row & Jn[o] Cutler jun[r], by Ord[r] of the above Said Committe, & Jn[o] Mousall & Jame[s] Lowden Carryed the Chaine, I say by mee,

　　　　　　　　DAVID FISKE, *Surveyo[r]*.

Att a Legall meeting of the proprieto[rs] of the Stinted pasture in Charlestowne, on this side menotamie[s] River, March 8th, 1685-6.

Then was the wor. James Russell Esq[r] Chosen moderato[r] in the S[d] Assembly or meeting, And Jn[o] Newell Clerk to them.

[**251.**] Charles Town, 1686. Like wise it was then put Unto Vote Whether they would put or leave the managem[t] of the sd pasture into the hands of the present Selectmen for this year, &c. — Voted in the negative.

Like wise they Voted for A Committe of ffive men to manage the Affaire[s] of S[d] pasture for one full year Ensueing, According to the instruction[s] Shalbe given to them by the sd proprietor[s].

The Committe Chosen are viz., m[r] Joseph Lynde, m[r] Elias Row, M[r] Tho Graves, Serg[t] Jn[o] Cutler, & Serg[t] Jn[o] Fosdicke.

Like wise they Voted this Committe to treat wth those p[r]sons

---

[1] This page 77 is our page [243]. — ED.

named by the dissatisfied proprietors, viz., Capt Jno Phillips, me Solomon Phipps, Josiah wood, mr Jonath Cary, & Samuel Ketell, for A freindly Issueing of the diffrences between the major part & minor prt of the proprietors.

Then they Voted these following perticulers in the Affirmative.

1.   That the Comon pasture, may be fenced into three pastures or enclosurs, thereby ffenceing of all Country highwayes, this to be done as soon as it can wth Convenince.

2.   That the Committe be impowerd to Chuse Comon drivers.

3.   That they Agree with Benl Bowers as to ffeeding in, or fence of the Sd Stinted pasture for the year Ensueing.

4.   That the Sucureing of the out ffences of the Sd Comon or pasture be Left to the management of the Committe

5.   That the Committe proportion the Divissions of the fence About the three pastures, to the respective proprietors according to Each mans proprietie in the Said pastures [this Voted. prformed as may be seen by A list there of on file.]

6.   That this Committe Look after & indeavour to prevent incroachments on the sd pasture.

7.   That the range or drift wayes in the first divission of the Stinted pasture, remaine this Ensueing year, as they were the Last & former years.

Jno NEWELL, Recordr.

This meeting Adjournd till the 22d of this March.

Att A meeting of the proprietors of the Stinted pasture, March 22d, 1685-6.

It was then Voted yt the ffence proportioned by the Committe about the three pastures (wch was Accepted by proprietors), be fenct in by the first day of May, 1687, wch if not done in that time then each proprietor may fence in perticuler.

Like wise they then Voted the Committe Above named to manage the (Or any Law) Suit that may Arise between the proprietors & ye inhabitant of the Town this year.

They then Chose for drivers of the sd pasture & to view the fences,

NATHL HUCHISON,
JOSEPH FROST,   } Viewrs — Driver { JAMES LOWDEN,
                                      THo PEIRCE.

[SURVEY OF 1713-14.]

[**252.**]   In Persuance of a vote of the Inhabitants of the town of Charlestown at their genneral meeting, march th 1st, 1713-14 — Impowering us the Subscribers to be a comitte to prevent incroachments : also to veiue and to measure the breadth of the ﬞtreets, Lanes & highwayes, &c., in sd Charlestown : and having proceeded in the Said work so farr as within the neck, make this return as followeth —

FISH STREET. — Att the ferry way from the northeast corner of Capt Jona: Dowses warff is 51 feet.

from mrs Huntings over to Benja Bunkers is 38 feet & 9 inches, mrs Huntings Seller doors in the highway.

from Benja Bunkers Westerly corner to Edward Larkins is 40

foot, and from m^r henry Phillipses westerly corner to m^r Russells Shop is 45 foot 3 inches:

The way ishuing out of fish street to low watter mark between Mr Russells Shop and Larkins is 37 foot from Russells warf to the Salt house is agreeable to the former record: Mr Russels Seller doors in the highway.

From Capt Phippses Southerly corner to Codmans fence & gate is 57 foot & from Capt Phippses Westerly corner to Perkinses North Corner is 54 foot, Mr Phippses Seller doors in the highway:

From Capt Chamberses corner (formerly allins) to Stephen Watters (formerly Carters) is 45 foot & 9 inches, the Seller doors in the highway:

MARKETT PLACE. — From Capt Chamberses South west corner to Ebenezer Breeds Noth east corner of his new house 98 foot & 3 inches, both Breeds Seller doors in the towns lands:

From Capt Chambers north corner of his house to the northeast corner of Longs new house 94 feet & $\frac{1}{2}$, S^d Longs Seller door in the towns land:

ffrom the Northeast corner of Longs new house to Epharim Breeds fence by the meeting house is 184 foot:

ffrom the Corner of Stephen Watterers (formerly Carters) to Eben^r Austins house is 194 feet & a $\frac{1}{2}$: Capt Chamberes, widow Phillipes & Benj^a Peirces, all their Seller doors in the towns land: Peirce p^d one penney acknoledgement: Samuel Knights porch in the high way: Ebenezer Austins Seller doors in the high way:

ffrom Knights to Joseph Phillipses, next to Soleyes, is 290 foot and 9 inches:

ffrom Joseph Phillipses to Longs new house is 120 foot 9 inches:

ffrom Capt Jon^a Dowses to Mrs Longs garden fence by the meeting house is 132 feet & a $\frac{1}{2}$:

ffrom Benj^a Peirces, where he now Dwells, to Sheppards, Lately bought peirces, is 268 foot: Jon^a Dowses Seller doors in the highway.

[**253.**] Charlestown 1714: ffrom cap^t Jonathan Dowses to the corner between Peirce and Hall, wch was formerly Sheppards, is 54 foot & a $\frac{1}{2}$.

MARKETT STREET. — ffrom Johnathan Dowses new house ware Benj^a Dows dwells to Stephen Halls is 37 feet & $\frac{1}{2}$, Said Halls Seller doors in the high way he Acknoledged & paid two pence:

Eleazer Phillipses Seller doors in the highway:

ffrom the house ware Patten Lives, formerly Capt Spragues, to Hiltons 25 foot & from^r Mr Nathaniel Dows to Hiltons 34 foot, allowing said Dows 4 foot from the corner of his house.

ffrom s^d Nathan Dowses to prices is 40 foot: prices Seller doors in the high way, she acknowledged she paid a penney:

ffrom Dadies great house to William Smiths old house where Scottow Lives is 46 foot & 3 inches: dadies Seller doors in the highway:

ffrom Thomas Lords to Jno Edmandes is 56 foot.

ffrom Treadewayes to William Smiths 60 foot: Smiths Seller doors in the high way.

ffrom Robbert Cutlers shop to vincent Carters 56 foot & a ½: Carters Seller doors in the high way: acknoledged & p⁴ a penney.

ffrom Mʳ Leṁons to Knells 53 foot, Leṁons hors block in the highway he acknoledged and paid one penney:

ffrom William Ketteels to Jonª Ketteels is 54 feet: William Ketteels and Daṁons Seller doors in the high way.

accknoledged and paid one penney: Jonª Ketteels Seller doors in the high way:

ffrom Nathⁿ Ketteels to Caleb Carters 53 foot: Carters Seller doors in the highway acknoledged and paid one penney

ffrom the east corner of Eleazer Johnsons house to Joseph Rands is 86 foot:

ffrom Isace Johnsons to Benjª Lawrences is 58 foot & 7 inches allowing 1 foot from Johnsons house

ffrom Mʳ Jonª Caryes to Capᵗ Phippses fence 62 foot & ½:

ffrom Capᵗ Caryes old house to the Southerly corner of heatons house 56 foot & ½: Heatons Seller door & hors block in the high way:

ffrom Mʳ Ausburys Porch to Heatons garden fence is fifty two feet & a half:

from Simsons over to Coll Phillipes orchard fence 93 foot ½ —

ffrom Jn° Rands to Coll Phillipes West corner orchard fence 56 foot. [The Land¹ built by John Rand 3ᵈ nott aproved.]

ffrom Chalklyes old house to Mʳ Greens is 50 foot.

from Woods barn to the Buriall hill fence is 64 feet.

from Richᵈ millers formerly Sollomon Phipses barn to the Buriing hill fence is 64 feet.

from Seth Sweetsirs house to the buring hill fence is 59 foot.

from Benjª Sweetsirs barn to John Rands Land is 75 foot ½.

from the Corner of Seth & Benjª Sweetsirs to the buring hill Bars Barrs is 64 foot ½:

[254.] from Kebes to Samuel frothinghams is 48 foot.

from Benjª Phillips to benjamin Sweetsirs fence is 50 foot.

from Mʳ Stimsons to James Ketteels is 55 foot & ½: Stimsons Seller door and hors block in the high way: Nathaniel frothinghams Seller doors in the high way:

from Wyers garden fence to Whites barn 93 foot: Mʳˢ Wyers Hogg pen & part of the Collash² house in the high way acknoledged & paid one penney.

from the North east corner of Blaneys fence to Whiers barn is 87 foot.

from the Northeast corner of said Blaneyes fence to Thomas Whites fence is 74 foot.

from the Northwest corner of Blanyes Land to ffrothinghams land is 74 foot ½.

from Blaneyes land to Jn° Stimpsons is 75 foot & ½. Said Stimsons 2 pair of Staires acknoleged & paid Two pence.

from the corner of Carys marsh (now Webbs) to Nathⁿ: Huttchinsons South corner of his land 69 foot & ½.

---

¹*Lane* or *Landing-place* may have been intended. — ED.
²*Calash* is perhaps intended. — ED.

from the Northerly corner of Lowdens marsh to Hutchinson ffence att the West corner of his land is 53 foot ½.

ffrom the pound to Lowdens orchard 50 foot.

ffrom Hutchinsons house to James Lowdens 42 foot ½: & ½ of s^d Lowdens fence att the Southerly corner of his Gate one foot in the high way.

Jn° Penny incumbred the way with stones and wood.

ffrom Thomas Calls house to Rands Orchard is 64 foot.

ffrom Mrs Cutlers house to the fence of Larkins march is 55 foot the Corner of Larkins marsh att the end of the Cassway to Mrs Cuttlers fence is 71 foot.

from the old gate post att the Caseway to Mrs Cuttlers fence is 68 foot.

ffrom Capt Jonathan Dowses fence by the barn to the edge of the bank att high watter mark is 52 foot.

ffrom the old stump of the tree att the corner of Mr Dowses Land formerly Bunkers, att the Landing place Called Bunkers point, along the bank to the northerly point of the Landing place is 160 foot.

ffrom Mrs Cutlers ffence over against the old gate post along the Caseway to Joseph Whittemores Corner of his land is 463 foot. [the s^d 463 foot being ye highway & the front of ye towns marsh wch goes to low watter mark].

BRIDGE STREET, Leading from fish street to the Swing Bridge. — from Mr Bunkers to Henry Phillipes 31 foot & 10 Inches — Said Bunkers Seller doors in the high way acknoledged & paid one penney : Henry Phillips Seller doors in the highway acknoledged.

from Dassets house to henry Phillipses house 26 foot.

from said Phillips shed to daniel Lawrances house is 29 foot & ½ : Lawrances Se[ller door]s in the highway.

[255.]   Charlestown 1714 : ffrom Cap Gills warehouse to Mrs Sheaths garden ffence is 23 foot, & from said Sheaths new house to Capt Gills fence is 18 foot and ½ : the Corner of Mrs Sheaths porch in the highway 15 Inches :

ffrom the Corner of Capt Chamberes warehouse to the Corner of Capt Gills ffence 32 feet, leaving 1 foot & 20 inches to Capt gill at the part of his fence against Capt Chamberses war house.

ffrom Chittys Westerly corner to Chapmans is 19 foot, from Chittys North corner to Capans 18 feet :

JOYNERS STREET. — From Chapmans Corner to the corner of Capt Gills fence entering into the s^d street out of bridge street is 21 foot & 10 inches.

ffrom Mr Hurds to Mr Ivoryes is 20 foot & 4 inches.

ffrom Edward Sheaths to the Westerly corner of Ivoryes barn is 23 foot.

from Benj^a. Hurds to John Griffins Land 20 feet & ½.

from Samuel Adames corner, allowing 6 Inches from it to the Westerly corner of James Capens New house, is 29 foot & 3 inches.

STREETERS LANE. — from : att the entring in att the markett place between Joseph Phillipes & the old house belonging to Joseph

Lemon is 10 feet & $\frac{1}{2}$, said Lemons fence $\frac{1}{2}$ a foot in the Lane, M^r fosters fence 1 foot.

from James Capens Capen West corner to John Loguns, 30 foot 3 inches.

from the North corner of James Capens to the East Corner of Benj^a Ketteels, formerly Dea. Joseph Ketteels, is 53 foot.

from Samuel Adameses to ffosters fence, at the lower end of Streeters lane, is

HEBBORNS STREET. — Between Capt Nathan^{ll}. Dowses & Capt Spragues is 18 foot, Sd Dowses Seller doors 18 inches in the high way.

Att Deac^n Sam^{ll} Dowses 22 foot: Seller doors in the highway acknoledged & p^d one penny.

from Deac^n Joseph Ketteels to davises 28 foot $\frac{1}{2}$; davises Seller doors & Mrs Jones in y^e highway, davis acknoledged & paid.

BACK STREET. — from James Austins Corner over to Davises is 72 foot $\frac{1}{2}$, allowing two foot from the Corner of Davises house.

from John Edeses (formerly Clows) to Davises 50 foot $\frac{1}{2}$, Eades Seller doors & Steps in the high way.

from John Calls to Daniel Edmandes pasture 50 foot.

from the Corner of Edmandes to Nathan^{ll} Dowses barn is 44 foot $\frac{1}{2}$.

from Ruth Waits corner to Richd Boylestons corner 47 foot.

from Sam^{ll} Trumballs to bakers is 43 foot: Said trumballs porch in the highway: Acknoledged & paid one penny.

from trumballs Land to Vincent Carters 42 foot; said Carters dungheep inclosed in [the highway] ; acknoledged & paid one penny.

[**256.**] from Long's pasture to Mrs Lemons 43 foot & $\frac{1}{2}$.

from the South east corner of Lemons pasture to Caleb Carters is 44 foot.

from Benj^a Lawrances Barn to Lemons pasture 50 foot, said Lawrances privcy att the end of his barn, all in the highway.

from the South East corner of Coll^n Phillipses Orchard to Capt Phippses medow 44 foot $\frac{1}{2}$.

from Heatons Corner to Coll^n Phillipes Orchard fence 25 foot. Said Heatons fence 9 inches in the highway.

Att the entring of back striet from Coll Phillps Orchard fence to a stake driven down at Simsons Land 31 foot & 10 inches. [The stakes sett down & way not aproved. — Side note.]

from Simsons in wast street accross the way to a stake, is 55 foot and 8 inches. [The same as above. — Side note.]

from Simsons, Cross both the wayes, to Coll Phillips Orchard fence, is 93 foot.

COLES LANE. — From William Smiths corner to John Edmandes Corner is 34 foot att the Lower end. Between Boylestons barn & Nath^{ll} Dowes barn, is 40 foot; Boylestons fence nine inches in the highway.

WAPPING STREET. — From James Austins Corner to Henry Phillipes (formerly Huzzies) is 40 foot.

from Joseph Hopkines to Hitts house is 39 foot, & the same bredth from heymans to Bentleyes: Hitts & Pratts Seller doors in the high way: Accknoledged & p^d one penney.

from Heymans to Lathrops is 37 feet, Sd Heymands horse block in the highway : acknoledged & paid one penney.

from Brigdens to Nelsons fence is 33 foot & $\frac{1}{2}$.

from the Northeast Corner of Brigdens to harberts fence is 30 foot $\frac{1}{2}$; the Northeast corner of Brigdens Shop 2 foot $\frac{1}{2}$ in the high way.

from the east end of Brigdens house to harberts is 33 foot : the Way between Brigdens house & Jn° Smiths land, down to the dock, is 24 foot & a $\frac{1}{2}$.

from John Smiths Land to Webbers is 33 foot.

from Taylors Corner to Jonᵃ Shearmans barn 36 foot.

ffrom ffosters to Stephen fords & Jonᵃ Shearmans is 40 foot; between Stephen fords East corner & ffosters land is 41 foot.

from Daniel Smiths Corner over to Coffins is 49 foot.

from Goodwins Corner to mʳˢ martins is 39 foot $\frac{1}{2}$.

From Samuel Blunts to Coll Phillipses old house, 32 foot 9 inches.

from Collⁿ Phillipses to Capᵗ Rowses is 25 foot $\frac{1}{2}$.

from King Corner to Blackmore, now Coll Lyndes, 21 foot; the Landing place att Kings Corner is 51 foot.

Att Kings Corner going down to Elias Stones, is 28 foot.

Between Capᵗ foyes & his ware house is 28 foot.

from Galpins gate to the ware house is 31 foot.

from Walkinses to Collⁿ Phillips old whare house Elias Stones, is 26 foott, 2 foots incroached.

[257.]   Charlestown, 1714.   Att Elias Stones corner, turning into the feild 28 foot, there is one foot & a half incroached by Wilsons fence.

The way between Mʳˢ Smiths & fords going out of Wapping to Trumballs between fords & Smiths 19 foot 9 inches, between Mʳˢ Smiths & foards there is 6 Inches incroached, by Stephen fford :

from Vines to Royalls Land 20 foot & $\frac{1}{2}$.

from Mʳˢ Trumballs to John Green 20 foot, att the Corner 19 foot.

from Mʳˢ Trumball corner to Greens (heires) Land 18 foot.

from Mʳ Trumballs garden fence to the head of Greens Dock 18 foot, the way much incumbred by Mʳ Tho's frothinghams & Capt Dowses Timber.

from the Corner of Ballards fence to fosters Land is 18 foot & Runns on a Streight line that breadth to Low watter mark :

The Street from the said Way to the bridge is from the midle of Ballards land on a line to the dock : by Thomas ffrothinghams Land 16 foot wide at the Lower end by Wards, 16 foot to the dock, & there it turns on a Squar 16 foot to the foot of the bridge : Mʳ frothing & Dowses Timber incumbers the highway.

BATTERY LANE. — from Trumballs to Vines is 15 foot.

from Trumballs to Leamans 13 foot, 1 foot incroached on the high way : Mʳˢ Smiths & Royalls Seller Doors in the highway : Samˡˡ Austin incroached on the high way $\frac{1}{2}$ a foot wᵗʰ his fence.

Att the End of the lane by Ballards is 14 foot.

The Way from the South Corner of Ballards Land to the battery is 18 foot.

Att the uper or northwest corner of the battery over the 18 foot way to ballards land is 43 foot: the Land for a privilidge to the battery att the Upper end by ballards Land to the West corner of the battery house 36 foot.

from the North Corner of the Battery by fosdicks Land 20 foot over and Above the Eigteen foot way:

BATTERY STREET. — Between fosdicks house & garden incroached by fosdick 2 foot, being so much wanting of the 18 foot.

Att the end of the way between Coll Lyndses (formerly Blackmores) house & garden incroached 6 Inches.

the Enteranc of Battery Street by ballards corner 18 foot.

SHIPPIES LANE. — Att the Lower end from taylors Corner to m^{rs} benitts 29 foot and 2 foot incroached by taylors fence, acknoledged & p^d a peny. Mrs Bennitts Leanto $\frac{1}{2}$ foot and her fence, 1 foot in the highway: Jno Taylor bank at the end of his house in the highway.

[**258.**] from Watter's barn to Jonathan ffosdicks 24 foot.

from Sheppies garden fence to watteres house 25 foot $\frac{1}{2}$.

between Shippies and Atwoods is 27 foot, attwood fence $\frac{1}{2}$ foot in the high way: hoppings fence incroached 1 foot.

from fosters Lands to Harberts Land 23 foot $\frac{1}{2}$.

TRAINING FEILD. — the East corner of the training feild: from the corner of Deericks & eades Land to the butten pare trees is 23 foot.

the upper side being the Northeast Side of the training field is 355 foot: the South east side by Mrs Heymans Land is 372 foot.

the South West side by Edmandses land is 224 foot $\frac{1}{2}$.

the North West side by Fowles & Lawrances Land is 284 foot.

The Upper end of the Lane going into the training field between Edmandes Corner & Lawrances Land is 21 foot.

from Waites garden to Edmandes Land 18 foot: Mrs Waites fence incroached 2 foot, acknoledged & p^d one peny.

Att the Lower end entering on Back street 36 foot $\frac{1}{2}$ and runs on a bevell to the Corner of waites garden fence, where it is 20 foot.

Ther is a way ishuing out of Wapping street Att the Dock head by Henry Phillips house, formerly m^{rs} Hurries, fronting on Wapping Street 24 foot from s^d Phillipses Corner to the dock: att the Lower end of Phillipes Land next to Benlys 8 foot $\frac{1}{2}$ & so runs on a straight line to the dock: the Said way inclosed: by s^d Henry Phillips all the way Against his own land: the s^d way incroached & incumbred with Benleyes wo[od] house: m^r Isacefowle Representing Benleys Children, Accknoledged & p^d 6^d. Accknoledgement.

THE LANE down to Moltons point: Att the Entring of the lane, between Mr Hoppings & Peirces Close 22 foot, between Mr Hopings garden fence & peirces fence 16 foot $\frac{1}{2}$, from Wilsons Land to Ebenezer Austin 14 foot, 2 foot $\frac{1}{2}$ incroached partley by both. Between Capt foyes & the Land now in the inprovment of Joseph Austin 16 foot $\frac{1}{4}$: between Knowles & Whattkins 16 foot: Elias Stones

Wall 2 foot in the highway and so runs 16½ foot allong untill it comes unto the North part of the said Stone Wall and that 2 foot in the high way:

The High way Stakt out by the former Comittee Leading down to Moultens point Anno 1670, & 1696, we find inclosed and shut up by Joseph Austin from the point to Stephen Watters pasture & then the said way inclosed by Stephen Watter to Richd Boylestons Land: & then Six foot of the said way inclosed by Richd Boylestons fence:

The fence of Longs Land against the towns marsh, Called the horse pasture, incroached att Sundry places on the towns Land Some 6 Inches & some 12 Inches:

Between Longs Land & hills incroached 3 foot ½ by hills fence.

The way from Moultens point 16 foot ½ all the way untill it comes to Jon^a Ketteeles against Longs Land: & there incroached 2 foot ½: also 1 foot ½ incroached between s^d Jon^a Ketteeles & Chambers's Land, it Seems to be by Capt Chambers fence between Longs Land & Jon^a Dows Land 1 foot incroached.

[259.] Charlestown 1714: THE WAY through the feild. The way is 16 foot ½ untill it comes between Eleaz^r Johnsons: land and Capt Phippes Land: Johnsons incroached 1 foot also one foot incroached between Dadyes & Boylesons pasture.

The way between Jon^a Dowses Land & Vincent Carters land in the low and Springey ground is 24 foot.

Between Austins land & Ivoryes is 30 foot & so that bred^th allong to Capt Rowses & Cuttlers Land.

Between Rows & Simsons Land is 16 foot ½, there is ½ a foot Incroached by s^d Rows:

Att the entering or coming in of the Other feild way between Rowses pasture & Jno Rand is 16 foot ½, incroached by Rowses fence 1 foot ½:

BUNKER HILL ST. — The way over Bunkers hill is 16 foot ½.

Between Davises land and Henry Phillips Land incroached 1 foot by Davises fence:

Between Ausbury & Thomas Call 1 foot incroached by Call.

Between James Lowden & Jon^a Dowses Land incroached 2 foot, ½ by Lowden, about 9 poles together, against m^r ffrothinghams land:

Jon^a Dows incroached ½ foot against Lowdens Orchard.

Att the uperend of Rands Orchard att the gravell pitt incrocht by James Lowden aboute 1 foote ½, most part of the way he borders on the gravell pitt:

from Cutlers fence to Rands Orchard against the midle of the barn is 33 foot: Mr Dowses fence against the gravel pitt is 2 foot in the highway:

from the North Corner of Rands Orchard to Dowses fence is 3 8 foot:

THE GRAVELL PITT: the Lower end of the gravel pitt being the Westerly end from the highway to Lowdens Land at the Southeast corner of Rands Orchard is 84 foot : & from thence it Runs to a point to the high way att the north Corner of Lowdens Orchard :

The way : Leading out of the feild att the Lower end — between Jn° Rands Corner & Phillip Cutlers Corner 16 foot ½ the said feild way to be 16 feet ½ all the way to greens hill, Jn° Rand, Junr, incroached 1 foot : Jn° Rand, Senr, incroached on the high way.

Between Jn° Rand, Junr, & Thomas White : ye said White incroached 3 foot : & ½ foot incroached by s^d Jn° Rand, Junr :

Nath^ll heaton incroached 2 foot ½ against Jn° Rands Land att the Northeast corner of his Land by Whites Lands — by Greens Orchard between heatons & Jn° Rands, Junr, incroach^d on the high way by both Heaton & Rand :

[260.] from greens orchard to William Smiths 13 foot, incroached by William Smith 3 feet ½ :

GREENS LANE. — Should be 16 foot & ½, incroached by Greens fence att the Upper end 2 foot ½ : in the midle of the lane Should be twenty 3 foot. Incroached by Greens fence from the porch upwards aboute Two foot all the way :

Att the Upper end of Greens lane the way Leading into the training feild 16 foot ½, incroached by William Smith 9 inches and most of the way Against Smiths Land incumbred wth rocks.

Between Ebenezer Austins & Samuel trumballs incroached 1 foot & ½ all the way.

Between Capt Phippses Land & trumbales Land incroached by Said Trumball 1 foot.

Capt Phipps his fence incroached 1 foot against the gravel pitt.

Between Capt Phippes fence across the way & gravel pitt att the Norwest Corner of fowles Land is 40 foot ½.

from Fowles Orchard fence cross the way & gravel pitt to fowles other land on the Southwest side of the gravel pitt is 42 foot ½.

Mr Isaac Fowle hath lately incroached the gravel pitt all the way against his land :

Joseph Mirick hath incroached the remainder of the gravel pitt, or towns Land, parrelell wth fowles new fence, Said Mirick incroached att the Upper end of his house by a post 1 foot & ½ : incroached att the Corner of the training feild by mirick 1 foot.

HILL STREET. — By Thomas Lords 12 foot treadewayes Seller doors in the high way acknoledged & paid one penney : Likewise 2 inches of his house incroached : the Upper end of the Lane Between Lord & Robbert Cutler 15 foot :

GRAVEL LANE. — Between Mr Halls & Mr Phillipes 6 foot ½ att the Lower end : att the Upper end 5 foot :

from Mrs Cookreyes garden fence by the meeting house to Mr Ephraim Breeds fence 31 foot.

from the Corner of Cookreyes house to said Breeds Corner is 26 foot.

GRAVE STREET. — from Graveses Corner to Samuel Counces is 21 foot —— att the lower end by graves house 23 foot.

from thence away to M Burrs (formerly Brigdens) Called prat's lane, 6 foot wide : the said Lane incroached by Mr Burrs fenc^e 2 foot : & the Southerly Corner of Isaac parkers new Kill house on the said way 3 foot att the least.

BRIGDENS LANE. — According to Reccord Should be 12 foot : incroached on both Sides So thatt there is 3 foot & ½ wanting most of the way.

Samuel Counces pump, mostly in the high way, acknoledged & paid a penney :

HIGH STREET. from Breeds Corner to Knights & Doctor Graves is 20 foot, Mr Breeds fence on the highway 2 foot.

from m^{rs} Rows house to Cookries is 49 foot.

from Mr Breeds fence to Mrs Cutlers (formerly peachies) is 27 foot, incroached by Mr Breed 2 foot ½, acknoledged & p^d a penney.

[261.] Charlestown, 1714. from Capt Caryes to Peirces (formerly Shepards) 40 foot.

from Nathaniel Ketteels Barn to Caleb Calls barn is 22 foot — Caleb Calls shed or wood house in the high way :

from the Corner of Caleb Calls & Nathan^{ll} Ketteels over to step^n Kidders between the towns house & Calls barn is 40 foot :

from the Southwest corner of Nathaniel Ketteels house to the Northeast corner of Stephen Kidders litle Leantow is 59 foot, One Corner of Said Kidders litle leantow in the towns land :

MIDLE GATE [STREET]. — from Nathaniel Davises to Abraham millers is 32 feet ½ ; Zachariah Davises Seller doors in the high way : from Eleazar Dowses to Rands land is 39 foot, s^d Dowses Seller doors in the highway 2 foot.

from Rands lands to rands house, where John Lewises, from Corner to Corner, is 38 is (*sic*) foot.

ROPEMAKERS LANE. — Att the Upper end from Capt Caryes to Rands Corner 25 foot & holds the same breadth to Thomas Rands house where lewist now dwells : att the lower end from Benjamans to John Newels garden is 23 foot :

from Jno Newels to Stephen Badgers is 21 foot :

from Stephen Badgers to Elias Brigdens Should be 21 foot, butt incroached by Brigden : Elias Brigdens fence 2 foot & 3 Inches in the highway, Acknoledged & paid one penney.

Att the Lower end Between Coll^n Lyndes & Stephen Badgers is 30 foot, & So runs down to Low watter mark : Stephen Badgers fence 1 foot ½ in the highway.

BOW STREET. — from Stephen Kedders barn to Eleaz^r Johnsons barn 33 foot : from Ballcomes corner to Kidders is 43 foot.

from Davises garden fence to Mrs Lewises is 44 foot.

from heymans Corner to Eleazer Dowses corner, 34 foot.

from Mrs Jenneres house to Hiltons Land, formerly Lords, is 42 feet.

from John Newells to Benjamans is 34 foot.

from Stephen Badgers to John Newels garden, 38 foot.

from Clisbyes to Royes, 36 foot.

from Abrahams Hills barn to his garden fence att Ortons Corner is 25 foot, incroacht by hills fence 1 foot.

from m^{rs} Emersons Corner by Casswells is 26 foot, Casswells porch half in the high way.

HALES STREET. — Att the Upper end next Bow street 16 foot: & so goes that Breadth by the towns land that was Johnsons to low watter mark.

Between Mr Burrs Orchard & Mrs Clerks, 28 foot.

from Wid^o Cutlers to Ebenezer Austins the street to be 21 foot wide, encroacht by Austins fence & Building 1 foot & $\frac{1}{2}$.

Mrs Hills fence (upon that wch was formerly Ortons Land), 1 foot in the highway, acknoledged & paid one penney:

THE TOWN HOUSE HILL. — from the norwest corner of peirces Land (next Capt Caryes) to Jonathan Ketteels barn over against Millers land 289 foot.

from Millers land cross the highway so over to Marches land is 53 foot: from the South west corner of marches Land next to Ketteels to the northwest corner of Robert Cutters barn Leanto, is 112 foot.

from the Said Corner of Robbert Cutlers Leanto to the Southwest Corner of his Barn, 46 foot & a $\frac{1}{2}$.

[262.] Encroacht by s^d Cutler on the town hill above his Barn 3 foot, and so the encroachment runs to a point att the lanes end that goes down by Lords:

from the Corner of Robert Cutlers Barn over to m^r Peirces land 190 foot:

from Capt Caryes corner over the hill by the South Side of the town house to the Corner of halls land near gravel lane, 247 foot & a $\frac{1}{2}$.

from Mr Hiltons land over the hill north of the town house to Rands land is 256 foot:

The way before Mr Burrs through to the towns land, formerly Johnson, inclosed & shutt up by Mr Burr.

THE TOWNS LAND FORMERLY JOHNSON. — the Southerly front of said land by the watter side is 89 foot.

from high watter mark by the highway to Jenneres land att the northerly side is 95 foot: from Capt Caryes fence to Jenneres land or Orchard, the northeast corner, 73 foot:

on the east side next Jenners from the Upper corner to high watter mark is 100 foot.

WITHOUT THE NECK. — Att the northwest end of the Cassway from Joseph Whittemores land, to Croutches land, 47 foot.

from S^d Joseph Whittemores door of his New house to the North west Corner of Croutches land, 81 foot.

Said Whittemores Seller doors in the high way, paid acknoledgement.

Miller ffrosts Seller doors in the highway.

from the said miller frosts, formerly Goodwins, over to the Corner of Jno fowles garden is now 32 foot $\frac{1}{2}$.

Att the Corner between James ffowles & William Brown over to M^r Jno ffowles garden fence is 52 foot — and the said John fowle hath incroached on the town land or high way att the lower end of his garden fence 8 foot : & his tan yard all the length incroached and att and about the midle incroached on the highway 15 foot & $\frac{1}{2}$.

Mr Reeds house fronting to the com̄on measures from the porch to the street or highway, 10 foot.

Thomas Welches house, ware m^r Lampson now lives, from the door of the said house to the street is 18 foot & $\frac{1}{2}$.

Att Ralph mousells the Southerly Corner of his house to the high way is 21 foot.

Att the gate by Jno mousells going into the field — from the gate post over the highway to the east corner of Widow Wyers land is 129 foot.

from Jno mousells land by the door over the highway to Wyers land is 124 foot, said Mousells orchard fence 2 foot in the high way, paid a penny acknoledgment.

Paul Wilsons fence all the Length in the towns land.

[**263.**]   Charlestown, 1714.   from the west corner paul Wilsons Orchard over the way to the corner between between Wyer & harries land 164 foot.

from Shepards well acrose the highway over to harries land is 182 foot : the said Shepards fence is 4 foot in the high way : & p^d a penny acknoledgment :

from Harrises barn over to the East corner of Turners Orchard is 174 foot :

from the North weast corner of turners Orchard to Joseph Phippes Stone wall fence, 140 feet :

from widdow Redlands fence at the house over to Joseph Phippes fence is 115 foot $\frac{1}{2}$.

The towns land at the Spring or Wattering place by the highway from turners norweast Corner to the Eeat [East] corner of Joseph Phippes meadow is 135 foot.

The said Wattering place att the Spring the depth from the highway is 138 foot, & so goeth Square from the highway to Keteels land :

Cambridge Way. — from the Westerly corner of Crosswells house lott to the fence against the Marsh is 94 foot.

Att the brook by the Bridge from minotts Land over to the North west corner of Crosswells marsh att the highway to Wheelers marsh is 65 foot.

There a highway belonging to the town of one pole & $\frac{1}{2}$ wide from the Contry road to Wheelers marsh inclosed wth Caleb Croswells land :

The highway Between said Croswells Land (formerly tylers) to Phippes pasture 105 foot :

between Wood^s pasture & Caleb Croswells pasture at the Slow or Small Bridge is 87 foot :

The lane or highway going down to Braizers att the entering in att the highway by the Contry road from the White oak tree to Croswells land is 42 foot.

Against Braisers door from Lyndes fence to the Corner of Croswells land 43 foot.

from the said Crosswells Corner to Braisers orchard fence is 47. foot.

And the said lane or highway from Braisers all the way to James millers house is 39 foot in width.

Ther is a high way belonging to the town of two rods wide going from the lane or high way by James millers down to the Bullott & the head of the marsh lotts: the s^d way lyes between millers land & wards pasture: and inclosed in Wards pasture now in the hands of s^d miller.

There is a part of the Bullot or towns land of aboute half acre inclosed in the said wards pasture: the head line of the s^d peice of land as it Seems to be formerly staked out is 57 feet $\frac{1}{2}$, & the said line between Wards land & it from y^e head to millers land is 132 foot.

[**264.**] We find a high way of two poles wedth from the Bulot allong att the head of the marsh lotts between the marsh and the Upland for the accomidation of the said marsh lotts till it comes to Wards marsh at the Southwest corner of Henry Phillipes lott (formerly m^r Jamisons:)

There is a peice of towns land Laid out & left for a wattering place & — Sand — gravel, &c: between Joseph Kents land and m^r ffoxcrafts land on the Southerly Side of the highway, the wedth by the said high way is 245 foot, & so runing down to the brook, and the Wedth att the lower end by the brook is 140 foot: and a part of the said land is inclosed & Improved by the said Jo^h Kent:

There is one acre of land belonging to the town at the South West corner of William Rands land (formerly Sam^{ll} Lords), & one quarter of acre att the South east corner of Charles Hunnewells (formerly Thomas Welches:)

The said Hunewell hath incroached & inclosed of the high way against his Orchard: between his old house & the Slough or Small Bridge 8 foot att the least:

Also between the said Slough or bridge to. the Norwest corner of his land encroached & enclosed att least 14 foot in ye midle.

The highway Between Coll^n Lyndes Land & m^r Godards (formerly Boueres) is 4 poles Wide:

The highway at ye N^{o}west corner of Godards Land to m^r Kidders pasture is 70 foot wide:

Coll Lynds Encroacht 2 foot on the high way against his Orchard:

Mr Samuel Kidders pasture fence is 6 foot on the high way:

Jacob Whatson incroached on the high way at the corner of his fence next to goves land 15 foot: and att Sundry other places of his fence by the s^d highway: incroached & inclosed 16 foot at least which is greatly to the damage of the way:

The North west corner of Jon^a Bavericks land incroached on the high way 8 foot:

The land bordering on said Jonathan Baverick belonging to Mr Higginson in Sundry places incroached on the highway 12 foot: & that also in such places as doth much damage to the highway.

Jon^a: Goves Southwest corner of his lott or pasture near the Quarries incroached very much to the damage of the said high way: att the s^d. Corner near the elm tree 6 foot at ye least, & so continues the encroachment the same breadth all the way till he comes over against Whatsons corner of his pasture below the Quarry hill and there encroached at ye Least 14 foot, & so goes on and continues his incroachment till he comes [**265.**] a litle below Ralph Mousells Quarrie against an old brier bush & there it is 22 foot at the least: & against the said Ralph Mousells Quarrie pitt incroached 18 foot, & so all the way up the hill till he comes to the corner of Mallotts land:

M^r. Mallot incroached & inclosed of the highway over against Mr Cleavelands house aboute 12 foot, & so continues the incroachment untill he turns the way or road leading to cambridge over the Quarrie hill.

Mr Aaron Cleaveland incroached and inclosed on the highway leading out of the farm to cambridge on the northwest side of the said high way over Against his barn 6 foot att the least:

& there is Sundry Others incroachments very Apparent wch doth much damage to the high wayes: & is absolutely necessary to be looked after and regulated:

Mistick Side. — The Way at mistick side as followeth:

there is a Small peice of land belonging to the town left for a pound or any other use: lying between m^r James Barrets Land & m^r Tuffs land formerly Stoweres.

The high way or contry road leading down from Malden to peney ferery is wholly inclosed & improved by m^r Stowers Sprague & Accknoledged by him & he paid one shilling:

There is a highway of one pole wide bordering on the head of the lotts within Stowers Spragues land from the contry road or high way by a ditch between the lotts formerly Thos. Rand & s^d. Spraages land North west ward & so along till it comes to Phinneas Uphams land: and the said high way runs from the said Thomas Rands Marsh down till it comes over against the White Island: the s^d high way was for the Accomodation of the marsh lotts on the North & North westerly Side of the said Stowers Spragues Upland, And is all inclosed & improved by said Stowers Sprague:

Att the lower end of the said high-way by the river there being formerly an old thorn bush, & that being demollished & gone, wee have driven down a stake on each side the high way near where the said thorn bush stood: over Against the White Island:

There is a highway belonging to the town of one pole wide leading out of the contry road by Samuel Switsers through the said Switsers land, & so through m^r Benj^a Swittsers land by his house to wormwood point: the said high-way is one pole wide till it comes to the head of the marsh formerly Dowses & then turns on the said Benj^a Swittsers Upland: att the head of the marsh till it comes to the gate between m^r Swittsers land & m^r odleins land formerly mitchells, now in the possession of James Nicholls: & then the said high way is two poles wide down to wormwoods point untill it comes to the Southerly corner of Brattells marsh & there measures two poles.

from the Old Stump against the barn & then the way & towns
land is four poles wide for a landing place by the Watter side
round the point [**266.**] till it comes to the cove or harbour against
the door of the now dweling house :
   There is incroached and inclosed 7 or 8 foot of the towns land
by James Nicholls within his garden fence att wormwoods point. `
   MENOTEMY or feild line.   Aprill the 12th 1715 being desired by
the Select men to veiue & look after the high ways in menottamy
feild called formerly line feild :
   Wee find the high way called the Bridgeway wch goeth through
the feild incroached on in Sundry places & some part of the said
high-way ploughed up & sown wth indian corn by mr Dunster, &
other part ploughed & improved by Walter Russell, And one highway of two pole wide leading down from the bridge way to the
bank & river all inclosed by mr Dunster & denied by him to bee
any town way : hee being then present :
   And Charlestown part of the bank and landing place wee find to
bee thirtey Seven poles & ½ in length from the land formerly mr
Proutes : eastward to a black oak tree marked wth C on the Westerley side thereof and D on the East Side, the Said landing place
being 4 poles in wedth all the way by the river and extends 18 foot
above the said black Oak tree : ware wee drave down a stake, mr
Dunster being present : the Said blank & landing place was then
all incumbred wth timber & Lumber : mr Dunster then denied to us
that wee or the town of Charlestowne had any bank or landing
place there, he claimed it all to be his own :

JOHN RAND,
JOHN TUFFS,
ELEAZER DOWS,
AARON CLEAVELAND,
JOSEPH WHITTEMORE.

True Coppie Attst NATHLL Dows, *Town Clerk.*

MR CALEB CALL'S GIFT, of a way to the Town, 1772.   *Know all
Men by these Presents,* that Whereas I, Caleb Call of Charlestown,
in the County of Middlesex, &c., Baker : Have for the Accomo-
dation of the Inhabitants of this Town Open'd a Way four Feet
wide thrō my Land from School Lane going over the Town House
Hill to Middle-Gate Street, which Way adjoyns to the Land of Mr
Richard Hunnewell. I Do therefore Covenant for myself, my
Heirs, Executors & Administrators, That neither I nor they nor
any person under us shall at any Time hereafter Stop up said Way,
But it shall lay open forever for the Conveniency of the Inhabitants
of the Town as aforesaid.
   Witness my Hand this 27th. Day of April 1772.

CALEB CALL[1].

Witness
   SETH SWEETSER[1], Town Clerk.

---

[1] These are both autographs.— ED.

SURVEY OF 1767.

[**267.**]   Charlestown, 1767.   We the Subscribers being appointed by the Town of Charlestown at their Meeting in March, 1767, to assert the Town's Rights; have carefully attended that Service & do Report thereon accordingly.   We have also measured all the Streets & high Ways in said Town, also all the Lanes and privilege places in said Town & give this our Return thereon.

Fish Street. — We began at the Wharf opposite Mrs Lemmons Shop, just below the ferry Shed & measur'd over to Capt Barber's Wharff, 78 Feet 6 Inches.

From Deacon Brigden's Shop to Bunkers Wharff, so called, is 46 Feet, said Wharff being the extream part of said Bunkers Bounds towards Charles River, & by a Grant of the Town to him & his Heirs they are to reserve a Road on said Wharff and a Landing place for Hay or the like as may be seen in one of the Town's Book (Page 35).   The Town owns all from Bunkers Wharff to Low Water mark.

Then we began & measur'd from Frothinghams House over to Bunker's Land 38 Feet; Frothingham's Cellar-Doors in the high Way.

From the lower Corner of Larkin's Land to Bunkers is 39 Feet 6 Inches; Larkins Cellar Doors in the high Way.

From the upper part of Larkins Land to Cheevers corner is 45 Feet 6 Inches, Larkins Cellar Doors in the high Way.

From Larkins Corner to Russell's Corner next the high Way is 40 Feet leading down the Creek.

From the back Corner of Russells to the back Corner of Larkins House is 16 Feet.

From the upper Corner of Mr Russell's Warehouse to Mr Rusell's Wharff across the Slip is 15 Feet.

From the Lower Corner of Mr Russells Warehouse to his Wharff across the Slip is 18 Feet & so runs to low water Mark.

From Cheevers N : W : Corner to the Corner of Russell's House is 44 Feet 8 Inches.

From Conant's Southerly Corner to Codman's Shop is 57 Feet, Codmans Cellar Doors in the high Way.

From the West Corner of Sam^{ll} Conants Land to the North Corner of the late Capt Luists House 51 Feet, both their Cellar Doors in the high Way.

[**268.**]   From Mr Russells S.W. Corner of his Brick Shop to Hopkins Corner is 44 Feet.   Mr Wm Conants & Mr Devens Cellar Doors in the high way & Russells Cellar Doors in the high way.

Market Street. — From Russells S.W. Corner of his Brick Shop over to Breeds House 99 Feet — Breeds Cellar Doors in the high Way.

Market Place. — From Browns N.E. Corner to Doctor Russells N.W. Corner is 94 Feet, From Browns said Corner along by Mr Abbott and Prentice' Land to Breeds House or Shop is 182 Feet 2 Inches — Breeds Cellar Doors in the high Way.

From Austins Corner to Hopkins Corner is 192 Feet — Austin and Welsh' Cellar Doors in the high way.

From Mr Odin or Ballard's House to the Town House is 48 Feet — Ballard's, Mr Hall & all their Cellar Doors in the high Way.

From Mr Halls to the Town House is 40 Feet.

From Austins House to the Town House is 39 Feet.

From Welsh' House to the Town House is 38 feet.

From Mrs Lemmon's Shop, formerly Phillip', near Mr Welsh' House, to Nathl Brown's Door is 120 Feet.

From Mr Lemmons Shop along by the End of the Town House & by Mr Brown's House to Mr Richard Cary's is 147 Feet.

Fiom Dow'' South Corner along by the Meeting House Steps to Mr Abbot's Land is 130 Feet, Mrs Lemmons House joyning Dowse' Land, the Cellar Doors in the high Way.

From Capt Sheaffes House to Capt Eleazer Johnson's House, where Hopping lives, is 266 Feet, Sheaffes Cellar Door in the high Way.

MARKET STREET. — From the Easterly Corner of David Waits House, formerly Pierces, to the Westerly Corner of Nathl Dowses Fence, is 158 Feet, Waits Cellar Doors in the high Way.

From Sam^{ll} Swans N Corner of his House over to Widow Johnsons, South Corner of her House, is 37 Feet & an half, both Cellar Doors in the high Way.

From Capt Hendlys to the Estate of Doctor Greaves, deceas'd, 27 Feet, Graves Cellar Doors in the high Way.

From Mr Stevens South Corner to Huldah Eades 36 Feet, said Huldah Edes Cellar Doors in the high Way.

From Mr Stevens Door to Isaac Fosters near his Doorer Steps is 38 Feet 9 Inches, Fosters Cellar Doors in the high Way.

From Judge Fosters to Richd Boylston's is 47 Feet, both and all Cellar Doors in the high way.

From Benj^a Hurds to Mr Abraham's 56 Feet, Hurds Cellar Doors in the high Way.

[269.] From Lippingtons House to Eb^r Kents, from Corner to Corner, is 59½ Feet, Cellar Doors in the high Way.

From Fluckers to Adams' is 57 Feet.

From Mr Peter Edes' to Mr Lemmons 53½ Feet, Cellar Doors in high Way.

From the late Deacon Jon^a Kettells to Deacon Wm Kettells is 54 Feet, Cellar Doors both sides in the high way & Steps.

MARKET STREET. — From Mistick Caleb Calls,[1] to Doc^r Rand's is 53½ Feet, both their Cellar Doors in the high Way.

From the East Corner of Capt Johnson's to Nathl Rands is 86 Feet.

From Isaac Johnsons House to Sam^{ll} Hutchinsons is 60½ Feet. Johnsons Steps & Hutchinsons Cellar Doors in the high Way.

From Mr Austins, formerly Capt Cary's, over to Doct^r Rands House, bought of Capt Wyer, is 62½ feet, Austins Horse Block, Steps and Cellar Doors in the high way.

From Mr Abrahams Land to Jon^a or Nehemiah Rand's House is 59 Feet, Rand's Cellar Doors in the high Way.

From Capt Barbour' House to James Hay's Fence 55 Feet, Captain Barbours Cellar Doors in the high way.

---

[1] This man was termed "Caleb Call second" and "Mistic Caleb" to designate him from his uncle Caleb and his Cousin Caleb, "Esquire." See Wyman's *Genealogies and Estates* art Call groupes 18 20 and 21 pp 171 72 ED

From Codmans House over to Mr John Hay's, Land on a Range with Codmans Fence between Doc^r Rand & Codman, is 93 Feet, Codmans Cellar Doors in the high Way.

From Nich° Hopping's House over to the Corner of Jn° Hay's Pasture is 55 Feet, Hoppins Cellar Doors in the high way.

From Eleazer Dows' House over to David Woods Fence is 53 Feet, Dowse' Cellar Door in the high way.

From David Woods House over to Millers Marsh is 64 Feet, Woods Cellar Doors in the high Way.

From Richard Miller's Shop over to Jn° Stones House, formerly Miller's, 64 Feet, Stones Cellar Doors in the high way.

From Jn° Hancocks House over to Rands Land is 59 Feet.

From the Burying Hill Gate to Mr Sweetsers Land 64½ Feet.

From Mr Henders to Capt Barbours, formerly Sweetsers Corner, is 68 Feet, Mr Hender's Cellar Doors in the high Way.

From Jo^s: Frothingham's House to Capt Adams Rail Fence is 75 Feet, Frothingham' Cellar Doors in the high ways.

From Mr Chamberlain' House to the Land formerly Doc^r Greave' Land is 70 Feet.

From Pierces House to Tho' Woods Pasture 68 Feet, Peirces Cellar Doors in the high way.

From Tho' Woods over to Frothingham's is 51 Feet, Woods Cellar doors in the high ways.

From Mr Eaton over to Calleys is 54 Feet, Calleys Cellar Doors in the high Way.

[**270.**] MARKET STREET. — From the S. E. Corner of Wyers Garden to Frothingham' Shop is 93 Feet, Frothingham's Cellar Doors in the high Way.

From the North East Corner of the Mill Land to the Westerly End of Wyers Barn is 87 Feet.

From the N. E. Corner of said Mill Land to Mr Hussins Fence 74 Feet, Encroach'd by Hussing about 2 Feet.

There is a Privilege Way belonging to the Town 23 Feet wide to low water mark between Mr Wyers Barn & The peice of Land which Mr Green has encroachd & set a House upon — There is a Road or high way leading from the main Road to the Mills 25 Feet wide.

GREENS ENCROACHM^T. — Encroachd by Wm Green on the Towns Land Leading to the Mills. In the Front on said Way 64 Feet, in the Rear the same, N.W. End 30 Feet deep, N.E. End 49 Feet deep — We measured from said Encroachment till we come on a Line with the Mill House 250 Feet on said Road (next to the water), belonging to the Town which Runs to Low water Mark.

Then we measurd from Jn° Stimpsons House over to the Marsh belonging to the Mill owners 75 Feet, Stimsons Stairs in the high Way.

From the Division Fence between Mercy Frothingham & Jn° Stimpson & the Mill owners Marsh 70½ Feet, Encroached by said Stimpson & Frothingham 3 Feet.

From Swans S. Corner over to said Mill owners Marsh 69½ Feet, Encroach'd by Swan on the Corner 2 Feet.

From Mr Peter Edes Marsh to his upland below the Pound is 58 Feet.

From the Pound over to Mr Peter Edes' Land is 50 Feet.

From Penneys to Peter Edes Land 42½ Feet, Encroachd by Edes half a Foot.

From Jon^a Calls over to the Corner of Peter Edes' Land 64 Feet, Encroachd by Edes one Foot.

From Temples House to his Marsh or Fence 55 Feet, Encroach'd by Temple one Foot, said Temples Rails before his Door in the high Way.

LANDING PLACE AT BOTTOM OF CAUSEWAY. — From Temples Fence across to the Corner of his Marsh at the Causeway is 71 Feet.

From the High way along Temples Wall to the Landing place is 300 Feet, & so running to low water mark — 52 Feet Wide at high water Mark being upland & the Flats to low water Mark.

From Mallets Corner of the Garden Fence to the Front or on the Road to Temples Fence is 73 Feet, From the back Corner of Mallets Garden Fence to Temple's Fence is 57 Feet.

From Temples Fence to Lamsons Shop, formerly Whittemores Land, 454 Feet.

From the S.E. Corner of Mallets Garden below his Shop to Temples Marsh across the Causeway is 46 Feet.

From Isaac Mallets Door to Whittemore' Marsh across is 48 Feet.

From James Fosdicks Shop Door across to said Whittemores Marsh is 46 Feet.

WHARFFE & LANDING PLACE. — Then we measurd a Landing place that belongs to the Town lying between Lamsons Shop & Fosdicks Shop, measuring in the Front 33 Feet, 9 Inches, then measuring the back part or Wharffe 32 Feet, 4 Inches, & continues said With to low water mark, the North Corner of Fosdicks Barn encroach'd near the Wharffe & Lamsons Shop Encroachd the front Corner.

[271.] Then we measur'd from the S.E. Corner of M^r. Jabez Whittemores Land & measurd across to other Land of said Whittemore 47 Feet.

Then measur'd from said Whittemores fore Door across to the N.W. Corner of said Whittemores other Land, formerly Crouches, 81 Feet.

BRIDGE STREET. — From Mr Cheevers to Bunkers (now Kings) Corner is 31 Feet, 10 Inches, Cheevers Cellar Doors in the high way.

From Cheevers over to Harris or Goodwins is 26 Feet.

From Cheevers over to Capens 23½ Feet, Capen Cellar Doors in the high Way.

From Capt. Hardings house over to his Garden 23 Feet, Encumbered by Rails before his Door 4 Feet from the House, his Steps & Cellar Doors in the high Way.

From Nat Sheaffes Corner to the Corner of Gills Pasture is 24½ Feet.

From the Door of Sheaffe's old House or Kitchen to Gills Fence is 17 Feet 9 Inches.

From the Northerly Corner of Whites Wharff to the Corner of Gills Pasture is 20 Feet.

From W. Corner of Stones Land to Chapmans is 19 feet, Chapmans Fence Encroached one Foot.

From the Northerly Corner of Chapmans land to Stones is 18 Feet.

JOYNERS STREET. — From Hoppings Corner to Stones Northerly Corner near the Foot of the Bridge is 20 Feet.

From Chapmans Corner to the Corner of Gills Pasture is 21 Feet 10 Inches.

From Mr Welsh' over to Widow Frothinghams is 20 Feet 6 Inches.

From Cap. Cheevers House to Capt Sheaffes Land is 21 Feet 6 Inches.

STREETERS LANE. — From the Corner of Whittemores House to the Corners of Capens House, not Shop, is 30 Feet.

From the Corner of Capens House to the Corner of Newells House is 30 Feet 3 Inches.

From Whittemores Gate to Fosters Fence is 18 Feet 6 Inches.

From Mr Lemmons House to Mr Lemmons House, the upper End of Streeters Land next the Market Place, 10 Feet 9 Inches.

AUSTINS LANE. — From Austins House or Corner to Capt Eleazer Johnsons House, where Hopping now Lives, is 9 Feet 6 Inches.

From Mr Johnsons Land over to Austins Land, where the old barn stood joyning on Gill, is 11 Feet 6 Inches.

From Welsh' Land to Gills Land at the bottom of the Lane is 15 Feet.

CHAMBER'S LANE. — From Doc^r Russells House to Odins House at the Top of the Lane is 14 Feet 6 Inches.

From Mr Soleys to Widow Spragues is 16 Feet.

From the Upper Corner of Hardings House to Gills Fence is 17 Feet 6 Inches.

SOLEYS LANE. — From the lower Corner of Hardings House to the Corner of Gills Pasture Fence is 29 Feet.

At the Upper End from Soley's Gate to Gills Fence is 9 Feet 10 Inches.

At Gills Gate across to the pasture Fence is 11 Feet.

HEBBURN STREET. — At the bottom from Gills Garden to his Pasture Fence is 10 Feet.

Between Capt Hendleys House & Mr Stevens is 18 Feet 6 Inches.

Between Mr Steven' lower House to Capt Hendleys Barn is 22 Feet, Mr Steven's Cellar Doors in the highway.

At the bottom from Capt Hendleys Tallow House to Mr Kettells is 28 Feet 6 Inches, Kettells Cellar Doors in the high Way.

BACK STREET. — From Sam^{ll} Waits Corner over to Widow Kettells Corner is 75 Feet, having left 2 Feet to said Kettell as her Right.

From Bradishes Bake House over to Mr Reeds & all the way, 49 Feet 6 Inches, all the Cellar Doors in the high Way.

From Jon^a Bradishes House to Nat Austins Fence is 47 Feet 6 Inches, Bradishes Cellar Doors in the high Way.

From the lower Corner of Abraham's to Mr Edes Corner is 43 Feet.

From the N.W. Corner of Trumbals Garden to Boylston Barn is 46 Feet.

From Ja^s Trumbals old House, West Door, over to Widow Wyers House is 40 Feet.

From Capt Adams' Barn over to Fosters Fence 41 Feet, Capt Adams Dung Penn & Dung in the high way.

From Lemmons Barn to Fosters Land is 42 Feet.

[**272.**] Back Street. — From Doctor Rand's Barn & Fence to the South Corner of Lemmons Pasture is 44 Feet, & Encroach'd by Lemmon & Foster 9 Inches.

From Hutchinsons Barn to Lemmons Pasture is 48 Feet 3 Inches.

From the S. E. Corner of Gardner's Smoke House across the Way to Gardners Fence 46 Feet and an half.

From Nehemiah Rands Barn to John Hay's Fence is 31 Feet, Encroachd six Inches by said Jno Hays Pasture Fence.

Coles Lane. — At the Bottom from Boylstons Barn to the lower Corner of Abrahams Land Land is 40 Feet.

In the middle where Abrahams Porch is 34 Feet, Abrahams Porch in the high Way.

At the upper End between Abrahams & Capt Kents is 31 Feet 4 Inches, Kent Encroached 3 Feet.

Wapping Street. — From Saml Waits Corner to the House formerly Phillip's 40 Feet.

From Whittemores over to Jos. Sweetsers is 39 Feet, both Cellar Doors in the high Way.

From Mr Powars to Bodges is 37 Feet.

There is a Way leading out of Wapping Street between Whittemore's & Teel 11 Feet Wide, & so runs down to the Dock 133 Feet.

From the N.W. Corner of Mr Harris' Work House to Capt Millers is 33 Feet 6 Inches, but Encroach'd by said Harris 3 Feet 6 Inches.

From the N. E. Corner of Harris' Work House to Miller's Fence is 30 feet 6 inches, Encroach'd by Harris 2 Feet 6 Inches.

There is a Way Issuing out of Wapping Street to the Dock between Mr Harris' Work House & Kiln House 24 Feet 6 Inches wide all the Way.

At the Upper End, next Wapping Street, Encroach'd by Mr Harris' Buildings, 5 Feet 6 Inches, being a Landing Place that belongs to the Town & runs downs to the Dock or Creek.

From Grubbs Land to Capt Hendley's is 33 Feet.

From Miricks Corner to Capt Hendleys Land or Fence, 36 Feet, Encroach by Hendley 6 Inches.

From Foster's Land to Capt Hendley's & Fords, 40 Feet.

From Foster's to Stephen Fords East Corner is 41 Feet, Encroach'd 1 Foot by Foster.

From Capt David Wyers across the Road to Land lying Vacant 49 Feet.

From Abr^m Waters House over to Tim^o Goodwin^s Land is 39 Feet & an half.

From East End of said Goodwin's Land to N. W. part of Stantons House is 32 Feet 9 Inches.

From Capt Stantons Fence by the great Door to Capt Orrs House 25 Feet 6 Inches, Encroach'd by Stanton 6 Inches.

From Capt Orrs Corner to the House formerly Kings now possess'd by Mr Wheatley is 24 Feet.

MARDLING STREET. — Then we measur'd from Mr Mardlins House to Capt Fords House, leading from Wapping Street to the Dock is 19 Feet & 9 Inches across.

From Jonathan Cary's to Capt Hendley's Cooper Shop is 20 Feet.

From Hendleys Fence to Ivorys Fence of Land he bought of Trumbal, is 19 Feet, & then at the Bottom of said Street to the Eastward leading towards Charles River, we turn and run on a Straight Line between John Ivory's said Land and Land that was Danl Edes^s to low water mark, 18 Feet wide all the Way down to Charles River accross Battery Street.

BATTERY LANE. — From Jno Ivory's Land to Jon^s. Cary's House & so down to Battery Street 15 Feet wide, till you come to the Bottom of said Lane where it is but 14 Feet wide.

BATTERY STREET. — Then we measured across the Dock at the Bridge 37 Feet —— the Road is 16 Feet wide by the east side the Dock 'till you come to Harris^s, Store, & then t urns and runs along by said Harris^s & Edes^s House 'till you come to the 18 Feet Way which runs to low water mark, said Way being 16 Feet wide.

Then said Battery Street begins from said 18 Feet way which leads to low Water Mark and runs by the old & new Battery, & is 18 Feet wide 'till you come to Capt Orr's Wharffe, & from thence to the East Corner of Mr Foyes Bounds is 28 Feet wide, and from thence to Mr Dowse^s is 28 & 30 Feet wide.

[273.] OLD BATTERY LAND. — On said Battery Street between Mr Mardlings & Fosdicks Land there is a place belonging to the Town, formerly a Battery, the lower side next the River & on the upper side of said Battery Street, opposite said Battery Land, is a Piece of Ground belonging to the Town, on which stands the Battery House, measuring on said Street 20 Feet & 43 Feet back. There is also a peice of Land on the South Side of said Battery House, Land measuring 36 Feet, Southerly towards Battery Lane, bounding Westerly and Southerly on Mr Mardlins, and is 43 Feet back from said Battery Street and 36 Feet on said Street, on the Southerly Corner of said Land near the Saw Pit, we drove a Stake & run the line between Mardlin & the Town across the Road & so on a Bevel to the N E Corner of his Wharffe which was agreeable to his Deed & so runs to low water mark 167 Feet from Mardlins Line the lower side Battery Street. The N Corner of the Battery next Mr Fosdicks is 65 Feet & from said N. Corner runs to low water Mark, on a Straight Line with the N Corner of the Battery. on the upper side of Battery Street is a peice of Land joyning to the Battery House Land, measuring 12 Feet on said Street, & goes

14 Feet back, Bounded Northerly & Westerly on James Fosdick, which we staked out, and which is Encroached by said Fosdick, & he has built a Smiths Shop on the same. The distance from the N E Corner of Fosdicks encroachment to the Southerly Corner of the Towns Land on Battery Street (where we drove down a stake) is 76 Feet all Incumberd by Mr Mardlins Timber & plank; and we are of Opinion it wou'd be best for the Town to sell the above mention'd Lands.

Then we measur'd a Landing place on said Battery Street at the lower End of Wapping Street, joyning to N E side of Capt Orr's Wharffe, 51 Feet wide, & runs down to low water mark which belongs to the Town.

Then we measur'd the new Battery on said Battery Street, 90 Feet front, & the same Breadth to low water mark, as will appear by the Deed which is lodg'd with the Town Treasurer. At the bottom of Battery Street we turn round the East Corner of Mr Dowse' Land to the South Corner of Waits Damm, measure 16½ broad all the way.

WAY TO MOULTON'S POINT. — From said Corner to Dows' upper Pasture Fence is 19 Feet 6 Inches, and the Lane continuing all the Way towards the brick Kiln or Judge Fosters Pasture, 19 Feet.

From Judge Fosters E Corner over to Waits Wall is 40 Feet where Moulton's Point & Bunker Hill road meet, from said place towards Moulton's point is 18 Feet across, 'till we come to the W Corner of David Woods Pasture, where it is 16½ Feet, Encroached by Wood half a Foot.

From the middle of Woods Pasture to Waits Wall shou'd be 16½ Feet, is but 14 Feet, Encroachd by Wood and Wait 2½ Feet, which is a great Damage to the Town.

From the upper or or [sic] Southerly Corner of Woods to Waits Wall is 20 Feet.

From the Southerly Corner of Widow Spragues Pasture to Waits Fence is 16½ Feet.

From Conants & Harris' W Corner of their Pasture to Waits Fence shou'd be 16½ Feet — Encroachd by Conant & Harris 2 Feet — about the middle of Conants & Harris' Pasture should be 16½ Feet, is but 15½, Encroach by them 1 Foot.

Between Boylston & Conant & Harris the Way is 23 Feet at the West end of said Lands, and 27 Feet wide at the E End of their Lands towards the Point.

There is a Way leading towards the Point to Austin' Pasture 16½ Feet wide, measuring 205 Feet long, 4½ Feet of the width the whole Length Encroach'd by Doc^r Russell's Fence, & Harris & Conant's Fence, the rest by Austin shut up and & improv'd — said Way continues 16½ Feet & 352 Feet long, leading down to the point all taken in and improv'd by Austin & the Towns Right continues the same width to low Water Mark.

WAY TO BUNKER HILL. — Then we begun & measur'd all the Way from Judge Fosters pasture & Waits Point where Molton point and Bunker's Hill road meet, and find it 18 Feet wide all the Way until we come to the Bottom of Dizar's Land.

From Dizars N Corner to Capt Kents East Corner is 16 Feet 6 Inches, Encroach'd by Capt Johnsons pasture Fence 2 Feet, which pasture is improv'd by Hopping.

The Road is 18 Feet wide from Kent's Pasture, all the way 'till you come to Dowse' Orchard.

At the South Corner of Dow' orchard across the way is 24 Feet.

At the W Corner of Dowse' Orchard across is 30 Feet & so continues to the Southerly part of Capt Fosters Pasture.

At the W Corner of Capt Fosters Pasture across is but 17 Feet.

From the middle of Larkins pasture over to Nat Rand is 16 Feet 6 Inches.

Then all the Way from that to the Top of Bunkers Hill is 17 Feet wide 'till we come to Capt Barber's Pasture, David Wait has Encroach'd six Inches on his Corner.

[**274.**] WAY TO BUNKERS HILL. — Between Capt Barber & Josiah Austin should be 16$\frac{1}{2}$ Feet, Encroachd by them one Foot, said Encroachment is by Barber only. — Also one Foot Encroach'd by Jos. Rand, & one Foot encroach'd by Tho' Call to make the 16$\frac{1}{2}$ Feet wide

Then the Road holds 16$\frac{1}{2}$ Feet 'till we come to Tho' Calls small peice of Stonewall Encroach'd by said Call's Wall one Foot. Then encroachd by Tho' Call at his pasture across from the upper End of Mr Ede' Land as it measures but 15 Feet & should be 16$\frac{1}{2}$ Feet, encroach'd one Foot & an half — Encroach'd by Mr Peter Edes 1$\frac{1}{2}$ Foot of the Road & 200 Feet long, it being about nine Rods above the Pitt where the Gravel has been dug, as it measures but 15 Feet, & shou'd be 16$\frac{1}{2}$ Feet.

Then we measur'd from the lower part of the place where the Gravel has been dug, as it measures but 15 feet & shou'd be 16$\frac{1}{2}$.

GRAVEL PIT. — Then we measur'd from the lower part of the Place where the Gravel was dug down to the Bottom of the Lane or way across from Temple's House to Eade's Corner, and the way is 18 Feet, wide all the way encroachd by Mr Eade's Stone Wall at the lower Corner one Foot.

Then we measurd a Gravel Pitt Enclos'd & Improv'd by Mr Peter Edes with his land lying Bounded on the way leading over Bunker's Hill just opposite to Temple's Barn. We began about 8 Feet below the easterly part of his Mr Edes' Stone Wall, said Wall being on the Way from Temples leading over Bunker's Hill & measurd from said Wall 84 Feet about South, where we drove a Stake & from said Stake we measur'd on a straight Line to the second Post in the Fence above the Apple Tree or Bush which brings it to a point which Line measures 180 Feet, which Land so describ'd is belonging to the Town, as appears by the Records of the Town.

WAY OUT OF THE FIELD. — Then we measur'd the way out of the Fields at the lower End between Nathl Rands & David Wait's Corners, which is 18 Feet.

From the South part of David Wait's wall over to Nat^l Rand's Fence is but 14 Feet wide, shou'd be 16 Feet 6 Inches, encroach'd by Waits Wall 2 Feet 6 Inches in the high Way — At the South part of Waits Land is 16 Feet 6 Inches.

Opposite to Jos. Rands N Corner shoud be 16 Feet 6 Inches — encroach'd by Smith one Foot and then holds out 16 Feet 6 Inches to the End of the Lane.

Then we measur'd a privilege Way from Jos. Rands Corner & David Woods Land which are opposite W Northerly Leading to the back side of Mr Seth Sweetsers Orchard encroachd by the Fence the back of Millers & Souther's Land one Foot, said Privilege Way being 14 Feet wide, & from Mr Sweetsers Orchard 100 Feet of said Way is shut up & Improv'd by Deacon Brigden.

GREEN'S LANE. — Then we began at the Bottom of Greens Lane by David Wood ju^rs House, which shou'd be 23 Feet one half the Way up the Lane, but from said Woods Fence by the House is but 19 Feet across, encroach'd by said Fence by Wood 4 Feet, & from the Barn to the middle of the Lane encroach'd 3 Feet by said Wood ; at the Top of the Lane shou'd be 16½ Feet, but near the Top is but 13 Feet 6 Inches, encroach'd by Wood & Hay 3 Feet.

LEADING TO THE TRAINING FIELD. — Then measur'd the Lane above Green's Lane to the Training Field ; we began at Jos : Rand Corner to David Wood's Fence, is 19 Feet from David Woods S : Corner head of Green's Lane to Nath^ll Austins Stone Wall 21 Feet. From Jno Hay's Corner top of Green's Lane to said Austins Wall is 20 Feet.

Between Mr Lemmon's & Mrs Austins Land should be 16 Feet, 6 Inches Encroachd by Mr Lemmon one Foot & an half —

From Austins Pasture to Trumbal's shoud be 16 Feet 6 Inches, Encroach by Austin 1½ Foot, and said Way continues 16 Feet 6 Inches to the Training Field —

GRAVEL PITT. — Then we measur'd a gravel Pitt belonging to the Town which lies opposite side the Road to the Front of Boylston's Pasture just above Mirick's, enclos'd & improv'd by Capt Hendley & Mr Mirick as follows, viz., by Hendley 147 Feet along on the Road at the N West End 24 Feet wide — In the middle 30 Feet deep, at the S. East End next Mirick's is 21 Feet wide, all from the Road a straight Line — By Mirick's as follows, from Capt Hendleys Fence on a straight Line to the second Post in the Fence on the Road from Mirick's House is 44 Feet, from said Post along the Road to Capt Hendley's Corner is 44 Feet, all which Lines we have measur'd & drove down Stakes —

[**275.**] TRAINING FIELD. — From Mirick's Garden Fence Southerly to Capt Halls N E Corner of his Land, Improvd by Peter Edes, is 355 Feet — From Dizars to said Corner shou'd be 23 Feet, encroach'd by Hall one Foot — From Dizars Fence to Boyleston's East Corners is 168 Feet, shoud be 172 feet, encroach'd by Dizar one foot, by Boyleston 3 feet — From Mr Waits Land to Capt Hendley's is 221 Feet, shou'd be 224 Feet & an half, encroach'd 3 Feet, & an half — From Boylston's up to Hendleys Fence by the House S. W. Corner is 224 Feet. —

TRAINING FIELD LANE. — From Peter Eades Barn to Trumbals Fence is 21 Feet — From the middle of said Line to the Entrance of the Training Field is 21 Feet, Encroach by Trumbal & Hendley one Foot all the Way to said Entrance.

DIZARS LANE. — From N W Corner of Townsends old House to Dizars Fence is 24 Feet 6 Inches — From Townsend's Barn to Dizars Fence 15 Feet 6 Inches — From Townsend's N Corner to Dizars, 16 Feet, both shou'd be 16 Feet 6 Inches, encroach'd by Dizar —
The Lane all the way down to Waits Marsh is 16 Feet 6 Inches, Encroach by Breed one Foot, by Conant 6 Inches.

SHIPPEY⁸ LANE. — From Mirick's Corner to Hussey's Corner, 30 Feet, Encroachd by Mirick one Foot.
From Miricks House or Bank to Fosters lower Corner is 18 feet.
From Townsends Shop to Capᵗ Fosters Land is 21 Feet — From Fosters upper Corner to Townsends Land is 25 Feet — From Wᵐ Leathers juʳ, formerly Fosdicks, to his own Land the other side the Way, formerly Waters, is 24 Feet, Encroachd by said Leathers one Foot — From said Leather's juʳ upper Corner, upper Corner, [sic] to Townsend's Lower Corner is 25 Feet — From Wᵐ Leathers Senʳ House to Townsend's old House is 27 Feet, Encroach'd by Townsend one Foot — Encroach'd by the Corner of Leather's Garden Fence 3 Feet.

HIGH STREET. — Then we began & measur'd from Mʳ Richᵈ Cary's North Corner over to Ebenʳ Breeds Shop, is 22 Feet.
From Josiah Harris' N Corner over to Mʳ Prentice's W Corner, improv'd by Abrahams, is 49 Feet, Prentice's Cellar Doors in the high Way — From Austin's to Jenner's Land, formerly Cutlers, is 21 Feet.

JENNERS LANE. — Then we measur'd a Lane leading from the lower End of Bow Street towards Charles River which runs to low water Mark — At the Top between Austin & Devens is 15 Feet down to Pratt's Lane which leads through between Josiah Harris' Work H House & Kiln House, at said last mention'd place said Jenners Lane is but 12 Feet wide & same width to low water mark which is fenc'd by Jenner's & Improv'd as a Garden All the way below Pratt's Land to the Wharffe, which 12 Feet is from the Line on the East Side by Mʳ Austins & Jenners Land.

PRATTS LANE. — Then we measurd Pratts Lane running East from Jenners Lane to Mʳ Russells Fence or upper Corner of his little House, which is 6 Feet wide, encroach'd by Jenner's Garden Fence about one Foot.

GREAVES STREET. — Then we measur'd from the upper Corner of Mʳ Russells little House 136 Feet, which brings us to a Post which is Mʳ Russells Bounds on the Top of Greaves Street joyning to high Street — The Top of Greaves Street from Mʳ Russells to Josiah Harris' Land is 21 Feet. At the bottom of Greaves Street from Mʳ Russells Fence to Josiah Harris' Land is 23 Feet, Encroach'd by Harris' Work House 2 Feet.

BOW STREET. — From Devens' N. East Corner at the head of Jenner's Lane over to Jenner's Pasture or Garden Fence is 29 Feet.

MASONS STREET. — There is a Street call'd Mason Street, between Masons Corner & Jenner's Corner, leading to Charles River, which is 16 Feet wide & runs to low water Mark.

Bow Street, continued. — From the widow Woods W. Corner to Mr Masons House is 26 Feet.

From Abrahams N. Corner to Mr Batemans is 26 Feet.

From Hunnewells to Brazers is 36 Feet.

From Lewis' Door to Docter Rand's Land is 36 Feet.

From Badgers Corner to Docter Rands Corner is 37 Feet 6 Inches, should be 38 Feet, encroachd by Docter Rand 6 Inches.

From the lower Corner of Ja' Bradish's, Junr, Land to the Corner of Hay's Land, formerly Newells, is 42 Feet 6 Inches, shoud be 44 Feet, Encroach'd by Mr Hay one Foot & an half.

From Jenners Land to the widow Fuz's[1] Land 42 Feet.

From Nat^l Phillips' N.W. Corner to Jno Goodwin's S. E. Corner is 45 Feet.

2. From David Newells Southerly Corner to Mr Roads' Barn is 43 Feet.

1. From the widow Lee's Fence to Lynde's House or Bounds is 45 Feet.

From Capt Johnson's Barn to Kiddars Fence, where the Barn stood, 33 Feet.

From Capt Johnsons Corner of his House to the N. E. Corner of Kiddars Shop is 45 Feet 6 Inches.

From Capt Johnsons Corner to Mistick Caleb Call's[2] W. Corner next the Street is 43 Feet 9 Inches.

Middle Gate Street. — From the S. W. Corner of Caleb Calls House or Land over to the S.E. Corner of Kiddars House (not Shop,) is 63 Feet & an half.

From the N.W. Corner of Bradish' Shop over to the S.E. Corner of Kiddar or Roads House (not Shop) is 33 Feet & an half.

From the widow Lees House or Shop over to Newells Barn is 36 Feet, M' Lees Cellar Doors part in the high Way.

From Nat. Phillips' house over to Richd Hunnewells is 29 Feet 6 Inches, Cellar Doors in the high Way.

From Tho' Rand S. Corner to Hunnewells is 38 Feet.

From Barnabas Davis' Corner to Ja' Bradish' Corner is 40 Feet 4 Inches.

[**276.**] Rope Makers Lane. — From Mr Seth Sweetsers S. Corner of his Fence near his House over to the Corner of his Garden bought of Davis shou'd be 25 Feet, is but 23 Feet 4 Inches, Encroach'd by Sweetsers Garden 20 Inches.

From Davis tower or S.W. Corner over to Ja' Bradish, Senr, is 25 Feet.

From Ja' Bradish, ju^r, S.E. Corner over to Ja' Bradish, Senr, Land is 23 Feet.

From Ja' Bradish ju^m Fence just below his House to Doct^r Rand's Fence is 21 Feet, shou'd be 23, Encroach'd by said Bradish 2 Feet.

From the lower Corner of Bradish's Land, where Frothingham's Shop is, to Doct^r Rands Corner is 23 Feet.

From Badgers Corner over to Hay's Corner, formerly Jno Newells, is 23 Feet.

---

[1] She was Mary Waters and married Hugh Furss, a mariner, Nov. 5, 1734. The name was sometimes spelled *Furze*.

[2] See foot-note on page 221. — Ed.

Just below Badgers House to Mr Lynde's Land is 21 Feet. From Lyndes Land to the lower End of Badgers Land is 30 Feet, & so runs down to low water Mark, which Landing is the Town's property.

TOWN HILL STREET. — From Caleb Calls Barn over to said Calls Land is 22 Feet.

From the Door of the Prison House to Mr Whites Land is 30 Feet & an half.

There is a Piece of Land between the Goal Land & Deacon Kettell, dec^d, now Shippie Townsend, measuring on the above said Street 18 Feet, & so runs back towards the back part, where it comes on a Line with Mr Edes Buildings, it is 19 Feet wide; said Piece of Land belongs to the Town, & is enclos'd by Mr Peter Edes.

TOWN HILL. — From the Corner of the School House over to Osbornes Fence is 42 Feet.

From Osborns Fence along by the School House & Flukers Barn to Deacon Jno Frothinghams Barn is 170 feet.

HURDS LANE. — Then we measur'd about 8 Feet from the Top, is 15 Feet wide, & a little below it is 11 Feet 9 Inches, encroach'd 3 Inches, Frothinghams Cellar Doors in the high way.

TOWNS HILL. — From Capt Fords Fence along by Boylstons & Fosters Barn to the South West Corner of Gravel Lane is 176 Feet, Frothinghams, Boylston's & Fosters dung Places in the Town's Land.

GRAVEL LANE. — At the Top from Phillip^s to Swans is 5 Feet.

At the lower End from Phillip^s to Swans 6 Feet 6 Inches.

TOWN HILL, continued. — From the N. Corner of Swans Barn to the S.W. Corner of Fosters Barn is 79 Feet.

From the N.W. Corner of Swans Barn to the S^o Corner of the old Town House is 54 Feet.

From Doc^r Greaves' Estate, now improvd by Capt Cary, over the Hill the N. side the Town House to Mr Sweetsers Garden bought of Davis, is 253 Feet 6 Inches.

From Capt Sheaffes Tallow House across the W. side of the Hill to the S^o Corner of Flucker's Chaise House is 180 Feet.

From the N. Corner of Corner of Capt Sheaffe's Barn to the S.W. Corner of the School House is 140 Feet.

From Mr Snow's Shop to the Fence just below Mr Abbot's Gate is 25 Feet.

From Mr Prentice's to Conant's Barn is 20 Feet.

From Jenner's House to Breeds Corner, now Wyers, shou'd be 30 Feet, is but 27 Feet 6 Inches, Encroach'd by Wyer's Fence 2 Feet 6 Inches.

From the Corner of Mr Prentice's House to the Corner of Wyers is 26 Feet.

STREET BEHIND THE MEETING HOUSE. — From the Corner of Mr Prentice's little House by the Meeting House to Breed's House or Shop shou'd be 31 Feet, is but 28 Feet, encroach'd 3 Feet, uncertain by which — Breed's Cellar-Doors in the high Way.

From the Corner of the Meeting House to Capt Austin's, Improv'd by Tim^o Goodwin, is 26 Feet and six Inches, Austins Cellar Doors in the high Way.

From the Widow Austins Corner of her House to the N. Corner of the Meeting is 23 Feet, the Cellar Doors in the high Way.

THE DOCK [AT] BOTTOM OF JOYNERS STREET. — There is a Dock the Bottom of Joyners Street that belongs to the Town between Mr Elias Stones Wharffe & Mr Jnᵒ White's Wharffe, measuring 21 Feet 10 Inches on Bridge Street, & so running the same Width to low Water Mark, Encroach'd by Mr White 16 Inches the low End of his Wharffe.

THE COMMON. — We began & measur'd from the Door of Mr Jabez Whittemores House across the Road to the Rail Fence six Rods to the first Post, making a straight Line on Cambridge Road.

From said Post on a N.W. Line up to the Corner of Mallets Land is 77 Rods & one Foot.

From said Corner of Mallets Land or N.E. Corner a straight Line along by the range of Lots to the N. Corner of Stearns' Orchard is 71 Rods six Feet & 6 Inches.

From the N. Corner of Stearns' Orchard on a straight Line running by his Barn & House to the S. W. Corner of said Stearns' Orchard is 24 Rods.

From said S.W. Corner of said Orchard, being the Bounds between Minot & Stearns, [on a] Straight Line with the Partition Fence across the Road to Stearns' other Land is 6 [Rods].

From the N.E. Corner of Stearns Orchard over the Way to the Division Fence of L [and] Marsh, formerly Miller's & Stearns' other Marsh, is 18 Rods.

[277.] COMMON. — From the Gate in the Range of Lots the upper side the Common across to the Division Fence between Wyer & Lynde is 53 Rods & Ten Feet six Inches.

From the Division Line between Shed & Wyer's Marsh on Cambridge Road to Alfords Sᵒ Corner is 22 Rod & 1 Foot.

CAMBRIDGE ROAD. — Then we measur'd across the Road at the Bridge just above Stearns' House, from Minots Land to Stearns' Marsh is 4 Rods & 14 Feet.

MINOTS MARSH WAY. — Then we measur'd a Way leading from the high Way the East Side the Bridge leading to Minots Marsh, measuring 5 Rods & 7 Feet & an half & 1 Rod & an half wide, which is enclos'd & improv'd by Mr Stearns.

Then we measur'd from Mr Miller's Wall by his House across the Road to the Fence by the Range way, is 6 Rods 13 Feet.

From Mr Woods Corner, which leads to Stephen Miller, over across the Road to Sheds Land, is 4 Rods & 14 Feet.

LANE BY MILLER'S TO WARDS MARSH. — Then we measur'd the Entrance of the Lane from Woods Corner to Lynde' Corner 2 Rods & 8 Feet.

From the back Corner of Wood's to Lynde' Land is 2 Rods & 10 Feet.

From Wood's back Corner on the Turn between Wood & Shed is 2 Rods & 12 Feet.

From Woods Land to Sheds near the next Turn is 1 Rod 12 Feet 6 Inches.

From Miller's to Shed's after the turn more Southerly is 1 Rod 13 Feet 6 Inches.

From the Line between Lynde's & Shed across the Lane to Miller's Land is 2 Rods & 9 Feet.

From the Bounds between Lynde's & Miller over to Jaͣ Millerͨ Land is 2 Rods & 14 Feet.

From Miller's Land to Miller's at the End of the Lane near Miller's House is 2 Rods & 14 Feet.

At the End of said Lane there is a way turns about East leading down to the Land or Marsh called formerly Bull Lot, measuring 20 Rods and a half and is 1 Rod wide, then said Way turning Southerly measuring 24 Rods & 7 Foot one Rod wide, both improved by Stephen Miller; then said Way runs 11 Rods 5 Feet & an half, improv'd by Brigden one Rod wide, it being part of the Bull Lot sold him by Miller or running by or through said Land.

Then said Road runs beyond the Bull Lot 15 Rods 2½ Feet, 2 Rods wide Improv'd by Brigden.

Then said Road runs on a little Turn Easterly and then runs South, in the whole 41 Rods 7 Feet 6 Inches and two Rods wide, improv'd by Miller, which brings us down to a point call'd Wards Marsh.

CAMBRIDGE ROAD CONTINUED. — From Foster's Corner at the Entrance of 3 Pole Lane over to Lynde's House is 6 Rods & 2 Feet.

From the Partition Fence between Lynd's & Welsh across the way to Welsh's Land or Fence 7 Rods 11 Feet & an half, Lynde's Fence the W. side his House encroach'd about 4 or 5 Feet.

From Welshͨ over to Welsh's Land is 6 Rods 6 Feet.

From Codmans N. W. Corner over to Pierces Land is 6 Rods 3 Feet.

From Tufts S.E. Corner to Pierces is 6 Rods.

From Pierces Corner to Tuft's Chaise House the W. Corner near the Stone House is 8 Rods & 8 Feet.

From Russells Corner to Tufts Fence is 7 Rods 14 Feet 6 Inches.

From the Partition Fence between Russell & Tufts on a Line with said Fence over to Mͬ Russell's Land is 8 Rods and 8 Feet.

The S.W. side the Bridge from Mͬ Russells Land to Mͬ Russell's Land is 3 Rods & 14 Feet.

At the widest place just at the turn of the Corner just below Mͬ Russell's House is 5 Rod & 14 Feet.

From Mͬ Russell's N. W. Corner of his Barn across to his Orchard is 2 Rods & 8 Feet.

From the Division Fence between Mͬ Russell & Mͬ Tufts over to Mͬ Russells Land is 4 Rods and 1 Foot.

From the Division Fence between Hastings & Tufts over to Russell's Land is 5 Rods 8 Feet & an half.

From the Division Fence between Hastings & Frost over to Mͬ Russell's Land is 5 Rods 1 Foot & 6 Inches.

At the Line which make the Bounds between Charlestown & Cambridge is 4 Rods & 2 Feet.

Then we measur'd a Piece of Land between Codmans Corner & Tuft's Corner on the Creek as follows: —

CREEK ON CAMBRIDGE ROAD. — From Codman's Corner to Tufts Corner on Cambridge Road is 7 Rods & 9 Feet.

From Tuft's Corner Southerly to a Corner is 8 Rods.

Then Turning Westerly which brings us to the Creek 5 Rods.

Then Easterly this side the Bridge to the Creek 4 Rods.

Then measuring across from the Corner of Tuft's Fence or Wall which is 8 Rods from Cambridge Road to the lower Corner of Codmans Fence is 8 Rods & eight Feet.

From the Creek measuring N. to the front Corner of said Codmans Fence on Cambridge Road is 6 Rods.

RANGE WAY [BAC] K OF TUFTS [ORCH] ARD. — Then measur'd a Range Way belonging to the Town which begins at a Gate back side of Tufts Orchard, Codmans 4 Acres, Irelands 4 Acres, & to Codmans other Land or Pasture, it being 81 Rods in Length & 2 Rods wide, all which is Shut up & improv'd by Wm Tufts.

Then we began & measurd a Range Way between Shed & Codman's Land running down towards the Marsh 55 Feet, then turning East 15 Rods & 2 Feet, Improv'd by Shed & Codman, it being 1 Rod wide.

Then said Range Way continued, 9 Rods 2 Feet of the last mentiond, nixt Welshe's is 1 Rod & half wide, then runs at the Bottom of Welsh^s upland 1 Rod & $\frac{1}{2}$ wide, Continuing the above Line to Minots [Mars]h, measuring 10 Rods, Improv'd by Ebenezer Shed.

[278.] Then we began & measur'd the Towns way beginning on Cambridge Road.

KENTS STREET. — At Pierces House over to Mr Russells Corner is 4 Rods & continuing the same Width all along to Mr Kents.

CHOATS ENCROACHMENT. — Then we measur'd a Piece of Land on said Street belonging to the Town chiefly encroach'd & built upon by Mr Sam^{ll} Choate, which lieth on the W. Side the Road & is bounded as follows, vizt N. Corner of Mr Russells Land W. to Pierces Land 7 Rods, then running on the Road or Street Southerly till you come to Mr Russells Land is 14 Rods & an half.

WATRING PLACE BY PEIRCES. — There is a watring place of 3 Quarters of an Acre lying between the Land of James Pierce & Nathl Tufts on the Road N. side, Encroach by Pierce & Tufts which belongs to the Town.

WATRING PLACE BY MR. KENTS. — Then we measur'd a Watring Place that belongs to the Town that lies near Mr Kents House bounded as follows, vizt: from the Corner of his Shop on the Road to the Corner of his other Land on the same Road on a straight Line is 14 Rods & 8 Feet, then from said Corner of Kents Shop running Southerly to the back Corner of said Kents Fence is 19 Rods & an half, from the above said Corner by or across the Brook W. to said Kents Land 9 Rods.

From said Corner N. to the upper Corner of said Kents Land next the Road is 22 Rods, & 13 Feet & 6 Inches with a considerable Bend near the Middle, from said Bend over across to said Kents other Land Easterly is 8 Rods & 10 Feet.

THE QUARRY. — There is about an Acre of Land between Hunnewells & Rands:

East of the Range Way which belongs to the Town & measures as follow : —

From the Range Way N.W. we measur'd E. to Rands Wall is 9 Rods & an half.

Then S. by said Rands Wall to the high way 16 Rods.

From thence along the Range Way N. is 16 Rods to said Rands Land, the place we sat out at.

HUNNEWELLS ENCROACHMT. — There is 1 quarter of an Acre which belongs to the Town on the W. side of the Range way near Charles Hunnewells, as a quarry, which Land said Charles Hunnewell has enclos'd and encroachd.

Said Hunnewell has encroachd on the Road from said Encroachment of the Town's on said Quarry 'till you come opposite his House 12 Rods & 7 Feet long at the Range Way, 1 Rod & 4 Feet by his House, 1 Rod & 2 Feet deep. From the N.W. Corner of Wyers Lot over to Charles Hunnewell's Land we find encroachd 10 Feet & an half, $7\frac{1}{2}$ Feet by Hunnewell & 3 Feet by Noah Bow man. Then we measur'd from Hunnewell's W. Corner over to Noah Bowmans Land & find it encroachd 1 Rod by said Noah Bowan, & said Encroachment continues about 8 Rods along the Road but not quite the same Width further along.

The Road continues 4 Rods wide 'till we come to the Turn which goes towards Cambridge Bounds or Coopers.

From Coopers Land to Goddards Land at the Line between Cambridge & Charlestown 3 Rods 11 Feet & an half.

In the Middle of said Lane or Street 3 Rods 10 Feet & an half. From Cooper E. Corner to Goddards W. Corner is 4 Rods 2 Feet. From Coopers Corner on a Turn to Prentices is 4 Rods 8 Feet.

From Watson's Land to Watson's at the first Bridge is 4 Rods. From the Widow Goddard's to Watson's at the Second or little Bridge is 4 Rods. From the Widow Goddard's to Watson's by the Elm Tree is 3 Rods 13 Feet & an half. From the South Corner of the Quarry sold Watson 3 Rods 14 Feet 6 Inches.

From the Land sold Watson, formerly the Quarry Hill, over to Mallet's all the Way along, 4 Rods.

PENNY FERRY ROAD. — From Capt Hancocks to Alfords is 33 feet.

From Whittemore's Land, where the House formerly was, just above Lamsons, across to Alfords Fence, is 53 feet.

From the lower or N E Corner of Lamsons Barn to said Alfords Fence is 34 Feet, besides a small Encroachment of about 2 feet by said Alfords Fence. The said Road continues the same Width, or 36 Feet to the Ferry, & round the Widow Howard's House & up to Miller's Marsh.

MEDFORD ROAD. — Then we measur'd from Mousell's Gate to Mallets Corner of his Pasture is 129 Feet. From the Corner of Stearn's Wall over to Mallets Land is 126 Feet. From Mr Stearn's Line, or Bounds opposite his Door, to Mr Deland's land is 174 Feet. From Deland's House or Bounds, to Bradish^s E Corner is 172 Feet.

From the Bounds of Phipps opposite his House to Bradish^s is 140 Feet.

From Ja⁵ Trumbals House to Phipp's Corner, the other Side the Road, 118 Feet & an half.

WATRING PLACE BY BRADISH⁸ LAND. — Between Bradish & Phipp⁸ is a watering place that belongs to the Town on the S side of Medford Rode, which measures as follows, viz⁴, From Bradishes' N W Corner to the back part or S. Corner of said Watring place is 132 Feet S. Side of Bradish⁸ Fence, the S. of the Barn encroached 18 Inches. From Phipp⁸ S E. Corner to the back of said Watring Place is 145 Feet.

MEDFORD ROAD, CONTINUED. — From Bradish's N W Corner to Phipps S E Corner on the Road is 136 Feet. From Phipp⁸ to Bradishes in the rere is 136 Feet.

From the East Corner of Mr Prentices Land to Leakeys Land 128 Feet.

From David Woods Land over to Leakeys Barn 124 Feet.

[279.] From the N E Corner of 3 Pole Lane over to Leakeys Land is 136 Feet.

MEDFORD ROAD. — From Mr Wood's Land by the little Bridge to Mr Wood's Land is 140 Feet.

From the N W. Corner of Wood's Land by the next Bridge over to Priest's Land is 136 Feet.

At the Corner of the Range Way by Shadrach Ireland's to Priest's is 64 Feet.

From Mr Temples S E Corner over to Isaac Mallets Orchard is 129 Feet & an half.

From the Corner between Mallet & Hutchinson over to Temples Land or Wall is 7 Rods & an half, Encroach'd by said Mallet & Hutchinson by their Barrs 3 Feet.

From Temple's Gate to the N W Corner of Hutchinson's Land is 8 Rods.

From Tufts House to Temples Land is 6 Rods & 14 Feet. From Tuft's Land to Temple's Land, making a Corner at the Locust Tree leading to Medford, is 6 Rods & 04 Feet. From said Corner or Locust Tree over to the Barrs that makes the Point or End of Temples Land the other side the way, is 8 rods & 14 feet. From the above said Barrs or Point across the Road to a Corner of Temples Wall leading to Medford is 3 Rods & 2 Feet, except two Feet, which is encroach'd in the middle, & continues said Width all the Way to Medford Bounds.

MENOTOMY ROAD. — From Temples Barrs or Point over to Peter Tuft's Wall is 6 Rods. From Temple's Fence of his Farm, or his East Fence across both Roads by the Barrs or Point of his other Land over to Peter Wall, is 10 Rods & 8 Feet. From the Division Line between Temple & Royall over to Peter Tuft's Wall is 6 Rods & 12 Feet.

From the Range Way by David Woods Orchard over to Royalls Farm is 5 Rods & 13 Feet 6 Inches.

From the N. W Corner of David Wood's Orchard to Royalls Fence is 6 Rods & 3 Feet.

From the N W Corner of the Range leading into Lynde's Farm over to Royall's Fence is 5 Rods 12 Feet 6 Inches.

From Lynde's Farm to Royall's at the Bridge is 6 Rods & 9 Feet.

From Mr Nathan Tuft's to Mallets is 5 Rods.   From the Corner of Nathan Tufts Land, or point turning to Medford Road over to Mallets, is 4 Rods 4 Feet.   From said Corner of Tuft's Land to his other Land across is 3 Rods & 8 Feet, leading towards Medford Line.

At the Division Line between Medford & Charlestown, between Tuft's Land & Tuft's Land, 3 Rods 10 Feet & 6 Inches.

From Mallets Corner over to Tuft's Land, which makes the Way to Menotomy & Cambridge Road, is 3 Rods 13 Feet 6 Inches.

From Mallets to Watson's Land at Cambridge Road, 3 Rods 2 Feet, a little Distance from the Corner.

An Account of the 8 lower Range Ways & the middle way, which are belonging to the Town, vizt:

RANGE WAY FIRST. — We began at the first by Brandishes a [t] the watering Place.   At the Entrance is 18 Feet wide, & is shut up & Improv'd by David Wood, 29 Rods & an half, running Southerly.   By Capt Brigden still Southerly, Shut up & Improv'd 16 Rods by him.   By Peleg Stearns, 8 Rods & an half, shut up & improved.   By Eben^r Shed, 17 Rods & an half, shut up & improv'd.   By James Miller, 18 Rods, shut up & improv'd, which comes into Cambridge Road.

SECOND. — Three Pole Lane from Medford Road to Cambridge Road, holds 3 Rods wide, & no part Shut up.

THIRD. — Then we began at the Wat'ring place between Pierce & Tufts, & measur'd the third Range Way, viz.: Shut up & Improv'd by Pierce, 53 Rods, the Remainder of said Range is open till we come to the End on Medford Road.

FOURTH. — Then we began on Medford Road, & measur'd Southerly on the Range Way 89 Rods, shut up & Improv'd by Peter Tufts, ju^r.   Then we measur'd still Southerly 11 Rods, shut up & Improv'd by Sam^{ll} Rand.   Then we measur'd still Southerly 5 Rods, Shut up & Improv'd with the Church Lot by Shed.   Then we measur'd still Southerly 32 Rods, shut up & Improv'd by Fillebrown, which brings us into middle Lane, which is on the Top of the Hill, the rest of said Range Way leading down to Irelands on Kents Street is all open.

FIFTH. — Then we began on Kents Street by Sam^{ll} Rands, and find the fifth Range Way open all the way through to Menotomy Road.

MIDDLE LANE. — From the fifth Range Way along the Top of the Hill is a way running aCross the Range Ways till you come into the Way call'd 3 Pole Lane, open all the Way; said Way is call'd Middle Lane.

SIXTH. — Then we measur'd the 6th Range Way.   We began on Menotomy Road, and measur'd Southerly 66 Rods & an half, in-closd and improvd by Mr David Wood.   By Sam^{ll} Kent, still Southerly, Shut up & improv'd by him.   By Sam^{ll} Rand, still Southerly, shut up & improv'd by him 8 Rods.   By Joshua Rand, Shut up & improv'd by him Still Southerly 40 Rods.   By Peter Tufts, shut up and improv'd by him, Still Southerly 38 Rods and an half. From the last mentioned Place to the Quarrie Still Southerly 79 Rods, which is fenc'd each side of the way, but at said End of the Lane, Charles Hunnewell has put a Fence & Improv'd it, but not so as to hinder Cattle's passing thro. said Quarrie being on Kents Street.

SEVENTH. — Then we began at Menotomy Road, and measur'd the Seventh Range Way from said Road Southerly 42 Rods, shut up & improv'd by Mr Lynd. Then measur'd still Southerly 40 Rods & ¼, shut up & improv'd by Peter Tufts, ju^r. Then measurd still Southerly 12 Rods & 4 Feet, shut up & improvd by Mr Lynde.

[**280.**] SEVENTH RANGE, CONTINUED. — Then we measur'd still Southerly 11 Rods & 2 Feet, shut up by Mansfield Tappling & improv'd by him. Then we measurd still Southerly 20 Rods, Shut up & improv'd by Lynde. Then we measur'd still Southerly 36 Rods, Shut up & improvd by Jon^a Hill, of Cambridge, from that to Kents Street open.

EIGHTH RANGE WAY. — Then we began at Kents Lane & measur'd to Lynde's House, is not shut up, & from thence Northerly 168 Rods & ¼ shut up & improv'd by Lynde. then we measur'd still Northerly till we came to Menotomy Road 28 Rods & ¾, shut up & improv'd by Nathan Tufts.

MENOTOMY ROAD, CONTINU'D. — From Nathan Tufts to Watson's, formerly Quarrie Hill, a little way from the Corner leading to Menotomy is 4 Rods & 4 Feet. From the N W Corner of said Watson's Land by the Brook to Mr Russell's Land, is 4 Rods & 4 Feet.

From the Range Way just beyond the Brook across the Road is 4 Rods & 11 Feet.

From Mr Russells House over to Cookes Land, 4 Rods.

From the Range way by Walter Russells over is 4 Rods wide; said Walter Russell encroach'd 4 Feet.

From Patten Russells over to Teels, 4 Rods & 8 Feet.

Down at Menotomy or Fillebrowns Bridge, from Fence to Fence, is 8 Rods and 10 Feet, and so runs quite to the Brook, which makes it 5 Rods. But Mr Dicksons has fenced off a piece, the lower side the Way, which prevents the Ro[a]d on that part coming to the Brook, and says he has a Deed of it, but we are of Opinion, according to former Records, & by the Situation of the Place, it belongs to the Town for a fishing place.

There is a Piece of Land of 5 Rods on the Brook the other side the Bridge belonging to the Town which we cannot particularly describe, for want of the plan, which is mislaid by some persons.

Then we measurd 3 Range Ways in the upper Part of Charlestown, between Menotomy Road & Medford River.

FIRST RANGE WAY. — We began on Menotomy Road, near two penny Brook or Walnut Tree Hill, & measur'd the first Range Way, Northerly 90 Rods & ¾. Shut up and improv'd by Mr Russell; then still Northerly 24 Rods, shut up & improv'd ½ by Mr Russell & ½ by Mr Fosdick; then running still Northerly 5 Rods, shut up wholly by Mr Fosdick & improv'd by him; then we measur'd still Northerly, this being Medford Bounds, 85 Rods, shut up & improv'd by Nathan Tufts; then still Northerly 169 Rods, shut up & improv'd by Brigadier Royall, which brings us to way which passes by our Fish Place on Medford River.

SECOND RANGE WAY. — Then we began at M^r Ja^s. Tufts near Medford River, & measur'd Southerly 120 Rods, shut up & improved by Ja^s Tufts, which brings us into Charlestown; still Southerly we measur'd 142 Rods, which brings us to Menotamy Ro[a]d, shut up and improvd by Mr Russell.

THIRD RANGE WAY. — Then we began on Menotomy Road, & measurd the third Range Way Northerly, partly open, & then still Northerly, shut up, 20 Rods, partly by Dickson, partly by Smith, this being Medford Bounds. Then proceeded still Northerly to Medford River to a Rock, which measures 160 Rods, shut up & improv'd by the Revd Mr Smith.

There is by the Records a place for Gravel about $\frac{1}{2}$ an Acre of Land on Mistick River just above the Bridge bounded as follows: Westerly by Land formerly Jonathan Tufts^s, now Brigadier Royalls, 10 Rods, & $\frac{1}{2}$ Northerly on said Tufts^s Land next the Marsh, 7 Rods, from whence a 2 pole way, running down to the River, Butting Easterly on the Country Road 5 Rod & $\frac{1}{2}$, and Southerly upon the way that Leads to the Ford or Landing place 9 Rods, which way is 2 Rods wide to the Landing place, now improvd by Eb^r. Marrow, and which he challenges as his property.

There is a piece of Land about $\frac{1}{2}$ an Acre belonging to the Town for a Landing or a Fishing place on Medford River, which is Bounded as follows, vizt: on Land formerly Mr Jon^a Tufts, now Brigadier Royalls, measuring from the Road at east End back to the River Northerly 8 Rods, from said East End along the Road to a stake, measuring 24 Rods Westerly, and from said stake Northerly to the River is 2 Rods, all straight Lines.

There is a p'ce of Land belonging to the Town, upland & Marsh; the Pound standing on one Corner of it, containing about 2 Acres, bounded as follows, viz: Easterly on the high way, Westerly on Nat^l Browns Land, and, as the Creek now goes, runs into the Mill Pond Southerly upon Peter Edes^s from the high to the Mill Pond.

There is a wat'ring place belonging to the Town lying on Medford River, bounded as follows: Bounded on each side by the Land of Mr Wm Smith S: W: 29$\frac{1}{2}$ Rods N: E, 28 Rods & $\frac{1}{2}$ South East on the Range Way, leading to the River 2 Rods, the Breadth at the Bottom next the River Northerly 13 Rods & $\frac{1}{2}$, which lyes a little to the Westward of Smith's house.

[281.] MENOTOMY ROAD CONTINUED. — From Dixson's to Mr Russells Land the West side the Bridge is 2 Rods & 9 Feet.

Between old Mr Dixson & his son 28 Feet, Encroach'd by both of them considerably as it shou'd 3 Rods.

From the W Corner of Dixson's Land across 2 Rods & 12 Feet, Encroach'd 4 Feet and an half.

From the W Corner of Deacon Cutlers, now Lying common, across the way, 2 Rods six Feet.

At the S. E. Corner of Winships Land, formerly Cooks, over across the way, 2 Rods & seven Feet.

From the S° Corner of Jos : Adam' Land, over the Way to Town' Landing by Cartwrights, 2 Rods 2 Feet.

From Winships Land to Belknaps across is 2 Rods 14 Feet.

From George Cutters to Winships across at the Entrance which Leads to Menotomy, 3 Rods.

From Cutlers across to Adam' as you go to the Wares, 3 Rods.

From Cutlers Barn to Joseph Adams across, 2 Rods 15 Feet.

From the N E Corner of Holden's House across is 2 Rods & 12 Feet.

At the Bridge is 2 Rods and 8 Feet across ; the Road between Holdens & the Bridge encroach in several places.

WAY FROM CAMBRIDGE BOUNDS TO WOBURN BOUNDS. — Then we measur'd the Way from the little Bridge which makes Cambridge Bounds towards Sam[ll] Cutters to the Top of the Hill, making a Corner which leads to Cutters Mill.

the Road is 2 Rods & half wide all the way.

At the Bottom of said Hill leading to said Cutter's in the Valley is 2 rods & 2 Feet ; at the Bottom of said Hill or Valley S of said Cutters House is 3 Rods and 10 Feet ; at the S° Corner of Cutters House from Fence to to Fence across is 2 Rods & 3 Feet ; at the N E Corner of Cutters House across from Fence to Fence is 4 Rods ; said Cutter hath fenced off a piece of the way for a Garden.

Between Francis & Cutter is 3 Rods 10 Links, Between D° further along is 2 Rods.

Between Adam's & Sam[ll] Cutter is 2 Rods & 3 Feet.

From the House formerly Dan[l] Reeds across the Road is 3 Rods & 2 Links.

At the foot of the Hill is 2 Rods & 12 Feet across, at the Top of the Hill towards Seth Reeds across, 2 Rods 6 Links. At the S° part of said Seth Reeds House across is 2 Rods & ¼. At said Reeds Barn across the Way is 2 Rods 9 Feet. The Road between Reeds Land rising the Hill 3 Rods 6 Links across. The road above the Brook across is 2 Rods, but encroach'd on Link by Reed.

At the Brook between Adams & Swan is 3 Rod 1 Link. From the S° E: Corner by Swans House to Adams Land is 2 Rods 10 Feet.

At the Top of the Hill between Hartwell & Hartwell is 2 Rods, 13 Feet. Between D° at the Brow at the Brow [sic] of the Hill 2 Rods, but encroach'd by Hartwell 18 Inches. At the Bottom of the Hill between D° is 3 Rods & 8 Feet. Further along between D° is 2 Rods & 14 Links.

Between Gardners & widow Hartwells thirds is 2 Rods 13 Feet.

At the lowest Corner of Gardners Garden over th the Wall by the Cyder press is but 29 Feet, should be at least 2 Rods, encroach'd by said Gardner on the Way at least 4 Feet by the Wall near the Cyder press

At the S° Corner of Gardners House across the Way 3 Rods 2 Feet. At the Bounds of Woburn from Corner to Corner of Gardners Land is 3 Rods & 2 Feet.

We have carefully measur'd every Place, & find as we have reported in the above & sheets annex'd, & have taken great Care & Pains to Search the Towns Records relative thereto.

SAMUEL KENT.

JOHN CODMAN.

JOSIAH WHITTEMORE.

CHARLESTOWN, March 2ᵈ, 1767.

We the Subscribers being appointed to assert the Towns Rights report as follows : —

+1ᵗ. That the Wharffe & Landing Place at the Bottom of Rope Makers Lane between Mʳ Lyndes & Badgers is the Towns Property to low Water mark.

2ᵈ. That the Landing Place the Bottom of Masons lane between Foster & Goodwin is the Towns Property to low Water mark.

+3ᵈ. That the Wharffe & Landing Place at the Bottom of Jenners Lane, between Jenners Land and Jenners Land, belongs to the Town to low Water mark.

4ᵗʰ. That the Creek between Mʳ Russels Wharffe & Ware House to low Water mark, belongs to the Town.

5ᵗʰ. That the Dock for the Ferry' use from Lemmons Wharffe or Goodwins over to Barbers Wharffe, & so running down to low Water mark, is the Towns Property. That Bunkers Wharffe is built to its utmost Bounds, & that on condition of leaving a sufficient high Way across, & not to hinder landing Hay, Wood, or any thing on the Same.

+6ᵗʰ. That the Dock at the Bottom of Joynes Street, between Mʳ White & Mʳ Stone, belongs to the Town, & runs to low Water mark.

7ᵗʰ. That the Dock call'd the Towns Dock at the Swing Bridge & upwards belongs to the Town & runs to low Water mark.

[282.] 8ᵗʰ. That there is a landing Place at the Bottom of the Lane between John Ivory' Land, formerly Trumbals, & the Land formerly Danˡ Edes, in Charles River, which belongs to the Town, & Runs to low Water Mark, which Lane runs across battery Street to Charles River.

9ᵗʰ. That there is a piece of Land the lower side Battry Street which runs to low Water Mark ; also a Pice of Land the upper side said Street, belonging to the Town, Improv'd by Mʳ Marɪllin, all which we advise the Town to dispose of, which belonged to the old Battry.

10ᵗʰ. That there is a Landing Place on Battery Street, the bottom of Wapping Street, which belongs to the Town & runs to low water mark.

11ᵗʰ. That there is a Place improv'd for a Battery on Said Battery Street, just below Mʳ Foye's, which belongs to the Town, which runs to low water mark.

12ᵗʰ. There is a way at Molton's Point, between Mʳ Harris' & Conants Land & Mʳ Jos. Austins Heirs Land towards Chelsea, & runs to low Water mark, which belong's to the Town, and is shut up & improv'd by Austins Heirs chiefly.

13ᵗʰ. There is a Landing Place near the Bottom of Streeters Lane on wapping Street, which runs to the Dock between Mʳ Harris⁸ Kiln House & work House, opposite Mr Grubbs House, which belongs to the Town.

14th. There is a Landing Place issuing out of Wapping Street, between Mr Teel & the widow Whittemore, which belongs to the Town.

15th. The head of the Town Dock which is at the Bridge, the upper End of Wapping Street, belongs to the Town & is 22 Feet wide, and runs to low Water mark.

15th. That the Place called the Market Place belongs to the Town, reserving a public highway thro' the same.

16th. That the Towns Hill (so call'd) on which the old Town House stands, That the two ministerial Houses & the Land on which they stand & which is improvd by the Ministers with said Houses, belongs to the Town

17th. That the Land on which the School House stands & Alms House or Work House stands or improv'd by them are all belonging to & improv'd by the Town.

18^t.. That there is a Piece of Land between the County's Land and Mr Townsend's or the late Deacon Kettells Land which belongs to the Town and is shut up and improv'd by Mr Peter Edes.

19th There is a Piece of Land belonging to the Town, call'd the Training Field, & improv'd for Military Exercise.

20th. There is a Piece of Land belonging to the Town, formerly a Gravel pit, which is fenc'd & improv'd by Capt Hendley & Mr Mirick, near the Training Field, which we advise the Town to dispose of. There is also a Gravel pit Enclos'd by Mr Edes belonging to the Town by Temples.

21st. There is a Hill call'd burying Hill which belongs to the Town, only Mr Rand has a Right to Feed the Same, with a broad way & a way to the Lime Kiln.

22^d. There is a Landing place on the way to the Mills from Mr Wyers Bounds to at Line with the first Corner of the Mill House to low water mark, which belongs to the Town, on which Mr Green has built a House.

23^d. There is a Landing at the lower End of the Causeway running by Temples Fence to low water mark, & all the Flats, which belongs to the Town & might be improv'd to some profit.

24th. There is a wharffe and Landing Place between Mr Fosdicks Shop & Mr Lamsons Shop, which runs to low Water mark, which belongs to the Town.

25th. The Common Land lying unfenced belongs to the Town.

26th. There is a wat'ring place by Mr Bradlish House, Formerly Turners, which belongs to the Town.

27th. There is a way on Cambridge Road to Minots Marsh belongs to the Town, Improv'd by Mr Stearns.

28th. There is a way near Stephen Millers, leading to Bull Lot & other Lots, which the Town might sell part of without Injury to any one.

29th. There is a way between Mr Sheds & Mr Codmens, leading to the marshes, shut up by Codman and Shed, but chiefly by Shed.

30th. There is a Square or Piece of Ground by the Bridge, between Codmans Land & Tuft's Land, belonging to the Town.

31st. There is a way over the Bridge, between Wm Tufts Land

& Tho⁸ Ireland's & Codmans Land, enclosd & Improv'd by said Tufts, which belongs to the Town.

32ᵈ.   There is a Triangular Piece of Ground in Kents Lane, the Corner of Mʳ Russells Orchard, on which Mʳ Choate has built an House, which belongs to the Town.

33ᵈ.   There is ¾ of an Acre of Land, more or less, for a wat'-ring place at the bottom of the Range Way between Pierces & Nat: Tufts, improv'd cheifly by said Pierce & Tufts, which we advise the Town to dispose of.

34ᵗʰ.   There is a watring place just by Mʳ Kents House, which belongs to the Town.

35ᵗʰ.   There is a square piece of Land for a Quarry, between Joshua Rands Land & the Range Way, which belongs to the Town.   There is a Quarter of an Acre of Land for a Quarry, be-tween said Range way & Charles Hunnewells Land, enclosd & improvd by said Hunnewell, with a considerable piece of the high way, which belong to the Town.

[285.]¹   36th.   There are eight Range Ways between the Common and the Powder House and one middle way all belonging to the Town, the middle way and 2 of the Range Ways kept open ; all the rest shut up and improv'd by sundry Persons.

37th.   There are 3 Range Ways in the upper part of Charles-town, from Walnut Free Hill to menotamy Road, over to Medford River, which belong to the Town, & are shut up by sundry persons, & improvd by them, some in Charlestown & some in Medford.

38th.   There is a fishing place on Medford River, at the End of the first Range which belongs to the Town.

39th.   There is wat'ring place near the End of the third Range Way. which is enclos'd by Mʳ Smith⁸ Farm, which we woud have the Town dispose of as it may be done without Injury to any Body.

40th.   There is a Landing just below the wares, & a way to it, which Way Capᵗ Cartwright has shut up & improves the Landing, calling them his own, all which appear from the former Surveys to belong to this Town, & are of considerable Consequence to the Town.

41st.   There is a fishing place at Menotomy Bridge, South Side, which appears to belong to the Town, but Mʳ Dixson has put up a Fence & enclosed the most of it.   There is a piece of Land the other side of the Bridge, which belongs to the Town, which we cannot certainly describe for want of the Plan which is mislaid.

42d.   We find in the smallest Town's Book, Folio 40, That the Place for getting Sand by Leakies, opposite Mʳ Wood's Land, was laid out for that Purpose.

SAMUEL KENT.
JOHN CODMAN.
JOSIAH WHITTEMORE.

Attest:

SETH SWEETSER, *Town Clerk.*

A copy from the original & recorded agreeable to a Vote of the Town.

---

¹ The Survey of 1767 here goes to p. 285, skipping pp. 283 and 284. — ED.

BOUNDS BETWEEN CAMBRIDGE AND CHARLESTOWN.

[283.] The Bounds between the Towns of Cambridge & Charlestown, as shewn to me by the Select Men of Each Town, Sepr 17 & 18, A.D. 1771, vizt : —

	Degrees	Minutes		Chains	Links		Marks	No.	
							a Cedar Post	1,	about 3 Rods from the Sedge Bank.
thence North,	64	15	West,	15	90	to a Post		2,	near the Fence ———
thence N.,	76	30	W.,	15	45	to a Post		3,	near a White Oak Tree
thence N.,	79	15	W.,	10		to a Post		4,	near a large Stump mark'd C. C.
thence N.,	75	45	W.,	9	73	to a Post		5,	near a gray Oak Tree.
thence So.,	89	0	W.,	6	30	to a Post		6,	near a crotch'd White Oak Tree.
thence N.,	83	45	W.,	12	43	to a Pdst		7,	at a Corner.
thence N.,	30	30	W.,	25	70	to a Post		8,	by the Country Road.
thence N.,	30	30	W.,	4	53	to a Post		9,	in the Meadow.
thence N.,	34	0	W.,	14	90	to a Post		10,	near a Walnut Tree.
thence N.,	33	0	W.,	7	80	to a Post		11,	the Corner of Mr Foxcrofts pasture.
thence N.,	32	0	W.,	23	50	to a Post		12,	aCross a Meadow.
thence N.,	24	0	W.,	10	58	to a Post		13,	——— ———.
thence N.,	30	45	W.,	23	31	to a Post		14,	near the widow Goddards.
thence N.	34	0	W.,	6	37	to a Post		15,	at th S. W. of Ebr Thwings House.
thence N.,	31	30	W.,	20	50	to a Post		16,	near an old Stump.
thence N.,	25	0	W.,	22	0	to a Post		17,	the Corner of Isaac Watsons Orchard.
thence N.,	26	0	W.,	30	0	to a Post		18,	by a Stone Wall between the Land of John & Edward Dixson.
thence N.,	36	0	W.,	15	0	to a Post		19,	by John Dixson's Stone Wall.
thence N.,	34	30	W.,	17	50	to a Post		20,	over the River and Meadow.
thence N.,	29	45	W.,	10	92	to a Post		21,	by the Wall between Cutter & Lock.
thence N.,	33	30	W.,	33	30	to a Post		22,	by the Country Road.
thence N.,	34	0	W.,	28	50	to a Post		23,	on the Northerly Side of the Road leading to Medford.
thence N.,	34	0	W.,	18	60	to a Post		24,	by the Road near a Stone Bridge.
thence N.,	34	15	W.,	7	0	to a Post		25,	near the widow Cutters Field.
thence N.,	37	30	W.,	22	75	to a Post		26,	near ye Fence between Am^h & Sam^{ll} Cutters Land.
thence N.,	37	15	W.,	11	90	to a Post		27,	on a Hill near a bass Wood Tree.
thence N.,	36	0	W.,	8	11	to a Post		28,	S^o of Ensign Adams's Pasture.
thence N.,	39	0	W.,	16	19	to a Post		29,	in Amma Cutters Pasture.
thence N.,	34	45	W.,	18	0	to a Post		30,	where three Walls meet.
thence N.,	26	0	W.,	6	78	to a Post		31,	where 3 Walls meet ye West Corner of Seth Reeds Pasture.
thence N.,	20	15	W.,	8	0	to a Post		32,	by a Wall between Bowman & Adams.
thence N.,	36	30	W.,	23	0	to a Post		33,	near an old black Oak by the Road.
thence N.,	41	45	W.,	13	70	to a Post		34,	by the Wall in Tho: Wright's Land.
thence N.,	31	0	W.,	9	50	to a Post		35,	at Thos Wrights Corner at Woburn Line.

N. B. 25 Links make one Rod — 4 Rods make one Chain. — There being Trees between several of the aforementioned Stations, & that prevented the Seeing some of them at the next Station, which makes it uncertain whether all the Stations or Posts aforemention'd are in the exact Course aforemention'd, but the Variation from the same can be but very little, if any.

AB^R. FULLER, Survey^r.

February 24th, 1772. We, the Subscribers, Select Men of the
Towns of Cambridge & Charlestown, Committees chosen by the
respective Towns to run the Lines between said Towns, have, according to the Votes pass'd by said Towns in May last, attended
the Service therein assignd us, & the boundary Line between the
Two Towns aforesaid is contain'd in the above and foregoing
paper: 1. W^m. Brattle; 2. Eben^r Stedman; 3. Edward Marritt;
4. Joseph Willington; 5. Joseph Adams, Ju^r.; 6. Alijah Learned;
7. Thos. Gardner.

William Conant, Nathaniel Gorham, Nehemiah Rand, Nathl.
Frothingham, David Wood, Peter Tufts, ju^r., Stephen Miller. ——
The foregoing is a True Copy from the Original, & recorded
agreeable to a Vote of the Town at their meet^g June 2^d, 1772.

Attⁿ: Seth Sweetser, Town Clerk.

BOUNDS BETWEEN CHARLESTOWN AND MEDFORD

[284.]¹   Novr 1771.

We, the Subscribers, being appointed by the Towns of Charlestown & Medford to perambulate the Line between the Two Towns
& fix some certain Monuments & Marks in said Line, met this Day
and proceeded as follows: —

Set out from the River called Medford River, Course South 38½
Deg: West, Distance 7 Rods to a Post between Col°: Royall's
Farm & Mr Temple's Farm, markd N° 1 with the Letters C. &
M: — From thence on the same Course to the Country Road, 84
Rods to a Post N° 2, mark'd C. & M: on the same Course to
another Post N°. 3 at the South West Corner of said Royall's
Farm, mark'd C. & M., Distance 25 Rods. Then turning North,
62 Deg. West, to a Post N°. 4, near the Wind Mill, Distance 279
Rods on the Country Road — Then running North, 50 Deg. East,
Distance 31 Rods to a Post N°. 5, mark'd C. & M., at a Stone
Wall & Gate bounding Col° Royall's Farm. Then North. 25
Deg. West, Distance 20 Rods across the *Country* Road, a circular
Line to a Post N°. 6, mark'd C. & M: From thence North, 5
Degrees East, Distance 49 Rods a circular Line to a Post N°. 7,
Mark C. & M., between said Royall's Land & Mr Nathan Tuft's
Land — Then North, 58½ Deg: West, Distance 70 Rods across
Tuft's Land & the Range Way to a Post in Mr Peter Tuft's Land
N°. 8, Mark'd C. & M. Then South, 31½ Deg. W., Distance 5
Rods by the Range Way to a Post in the Hon^b. James Russell's
Land N°. 9, Mark'd C. & M. Then North, 60 Degs. W: Dis-
tance 41 Rods to a Post N°. 10, in a corner of Peter Tuft's Land,
Mark'd C. & M. — Then North, 30½ Deg: East, Distance 7¼ Rods
to a Post N°. 11, Mark'd C. & M., in said Tuft's Land. Then
North. 60 Deg: W., Distance 42 Rods to a Post N°. 12, mark'd
C. & M., on A Range Way. Then North, 31 Deg: East, Distance
23 Rods to a Post N°. 13, markd C. & M. Then across said
Range Way North, 59 Deg: W., Distance 43 Rods to a Post N°.
14, Mark'd C. & M.: in a Corner of the late James Tuft's Land,
adjoyning Smith's Land. Thence South, 29 Deg: W., Distance 17
Rods to a Post N°. 15, the South West Corner of Smith's Farm,
Mark'd C. & M. — Thence North, 39 Deg: W., Distance 43½
Rods to a Post N°. 16, mark'd C. & M: at the Range Way —

---

¹ See Foot note on page 244.—Ed.

Thence North, 33 Deg: E., Distance 38½ Rods to a Post Nº. 17, by the Range Way in Smith's Farm. Thence North across said Range Way, 59½ Deg: W., to a Post Nº. 18, mark'd C. & M., against the N. West Corner of Smith's Farm, Distance 52 Rods — Thence North, 35½ Deg: E., Distance 87 Rods to a Post Nº. 19, near Medford River, mark'd C. & M. — Thence on said River & Medford Pond, to Symmes' River, and on said River to a Post Nº. 20, at the Easterly Corner of Gardner's Farm, near Symmes', mark'd C. & M. — Thence North, 25 Deg: W., through a Swamp, Distance about 80 Rods, to a Post Nº. 21, between Gardner, & Symme's Farm, markd C. & M., & on the same Course 72 Rods to a Post Nº. 22, on Woburn Ro[a]d, marked C. & M. — William Conant, Nehemiah Rand, Peter Tufts, juʳ., Stephen Miller, Committee for Charlestown. — Seth Blodget, Nathan Tufts, Willis Hall, Committee for Medford.

EBENEZER BROOKS, Surveyor.

N. B. It is further agreed by the Committee of both Towns that Charlestown shall maintain the first Eleven Posts, beginning at Nº. one, & Medford the other Eleven, beginning at Nº. 12. — The foregoing is a true Copy from the Original, & recorded agreeable to a Vote of the Town at their Meetᵍ., June 2ᵈ, 1772.

Attⁿ. SETH SWEETSER, Town Clerk.

Page [286] Blank.
Page [287] Blank.

SURVEY OF 1802.

[288.] In conformity to a Vote of the Inhabitants of Charlestown, at their Meeting on the 1ˢᵗ. of March, 1802, authorizing the Selectmen to appoint a Committee to ascertain the Town's rights: We, the Subscribers, being appointed for that purpose, most respectfully submit the following report.

We began at Mʳ Benjamin Goodwins line, and measured over the Dock to Thomas Hoopers Wharf 74 feet, encroached by Hooper 2 feet 6 inches.

From the East corner of Mr Andrew Stimpson's house to the South Corner of Mrs Gardiner's is 43 feet, the house being ten feet, or thereabout, from the Cap of the Wharf, being the extreme bounds of Mrs Gardner's land towards Charles river.

From the north Corner of Mr Brigden's house over to Mr Ebenezer Austin's fence is 37 feet 9 inches. Mr Ammi Tufts' house has encroached 9 inches, and cellar doors in the street.

MAIN STREET. — From Ebenʳ. Austin's, west of the house to Mr Charles Coles opposite, is 39 feet 6 inches. From the South corner of Mr Trumbull's house to Mr Thomas Russell's bounds is 44 feet — encroached one foot 6 inches. At the South extreme of the Square from Devens house to Mr Russell's land opposite is 50 feet.

Bringing the Square to a point from Deven's north east Corner, 26 feet 4 inches East of the house, to the west of the square at

John Austins' house 308 feet 6 inches; being South side of the Square.

From John Austin's, west corner of the Square, to the north corner, 7 feet South of Waitt's Brick wall, is 306 feet, 6 inches.

From the north corner of the Square at Waitt's house to the East corner of the Square at Whittemores is 284 feet.

From the East corner of the Square at Whittemores to the South corner at Devens' is 188 feet, 6 inches.

From David Waitt's brick wall over to the house belonging to the Estate of the late Thomas Russell, is 49 feet, formerly 50 feet, encroached one foot.

From the north corner of Mr Nath¹ Austin's store to Sam¹ Bradstreet's South corner is 49 feet, 6 inches. Broadstreet encroached 6 inches.

From Benjᵃ. Hurd, junr's, brick store over to Rudburg's is 51 feet 8 inchˢ.

From Mr Richard Boylstone's over to Benjᵃ Hurd's north corner is 57 feet. From the East corner of Mr Thomas Brooks over to Nuttings Store is 52 feet. From Doctor Josiah Bartlett's over to Mr Nath¹. Austin's south corner is 61 feet. From the east corner of Mr. Amos Tufts', over to the South corner of Eliphalet Newell's (called Warren Tavern), is 98 feet 4 inches.

[289.] From the east corner of Mrs Bradish's house over to Moses Hall's garden fence is 64 feet 6 inches. From the west corner of John Hay's house over to Mr James Green's front door is 60 feet.

From the South corner of Page's tavern, corner of Green's lane, to the opposite side across the street, is 72 feet 5 inches.

From Mrs Bradshaw's horse block, over to Chapman's land, is 62 feet 9 inches. From Solomon Phipps' front door over to the the corner of Harrisons fence, going up to the new Baptist Meeting house, is 82 feet. From the east corner of Mr Thomas Frothingham's house to the South corner of his shop opposite is 59 feet 4 inches.

From the north corner of Major Benjamin Frothingham's over to Richard Frothingham's land opposite, is 83 feet 3 inches.

MAIN STREET. — From the north corner of Mitchel's house over to the South corner of Richard Frothingham's house, is 126 feet. From the south corner of Cox's land leading to the Mill, to Richard Frothingham's garden fence, is 142 feet. From the east corner of Cox's land to Richard Frothingham's garden fence opposite, is 72 feet.

From the east corner of Cox's land over to Keith's north corner of his house is 88 feet 9 inches. From Mr Joseph Newell's house to the Mill land is 75 feet. From the South of Mr Samuel Swan's land over to Mr Austin's marsh, at the east corner, is 68 feet 6 inches, encroached by Swan one foot. From the east corner of the pound over to Edes' land is 81 feet. From Edes' land over to Penny's is 72 feet. From Edes corner at Bunker's hill lane over to Mr Nath¹ Austins land, formerly Call's, is 65 feet 3 inches. Pierces' steps are in the street. From Mr Mallett's, formerly Temple's, over to Pierces' marsh, formerly Temples, is 55 feet. From the corner of Mallet's, formerly Temples, leading to the beach over to Pierces marsh opposite, at the entrance of the causeway, is 120 feet. From the South corner of Mallett's store, improved by Capt. Waters, over to Pierce's marsh, opposite, is 90 feet. From the South corner of Sam¹. Swan jun'rs house over to Sam¹. Swan's marsh, opposite, is 90 feet. From the upper corner of the Causeway of the road leading to Cambridge to Mrs Whittemore's house, opposite, is 87 feet 9 inches. Length of the Causeway from the South corner of Mrs Whittemore's house to the South corner of Mallett's land is 463 feet.

[**290.**] WATER STREET. — From Mr Richard Trumbull's south corner of his house to Eben'. Austin's, opposite, is 40 feet, and should continue forty feet through the street. Mr Benjamin Goodwin has encroached at the north corner of his house 2 feet 4 inches. The north corner of the late Thomas Russell's Esq'. store has encroached 4 feet 6 inches.

OLD WAPPING STREET. — Then we began at the bottom of old Wapping street, at the extreme of the Navy Yard, 24 feet, running down to low water mark, bounding upon Mr Isaac Carleton and the Navy yard.

From the west corner of Capt. Thomas Edes portico's stone work to Isaac Carleton's east corner of his house, or bounds of the street, making the corner between water street and Old Wapping street.

From the South corner of Mr. Barker's bounds over to Mr Isaac Carleton's Cellar Wall is 30 feet. From Capt. Waters over to Mr Thomas Brooks, opposite, is 24 feet, 6 inches, ought to be 39 feet 6 inches, encroached by Brooks and Gibbs 15 feet. From Mr Thomas Harris' land, formerly Wyer's, over to Mr John Harris' land, at the corner of Madlin street is 23 feet, formerly 49 feet, encroached by Mr John Harris 26 feet. From Brown's over to Turner's is 40 feet. From Townsend's corner, formerly Pilcres, over to Doctor Putnam's, is 49 feet.

JOINERS STREET. — From Mr John Edmand's bounds over to Mr Isaac Mallett's is 30 feet. From Mr John Welch's over to Joseph Cordis is 23 feet. From Capt Chapman's land over to Mr Gill's land is 21 feet 10 inches. From Mr Nath¹. Austin's land over to Nathan Whittemore's house is 20 feet.

GILL STREET. — From Mr John Welch's land over to Mr Gill's is 20 feet. length of the street 214 feet.

CHAMBERS LANE. — From Mr Eben'. Breed's house over to Newell's, opposite, is 30 feet, and so continues through the street.

GRAVES LANE. — From John Harris' house over to James Russell Esq''s is 21 feet. Mr John Harris portico partly in the street. the length of the street from Mr Russell's bounds to Pratt's lane is 136 feet.

PRATT'S LANE. — From the bottom of Grave's lane there is a lane 6 feet wide running to Jenner's lane, called Pratt's lane. The west corner of Mr John Harris' stable is encroached 4 inches. The north west corner of Austin's garden fence encroached 4 inches. JENNER'S LANE. — At the head of Jenner's lane it is 15. feet. Against Pratt's lane it is 12 feet down to low water mark.

[291.] MASON STREET.[1] — The Entrance of Mason street, from James Edmands over to Mr Warren's, is 16 feet. Mr. Edmands encroached at the bottom of his garden fence. From the north west corner of John Austin's land, by Jenners lane, over to Mr Thomas Harris land, at the watch house, is 21 feet.

Bow STREET. — From Mr Devens house over to Thomas Harris land is 29 feet. From Mr Dunckley's house over to Curtis house is 26 feet. From Capt. Thomas Harris' house over to his land, opposite, is 26 feet. From William Goodwin's house over to Isaac Williams' fence, opposite, is 36 feet. Goodwin's shed encroached 2 feet 8 inches. From Mr John Lewis' over to Mr Conn's is 36 feet. From Mr David Edmands over to Moody Whitings is 38 feet. From Deacon James Frothingham's over to Arch^d. McNeill's is 44 feet — encroached one foot by Frothingham. From Mr Jonathan Calls over to Mr Archibald McNeill's is 42 feet; encroached by McNeill 6 feet 2 inches. From Richard Devens Esq^{rs} over to Arch^d. McNeills is 45 feet — encroached by Richard Devens Esqr. on the South line 16 feet; on the north line 5 feet. From Mr Daniel Smith's, across the street, is 45 feet. Smith encroached at the south line 5 feet 5 inches. From David Fosdick's South corner over to Mr Jacob Rhodes' South corner is 43 feet. Fosdick encroached 7 inches and Cellar doors in the street. From the South corner of Mr Amos Tuft's fence over to Mr John Kidder's is 33 feet. Kidder encroached 7 inches. From Amos Tuft's east corner over to Kidder's is 45 feet 6 inches.

ROPEMAKERS LANE. — From north corner of Richard Devens Esqr's house over to Capt. David Goodwin's land is 26 feet 3 inches. Devens west corner of his house encroached one foot, steps and cellar door in the street. From the east corner of Dea: James Frothingham's over to Mr William Wiley's north corner is twenty four feet.

From the South corner of Dea: James Frothingham's land over to Mr Moody Whitings is 26 feet. From Mr David Edmand's north corner over to McNeill's land, opposite, is 24 feet 8 inches. From the lower part of David Edmand's land over to Mr McNeills is 21 feet. From Benj^a. Hurd's land over to McNeill's land is 30 feet, and so continues to low water mark.

MIDDLE GATE STREET. — From Mr John Kidders over to Mr Amos Tuft's blacksmith Shop is 34 feet 8 inches. From the east corner of Mr Daniel Smith's land over to Mr John Goodwins is 36 feet — encroached by Smith 7 inches. From William Smiths (black-man) over to Capt. David Goodwin's, opposite, is 40 feet 5 inches. From Dea: James Frothingham's house over to Mr John Netting's is 40 feet 10 inches.

---

[1] Mason Street: this street is 16 feet wide to low water mark. — *Marginal note in handwriting of Phillips Payson, Town Clerk.* — ED.

[**292.**] TOWN HIL STREET. — From Mr John Goodwin's house over to Doctor Josiah Bartlett's land is 32 feet 7 inches. From the east corner of Mr John Goodwin's over to Mr Palmers is 46 feet 2 inches. From the South corner of the new School house over to Capt. David Goodwin's fence is 48 feet. From the east Corner of Mr Ezra Welsh's house over to Doctor Morse's fence is 43 feet 6 inches. From Mr Matthew Bridge's east corner to Doct^r. Morse's fence is 46 feet 6 inches. From the north corner of Capt. Thomas Harris' land, at the turnpike, over to Doct^r. Morse's fence is 44 feet 3 inches. From Mr Thomas Robbins' barn over to Capt. Thomas Harris land is 35 feet 2 inches.

GRAVEL LANE. — From Mr Cotton Center's house over to Major William Calder's land, or house, is 7 feet; at the west end of the lane is 6 feet 4 inches.

NEW STREET TO MEETING HOUSE. — From the west corner of Dea : John Larkin's barn, at the east end of the meeting house, over to John Edmand's is 30 feet; John Edmands has encroached 6 inches on the street; the street continues 30 feet wide to the main street. Mr Phillips Paysons's office steps in the street.

HURDS LANE. — From the west corner of Mr Joseph Hurds barn over to the South corner of his garden is 12 feet 5 inches : at the main street is 12 feet 3 inches.

HENLEY'S LANE. — From the west corner of Henley's house on the main street over to Mr Benj^a. Hurd's brick store is 38 feet : should be 40 feet; Hurd's Cellar doors in the street. At the north corner of Henley's house to the east corner of Hurd's store is 39 feet. From the north corner of Henley's garden fence, at the bottom of the street, over to the east corner of Mr Hurd's barn, opposite, is 40 feet.

PHILLIPS' LANE. — From the south corner of Mr Joseph Hurd's store, in the square, over to Mr John Harris' store is 24 feet 9 inches ; encroached 3 inches. From the corner of Mr Joseph Hurd's barn over to Mr John Harris garden fence, opposite, is 25 feet. From the corner of Mr Bradstreet's house over to Mr Isaac Mallet's bound is 28 feet. Bradstreet's Cellar doors in the street.

BACK STREET. — From the west corner of Hadley's cellar over to Henley's land is 33 feet 3 inches. From the west corner of Mr Daniel Tuft's house over to Mr Hurd's barn, opposite, is 59 feet 8 inches. From Mr Chubb's house over to Mr Hurd's land is 48 feet ; encroached 1 foot 6 inches. From the house of the late Thomas Russell Esqr. over to Mr Caleb Swan's land, east corner, is 46 feet ; encroached 1 foot 6 inches. From the north corner of Mr Richard Boylstone's land over to Major William Calder's barn is 43 feet 6 inches.

[**293.**] BACK STREET. — From the east corner of Mr Richard Boylstone's land over to the dye house is 46 feet 7 inches. From the widow Hannah Newell's over to Dea : John Larkin's fence is

Oct. 3, 1831. — This Street & part of Salem Turnpike, so called, named "Back Street." See vol : 12, page 140. Afterwards, to wit, March 3, 1834, named "Warren Street." See vol. 12, page 256. — *Marginal Note in handwriting of David Dodge, Town Clerk.* — ED.

41 feet. From Dea: John Larkin's barn over to the South corner of Mr Nathan Adams' land is 41 feet. From Mr Jonathan Nuttings barn over to Mr Nathan Adams' land is 41 feet. From Mr Nath¹. Austins' barn over to Mr Andrew Kettell's land is 44 feet. From Mr Timothy Tompson's shed to Tompson's land, opposite, is 48 feet; encroached by Thompson 1 foot. From Dea: Moses Hall's land over to Mr Tim°. Thompson's land, opposite, is 46 feet 6 inches; Thompson and Hall encroached 2 feet. From the east corner of Mr John Hay's land over to his land opposite, is 30 feet 6 inches. From the north corner of John Hay's house over to the South corner of Mr Stephen's house is 35 feet 2 inches.

COLE'S LANE. — From the west corner of Mr Richard Boylstone's house over to Dea: John Larkin's South corner is 31 feet 4 inches; Larkin's portico and cellar doors in the street. From the north corner of Mr Richard Boylstone's land, at the bottom of the lane, over to Boylstone's land opposite, is 41 feet; in the Center it is but 34 feet.

TRAINING FIELD LANE. — From Major William Calder's barn over to the dye house is 21 feet; in the middle it is 19 feet 4 inches; encroached by Trumbul 1 foot 4 inches.

TRAINING FIELD. — From Raymond's, running Easterly to the South corner of the Alms house fence, is 356 feet 6 inches. From the South corner of the Alms house fence to Mr Gould's fence is 26 feet 6 inches. From the South corner of the Alms house fence to Mr Richard Boylstone's land, on a westerly line, is 378 feet 4 inches. From the east corner of Mr Richard Boylstone's land, on a northerly line, to Henley's land, is 232 feet. From the entrance of the training field at Henley's land, in an easterly direction, to Mrs. Wallace's or the first mentioned bounds, is 286 feet.

HIGH STREET. — From the West Corner of Dea: John Larkins' land or stone wall, over to Col. David Wood's pasture, is 36 feet; should be 40 feet, Wood's fence not being moved. From Col: David Wood's board fence over to Dea: John Larkin's wall is 40 feet. From Col: David Wood's land, at the head of Greene's lane, over to Dea: John Larkins' land is 40 feet. From the east corner of Mr Alexander's land over to the west corner of Mr Noble's garden is 40 feet. From the east corner of Mr Zabdiel B. Adams' land over to Mr Noble's is 40 feet. From the east corner of Mr Joseph Johnson's half acre, over to Mr Nath¹ Austin's land, opposite the monument, is 40 feet.

[**294.**] HIGH STREET. — From the South corner of Mr Nath¹ Austin's land, by the lane over to Trumbull's pasture is 40 feet. From the South corner of Mr Richard Boylstone's land over to Mrs Henley's land is 40 feet.

From the middle of Mr Raymond's barn over to Mrs Wallace's fence, is 27 feet 9 inches. From the east corner of Mr Raymond's house, on a straight line from the barn, over to the west corner of Mrs Wallaces house is 22 feet 2 inches.

SHIPPIES STREET.¹ — From Capt. John Thomas' land over to Mr Sam¹ Townsend's land is 34 feet 7 inches. From the South corner of Richard Devens, Esqr's, land, over to John Austin's land, is 30

¹ March 14, 1831, the name of "Townsend Street" was by the selectmen given to Shippie Street. — *Marginal note in handwriting of David Dodge, Town Clerk.* — ED.

feet 3 inches.   From the east corner of Richd Devens Esqr's land, over to Mr. John Austin's north corner, is 32 feet 7 inches.   From the lower corner of Mr Leather's land over to Mr Saml Townsend's gate before his house is 30 feet 10 inches.   From Mr Leather's fence, within 8 feet of the north east corner of his house, over to the north corner of Mr Saml Townsend's upper garden fence, is 30 feet 7 inches.

SULLIVAN STREET. — From Mr Saml Townsend's garden fence, north corner, to the west corner of Mr Sullivan's garden fence is 44 feet.   From the east corner of Mr Sullivan's garden fence to Capt. Thomas Harris' fence is 38 feet 3 inches.   From the east corner of Mr Eben^r Breed's land over to the Navy Yard is 37 feet 3 inches.

MOLTON'S POINT ROAD. — From Mr Eben^r Breed's stone wall to Mr Caleb Swan's is 19 feet 6 inches.   At the point where Bunkers Hill and Molton point roads meet is 42 feet.   The road to Molton's point is 18 feet wide a little east of the Rope walk, from thence 16½ feet wide till it meets the Navy yard.

BATTERY LANE. — From Mr Jacob Rhodes' land over to Mr Thomas Edmands land is 15 feet, and continues through the lane the same width.

MADLIN STREET. — From Mr John Turner's east corner over to Mr John Harris land opposite, is 19 feet 9 inches.   From Mr Cary's over to Doct^r Putnam's land is 20 feet, Putnam has encroached 9 inches.   At the turn between Putnam and Edmands the street is 18 feet wide till it meets Water street.

GREEN'S LANE. — From the South corner of Mr Page's tavern over to the west corner of Mr. Giles Alexander's land is 34 feet. From the upper end of Page's hall to Alexander's fence is 28 feet 7 inches.   From Alexander's gate to Woods fence is 28 feet. From the north corner of Mr Alexander's Coach house to Mr David Wood's fence opposite, is 39 feet 4 inches.

HOLDEN STREET. — From the west corner of Dea : John Larkins land over to Mr Oliver Holden's land is 40 feet — this street was laid out to be 40 feet through ; at the Northeast end it is 39 feet 4 inches.

[**295.**]   From Mr Eben^r Breed's land to John Waitt's point of land is 18 feet ; Breed and Waitt have encroached 4 feet in some parts.   From Mr Sullivan's land over to Mr John Harris' is 17 feet 6 inches.   From Mr Richard Boylstone's land over to Mr Nathl Austin's is 16 feet 6 inches.   From Mr Nathan Tufts land to the west corner of Mr Nathl Austin's is 30 feet, and so continues till we come to the South corner of the Poor's land.   At the west corner of the Poor's land to Mr Joseph Hurd's land is 17 feet. From the middle of Mr Larkins pasture over to Mr Joseph Hurd's land is 16 feet and an half

BUNKER HILL.^{1} — From the west corner of Mr Edes' land, at Bunker's hill lane, over to Mr Isaac Mallett's house is 18 feet, and so continues to the gravel pit or School house, from thence encroached from 2 feet to 2 feet & an half, till we come to Mr Saml Swan's, opposite to where the old fort was.

MILL LANE. — From the north corner of Mr Timothy Keith's

---

^{1} Now Charles Street. — *Marginal Note.* — ED.

house to Mr John Greene's is 21 feet 10 inches; encroached by Green in front 14 inches. From the east corner of Mr John Greene's to the west corner is 68 feet, encroached by Greene 20 inches. From the west corner of Mr John Greene's land, leading to the Mill, is 250 feet, to a stake, drove, all which belongs to the town to low water mark. The road to the mill is 25 feet wide; encroached at the east end by Mr. L. Cox 3 feet — in the middle 6 feet 3 inches. Mr Timothy Keith encroached on the Town's land, at his Slaughter house, 5 feet.

MALDEN BRIDGE ROAD. — From the west corner of Mr Charles Coles' over to Mr Beachum's land is 33 feet. From the west corner of Mrs Anna Whittemore's land, or Mrs Swan's, over to Mr Beachams is 53 feet. From the north corner of Mrs Anna Whittemore's, or Mrs Swan's, over to Mr Beacham's is 34 feet. Mrs Whittemore encroached at the north corner 5 feet. From the last mentioned bounds (Beacham's.) as the fence now stands to Malden Bridge, down to low water mark belongs to the Town, and from thence to dirty marsh around the beach.

CAMBRIDGE ROAD. — From the north corner of Mrs Anna Whittemore's, alias Swan's, land, at the turn of Cambridge road, to the east corner of Mr Russell's bounds, opposite Mr Beacham's on Medford road, 280 feet. From thence on Mr Russell's bounds to a turn in Mr Russell's garden fence, on Cambridge road 225 feet, meeting the measurement from the north corner of Mr Caleb Swan's land opposite, formerly Wyers, is 109 feet. From the south end of Mr Russells garden fence [**296.**] CAMBRIDGE ROAD, over to Mr Caleb Swan's land opposite is 98 feet. There is a Range way through Mr Russell's land (formerly the Common) 16½ feet wide to Mr William Smith's land (formerly Hay's land). From the said Range way over to Swan's land, opposite, is 102 feet. From Russell's land (formerly the Common) over to Mr Lynde's land is 101 feet 7 inches. Then we measured from Mr Russells first encroachment, at the before mentioned Lyndes', 743 feet on the road leading to Cambridge to the extreme bounds of Mr Russell's land, then Mr Russell has encroached 16 feet: from which place, across the road to Stearn's marsh or stone wall is 83 feet, by the Elm tree in the road. From the corner of the Stone wall, dividing the land between Stearns & Lynde, is 108 feet (this should be entered before the next above.) From the South corner of Mr Russells land to Stearn's fence opposite is 76 feet 6 inches. Then we measured the Quarrie belonging to the Town, bounding on Mr Russell's land, formerly the Common, 182 feet. From Mr Russell's west corner, bounding upon Smith, in a Southerly direction upon Stearns and Ireland, 514 feet. From Ireland's stone wall, at the end of the 514 feet above-mentioned, across the road to Stearn's fence by the marsh is 71 feet.

Then we measured from Ireland's, east of the Bridge, to the opposite side, at a Range way leading down to Minots marsh, 78 feet; encroached by Ireland 2 feet. From Mr Joseph Barrell's wall over to the Range way, at the South corner of Mr Joseph Miller's land, is 108 feet; encroached at the corner of said Range way, by Miller, 4 feet. From Mr Joseph Barrell's stone wall (formerly Wood's) over to Mr. Eben[r] Shed's land is 77 feet 6 inches; encroached by Mr. Barrell 2 feet 6 inches. At the corner of Threepole lane over to Mr. Joseph Barrell's stone wall is 102 feet. From the north corner of Mr Eben[r] Shed's land over to Mr John Harris' land is 127 feet. From Mr Eben[r] Shed's stone wall, or fence, over to Mr John Harris' house is 107 feet — said Harris encroached against the Elm tree 2 feet 6 inches. From the north west Corner of Codman's land, leading to Bullard's Bridge, to Mr Samuel Shed's land is 90 feet. From the South corner of Mr John Stone's bound, on Milk row, over Mr John Tuft's stone wall, or fence, is 136½ feet: encroached by Stone 3 feet 6 inches at said corner; also a yard enclosed, at the east corner of Stone's house, in the road. From the the east corner of Col. Nath[l] Hawkin's land over to Mr John Tufts' is 129 feet 6 inches. From the partition wall, between Hawkins and Tufts, over to Hawkins, is 105 feet 6 inches. From the Southwest side of the Bridge, below Hawkins, across the road over to Hawkins' land is 78 feet. From Col. Nath[l] Hawkins front door to his land opposite is 93 feet. From the Elm tree at the upper corner of his [297.] house yard over to the barn yard is 58 feet. From the South west corner of Col. Hawkins' barn to his land opposite is 41 feet. From the division fence, between Mr Sam[l] Tufts & Col. Hawkins, over to Hawkins, is 67 feet; encroached 1½ feet on the north side.

CAMBRIDGE ROAD. — From the division fence, between Mr Sam[l] Tufts & Hastings, over to Hawkins' should be 90 feet: encroached 8 feet by Tufts. From the division fence, between Mr Gideon Frost & Sam[l] Tufts, over to Hawkins' land is 80 feet; encroached by Hawkins 1 foot 6 inches. On the boundary lines, between Cambridge and Charlestown, at Pillion bridge, from Frosts land to Col[o] Hawkins's across the road is 65 feet, should be 68 feet: encroached 3 feet by Hawkins.

THE WATERING PLACE — MILK ROW. — From the east corner of Col. Nath[l] Hawkins' land over to Mr John Stones' is 66 feet — From Mr Jon[a] Ireland's house to Mr Sam[l] Tufts is encroached 2 feet upon each side.

From the north corner of Mr Kent's land, on milk row, on a Southerly direction 20 Rods & 2 feet; from thence a westerly direction 9 rods across the brook; from thence running northerly 23 rods 3½ feet: from thence on the road to the first mentioned corner is 14 rods & 13 feet. From the west corner of Mr Caleb Rand's land over to Mr Kent's is 63½ feet.

QUARRY HILL. — Then we measured the Quarry hill between Mr Caleb Rand's and Mr John Harris'. From the west corner of the Quarry, bounded on the Range way, in an easterly direction to Rand's land is 9 rods & an half: from thence Southerly, bounding upon Rand's land is 16 rods. 7 feet to the road: from thence westerly on the road to the Range way is 12 Rods 6 feet: from thence northerly to the first mentioned bounds on the Range way is 16 Rods.

MILK ROW. — From the South corner of Mr John Harris land, on the Range way, over to Mr Sam[l] Kents land is 79 feet — Mr John Harris, at the corner, has given in 13 feet of his land — on the road.

From the west corner of Mr John Harris' fence, on the road by his house, over to Kent's land is 49½ feet. From the north west corner of Mr Wyer's land over to Mr John Harris' land is 62 feet, 6 inches. From the north west corner of Mr Wyers' land to Mr John Harris' new Wall is 79 feet. From the west corner of Mr John Harris' land over to Mr Noah Boardman's formerly, now Frost's, is 51 feet, should be 66 feet, encroached by Frost 15 feet; and so continues 8 rods, more or less, through. From the west corner of Harris', bounding on the Range way, to Frost's land is 58 feet, encroached by Frost 8 feet. From the east corner of Mr Stephen Goddard's land over to Tim° Tufts Esqr's land is 67 feet.

[**298.**] POWDER HOUSE ROAD. From the east corner of Mr Wellington's land over to Dea: Frost's land across the road is 78 feet. From the division line *post* between Charlestown and Cambridge over to the land opposite is 67 feet. From Mr Peter Tufts' land by a small bridge, over to Mr Goddard's is 64 feet. From the South corner of the quarry sold to Watson, over to land opposite is 64 feet. From quarry hill belonging to Russell, to Peter Tufts' land opposite is 66 feet, and continues 4 rods all the way to Tufts' fence on the Menotomy road. From the South corner of Mr. Beacham's land, leading to Malden Bridge, over to Russell's is 90 feet. From Mr Lamson's gate to the east corner of Mr Smith's land, opposite, is 125 feet, encroached by Smith 4 feet. From the South corner of Mr Stearns' land over to Mr Isaac Smith's land, opposite, is 126 feet.

MENOTOMY ROAD. — From the corner of Mr William Stearns' fence, near the house, over to Smith's is 172 feet. From Mr Benjᵃ Goodwin's stone wall over to Mr John Stevens' land across the road, is 168 feet; encroached by Stevens 4 feet. From Mr Joseph Phipps' over to Mr Benjamin Goodwin's land is 137 feet. encroached by Phipps 3 feet.

WATERING PLACE. From the north corner of Mr Benjamin Goodwin's fence on a Southeasterly line is 135 feet, on the South west line is 135 feet, on the northwest line, bounding on Phipps, 145 feet.

MENOTOMY ROAD. — From the north east corner of Mr Joseph Phipps' land, by the watering place, to Phipps' land opposite is 118 feet. From the east end of Mr Joseph Phipps' stone wall over to Thomas Edes land is 110 feet, encroached by Edes 18 feet. & so continues to Phipps' line. From Tufts land over to Edes is 122 feet; encroached by Edes 2 feet. From the north east corner of three pole lane over to Mr Timothy Tufts' land. formerly Leekey's, is 132 feet; encroached 4 feet. From Mr Tim° Tufts' land over to Capt George Lane's is 9 rods or 152 feet 6 inches. From Capt George Lanes' stone wall, little above the willow trees, to the north corner of Tuft's wall opposite, at the Range way, is 9 rods 13 feet. From Lanes fence over to Adams land is 7 rods 3 feet; encroached by Adams 5 feet. From Capt. George Lanes' gate over to the division wall, between Mr Joseph Adams and Tufts, is 8 rods, or 132 feet.

MEDFORD ROAD. — From the west corner of Mr Lane's land, turning to Medford, to the land opposite, is 51 feet 6 inches, and so continues to Medford bounds.

MENOTOMY ROAD. — From Capt. George Lane's fence at the turn of the road to Medford, over to Mr. Joseph Tufts fence is 6 rods 3 feet; encroached 1 foot. From Mr Joseph Adams', near his house, over to Royals land, at the South post making the division line between Medford & Charlestown, is 6 rods 13 feet, & so continues the wedth to the Powder house as formerly, the road being part in Medford and part in Charlestown.

[**299.**] MENOTOMY ROAD AT FIRST RANGEWAY. — From Walter Russell's land, called quarry hill, near the corner, over to Mr Peter Tufts' gate is 4 rods. From Walter Russells land at the bridge to Peter Tufts' opposite is 4 rods 6 feet. Above the bridge, at the Rangeway, over to Walter Russell's land opposite is 4 rods 11 feet. From the late Thomas Russell's Esq^{rs}. garden fence over to his land opposite is 4 rods.

SECOND RANGEWAY. — From the Range way above Mr. Russell's house, from the South corner of Mr. Dixon's land over to the wall opposite is 4 rods.

MENOTOMY ROAD. — From Philemon Russell's land over to Mr Teel's land is 4 Rods 3 feet. From the west corner of Mr James Russell's land, bounding on the 3d Rangeway, to the land opposite is 4 rods 4 feet. Mr James Russell has encroached at the Range way 10 feet — and Mr. Philemon Russell, on the opposite side of the Rangeway, has encroached 7 feet.

At the east side of Alewife bridge, from Teal's land over to Mr Philemon Russell's opposite is 8 rods & 10 feet, and so continues to the Brook.

Then we measured, by Mr Dixon's house, upper side the bridge, to the land opposite is 4 rods 10 feet. From the west end of Mr Dixon's barn to the land opposite is 6 rods 1 foot. From the Wall at the west end of the School house, by a cherry tree, over to Dixon's land opposite is 11 Rods 7 feet. From the east corner of Mr. Samuel Whittemore's wall, in the hollow, to Mr Jon^a Teel's wall opposite is 11 rods. At the old wall, at the north corner of Mr William Dixon's house, over to Mr Saml. Whittemore's wall opposite is 6 rods 13 feet.

From the cherry tree in the road above Mr Dixons, in the hollow, to Dixons land opposite is 4 rods 13 feet. From the west corner of the Range way across to the two roads is 9 rods 8½ feet. From an oak tree, at the parting of the road, across is 3 rods 5½ feet. At the division Post, dividing the line between Cambridge and Charlestown, to the wall opposite, is 2 rods 15 feet; encroached 4 feet at the east end of Isaac Cutters land. From Josiah Whittemore's land, at the end of the road leading to Menotomy over to Mr Amos Warren's is 3 rods; Mr Amos Warren has encroached 11 feet.

GARDNER'S ROAD. — At the bridge near Mr. Cutter's mill, at the post making the division line between Cambridge & Charlestown, is 2

rods across the road, encroached on the north side of the road 8 feet.
At the valley south side of Mr. Cutter's is 32 feet; encroached
3 feet.   At the bend of the road, at the south of Mr Eben' Cutter's
house, across the road is 3 rods 10 feet.   At the south of Mr
Cutter's yard, at an Elm tree opposite is 2 rods 2 feet.   From the
north east corner of Mr [**300.**] Ebenezer Cutters yard to the
land opposite is 2 rods 9 feet, should be 4 rods; encroached
by Cutter 24½ feet.   At the bend above Cutters is 2 rods.   From
Joseph Wyman's house to the Wall opposite is 3 rods.   At the
foot of the hill, South of Mr Daniel Reeds is 2 rods 12 feet.
From the north corner of Mr Daniel Reed's, at the button wood
tree, to the wall opposite is 2 rods 6 feet.   From the north corner
of Mr Seth Wyman's over to the land opposite is 2 rods 11 feet.
From the north corner of Mr Seth Wyman's barn to the wall opposite is 2 rods 3 feet — about three rods above the School house
the road is 2 rods wide.   At the Brook it is two rods 8 feet.
From the South east corner of Mr John Swan's land to the wall
opposite is 2 rods 13 feet.   At the top of the hill between Seth
Wyman's & Gardner's it is 2 rods 12 feet.   Between Wyman's
and Wyman's land the road is 2 rods.   Between Wyman's and
Gardner's land it is 2 rods 13 feet.   Below Sam¹. Gardner's some
person has put a Blacksmith's shop nearly all in the road.   At the
South of Mr John Gardner's house across the road is 26 feet;
should be 33 feet; encroached by said Gardner, 7 feet.   From the
South corner of Mr John Gardner's barn yard fence across the
road is 3 rods 4 feet.   At the bounds of Woburn & Charlestown
from the north corner of Mr Gardner's wall to the opposite wall is
3 rods 2 feet.

HUTCHINSONS ROAD.—Mr John Hutchinson's road is 2 rods
from his house to Mr Seth Wymans, except, encroached by Mr
Hutchinson's Cow yard 1 rod.   And Mr Daniel Reed, opposite to
Mr. Seth Wyman, 7 feet.

FIRST RANGE WAY.—At the entrance of the first range way, on
the Menotomy road, near the late Tho°. Russell Esqr's land, to the
Southward of the house, is 20 feet; should be 33 feet; and continues 33 feet to Medford bounds — encroached by Mr Peter Tufts
13 feet.

SECOND RANGE WAY.—At the east corner of the Range way on
Medford bounds is 33 feet, inclosed and improved by Mr Jonathan
Teal.

From the west corner of the Church Lot to Mr Jon° Teel's land
opposite is 25 feet; encroached by said Teel 8 feet.

THIRD RANGE WAY.—At the entrance of the third Range way,
on Menotomy road, from Mr Philemon Russell's wall to Mr. James
Russell's is 23 feet; encroached 10 feet.   At the east corner of the
Range way on Medford line is 33 feet, enclosed by Smith and Benjamin Teel.

FIRST RANGE WAY.—Then we measured from the South west
corner of the watering place, on Medford road, opposite Mr

☞ These leaves were torn out before the record of this report was made.—*Marginal note on page 300 by Phillips Payson, Town Clerk.*—ED.

Joseph Phipp's in a Southerly line 54 rods, open. Then we measured still southerly 37 rods & 6 feet, enclosed by Michael Brigden. Then, southerly 7 rods, improved by Mr. William Stearns; Then still southerly 39 rods 8 feet, improved by [**301.**] Mr Samuel Ireland and Joseph Miller.

SECOND RANGE WAY. — Three pole Lane is open through out.

THIRD RANGE WAY. — Then we measured from Medford or Menotomy Road, Southerly and found the way open to the Widow Smiths Land; then we measured 27 rods, enclosed and improved by the Widow Smith; then we measured, still southerly, 48 rods, inclosed & improved by John Stone, ending at Milk row.

FOURTH RANGE WAY. — Then we began at Milk row, at Mr Jonathan Ireland's, from thence to the cross road at the top of the hill, is open, it being a northerly direction. Then we measured from the north east corner of said Ireland's stone wall. Then we measured from the cross lane, top of the hill, northerly, 57 rods, 4 feet, inclosed and improved by Mr John Tufts. Then still northerly 91 rods 6 feet to Menotomy or Medford road, inclosed and improved by Joseph Tufts.

FIFTH RANGE WAY. — Then we measured the fifth Range way, on Menotomy road on Winter Hill, being 2 rods across the Range way, it remains open throughout; encroached by Col. Hawkins by a short rail fence, in order to make a stone wall. On milk row Mr. Thomas Rand has encroached 7 feet 4 inches.

SIXTH RANGE WAY. — Then we began at the Range way, at the entrance of the Range way above the quarry, 63 Rods, fenced on both sides, at the south and enclosed by barrs; from thence, still northerly, 56 rods and an half, inclosed and improved by Samuel Tufts from thence 4½ rods, improved by Sam¹ Kent and Mr. Thomas Rand; from thence, still northerly, 46 rods 6 feet, inclosed & improved by Doct: William Stearns; then still northerly 51 rods, inclosed and improved by Mr Joseph Adams, ending at Menotomy road.

SEVENTH RANGE WAY. — Then we began on Menotomy road, the Seventh Range way, measuring Southerly 42 rods, inclosed and improved by Timothy Tufts, Esqʳ; still Southerly 40 rods 4 feet, inclosed & improved by Mr Joseph Tufts; still Southerly 12 rods, inclosed and improved by Timothy Tufts, Esqʳ; still Southerly 11 rods, inclosed and improved by Walter Russell; then still Southerly 42½ rods, inclosed and improved by Timothy Tufts, Esqʳ; from thence to milk row is open.

EIGHTH RANGE WAY. — Then we began at the upper end of milk row, a little above Timothy Tufts, Esqr's house, to measure the Eighth Range way, at the extreme of which it is inclosed by a wall and barrs.

[**302.**] EIGHTH RANGE WAY. — from thence we measured northerly 111 rods & 12 feet, enclosed and improved by Timothy Tufts, Esqʳ; then still northerly 65 rods inclosed and improved by Dea: Gideon Frost; then still northerly 20 rods, inclosed and improved by Mr. Peter Tufts, to Menotomy road.

CROSS LANE. — Then we began at the fifth Range way, at the

top of the hill, easterly to three pole lane, and measured 42 rods 12 feet, inclosed by Mr John Tufts ; then still easterly 20½ rods, inclosed and improved by Mr Jon^a Ireland ; then still easterly 20 rods 12 feet, inclosed by Mr. John Tufts and improved till we come to the fourth Rangeway ; then we measured on said Range-way southerly 10 rods till we come to the Church Lot, at the westerly corner ; then measuring easterly 119½ Rods till we enterd Fosdick's square, (so called) ; then we measured the square, the westerley side 7 rods 7 feet ; the south side 5 rods 3 feet ; easterly side 7 rods 6 feet ; the northerly side 5 rods 3 feet ; from thence to three pole lane is 39 rods 6 feet ; it appears that it is 1½ rod wide through the whole lane.

MINOT'S MARSH ROAD. — Then we measured the passage way leading to Minot's marsh (so called), east side of the bridge, east of Capt. Joseph Miller's house on Cambridge road, 11 rods 5 feet long, one rod & a half wide.

DIRTY MARSH. — Then we measured the road leading to dirty marsh (so called), from Mousell's gate, or Lamsons, through Mr. Andrew Kettell's land, 47 rods 11 feet, in a northerly direction, 1½ rods wide ; then we turned northwesterly and measured 85 rods 11 feet, till we came to a square piece of land, formerly called High Fields, measuring as follows : South-east side 7 rods 8 feet ; north-east side 7 rods 9 feet ; north west side 7 rods ; the south-west side 6 rods ; from the east corner of the north east side of the square there is a way 1½ rod wide, leading down to Mystic river, in a northerly line.

COMMON WAY BY BULLARD'S BRIDGE. — From the west corner of Mr Cragie's land on Cambridge road, formerly Mr. Codman's, over to the east corner of Mr John Tufts stone wall is 7 rods 13 feet ; from the east corner of Mr. John Tuft's land above men-tioned, in a southerly direction 7 rods 11 feet ; then turning westerly 5 rods to the Creek ; then easterly, north side of the bridge, 4 rods to the Creek ; then measuring across from Mr. John Tuft's fence or wall over to Mr Cragie's fence 8 rods 8 feet ; from thence by the Creek to Cragie's west corner, on the road to Cam-bridge is 12 rods. From Bullard's bridge (so called) to where the gate formerly stood, leading to Leachmore's farm, is open, but encroached by Mr John Tufts 8 feet, and Col. Nathl Hawkins 4 feet. From the gate there is a way to Mr Craigie's upper pasture 2 rods wide, but not on a Straight line.

[**303.**] RANGE WAY BETWEEN CRAGIE & SHED. — There is a way, between Mr Cragie's land and Mr Eben^r Shed's leading to the marsh from Cambridge road, one rod wide.

BURYING PLACE. — There is a way from the main street leading to and around the burying place, down to low water mark, and the flatts below belonging to the Town.

At the Entrance of the road leading to Mystic river, between Mallet and Mallett, is 22 feet, at the extreme bounds of Malletts land, measuring 112 feet from the main road towards Mystic river ; from thence to the east corner of Mr Mallett's bounds over to Malletts fence or stone wall is 47 feet 6 inches. From the entrance of the main street to the South corner of the Land sold to Mr Hagar is 275 feet; all the land and flatts between Mallett's and Hagar's belongs to the Town; also all the flatts below Hagar. From the South corner of Hagar's land over to Mallett's is 25 feet, and so continues to low water mark. Mr. Jotham Johnson and William Maxwell have encroached by setting a barn on the road.

There is a way leading from Cambridge road on the South side, near Mr. Samuel Ireland's through Joseph Barrell, Esqr's land, down to Ward's marsh (formerly so called); at the last measurement, at the entrance it was 2 rods and 8 feet wide; at the back corner of Woods Lot 2 Rods 10 feet; then between Wood and Shed's, at the turn, was 2 rods and 12 feet; from Wood's land to Shed's land, near the turn is 1 Rod 12 feet 6 inches; from Miller's to Shed's near the turn is 1 rod 13 feet 6 inches; from the line between Lynd's and Shed's over to Miller's is 2 rods 9 feet; from the bounds between Lynd's & Miller, over to James Miller's was 2 rods & 14 feet; from Miller's to Miller's near Miller's house is 2 rods 14 feet; at the end of said lane, there is a way leading about east to the Bull Lot (formerly so called), measuring $20\frac{1}{2}$ rods in length & one rod wide; then said way turns southerly measuring 24 rods 7 feet, one rod wide; these were improved by Stephen Miller formerly; then the said way runs 11 rods $5\frac{1}{2}$ feet; formerly improved by Brigden the same width; it being part of the Bull lot to Brigden by Miller; then the said road runs beyond the Bull lot 15 rods $2\frac{1}{2}$ feet, two rods wide, formerly improved by Brigden; then the said road is a little turning east and then runs Southerly, in the whole 41 rods 7 feet 6 inches, and two rods wide, which brings us down to a point called Ward's marsh.

[**304.**] There is a tract of Land belonging to the Town, in Stoneham at the upper part of Spot pond, called about Seventy acres.

There are three pieces of land in Medford, bounding on Mystic river, mentioned in the late records; it is said to belong to the Town of Charlestown —

Bounding as follows:

First — on the river above the Bridge: Westerly by land formerly Mr. Jonathan Tufts, now Col. Royal's, measuring ten rods & an half; Northerly on said Tufts land next to the marsh seven rods, whence a two pole way runs down to the river — butting easterly on the Country road five rods and an half; and Southerly on the way that leads to the ford or landing place nine rods, which way is two rods wide to the landing place; improved by Mr Hezekiah Blanchard.

Second — There is a piece of land, about half an acre, belonging to the Town for a fishing place on mystic river, which is bounded as follows: bounding upon Royall's, measuring from the road at the east end back to the River eight rods; from the said east end, along the road to a stake, measuring twenty four rods, Westerly; and from the said stake to the river is two rods, all straight lines.

Third — There is a piece of Land lying upon Mystic River,

belonging to the Town, bounding each side upon the hon'ble John Adams Esqr's land, measuring Southwesterly twenty rods and an half; Northeasterly twenty eight rods and an half; Southeasterly on the Range way leading to the River two rods; the breadth at the bottom next to the river, northerly, thirteen rods and an half; which lies a little to the westward of Adams' house.

(signed   Nathl Hawkins ⎫
           Richd Frothingham ⎬ *Committee.*
           John Carter ⎭

A true Copy from the original on file.
      Attest,   Phillips Payson,
                      Town Clerk.

Recorded by Vote of Town, passed May 2^d, 1803, which Vote is recorded in Vol. 9, page 521, of Town records.

INDEX.

INDEX.

INDEX.